D1522545

This collection of Sir Geoffrey Elton's articles and reviews, published between 1983 and 1990, follows three previous volumes. Volume IV contains a group of pieces on sixteenth-century government and politics, and more especially on aspects of the Reformation, on the continent as well as in England, with some attention to Martin Luther and an essay on Lancelot Andrewes. Several pieces deal with Parliament under the Tudors. A second group, 'On Historians', reprints an appraisal of Sir Herbert Butterfield and three substantial reviews on historiographical problems.

STUDIES IN
TUDOR AND STUART POLITICS
AND GOVERNMENT

VOLUME FOUR

STUDIES IN
TUDOR AND STUART POLITICS
AND GOVERNMENT

G. R. ELTON

VOLUME FOUR

PAPERS AND REVIEWS 1983–1990

CAMBRIDGE
UNIVERSITY PRESS

Published by the Press Syndicate of the University of Cambridge
The Pitt Building, Trumpington Street, Cambridge CB2 1RP
40 West 20th Street, New York, NY 10011–4211, USA
10 Stamford Road, Oakleigh, Victoria 3166, Australia

Printed in Great Britain at the University Press, Cambridge

*A catalogue record for this book
is available from the British Library*

Library of Congress cataloguing in publication data

Elton, G. R. (Geoffrey Rudolph)
Studies in Tudor and Stuart politics and government.
Vols. 1–2 have subtitle: Papers and reviews, 1946–1972.
Includes bibliographical references and indexes.
Contents: v. 1. Tudor politics / Tudor government – v. 2. Parliament / political
thought – [etc.] – v. 3. Papers and reviews 1973–1981 – v. 4. Papers and reviews, 1983–
1. Great Britain – Politics and government – 1485–1603.
2. Great Britain – Politics and government – 1603–1714.
JN181.E48 942.05 73-79305

ISBN 0 521 41832 1 hardback

UP

CONTENTS

PREFACE

I am grateful to the Syndics of the Cambridge University Press and especially to Mr William Davies for undertaking to publish a further collection of my articles and occasional pieces, and I repeat my earlier hope that their generosity will not come to appear misguided. In editing the material I have followed the principles explained in the previous prefaces, using square brackets to add explanations and corrections. I have also converted American and German printing conventions, especially in footnotes, into my standardised English practice, in order to achieve a seemly conformity. In view of what one or two reviewers of the third volume said, I think I must apologise for including three untranslated pieces in German, but that was the form in which they were published and moreover delivered: all three were lectures, one of them unscripted (and, owing to the failure of the tape-recorder, recalled from memory).

Clare College, Cambridge   G. R. ELTON
July 1991

ACKNOWLEDGMENTS

The author and publisher are grateful to the following for permission to reprint material first published by them:

Charles Scribner's Sons (49)
Basil Blackwell Ltd (50)
The Board of Trustees of the University of Illinois (51)
The Hon. Society of Cymmrodorion (52)
University of Wales Press (53)
R. Oldenbourg Verlag (55)
The Folger Institute (56)
The Master and Fellows of Pembroke College, Cambridge (57)
Herzog August Bibliothek Wolfenbüttel (59)
Longman Group UK (60)
Güttersloher Verlagshaus Gerd Mohr (61)
Klett-Cotta Verlag (62)
The American Scholar (65)

ABBREVIATIONS

AM	John Foxe, *Acts and Monuments*. ed. J. Pratt (London, 1870)
BIHR	*Bulletin of the Institute of Historical Research*
BL	British Library
CJ	*Journal of the House of Commons*
DNB	*Dictionary of National Biography*
EHR	*English Historical Review*
HJ	*Historical Journal*
HLRO	House of Lords Record Office
HMC	Historical Manuscripts Commission
LJ	*Journals of the House of Lords*
LP	*Letters and Papers, Foreign and Domestic, of the Reign of Henry VIII*, ed. J. S. Brewer, J. Gairdner, R. H. Brodie, 21 vols. (1862–1932)
OA	Original Act
Parliament	G. R. Elton, *The Parliament of England 1559–1581* (Cambridge, 1986)
PRO	Public Record Office
Reform and Reformation	G. R. Elton, *Reform and Reformation: England 1509–1558* (London, 1977)
Reform and Renewal	G. R. Elton, *Reform and Renewal: Thomas Cromwell and the Common Weal* (Cambridge, 1973)
SR	*Statutes of the Realm*, 11 vols. (1810–28)
STC	*A Short-Title Catalogue of Books Printed 1475–1640*, 2nd edn by W. A. Jackson and K. Pantzer (London, 1976, 1986, 1990)
TRHS	*Transactions of the Royal Historical Society*
TRP	*Tudor Royal Proclamations*, ed. P. L. Hughes and J. F. Larkin, 3 vols. (New Haven, 1964, 1969)
Tudor Constitution	*The Tudor Constitution*, ed. G. R. Elton, 2nd edn (Cambridge, 1982)

I

POLITICS AND THE REFORMATION

49

THE STATE: GOVERNMENT AND POLITICS
UNDER ELIZABETH AND JAMES*

CENTRAL GOVERNMENT

The England of Shakespeare's day was a monarchy, but a monarchy of a special kind. Though the king or queen ruled without question and stood isolated at the apex of the social and political pyramid, that rule had to be exercised within quite well-defined limitations: it was in no sense despotic, though it could be autocratic. The most formal conditions of restraint existed in the law of the land, called the common law, and its accepted conventions. Though the monarch possessed special rights not available to his subjects, these so-called prerogatives themselves received definition in terms of the law.

Royal prerogatives – rights enjoyed by that person whose duties were special and could not be discharged without such rights – were usually divided into two kinds, ordinary and absolute, which refer to the relationship between royal rights and the law. *Ordinary* (meaning ordained) signified 'defined in the law of the realm'; *absolute* (free of the law) meant 'not so defined', the implication being that they could not be defined because they touched upon unpredictable needs of the state that the ruler must be able to meet. Ordinary prerogatives included the fiscal rights of the crown, the power to appoint to office, the right to dispense justice and the regulation of trade. Absolute prerogatives included the making of peace and war, but also (more ominously) the taking of necessary action against alleged enemies of the commonwealth, as, for instance, imprisonment and examination under torture. The absolute prerogative unquestionably had autocratic and even tyrannous possibilities; it needed to be used with tact and without arousing dangerous dissatisfaction, the more so because this monarchy disposed of only a minimal establishment of armed force. That is to say, political action, as it always does, required skill and good sense.

The legal doctrine that the king can do no wrong sounds like despotism. In reality it meant only that, since no man can be sued in his

---

* [*William Shakespeare: His World, His Work, His Influence*, ed. John F. Andrews (New York, 1985), I, 1–18.]

own court and since the courts of the realm were the king's, it was not possible to bring an action at law against the king; being unremediable in a court, the king's actions must be presumed never to do wrong. As a judge put it in a case tried in 1562: 'The king cannot do any wrong, nor will his prerogative be any warrant to him to do an injury to another.' This was all very well in principle, but suppose the king – or his agents – did do such a wrong, perhaps inadvertently, and no remedy lay against him in a court of law: what redress was there in such a case? On the death of a man possessed of land whose heir was a minor – a very common event at the time – an enquiry might discover that a part of the dead man's real estate was held of the crown in knight's service. The heir and all his property then became subject to the very burdensome royal right of prerogative wardship, and, as the phrase went, the lands were immediately taken into the king's hands, so that their income was lost to the heir's family. The verdict of the enquiring jury might be wrong – malevolently so, through corruption or intimidation, or quite innocently through ignorance or error – yet the king could not be sued for illegal entry, forcible disseisin, or any of the other ways in which such injustice could be remedied between two of his subjects.

The law nevertheless provided a remedy to prevent the king from 'doing wrong' – a remedy derived from every subject's right to petition the king. The law knew two kinds of petition. A petition of grace asked the king to do something that lay within his free choice, such as granting an office or bestowing a piece of land. Such a petition asked for something that the petitioners wanted but had no existing right to have until the king had responded favourably. A petition of right, on the other hand, declared that a right already existing at law had been offended and asked that the right so lost be restored to the petitioner. Such a petition obviously applied if the grievance concerned an erroneous verdict that had transferred some lands from the petitioner to the king. There was a standard procedure for these petitions that produced a proper review of the case and a restoration of the property if the investigation showed that the petitioner had indeed been wronged.

Thus the subjection of the crown to the law had positive reality, and the English monarchy, though often described as absolute and manifestly powerful, was a law-defined and therefore a law-restrained monarchy. Cases arising out of these circumstances were naturally not common, and as a rule the power of the crown showed more plainly than the limitations upon it. Kings reigned and ruled; government and politics flowed from the personal position and actions of the monarch. However, in these respects too, kingship was not unrestrained both in theory and in fact. The government of the realm was indeed in the fullest sense royal, but it had to be exercised in ways that limited the power of the monarch to do as he pleased. These ways appear in two kinds: the formal limitations of the instruments of government, which dictated the shape that political action could take; and the informal but all-pervasive conditions imposed by the mutual relations between ruler and ruled. First we shall consider the former: the structure of government and its agencies.

Elizabeth and James bore titles that define them as monarchs of England (not to mention France and Ireland, and in James' case of Scotland too) as well as supreme governors of the Church of England. This duality raised no problems because it simply described royal rule over one set of people who in their bodies constituted the commonwealth of England ruled by the king, and in their souls made up the Church of England ruled by its supreme governor. For both purposes, kings commanded machinery for the exercise of these supremacies, while beyond and behind them, in the Parliament of England, there stood machinery that united commonwealth and church, as well as king and governor.

The chief instrument of rule was the Privy Council. Technically a body of advisers chosen by the monarch and sworn to his service, it had in fact a corporate existence of its own as well. It emerged during Thomas Cromwell's reform of the administration in the 1530s, replacing the very large medieval king's council that Henry VII had reconstituted as the centre of a highly personal government. The reformed Privy Council constituted one of the clear indications that such personal rule was to be replaced by government through established institutions. Composed of the leading officers of state, including the top officials of the Royal Household whose posts were sinecures, it in fact consisted of politicians engaged in governing the realm. Elizabeth followed Cromwell's example by using a small Council of never more than twenty members, reduced at the end to thirteen by her failure to replace old men who died before her. James, pressed by men of ambition, understandably found it advisable to enlarge the body, even to unmanageable size. At all times, some privy councillors carried more weight than others – men of outstanding abilities or in the monarch's special confidence, but, above all, men sufficiently devoted to the work to attend meetings regularly. The chief active councillors were the (commonly two) principal secretaries, or secretaries of state, who usually prepared the agenda and carried out most of the decisions taken. Under Elizabeth, the secretaries included such leading councillors as the two Cecils – William Lord Burghley and his son Robert, later earl of Salisbury – and Sir Francis Walsingham; but, even so, the office never enjoyed the highest formal standing that rested rather with the three great officers of state – the lord chancellor, the lord treasurer, and the lord privy seal. Under James, leading statesmen spurned the secretary-ship, which came to be held by working bureaucrats of relatively low standing. During the reigns of Henry VIII and his two successors, the problems of the Reformation had made it essential to have leading bishops on the Council, but Elizabeth kept them off it until she found a congenial churchman in John Whitgift, archbishop of Canterbury from 1583 to 1604; thereafter the spirituality had always at least one man on the Council.

The councillors exercised their nominally chief function of advising the monarch as individuals or, more commonly, as a body. Elizabeth generally relied on advisers who had been formally appointed to the Privy Council. James resorted to the older practice of obtaining extraconciliar advice from court favourites and even from foreign ambassadors; altogether his government could be said to be more distinctly personal, even quirky, than his predecessor's.

The Tudor-Stuart Privy Council had independent powers unusual in the administrations of the age. Unlike the councillors of the kings of Spain and France, who could only advocate actions all of which required formal sanction by the king, English privy councillors discharged many tasks of government on their own authority. It would not be far wrong to say that, while the making of policy (especially in foreign affairs) involved the monarch's direct participation, the running of the country was supervised by the Council, which activated executive agencies by means of instruments – Privy Council letters – in which the monarch played no part. In fact, the Council did many things, especially in the supervision of justice and finances, of which the sovereign remained ignorant. So long as the Council was purposeful and efficient, this was a sensible arrangement: kings and queens of England saw no reason why they should involve themselves in every detail, and government was not, as in Spain, subjected to the endless delays that resulted from having to seek the king's signature on every act of state. Privy councillors, then, were men of very superior standing in the realm, often independent actors in matters political and social, rather than mere creatures of the royal will. Their personalities and opinions mattered; what mattered especially was their inclination to pursue personal advancement and to promote particular policies by forming associations within the Council. Elizabeth on the whole succeeded in balancing these so-called factions (about which more later on) against one another and in maintaining the principle that the service of the state overrode other concerns, but the enlargement of the Council and the decline of respect for the monarch that came with the next reign meant that the standing of the councillors deteriorated together with their efficiency. As James encouraged political dominance by court favourites, the Council, though never negligible, became an arena of personal rivalry rather than a formidable instrument of royal government.

The Council worked through regular government departments charged with particular functions. The oldest, and in its way the most important, was the Exchequer, first organized in the reign of Henry I and most recently reformed in a general review of the financial offices under Mary I. In Elizabeth's reign it underwent piecemeal and never entirely successful reforms at the hands of Lord Treasurer Burghley. The Exchequer was a ministry of finance in the narrow sense, responsible for collecting, spending, and accounting for the revenues of the crown, but not responsible for financial policy, the province of the Council.

The crown (always in this age underfinanced) enjoyed certain revenues as of right, all but one of which were administered by the Exchequer. The crown lands, a mainstay of early Tudor finance and enormously augmented by the dissolution of the monasteries under Henry VIII, now represented a wasting asset. After her first few years, Elizabeth tried to avoid selling this capital but had to countenance leases favourable to the lessees. In the war years at the end of her reign, she was forced to resume selling, and James made no effort to hold the vast landed estate together. By the early seventeenth century the crown was no longer a major national rent-collecting landowner, though of course some lands continued to generate income. By then, the most important, because most buoyant, sources of revenue were the customs on imports and exports granted to each monarch for life in the first Parliament of every reign. This income was augmented, especially under James, by new 'impositions', which the government justified rather speciously as a means to control trade (a right vested in the prerogative) rather than raise revenue (which required parliamentary consent). Impositions, declared lawful in a collusive action arranged with a cooperative merchant in 1606 (Bate's Case), caused an uproar in Parliament in 1607 and 1610 but remained embedded in the customs. The post-Reformation church contributed to the royal coffers an annual 10 per cent income tax (the clerical tenth) as well as the 'first fruits' payable by every cleric (from parish priest to archbishop) appointed to a new benefice, and valued as a rule as equal to one year's income from that benefice.

All these and a variety of lesser sources – especially the fines, forfeitures, and amercements arising from legal suits – fell within the province of the Exchequer. The one item that did not was what we call the 'feudal revenue,' which was based on the principle that the sole owner of all land in England was the king, from whom the real owners technically 'held' their properties on various terms. Feudal revenue is best described as a collection of death duties, because it fell due only on the death of a crown tenant. If there was no heir, the property returned to the crown (escheat). If there was an heir, and he was of age, he had to pay a standard sum (the relief) for the formal confirmation of his inheritance. If he was under age, he became a royal ward and the revenues of his lands were either administered by the crown or (more commonly) sold to a purchaser, often but not always a relative of the ward. This revenue constituted the province of the Court of Wards and liveries. Wardship, which could threaten disastrous consequences to a family estate, always benefited the crown, but it was attractive also to others because it represented a potentially profitable area for investing surplus capital. Thus, though often resented, very haphazard in occurrence and a cause of much uncertainty for landowners, it survived as a fiscal remnant of feudalism until the earl of Salisbury tried to increase its yield. His plan to amortise feudal rights in exchange for a parliamentary tax (the Great Contract of 1610) failed, but a start had been made on removing an awkward fossil. The Court of Wards was abolished in 1646 and not revived at the Restoration (1660), when an arrangement similar to that proposed by Salisbury a half-century before came into existence.

During the years under discussion here, the notion that the state should be financed as the public but personal concern of the crown, by means of money due to the prerogative, endured despite its manifest inadequacy. In fact, actual government financing increasingly depended on parliamentary taxes, on borrowing in anticipation of revenue and on such windfalls as the capture of Spanish treasure ships or pensions (bribes) obtained from foreign powers. By dint of a frugality that rarely extended to her personal needs but in the realm at large looked like miserliness, Elizabeth avoided bankruptcy even in the war that left a legacy of debts both owed and owing. James, who evidently believed that in England money grew on trees, never came within hailing distance of making ends meet, a folly that, more than anything else, undermined the stability of monarchic government.

War apart, the greatest drain on royal resources – the largest spending department financed out of the Exchequer – was the Royal Household, or, in the reign of James, who had a wife and children to look after, the several Households. The Household maintained the king's court, that political centre of England; it comprised a vast inner bureaucracy ranging from kitchen boys to gentlemen of the Privy Chamber, lord chamberlains, and lord stewards. In the reign of Henry VII it had also been the centre of the actual government of the realm; that role had disappeared in the wake of Cromwell's administrative reform in the 1530s, though some functions of state (especially those connected with war) remained in the charge of Household officials, as did the Privy Purse, the monarch's private financial reserve. By the reign of Elizabeth, the normal government of the realm was managed by a regular bureaucracy of agents employed by the crown in organised departments. Two kinds of departments call for mention here – the secretarial offices and the courts of justice.

The secretarial offices were responsible for conveying the decisions of government in writing to others – officers in the localities, envoys abroad, foreign powers, and private individuals. The oldest and largest of these offices was the Chancery, which occupied the better part of its time in the conduct of judicial business.

In matters secretarial it acted by this time only as the issuer of formal documents that required the application of the Great Seal of England. It produced the letters patent that certified grants of the royal patronage – awards of offices, lands and so forth – and the transfer of executive powers by royal commissions. It also kept the massive rolls on which these activities of the crown were registered.

Its clerks received their instructions mainly from the Office of the Privy Seal, a lesser royal seal that had at one time been the crown's chief executive instrument but now mainly carried out formal and really superfluous duties – receiving and transmitting orders for the making of letters patent. Its only effective function was financial: while routine payments out of the Exchequer relied on standardised writs under the Great Seal, special disbursements were usually authorised by Privy Seal letters on the orders of the Privy Council or the lord treasurer. The Privy Seal also authenticated the bonds used in raising repayable loans to the crown negotiated within the realm.

Behind the Privy Seal stood the king's third seal, the Signet, kept by the secretary of state. Most regularly its clerks wrote out orders to the Privy Seal on instructions embodied in petitions to the crown that had been approved by the royal signature (sign manual bills), another of the strictly superfluous links in the chain that produced letters patent The Signet retained original powers, however: in particular, it authenticated the monarch's 'private' letters, especially correspondence with foreign rulers and with English ambassadors. Thus the Signet was the instrument of diplomacy and the formal emblem of the secretary's function as a minister for foreign affairs. Furthermore, letters under the Signet could convey specially important decisions in domestic matters (the secretary's other province) – items for which Privy Council letters or the secretary's private correspondence were thought insufficient, more particularly orders for arrests in matters of state. The three seals and their staffs thus formed an interlocking but flexible series of instruments for executing the will of government.

The courts of law dealt with conflicts that arose either between the crown and a party or between party and party. The central courts at Westminster comprised the ancient courts (or courts of record) and the more recent courts sprung from the duty of the Council to respond to appeals for justice withheld or unobtainable, and therefore commonly called the conciliar courts.

The three ancient courts, in order of repute, were the King's Bench (theoretically for cases involving the crown and therefore, among other things, the chief criminal court), the Common Pleas (for disputes between party and party, by this time concerning mostly debts but also titles to land) and the Exchequer (for disputes arising out of the royal revenue, especially so-called debts to the crown that were really revenue unaccounted for). These courts applied the common law of England.

The conciliar courts practised what was known as equity, originally a means for doing justice if the law failed to provide it, but by the period under review settling into a subsidiary system complementing the common law. The conciliar courts were the Chancery (civil pleas, especially over landed property, contracts and the personal rights of people ill protected by the law, such as women and children), the Star Chamber (in effect the Privy Council sitting as a court and controlling public order with jurisdiction over violent breaches of the peace, perjury, slander, corrupt juries, and miscreant officials), and the Court of Requests (for lesser equitable matters). The Exchequer also developed an equity side from the middle of the sixteenth century. In addition, the Court of Wards adjudicated disputes arising out of lands held in wardship, and the Duchy Chamber of Lancaster dealt with litigation over its large and scattered properties vested in the monarch as duke of Lancaster.

Common law and equity were not hostile to each other but complementary, and the working of both systems lay altogether in the hands of people trained as common lawyers at the Inns of Court. Only Requests used judges from the ranks of both the common lawyers and the practitioners of the Roman law (as taught at the universities), called civilians. (The chief resort for civilians as working lawyers was the High Court of Admiralty, which heard litigation over maritime and commercial disputes occurring outside the realm and therefore not triable at common law.) Though important differences existed between the two sets of central courts in matters of procedure and power, these did not lead to confrontation. Generally speaking, the conciliar courts acted more directly and swiftly, but in civil pleas they could issue only intermediate orders technically reviewable at common law if the unsuccessful party liked to go on. Thus Chancery could prevent a man from taking another man's lands but could not safely settle title. Similarly, Star Chamber, although widely regarded as the most formidable of courts, could fine and imprison a rioter or a perjured juryman, but it could not hang a thief or a murderer, rights reserved to the common law.

These courts were financed by fees payable by litigants and therefore needed to compete for business. In the earlier part of the sixteenth century the equity courts had prospered because the older courts had failed to keep up with changes in society and the evasive devices of attorneys, so that they became useless in a great number of cases. In particular, the ancient courts could offer no remedies for disputes arising out of property arrangements largely invented to evade the rules limiting a man's right to dispose of lands (by sale or bequest) that technically he did not own but held from a superior lord (especially the crown). The backwardness of common law then made the fortunes of Chancery and Requests. The old law reacted in two ways: it invented new remedies for new situations, and its courts – especially King's Bench and Exchequer – developed various fictions to empower themselves to hear cases that technically were outside their purview. Thus by the end of the century there was a marked recovery in the business handled by those courts at the expense of Common Pleas and Requests.

This competition for litigants could be dressed up as a battle of principle. When Sir Edward Coke became chief justice of Common Pleas he set himself to limit the activities of Chancery, whose attraction to litigants constituted the heaviest drain on the business of his court. In 1616, however, thanks to the king's personal intervention, Coke lost that battle with Thomas Egerton, Lord Ellesmere, one of the founding fathers of the established court of Chancery.

The Tudor-Stuart machinery for waging war remained somewhat underdeveloped. There existed a Royal Navy – ships belonging to the queen – and a somewhat rudimentary administration for it: the Navy Board, which consisted of officers separately responsible for building ships, staffing and victualling them, and supplying ordnance. But the running of the navy came under a lord admiral and his deputies, appointed for each of the coastal counties. They had no link with the Navy Board, and there was no career system for naval officers, though the experience of the long war with Spain began to produce professional captains out of the amateur gentlemen (often trained in careers of exploration and piracy) who commanded the queen's ships. In actual war, the Royal Navy was always augmented by privately owned vessels licensed by the crown.

The army, such as it was, had even less organisation, though the Ordnance Office was created early in Elizabeth's reign to administer the newly important weapon of artillery. Military administration had traditionally been the task of the Royal Household and, in a manner, remained so, with the master of the horse providing a species of military expertise, but in reality defence and war were managed by the Privy Council. Tudor and early Stuart armies consisted of contingents raised by commissioners of array in the countries, and of mercenaries hired at home and abroad. The general militia duty imposed on all males between the ages of sixteen and sixty, and supposedly supported by regular county musters and exercises supervised by the lords lieutenant and their deputies, produced only troops for domestic defence; these largely imaginary forces could not be compelled to fight abroad, though they provided material for the real armies recruited by the array.

Military administration was a thicket of malpractice, involving much inefficiency and vast corruption, though it should be remembered that the reality cannot have been quite as desperate as many accounts suggest – or as Shakespeare caricatured it in Falstaff's recruiting efforts in *Henry IV, Part 2*. Soldiers quite often went ill-shod and poorly fed, long waits at ports of embarkation resulted in regular and often massive desertions, contractors made their usual illicit profits, and captains of companies cheated the crown by drawing pay for non-existent soldiers on their roster (dead pays). Nevertheless, by the end of the century English armies were fighting quite effectively in the Netherlands, Normandy and Ireland, proving a severe drain on the resources of the crown and the taxpayer but also displaying a gratifying degree of professional competence.

LOCAL GOVERNMENT

From the point of view of the common man, the agencies of local government mattered more immediately, and more frequently, than those at the centre. Most of these authorities belonged to the royal machinery, though some did not. In the reign of Henry VIII, efforts to control the particularly troublesome parts of the realm along the Scottish border and in the Welsh Marches (along the Severn and on to Cheshire) had produced two supervising bodies – the Council of the North (at York) and the Council in the Marches of Wales (at Ludlow). Both were created by royal commission, with powers of civil and criminal jurisdiction; they were not offshoots of the Privy Council but subject to its authority. In the shires under their charge they acted by Elizabeth's time simply as superior courts of law, also receiving pleas remitted from the centre; they had powers both at common law and at equity. Wales itself had its own system of established courts – the four courts called Great Sessions – that was set up during the reorganisation of 1536 to 1543, when Wales was incorporated into England. These, however, were the exceptional means of local government, designed to deal with unusual areas and problems.

The ordinary diffusion of royal authority throughout the country flexibly and very successfully employed the principle that the king could delegate his rule by commissions empowering named persons to do specified work in his name. At the top of this system stood the assizes. Twice a year, judges of the central courts perambulated one of the six circuits into which the country was divided for this purpose. Usually associated with leading gentlemen from the counties in question, the judges carried three commissions (assize, oyer and terminer, jail delivery), which authorised them to try both civil and criminal pleas at the sessions resulting. In civil pleas, always decided by the verdict of local juries, a case had much better expectations of completion if the plea was brought to that jury in its county than if efforts were made to bring the jury to Westminster. Also, crimes had nearly always to be tried in the shires in which they were committed, which meant that, after the King's

13

Bench settled at Westminster in the early fourteenth century, it had to exercise that jurisdiction by delegation.

The best known of all the commissions was that of the peace, a regular annual instruction that set up courts of quarter sessions in every shire. For reasons of prestige privy councillors and bishops were included in the list where suitable, but most justices of the peace were local gentlemen; some were chosen for their legal experience. Between sessions, individual justices had powers to police the shire and collect material for trials at quarter sessions and assizes. By the 1590s, all felonies were tried at assizes, before a royal judge and his associates. Sessions dealt with lesser misdemeanours as well as the enforcement of controlling statutes, such as those concerned with the fixing of wages and the organising of apprenticeship. In effect, justices of the peace managed the counties for the crown, and since membership on the commission constituted an important aspect of local standing, the crown's control over the composition of the commission helped to preserve its hold over localities.

The executive officer of all these local bodies was still the sheriff. Though no longer the master of his shire, he remained responsible for finding juries, guarding prisoners and producing them for trial, hanging convicted felons, executing all royal writs sent down to the shire, and arranging elections of members of Parliament for the county. A serious study of the Tudor sheriff is overdue.

These were the standing commissions for carrying out local government, but special commissioners abounded – to deal with a particular case, to control river navigation, to investigate complaints, to assess and collect taxes and so on. Writs of commission provided for a flexible and inexhaustible transfer of authority from the centre to the localities and therefore for the extension of royal rule over all the realm. Of course, their effectiveness depended on the willingness of the amateur and unpaid gentlemen so commissioned (often, as at assizes and sessions, assisted by a paid and professional clerk) to carry out the burdensome work demanded by the crown. Though lapses occurred and private favour could frustrate justice, there is no reason for doubting that the system generally worked very well.

We should also note the multiplicity of local courts independent of any exercise of the royal will, at least in their existence and powers, though not necessarily in the work they did. Cities and boroughs ruled themselves under mayors and aldermen who held regular courts for their towns. Those feudal remnants, the courts of the leet and the manor, provided rule and justice (as well as much ordinary administration, for instance over admission to manorial landholding) at the level of the village. They settled the small disputes over boundaries, casual violence, or neighbourly hostility that, to the people at large, mattered more than the occasional greater crimes or litigious disputes that reached the king's courts. In these village tribunals, leading local men – peasants often of small property acting as guardians of the rules (the custom of the manor) – conducted a measure of self-government for the common man that has been insufficiently recognized in social studies of the period.

Two things become apparent as one surveys the working of this sometimes well organized, sometimes haphazard structure of authorities for the government of England. Though the ultimate control vested in bodies such as the king and the Privy Council, whose function and ethos were political, the instruments charged with the application of political power were all in form courts of law – agencies for the settlement of disagreements and claims of right according to known rules. Even the Privy Council, quite apart from its *alter ego* appearance in Star Chamber, often acted as a quasi court, as it responded to petitions put before it by individuals seeking justice. This was government not only under the law but by the law.

Parties to a dispute often tried to avoid the costs and delays involved in using the courts by agreeing to abide by the decision of one or more persons of eminence whose oracular pronouncements carried no powers of enforcement but nevertheless quite frequently terminated a dispute. Arbitration is another subject so far insufficiently studied.

CIVIL SERVANTS

Although many government administrators were unpaid amateurs, the system also provided for a considerable number of salaried professionals. The great Royal Household, the offices of Chancery, the Exchequer, the secretaries of state, and the central courts between them employed men by the hundreds. Most of them had other personal interests and wished to set themselves up as landed gentlemen, investing the profits of office in the only form of wealth that gave social status. Many of them went in and out of office in the wake of their superiors. Some of them, in fact, behaved like members of an American-style spoils system, while others more closely resembled the officials of nineteenth-century Britain, but all were nonetheless civil servants of the crown. Their kind is also found in the localities: officers of the Exchequer (customers and their colleagues in the ports, receivers of land revenue), representatives of the Court of Wards and clerks of assizes and sessions. In the greater departments definite career courses can be discerned as men rose through the ranks, whereas some offices provide interesting evidence of dynastic practices: men would get patents of survivorship or reversion, which enabled them to associate their sons in the office with themselves and thus to create a family preserve that could extend over several generations.

This civil service drew its income from two sources. The crown paid salaries, but these were never meant to be adequate and always lagged behind the steady inflation of prices. The major profits of office arose from the fees paid by people who used the offices. Fees were payable for the issue of all government documents solicited by the public (writs, letters patent), for all enrolments, for every step taken in the paying of revenue. In a case at law, litigants owed regular payments to the officers of the courts as well as to their own attorneys and counsel. Fees were supposedly fixed and indeed were posted in offices, but throughout the period complaints multiplied that officers arbitrarily increased the official scales – as they had to do if they wished to keep up with inflation. In James I's reign, many officers overcharged for their services, but efforts to control their greed achieved very little, while the value of crown office increased markedly.

Though unauthorised increases should not have been tolerated, the fees system by itself constituted no sort of corruption; it reflected the principle that at least a part of the costs incurred by the king's government should be borne by those who specifically made use of it for their own purposes. It has been calculated that around 1625 the official fees collected amounted to about £50,000 a year, or close to a sixth of the regular income of the crown. In addition, beyond any doubt, improper gifts and bribes were paid by people who sought to tip a decision in their favour or at least accelerate the operations of government, but it is understandably difficult to get firm evidence for this. Gifts were no doubt frequently of money, but what we can learn of them shows that presents in kind – a bolt of cloth, a cheese, a quantity of wine, or a piece of venison – very often served, changing manifest corruption into kindnesses bestowed on friends. Frequently promises of compensatory services sufficed, or even kind words about prayers offered or memories recalled.

Some historians have wildly exaggerated the extent of true corruption. While probably fairly rampant at the top, it seems to have played far less part within the civil service proper. Thanks to the survival of the correspondence of Sir Michael Hickes, secretary to Lord Burghley and later assistant to Robert Cecil, we know that the sale of wardships put money that should have gone to the crown into ministers' pockets, and we learn of the sizeable gifts they expected to receive for their favours, though many of these gifts really did represent a proof of personal attachment. But the Cecils' opportunities were exceptionally great. The indications are that truly corrupt behaviour increased at the much looser court of James I, where several genuine scandals came to light. Unquestionably, privy councillors and men of influence thought it right to exploit the help they could give to applicants, and the general ethos of the day supposed that friendly services from one side justified expectations of friendly appreciation from the other.

The line of propriety excluded excessive greed (which was with reason charged against some of the favourites of James I), strikingly biased actions in return for bribes (the charge that ruined Francis Bacon in 1621), and blatant robbing of the royal till (the misbehaviour that brought down Lord Treasurer Suffolk in 1618). Though the worst cases did occur after 1603, it is plain that things improper by the standards of the time (not just by ours) happened under Elizabeth, too. The most systematic suppliers of bribes were foreign envoys intent on buying both favour and information; they found English courtiers exceptionally open to such offers, which the English seem to have treated as an agreeable and amusing way of fleecing the foreigner.

Moralising judgements about 'wholesale corruption' not only go well beyond the evidence but also obscure the realities of a system that incorporated the demands made by close personal acquaintance and relations, with palpable exchanges of favours, in the structure of civil government. The society involved in this work was small, and its members knew one another too well to remove all temptation to exploit acquaintance. Consequently, those less well acquainted needed to use more obviously corrupt methods to attract the attention of the men at the heart of government. Finally, it must be noted that successful careers in the civil service depended not only on favour but also very much on ability, though this encouraging aspect of the scene deteriorated as the monarch and Council distanced themselves from administrative affairs in the 1610s.

THE CHURCH

The king, as head of the commonwealth, thus disposed of a complex structure of government; as supreme governor of the Church of England, he similarly commanded a wide and well-articulated instrument of rule. Like the secular offices, those of the church were inherited from the medieval past but had gone through important transformations that testified to the end of medieval kingship some time in the 1530s. In the church, these changes had been called for after the Henrician Reformation removed the foreign authority of the papacy.

The two provinces of the English church, Canterbury and York, presided over by archbishops, consisted of bishoprics – eighteen in the south and four in the north – themselves divided into archdeaconries. The parishes, the lowest rung in this chain of command, were grouped in rural deaneries. The cathedrals, seats of the bishops, were independently managed by deans and chapters, whose members held 'prebends' and were termed 'prebendaries'. The relative simplicity of this hierarchic order was slightly complicated by the existence of 'peculiars' – parishes and manors lying within one diocese but subject to the bishop or archbishop of another. The archbishop of Canterbury, as primate of England, ranked above his brother of York but had no governmental means of control over him; the traditional organisation of the English church provided for no single instrument of unification, since before the Reformation that function had been exercised by the pope and his court at Rome.

Each province possessed a representative assembly called a convocation, which consisted of an upper house of bishops and a lower house of proctors (elected representatives) of the clergy. By this time the convocations, though they still commonly met during parliamentary sessions, retained no significant powers. If they passed laws for the church, these had no authority without parliamentary enactment. Even the taxes of the clergy, which it required their grant to make available to the crown, were always further embodied in an act of Parliament.

In terms of government, the church, like the state, operated essentially as a system of law courts, presided over by bishops and archdeacons, or in the first case usually by deputies (chancellors, vicars general, officials principal) appointed for the purpose. The courts were linked in a regular sequence of appeals from the lower to the higher, something the state did not possess. The law administered in the church courts stood in some confusion. In 1535 the study of the canon law of the universal church was prohibited at the universities as popish, and in 1545 lawyers trained in the civil (Roman) law were authorised to take the place of canonists as practitioners in the courts. Several attempts to provide a reformed code of law suitable to a Protestant church failed to gain authorisation, until the canons of 1604, agreed by the convocations but never enacted by Parliament, came, as a case of necessity, to be treated as applicable.

The church courts in the main dealt with four categories of cases. They enforced discipline on the clergy in matters of personal behaviour and uniformity of worship; they asserted the claims of the clergy on the laity in matters of money (especially the tithe); they adjudged the moral delicts of the laity, a competence that brought within their grasp not only such sins as adultery and fornication but also all matters arising out of marriages and defamation; and they presided over the probate of testaments so far as movables were concerned. (Land devised by will came under the common law after the Statute of Wills of 1540.) Because they impinged in many, often intimate ways on the life of the people, the church courts were not popular. Though their powers had declined since pre-Reformation days, they remained very active, especially in matrimonial, testamentary, and moral cases. The sanctions they could apply included excommunication (rarely used) and penances, very commonly commuted for money payments. These courts were necessary aids in the affairs of men, as well as somewhat oppressive instruments of social coercion; and clerical lawyers, civilians now rather than canonists, continued to do good business.

The system was inadequate in two important respects. The supposedly ultimate cause for the attention of the church courts – the matter that most concerned the church as an instrument of salvation – was the assurance of spiritually sound means of grace and the prevention of heresy; and by the time that Elizabeth settled her Protestant church, these courts found that they had effectively relinquished jurisdiction over such matters. The second weakness lay in the removal of papal authority, with the consequent loss of a unifying umbrella above the archbishops and a unifying court of appeal above their courts. In both areas, the new pope – the supreme head, and after 1559 the supreme governor, of the Church of England – intervened. The experiment by which Henry VIII delegated the whole of his quasi-papal authority to a vicegerent in spirituals was never repeated after the fall of Thomas Cromwell in 1540, but the statutory creation of an *ad hoc* court of ultimate appeal, called the High Court of Delegates and appointed each time such an appeal came forward, survived quite usefully into the nineteenth century.

For the rest, the crown predictably resorted to its well-tried power to delegate authority by commission. Royal commissions were created within the government of the church for specific occasions before the Reformation, but it was only in the reign of Elizabeth that their existence was regularised by the creation of occasional ecclesiastical commissions over dioceses and especially the setting up of Courts of High Commission for each archiepiscopal province. Possessed of powers to fine and imprison, the high commissions (composed of clergy and laity) dealt with the more serious offences triable at spiritual law and acted as general supervisors of order and uniformity within the church.

The problem of uniformity, however, proved insoluble. Doctrine was plain and simple: since all Englishmen composed one church, all should in matters of the faith behave alike, accepting the doctrines defined in the Thirty-Nine Articles (1563), worshipping according to the rites laid down in the Book of Common Prayer (1559), and obedient to the queen, the bishops and the rest of the established order. Not all Englishmen were willing to do so. Those who refused to accept the restoration of a Protestant church in 1559 and adhered to Roman Catholicism proved no problem for the church courts: their refusal to attend the services of the church (recusancy) and their involvement in actual or potential treasons were matters for the secular courts. Deviance among Protestants, however, called for rectification by the bishops and their courts. These were the instruments available for tackling the many and various failures to conform – ranging from a refusal to use the Prayer Book or some part of it to demands for a presbyterian church government in place of an episcopalian one – which are nowadays summed up under the name 'Puritanism'. These courts also dealt with the more extreme departures from the form of religion laid down in law, namely the growth of separatist sects that rejected the principle of a national church and regarded themselves as the only true Christian congregations ('gathered churches').

The term Puritanism should be reserved for those English Protestants who accepted the existence of a uniform, national church but who in one way or another regarded that set up by the settlement of 1559 as inadequately scriptural and therefore in need of further reform, whether that reform touched the wearing of clerical vestments, the role of prayer and sermon, the use of certain ceremonies reckoned to be 'rags of popery' (for instance, the use of the ring in marriage, the sign of the cross in baptism, or kneeling at communion), or the structure of church government. Few Puritans really looked for revolution, and the attempt made in the 1580s to set up a presbyterian government was easily repressed by Archbishop Whitgift and the high commission. But deviation short of revolution, fed by the ardent Calvinism of a younger generation of clergy coming from the universities, remained ineradicable because it often represented an active spiritual zeal that many in authority welcomed and wished to see at work in the church. Elizabeth herself always implacably opposed all visible signs of non-conformity while remaining indifferent to deviant opinion so long as it caused no public scandal. James, once persuaded that the Puritans did not seek to do away with bishops or undermine his own authority in the church, showed himself more receptive to the disputations ardour of those preachers. In his reign a strongly Protestant, very Calvinist state of mind sufficiently dominated the church, especially after the death of Archbishop Richard Bancroft in 1610, to inhibit energetic action against minor manifestations of non-conformity within the church. Separatists and sectarians were another matter: it was at this time that the English refugee congregations (from which sprang the Pilgrim Fathers of 1620) settled in the Netherlands.

PARLIAMENT

The government of England, secular and ecclesiastical, was very monarchical in its fundamental principles: everything derived from the king, and all lines led back to him. Even if this monarch was supposed to govern under and by the established law, and even though he commonly did so, he resembled a truly absolute king very closely. Jacobean theorists, from the king downward, regularly emphasised this quality in English kingship, though by *absolute* they meant not superiority to the law but only unlimited exercise of power within that law.

Political realities, however, made the king rather weaker in practice than in theory. He had no means of his own to alter the law. His proclamations, theoretically issued with the advice of his Council, could not, it was universally agreed, make new law or abrogate old. If on occasion Elizabeth transgressed this principle when urgent dangers to the state required action against dissidents, she always took care to have such innovatory breaches of the rules ratified as soon as possible by the only lawful means available – by act of Parliament. Though on occasion James favoured a very free doctrine of monarchy and would speak of

21

giving ultimate authority to his proclamations, he never attempted to turn such claims into reality.

The making of law lay with the English Parliament. (Scotland and Ireland, being separate kingdoms, though from 1603 all under one monarch, had their own parliaments.) It used to be thought that everything about that body had been fully worked out, especially by two historians of the previous generation – Sir John Neale and Wallace Notestein – but in the last twenty years their coherent and systematic account has pretty well totally collapsed. A new look, unencumbered by ancient presuppositions, at the various sorts of evidence has shown that they got things very wrong indeed, but the new look has not yet found expression as complete as theirs, for which reason old error persists in some places.[1] Neale and Notestein really confined their attention to the House of Commons, which they regarded as engaged in a struggle for independence and power; they believed that what mattered in the history of Parliament was the alleged rise of an opposition to the crown, achieved by developments in parliamentary procedure and privilege, and expressed in battles over religious and constitutional principles. They put the emphasis on very exceptional occurrences, which, in addition, they misread by evaluating them as signs of a conflict between autocratic rulers and constitutionalist leaders in the Commons – conflicts that supposedly grew steadily more serious and in the end produced the confrontation of the civil war. Convincing though this picture could be at a very superficial level, and reflecting though it did propagandist explanations first put forward by the parliamentary side in the war, it simply falsifies what really went on and has proved as misleading as it has proved persistent. The Parliament of England was a part of the king's government, brought into intermittent existence by his summons and dismissed or prorogued at his will. It constituted the ultimate manifestation of government in action, with total competence over all affairs of state and church. Parliamentary law defined not only treason but also the sole lawful form of religion. Although the initiative in legislating for aspects of government remained with the crown, the existence and role of Parliament certainly meant that in this ultimate exercise of his powers the monarch was associated with a representative of the whole governing order sitting in assembly. Although Parliament originated in the thirteenth century, it underwent a transformation between about 1484 and 1536. Out of this transformation came the familiar institution of three

[1] [But see now above, vol. III, no. 35, and G. R. Elton, 'Parliament', in *The Reign of Elizabeth I*, ed. C. Haigh (London, 1984), 79–100.]

equipollent partners – king, Lords, and Commons, each a part of the Parliament. The king, as head, had a place of formal pre-eminence, and the Lords were socially and politically superior to the Commons. In parliamentary terms, however, they were all equally essential to the existence and the work of the institution: while the king could veto what the other partners had agreed, so could either House kill bills passed by the other or urgently put forward by the crown. In constitutional principle, therefore, all three entities stood on one level, though in political reality the Commons came last and mattered least – true throughout the period in question.

The three parts had to agree for anything to be achieved, and of the three two consisted of scores or even hundreds of people. The necessary agreement, therefore, could be easily upset by even minor disagreements, so that Parliament required regular management and careful guidance by the king's ministers. Councillors always sat in Parliament, in one House or the other, responsible for seeing to it that the purposes for which the crown had called a Parliament were carried through. In this task they had the help of the Speaker of the Commons (then invariably a government appointee), of the judges and other lawyers who sat as assistants in the Upper House, and of men in both houses who, though not formally officeholders, were attached to leading councillors and worked on their behalf. We now call these unofficial leaders 'men of business', a term familiar in parliamentary history down to the later nineteenth century. They were regular attenders at sittings – a fact that distinguished them from the larger part of the Commons and a not negligible part of the Lords – and they made themselves responsible for seeing to it that the business of the session got done. No one, of course, could guarantee such success: opinion and interest varied greatly within Parliament, which could be managed but not coerced. Difficulties and conflict certainly occurred, but such incidents arose from immediate and often factious explosions; they did not constitute the really important history of Parliament as a body.

True to the conventional language of the day, Parliament was called a court – the highest royal court in the land – but its activities rarely resembled those of a genuine court, and when it acted curially it was the Lords who carried out that function. Its actual purposes were of two kinds: the granting of taxes and the making of laws. It had established its control over both functions in the middle of the fourteenth century. Taxes, supposedly for extraordinary needs (war or defensive preparation for war), had since the 1530s been regularly requested for the general costs of government. They consisted of the customs duties (voted in this age for the monarch's life in the Tunnage and Poundage Acts passed in the first Parliament of each reign) and the special income taxes (subsidies) granted as demanded on occasion. Elizabeth asked for money in all but one of the thirteen sessions of her ten Parliaments. James's four Parliaments and eight sessions voted only three grants of taxation, though his demands on those three occasions ranged higher. The penury of government and the consequent 'power of the purse' vested in the Commons have traditionally been regarded as the greatest bulwark of parliamentary freedom and the greatest weakness of the crown in facing the representatives, but it should be noted that these grants rarely caused any dispute at all and became something of a routine, provided they remained at the traditional level. They did, however, begin (in 1571) to provide an opportunity for bringing forward complaints and requests for remedies, which by the eighteenth century was to make tax bills an opportunity for general political discussion.

The making of laws took up most of the time of Parliament. Invariably the majority of bills presented failed to pass, usually because their originators abandoned them in the course of the proceedings or for lack of time. Bills originated with a great variety of promoters: the Privy Council, towns, particular mercantile or manufacturing interests, or individuals interested in matters of both general and personal concern.

Acts were either public (printed at the end of the session and thus deemed to be universally known) or private (not printed and therefore needing to be presented in a certified copy if pleaded in litigation). Public acts dealt mainly with the affairs of crown and state: confirmation of royal powers; settlement of religion; treasons and other crimes; the control and promotion of husbandry, manufacture, and commerce; and reforms of the law. Private acts, according to a ruling of 1607, could not affect more than three counties. They attended to the needs of the localities (for instance, the levying of town rates for bridge building or road repairs, or the embodying in statute of private agreements touching such things as riparian rights or the enclosing of open fields), or of individuals and their families (naturalisation, removal of disabilities, marriage settlements).

Thus the ordinary business of Parliament involved the interests of a great many people, individuals as well as communities (not to mention the community of the whole realm), and for obvious reasons the individuals in question tended to be propertied and therefore influential. A long absence of Parliament probably caused more annoyance because it prevented private legislation than because it was perceived as some sort of a threat to the liberties of the subject. Until 1628, any mention of liberty and privilege in Parliament almost always signified the liberties and privileges of its members, not of the community at large.

The making of laws, however, could have a wider political side to it, a fact that emphasises a further function of Parliament beyond the normal business of the session. In the common constitutional theory of the day, Parliament was the nation in assembly, present in person (king and lords, including the bishops) or by representation (knights for the shires, citizens and burgesses for cities and boroughs). The principle had been exemplified in the reign of Henry VIII when the creation of a unitary realm had been accompanied by the calling of members from hitherto unrepresented regions (Calais, Wales, Cheshire; only Durham was, inexplicably, left out). From its earliest days, the announced purpose of the assembly had included the bringing up of problems by the localities and the presentation of urgent matters by the crown; not without reason was Parliament often called the great council of the realm. For the king, it was an efficient national forum for hearing complaints and disseminating information. Inevitably, however, Parliament came to be involved in issues that concerned government – inevitably, naturally and justly, since it was itself a special instrument of royal rule. Thus all parts of Parliament cooperated in settling the Church of England (1559), considered the political problems raised by the treasons hatched around Mary Queen of Scots (1572, 1587), found themselves exercised over the prosecution of the Spanish war and its economic consequences (in 1597 and 1601 the cause of angry exchanges over burdensome monopolies granted by the crown), were approached when James wished to promote his dream of a union of England and Scotland (1606), and debated iniquities committed by the ministers of the crown (1621, 1624).

Normally these issues were brought forward by the crown managers, as were all but the third example mentioned above. Elizabeth, however, found that some members of the Commons were eager to initiate discussions on touchy subjects, such as the further reform of the church or the uncertainties of the succession. She therefore invented a distinction between matters of the common weal, properly raised in Parliament by anybody, and matters of state, which could be discussed only with her permission. By the next reign this distinction – untenable because the line of demarcation rested with the sovereign's arbitrary decision – had ceased to operate, though it should be noted that matters of state (Edward I's 'grosses besoignes') continued to be put before the

Houses by members of the king's government. Privy Council initiatives unleashed the troublesome parliamentary demand of 1566 that the queen should secure the succession to the throne, and Privy Council politics promoted the so-called impeachments of royal servants in James I's last two Parliaments.

Such controversies, and the constitutional debates occasionally arising from them, do not testify to the existence of opposition parties or the rise of the Commons, but to the fact that Parliament was not only a legislative body but also an important arena of politics – a place where problems of state and nation could be discussed, fought over and sometimes resolved by legislation. Parliament offered a convenient instrument for the antagonists in real politics, the politics of the king's court and Council. So-called opposition nearly always turns out to be a manoeuvre of councillors against councillors, or a more united attempt to force the sovereign into decisions that pressure in Council had not succeeded in making him adopt. The very occasional cases of opposition by one man or a small group not associated with government never got anywhere at all and were stifled by majority opinion in one House or the other. It is only toward the end of the period and really only in the reign of Charles I that a new kind of opposition began to make itself felt – the opposition of ambitious politicians seeking service under the crown and compelled by the monopoly of favour enjoyed by the duke of Buckingham to show themselves enough of a nuisance for king and duke to decide that buying them off with office was worth the candle.

So much for the structure of government. The discussion has now brought us to the highly complex and confusing problems that a systematic analysis of the means of rule tends to hide. Politics used the system but also altered and even perverted it.

POLITICS

The structure of courts, offices, secretaries, bishops, and high commissions worked effectively only insofar as it took account of the existing social structure and the distribution of power within it. This society was plainly hierarchic: every man's place and function were defined in relation to those above and those below him. Only the king had no superiors (except God), and only landless and masterless men had no inferiors. Movement up and down the scale was certainly possible for individuals and their families; fortunes in this 'mobile' society notoriously rose and fell, either through changes in a man's wealth or through the crown's ability to raise inferiors to higher places. But individuals moving upward, or for that matter down, did not alter the ladder on which their climbing and falling took place. By the later sixteenth century there was no truly unfree man left in England; serfdom had in fact disappeared under the pressure of economic facts, though it was never formally abolished. But the free men of England differed widely in status: each had a position in a many-layered structure of social degrees in which a term like *class* has no meaning. This structure is conveniently illustrated in the range of correct forms of address, from a duke's or archbishop's 'grace' to the husbandman's 'goodman'.

One great dividing line separated those who exercised rule from those who did not, the latter on the face of it composing the great majority of Englishmen; but since trial juries and village adjudicators included husbandmen, even this distinction lacked genuine precision. Another line divided men and women, for women in the theory of the law lacked all independence and stood permanently in the tutelage of their fathers or husbands; however, in practice many women, especially widows but also spinsters and even wives, controlled their own affairs and property despite the law and with the frequent assistance of the court of Chancery. One of the more piteous but not uncommon figures of the age was the great landowner whose mother survived his inheritance of the estate by thirty years or more, during which time she by law possessed at least a third of what was nominally his and in the process very likely ruined him.

Such a structure by degree is theoretically coherent but in practice needs a social glue if ambition and ruthlessness are not to make it fly apart. And what held it together is commonly called the patronage system. This familiar term is usually interpreted as either a bond of loyalties or a form of pervasive corruption, but in fact it was neither. It meant simply that the relations between superior and inferior were anchored in the possession by the former (the patron) of desirable goods that the latter (the client) sought to attain in return for supporting his patron's causes. The desirable goods ranged from outright gifts to the bestowal of profitable offices and landed possessions to protection and assistance in any difficulties the client might find himself in. The returns made by the client included both active aid – for instance, by voting in parliamentary elections or by supplying physical force for the patron's proceedings – and the less substantial but equally important support that the possession of a large following gave to a patron's standing. Every man of substance depended for his influence on attracting the services of inferiors and therefore on his ability, exercised or potential, to satisfy his clients' requirements.

These relationships and their political manoeuvres pervaded all society, especially among the ruling elite. In no sense did they amount to corruption, though abuse of the system had led in the fifteenth century to the emergence under the crown of lesser rulers with private armies and the means to subvert the instruments of the law for private advantage. Of this kind of corruption very little survived into the later sixteenth century, by which time the crown had firmly re-established its overall control of society. This control was possible because, of all patrons, only the king was nobody's client, and he possessed far and away the largest reservoir of the goods that clients wished to obtain.

Thus the patronage system underpinned the monarchy, but it also qualified the dominance of the monarch in two ways. In the first place, if the central government wished to make itself felt in the provinces, and especially if it wished to carry through the enforcement of law and order or the maintenance of religious uniformity, it needed to retain the active cooperation of the hierarchically ordered society over which it presided. Government might be 'bureaucratic' at the centre, with civil servants doing more or less as they were told, but its exercise in the localities meant using men who could not be ordered about in this fashion. The power of these men to carry into effect the commands received from the centre depended on their standing at the point of action: though possession of a royal commission enhanced their status, they could exact obedience as noblemen or leading gentlemen rather than as servants of the crown. This fact gave them a measure of independence and something of a bargaining counter when they wished to secure the recompences of the patronage system in return for doing the government's work.

The real power in the shires rested with the local aristocracy and gentry, often deliberately promoted by the crown against some hostile interest. They had to be kept reasonably content with favours, and their deeper convictions needed regard and respect. Much the same conditions, in a smaller way, applied to the oligarchs who ruled the towns, though few towns – London being the great exception – could afford to do without the patronage of some great man in the neighbourhood, who in turn derived prestige from holding an honorific sinecure in the towns within his patronage structure. The earl of Leicester picked up high stewardships of boroughs with the same zest that Lord Burghley applied to the high stewardships of the two universities. Royal power was thus clearly, if often unsystematically and unpredictably, limited by the need to carry 'the country' along in the framing and execution of policy. If orders were issued that went counter to the interests of the local rulers, they were either ignored or, if the government insisted on their execution, produced the sort of relentless pressure that threatened future loyalties.

In this respect a real difference should be noted between the age of Elizabeth and that of her successor. Elizabeth's government kept carefully in touch with the localities and knew both men and public opinion throughout the realm very well. Lord Burghley decorated a wall of his house with a map of the English counties that showed the leading families in every region, and his correspondence was in great part a continuing flow from and to the people who ruled locally. The inflow offered detailed information on what was going on or being said, as well as requests for favour; the outflow responded with exhortations, instructions, promises, and reassurance. In consequence Elizabethan government could expect its orders (which it tailored to circumstances) to be obeyed. It rarely needed to pander to independent men in the shires; it worked on known ground and through familiar people, preventing opposition or non-cooperation by anticipating such difficulties rather than by confronting them when they showed themselves.

James I and his ministers, especially after the decline of the earl of Salisbury in the later 1600s, lost this close touch with the people on whose cooperation they so manifestly depended. The results were uncertain relations, an inability to get orders carried out, a widening split on such basic issues as those of religious diversity, and ultimately an increasing alienation of the country from the court – an alienation that, as the next reign was to show, could easily supply disaffected court politicians with disquieting support in their political struggles at the centre.

Politics in the Elizabethan counties characteristically revolved around the efforts of local rivals to secure crown favour, a state of affairs that clearly improved the crown's freedom of action. All men of ambition wooed the court, which in return had very little wooing of its own to do, provided it continued to use its advantage with instructed care and informed good sense. In the next reign, shire politics increasingly testified to the existence of local parties, only one of which had much hope of enjoying court favour. The other tried vainly to break into what had become a charmed circle and thus came to regard king and court not with greed and loyalty, but with disappointment and distrust.

The other circumstance that limited the monarch's power of patronage sprang from the elementary fact that kings could grant only such requests as came to their knowledge. Petitions had to be presented before they could be answered. This gave great importance, at times amounting to political control, to the normal channels for such communications, and in the first place this meant the secretary or secretaries of state. Apart from preparing the Council's business and carrying most of its decisions into effect, apart from managing foreign affairs by their conduct of the necessary correspondence and their collection of intelligence, the secretaries enjoyed great power by virtue of their regular access to the sovereign.

Their only real rivals in this matter were the monarch's personal attendants – ladies and a few gentlemen of the Privy Chamber under Elizabeth (who quite deliberately withheld political power from her female companions), gentlemen of the Privy Chamber and Bedchamber under James I. Of course, men specially favoured – such as the earl of Leicester (Robert Dudley) under Elizabeth or the earl of Somerset (Robert Carr) under James – could at times bypass normal channels and offer a good service to urgent clients, but in the total operation of the royal patronage their interventions played a minor part. Even they quite often worked through the secretary or the Privy Chamber. It may be supposed that, as royal favourites, they could hope for a more compliant response from those necessary intermediaries than could most men, but the intermediaries remained necessary.

The rule of the Cecils at court (unsuitably unglamorous though their personalities were) extended with mild interruptions from 1558 to 1612, and it rested upon the possession of the secretaryship, alternating with solid alliances with other secretaries, such as Francis Walsingham. Walsingham died in 1590, and when the queen delayed for six years before appointing Robert Cecil to his place, old Burghley, while training his son for the job, reassumed duties he had formally dropped in 1572. Jacobean secretaries – generally men of lesser mettle, truly executive officers rather than leading politicians – did not forget the lesson taught by the Cecils. Their lack of lustre, has been mistaken for a lack of importance: behind the scenes, through their control of access to the king, they maintained an influence that historians seem to have failed to notice. James, admittedly, made himself generally more accessible than Elizabeth had done; he could be petitioned directly while on horseback, hunting at Royston or Newmarket.

This aspect of the patronage system subjected the king to the manoeuvres, desires and even conspiracies of men who were nominally servants but in practice could become masters. In the 1620s George Villiers, duke of Buckingham, worked to monopolise control of the king and with it control of the royal patronage. Buckingham's success proved disastrous because it alienated the neglected sector of the ruling caste, probably the chief single cause of the crisis of 1640–2. He secured his influence by the ruthless exploitation of the two things that shaped court politics – royal favour and the building of factions.

Factions were the visible organisation (perhaps too strong a word) of patrons and their followers for securing political and financial benefits. Factional organisation ran through the whole of this hierarchic society but became most manifest at court (where it organised the exploitation of patronage) and much less evident in Council (where it could supposedly organise the promotion of rival policies). In the shires, factions appear to have shifted rather loosely with personalities and in response to events, but family alliances at times gave them stability and endurance. Elizabeth, well aware of the difficulties that her dependence on others for information about the realm created for her, liked to balance her factions. James tended to fall into the hands of his factions, though for much of his reign he also managed to keep them dangling and to preserve some real freedom of action. The factions of court politicians stretched through the realm by the attachment to them of people and factions in shires and boroughs, and many political struggles of the day cannot be understood unless that fact is kept in mind.

At the same time, the prevalence and especially the permanence of factions can be exaggerated. The power of a leader depended entirely on his ability to produce the goods, and no following ever felt bound to adhere to a patron in adversity. Moreover, these followers included too many men themselves of weight and influence, both at court and in the country, for the nominal leaders to be able to act as they pleased. Even as the patronage system limited the power of the crown, so it also forced politicians to observe the limitations set by their clients' individual strength and status.

The influence of faction, weakened by the willingness of followers to switch allegiance if it seemed prudent to do so, was further reduced by the readiness of wiser politicians to address also men who technically did not belong to their clientele in terms of friendship, favour, and consideration. The Cecils throughout made a point of offering assistance to anybody willing to respond, without insisting that everyone so favoured should regard himself as a Cecilian: in a way, they copied the crown in refusing to confine themselves to a fixed set of useful acquaintances. On the other hand, people like Leicester, the Howard clan under James, and ultimately Buckingham, who tended to demand a firm attachment from those they aided, in the end ruined the usefulness and flexibility of the faction system. Efforts to create monopolies over benefits and to make them available only to those who humbly acknowledged their service to the patron put too high a premium on self-interest and too low a premium on friendship. Few even of Buckingham's clients had sufficient respect for him to give him loyalty, and he came to depend solely on the king's favour.

An earlier danger signal had appeared with the entry upon the political stage of Robert, earl of Essex, in the late 1580s. Essex tried far too blatantly to create a national network of faction for himself, a hectic enterprise that shocked solid politicians, surrounded him with men of neither weight nor sense, and aroused the fatal suspicions of the queen. His faction-building forced Robert Cecil to practise similar tactics, though it was largely Cecil's refusal to appear in public as a leader of a faction that gained him his victory at court and with his sovereign. If Essex had been successful, faction would have hardened into party, a state of affairs that no tenant of the throne could have tolerated – Elizabeth allowed Essex's fate to demonstrate that truth for the benefit of other ambitious men. The ruin of Essex enabled Cecil to return to the wiser policy of treating faction as only one element (and a fluid one at that) in the power structure upon which he rested his government of the realm in the first years of James's reign.

Faction both local and central thus grew out of the search for influence by means of which power and profit might be obtained. Because factions rather obviously embodied plain self-interest, despite all the professions of undying friendship, they never could be anything but fluid so long as kings avoided putting themselves into fetters by giving sole favour to one faction leader. Men calculating the advantages of the Tudor and especially the Stuart courts could not afford to let themselves be moved by loyalties and sentiments. Faction was therefore a poor instrument for the working out of policy; those who followed power in the search for wealth used faction, those who sought power for the purpose of directing affairs knew that faction by itself could not aid them.

Royal policy dealt in effect with two areas of government: relations with other kings and nations, and the control of the realm. It is quite evident that in the minds of kings and queens the former came first, which distinguishes royal concerns from those of modern historians.

Both Elizabeth and James saw themselves above all as members of an international clan of monarchs; the problems raised by these relations – diplomacy and war – preoccupied them. Internal policy necessarily included the assuaging of 'grievances' (that is, balancing of rival interests seeking wealth and welfare), though it should be noted that enough of these demands involved the protection of domestic trade and manufacture to have international implications. More strictly internal were the issues of public order and obedience, usually left entirely to the Council and its subordinate agencies. Aside from all this, there were the problems of the church – uniformity and dissent – which, thanks to the aggressive policies of the Counter-Reformation papacy and the European Calvinist network, also had their international aspects.

In these matters faction should have played little part: policy, it was generally agreed, was the work of a monarch presiding over a united nation in whose interest he or she governed, and successful monarchs managed to make a reality of the ideal, as Elizabeth usually did and the Stuarts usually failed to do. But policy also, of necessity, produced differences of opinion concerning both what should be done and how it should be achieved. Policy therefore supplied the one element to faction that made it more than a device for seeking power and wealth, the one constituent part that could give it endurance. That element was principle, or (as we are now taught to call it) ideology. Relations with other powers involved basic principles of alliance or opposition and always entailed the possibility of armed conflict; thus one can usually find peace and war parties at court and in Council who held to their convictions with persistence and assurance. In an age of religious wars, both foreign relations and the internal problem of uniformity infused policy with principles of the faith, and divisions among makers of policy often arose out of varying zeal for the Protestant cause. In the 1570s and 1580s, the threat of Spain, seen by some as an overbearing and by others as a Catholic power, created a real rift on the Council between those (Leicester, Hatton, Walsingham) who called for active resistance and war, and those (Burghley in particular) who regarded peace as essential to the survival of England and held that the cause of Protestantism could be better protected by diplomacy and guile. From about 1587 all policy was profoundly affected by the long war with Spain, complicated by the equally prolonged endeavour to re-establish English rule over all of Ireland. Though James concluded the former and inherited the accomplishment of the latter, his policies consisted in great part of reactions to the strains produced by the continued hostilities in the

Netherlands, by the rivalry of Spain and France, and from 1621 by the outbreak of what was to become the Thirty Years War, in which England was directly (though very ineffectually) involved through the marriage of James's daughter Elizabeth to the elector palatine, briefly king of Bohemia and thereafter (1620) an exile at The Hague.

High politics, then, responded much less to domestic issues or power struggles within the gentry and aristocracy than to the international stresses of a much disturbed age – stresses in which religion played a leading role. Even though some statesmen might try to write religion out of politics and pursue national or dynastic interests in bare purity, those whom they governed and on whose cooperation they depended very often made religion a principle that transcended self-interest. A typical effect of these complications can be seen when James made peace with Spain: he immediately and irreversibly aroused anger and distrust among both ardent Protestants and those (especially the organisers of maritime war and plunder) who had found the war profitable – sometimes, of course, the same men. The religious (or indeed the economic) concerns of the nation, represented at court by politicians who were more than faction leaders but less than independent statesmen, formed one of the conditions for policy. Another arose from the equally principled concerns of other powers, usually represented by strictly unprincipled agents; the politics of the English court derived in no small measure from the conspiratorial activities of foreign ambassadors seeking to exploit faction and to influence the English monarch's decisions.

There is still much to be learned about the manner in which policy was actually made and since the process often took place either in the monarch's mind or in unrecorded conversions, much of it will always remain obscure. Yet it seems clear that the role of faction can easily be overestimated. The Elizabethan and Jacobean factions found it difficult to accommodate principle because their whole essence lay in the pursuit of interest that an excessive devotion to principle could only hinder; it might easily tie a man to a declining patron and therefore destroy for him the very virtue of faction.

The so-called factions arrayed in the Council for the pursuit of policy ought not to be given that name. They were really groupings of individuals – leaders, not followers – that rested on perceptions of political problems and on genuine personal convictions that often derived from faith. Zeal for the Reformation animated many of them, and even more were certain that they faced a popish plot of one kind or another, an apprehension that became well entrenched after the arrival in England of Mary Queen of Scots (1568) and, thanks to the Spanish war and the Gunpowder Plot, easily survived her execution (1587). These attitudes determined much of the advice the monarch received and acted on. They pushed people into cooperation with like-minded colleagues and led to confrontations in Council and elsewhere, but they operated against the sort of factions that derived from local connections and purely material ambitions. The politics of the age revolved around two fundamental pivots – power and principle – and according to the problems faced were directed either by unprincipled aspiration or by inner convictions of an ideological kind. Only Queen Elizabeth seems to have been entirely immune to ideology, unless her vanity and self-assertion deserve that name; she alone conducted policy with an eye solely to her success as a monarch and a symbol of national unity. James, in person much less suited to act as such a symbol, shared her vanity, but in his case it took the form of claims to intellectual eminence, which made him an ideologue in matters of religion.

Thus the structure of its government made England a monarchy limited by the rule of the law, but not a constitutional monarchy limited by the counterweight of Parliament, which was really an instrument of royal government. In actual practice, the real limitations on monarchy sprang from political realities that rendered the king dependent on others for advice, cooperation, and effectiveness in rule; without the willingness to act shown by a hierarchy of people over whom no real means of compulsion existed, royal government hardly existed. The Tudors knew how to make their government much more effective than such generalisations might suggest; their control of patronage enabled them to hold the nation together and secure loyalties. Despite divisions and serious disagreements (visible at times in Parliament but more commonly in the everyday operation of political ambition and strife), the sentiments of nationalism and Protestantism were powerful bonds within the nation as well as between the nation and its head.

Doubts and more than doubts concerning this system of government have often been expressed, and some would call it ramshackle. This it never was, though by the standards of the twentieth century it was loose and flexible: it worked, provided it was operated with political awareness and skill. No king could afford to act as though the theory of absolute monarchy really described its practical possibilities, and no king could safely ignore the claims, rights, and demands of powerful groups or individuals within his society. Yet, by the standards of its own day, the England of Elizabeth and James was a coherent and much governed country, improving in internal order, in wealth and standing, and (not to be forgotten) in the production of a high culture.

LEX TERRAE VICTRIX: THE TRIUMPH OF PARLIAMENTARY LAW IN THE SIXTEENTH CENTURY★

Even before the sixteenth century, the king's high court of Parliament had become England's legislative instrument: that part of the king's government which defined the law of the land by making and repealing statutes that constituted the ultimate definition of the common law. The fact that law developed and changed much more commonly in the course of litigation or discussion among judges and counsel is here irrelevant. The pronouncements of Parliament may have been rare by comparison and may often have summed up innovations carried forward in the courts, but when it set its seal upon some item of the law it established a certainty far more definite than the precedents created by judgements. In the course of the sixteenth century, that certainty and control over the law grew noticeably more positive, as printing fixed the text of statutes and compelled all concerned to respect their precise wording. All this has been set out before,[1] but one important issue deserves further attention. Parliament might hold ultimate authority over the common law, but its universal authority over the realm for that very reason depended on the exclusive authority of the common law within that realm. At the beginning of the century that authority was still limited by the independent force of rival legal systems, ranging from local customs to the canon law of the Universal Church, with all of which systems the common law had before this engaged in battles without ever winning an outright victory. A hundred years later, local custom and canon law still operated in certain areas of litigation but by then they had all come to accept the superiority of the common law and in particular had all come to accept the power of that law's legislative instrument to dictate to them too. A proper understanding of what happened requires a study of the Reformation, but one which asks

★ [*The Parliaments of Elizabethan England*, ed. D. M. Dean and N. L. Jones (Oxford, 1990), 15–36.] This is an adapted and slightly expanded translation of my article, 'Lex terrae victrix: Der Rechtsstreit in der englischen Frühreformation', *Zt. der Savigny-Stiftung*, Kanonistische Abteilung 70 (1984), 217–36. I am grateful to Professor Martin Heckel for permission to reuse this material, hitherto not very accessible to English-speaking historians.

1 See e.g. *Tudor Constitution*, 235–40.

questions different from the religious, political or social ones usually investigated.

It is true that the English Reformation in the reign of Henry VIII can be analysed in various ways and that most of them have been tried. Among historians who regret that it ever happened it has commonly been seen as an unhappy consequence of the king's wayward lechery. Others have treated it as an act of state by means of which the monarchy overcame the last independent rival in power within the realm. Even for those scholars who will admit genuinely religious origins and judge the event within the general setting of the European Reformation, uncertainties and differences persist. Medievalists seem content to treat it as merely a continuation, at best consummation, of long-standing and highly predictable developments: an episode in the history of the nation so clearly derived from its past that its importance must not be overstressed. Did it witness the triumph of laity over clergy, of the king over the last limitation upon his absolute powers, of a new faith over an old? Lately there has been a tendency to believe that nothing much happened at all because the whole country cannot be shown to have swiftly turned Protestant, as though only instant conversion could justify speaking of the Reformation at all.[2] The very diversity of reactions and interpretations demonstrates the magnitude of that break with Rome, that emergence of an independent national church, even as the size of the event fully justifies the wide range of views about it. But among those views, which turn upon politics, faith and personalities, one line of approach has not been prominent, even though it lies nearest to the language and concepts current at the time. The Reformation has not been investigated as an event in the history of the law. Yet, whatever else may have happened, in the first instance there occurred a collision and conflict of laws.

It is necessary to distinguish the various stages of the Henrician Reformation with some care. The central issue in debate altered twice quite drastically, with the result that both the battleground and the aims of the combatants moved into different planes. In the beginning the real question arose from the king's request that the pope should terminate his marriage with Catherine of Aragon. Then, when the curia, under pressure from Catherine's nephew Charles V, refused a service in itself by no means unusual, there resulted that 'break with Rome' which had not in the first place been intended: the king took over the headship of

[2] Christopher Haigh (ed.) *The English Reformation Revised* (Cambridge, 1987); J. J. Scarisbrick, *The Reformation and the English People* (Oxford, 1984).

his territorial church and became pope in his own country, in order that his personal problems might be resolved by agencies staffed by his own subjects. The necessity of finding a justification in law for the unquestionably revolutionary transfer of dignities then called forth a search for the legal foundations of the supremacy. At each stage of this progressive crisis different questions of law arose, different even though they were interdependent and developed one from another. If we are to discover which kind of law – and therefore what kind of polity – in the end emerged victorious, we must study the three stages and their juristic problems separately. The final outcome was by no means inevitable or even visible from the first.

In that first crisis of the divorce only one of the existing European legal systems played any part: no rival concepts of law collided here but only mutually opposed interpretations of the canon law. All agreed that the Scripture (Leviticus 20:21) prohibited marriage with a brother's widow, provided the earlier union had been consummated. Hence the debate over the delicate question of whether Prince Arthur had in fact consummated his marriage with Catherine, and hence Henry's highly dubious attempts to prove an alleged fact which the queen resolutely denied. Dubious or not, there is no reason to think that the pope would not have accepted those proofs if he had been free of imperial pressure. It was his unwillingness to pronounce judgement that provoked the first conflict – still a conflict not between legal systems but between personalities. As the king explained to the pope, the parties were in dispute over the same law: 'Nostris et vestris sunt iidem libri, adsunt iidem interpretes'[3] (we share the same books and are served by the same interpreters).

A second problem arose in the course of this first stage: had Julius II's bull of dispensation removed the obstacles to the king's marriage? If it had, the king had lost his right. In order to obtain his ends, Henry therefore found himself compelled to deny the papal power to dispense from the law of God, an issue also contained within the purview of the canon law of the church. Both parties investigated the canonistic precedents, and English propaganda placed special emphasis upon the favourable verdicts collected from various European universities in the years 1530 and 1531. As late as December 1533 the authoritatively concise *Articles devised by the whole consent of the king's most honourable council* based their case on this point. Neither the pope nor any other

[3] Henry VIII to Clement VII, 28 December 1531: *Records of the Reformation*, ed. N. Pocock (1870), II, 148–9.

39

human being, it was stated, could do away with the laws of God and nature (meaning *lex divina* and *lex naturae* in their technical sense), with the result that Leviticus 20 allowed the king, who professed to have innocently fallen into sin, no escape from the dilemma of his invalid marriage.[4]

This interpretation of the *lex divina* naturally contradicted the papal claim, embedded in the canon law of Rome, to be able to dispense also from the law of Scripture. Henry's interpretation deprived the curia of part of its instruments for the government of the church. In addition, at a time when the sack of Rome (1527) had seriously impaired the main sources of papal income, the pope could not afford to surrender a financially very profitable claim. With the canonists unable to agree and the pope unwilling to dissolve his marriage, Henry put forward another concept of the canon law which would enable him legitimately to rid himself of his wife. He maintained that the divorce could be pronounced by the authorities of the church in England; such a judgement, he alleged, could not be appealed to Rome nor was Rome entitled to advoke the case from England. To support this proposition, Henry again cited only rules of the canon law, especially the canons of the early councils; at this point, no sort of schismatic notions were put forward. It was simply stated and proved from the documents of the law of the church that the provinces of the church did not in any way move towards separation from the Universal Church when they claimed that measure of independence which the law granted them. The king emphasised both the sound sense of this and the precedents allegedly in support of what he regarded as a perfectly normal entitlement: 'Mari et montibus a Roma disiungimur, et tamen Romam citamur, quod nunquam auditum apud nos est, regem fuisse citatum' (sea and mountains separate us from Rome, and yet we are cited to appear at Rome; that a king should be so cited was never heard amongst us). Such papal proceedings were oppressive when applied to a private person, but 'in principe vero non ferendum' (for a prince unbearable).[5] In this respect, too, the English propaganda always repeated reliance on the same canonistic principles, as for instance in the *Articles of the Council:* the decision to entrust the trial of the matrimonial dispute to the archbishops in England rested, it was claimed, upon the principle enunciated by the councils of the church 'that cases of strife or

---

[4] Ibid., 525.   [5] Ibid., 150.

controversy being once begun in any region shall there and in the said region be finally determined, and none other where'.[6]

Thus the issues involved in the grand case of the divorce itself – the case which triggered off the Reformation in England – remained from first to last problems in the interpretation of the canon law, with Henry maintaining that the claims of what he called the papal canon law could not be reconciled to the law of God upon which that of the church was meant to depend. As late as 1534, at a time when the second stage had long been reached, it was asserted that the king would never, of course, have proceeded against the pope 'except he had seen the law of God clearly on his side'.[7]

At this point, however, such a position no longer constituted the truth of the conflict. In 1527–9, and possibly into the spring of 1531, it was genuinely intended to reconcile the differences between king and pope upon an agreed solution within the canon law; the king was really convinced that the support offered to him by carefully selected universities in England, France and Italy would persuade Rome of the truth (as he saw it). The years of negotiations, during which Henry VIII displayed a barely believable patience, lived by this illusion. Meanwhile, however, it had become clear to others – especially to Thomas Cromwell, rising star within the administration – that this line of operations could not lead to success. What may be called the fraternal strife with the pope over the true meaning of canonistic detail developed irresistibly into a dispute concerning the general papal claims to authority in the church. And thus the schism appeared at the gates.

As we have already seen, the king's choice of proofs insensibly slid from the positive provisions of the canon law into the abstract laws of God and nature. Everyone agreed that the positive law of the church had to derive from those superhuman laws, with the implication that disagreements concerning the canon law should be resolved by reference to the laws of God and nature. The consequences of this somewhat naive conviction cause little surprise. While the canon law could be read in books, only opinions existed about the actual contents of those laws created by God; the law of nature more especially would readily adapt itself to any reading that might prove useful. Thus Christopher St German declared as early as 1523 that the common law of England

---

[6] Ibid., 525.
[7] Ibid., 545 ('The little treatise against the muttering of some papists in corners').

derived directly from the law of nature – or, as he glossed it, the law of reason.[8] The pope's power to dispense could be disputed within the framework of the canon law; but if one wished to question the pope's claim to act as the ultimate court in the affairs of the English church one needed to resort to other-worldly laws and confront the 'papal-canon law' with the law of God.

In this manner Henry made himself supreme head of the Church of England. The foundation of proof that he offered for his claim was entirely a priori and ran thus. The Universal Catholic Church consists of parts organised in polities ruled by kings. As souls the inhabitants (subjects) form a church which in extent agrees entirely with the commonwealth composed of their bodies. Over them, acting as God's deputy, there rules a monarch simultaneously king of the common-wealth and supreme head of the church. This theory of the constitution (reminiscent of early medieval views of *Landeskirchen*) appears fully worked out in the preamble of Cromwell's act of appeals (January 1533), whose enactment was concerned only with the prohibition of all appeals from English to foreign courts. The importance of this act has repeatedly been called in question, simply because the principle stated in the preamble did not lead to equally resounding practical consequences in the body of the act, but this is to misunderstand what was going on. When a statute which did little more than extend the provisions of the old praemunire laws opened with a comprehensive constitutional definition, it did so because that definition was new and needed to be resoundingly proclaimed. The clergy had accepted the supremacy title in 1531 and had thus removed all theoretical difficulties standing in the way of Henry's claim. Thus, when Cromwell insisted that 'this realm of England is an empire ... governed by one supreme head and king ... unto whom a body politic compact of all sorts and degrees of people ... be bounden and owe to bear next to God a natural and humble obedience',[9] he was not trying to make new law but stating a newly established foundation for the character of the unitary realm of England – an empire so recognised in the world and therefore totally independent of all external authority. However long the prehistory may have been of efforts to subject the Church of England to the royal authority and rule, the schismatical achievement of 1533 was nevertheless totally novel and

[8] Christopher St German, *Doctor and Student*, ed. T. F. T. Plucknett and John Barton (Selden Society, 1974), 13–19.
[9] 24 Henry VIII, c. 12.

called for the provision of proof.[10] By choosing statute for making that proclamation Cromwell placed the authority of the common law behind a particular political philosophy. But what grounds in law, beyond mere assertion, could be alleged to substantiate Henry's claim?

In the act of appeals Cromwell did not allege any named law; instead, and at first sight surprisingly, he produced the evidence of 'diverse ... histories and chronicles' which allegedly testified to the existence and constitution of that unitary state. The reference was, in fact, to the collection of historians' statements which had been in process of being compiled for some three years and was intended to provide support for the new situation; in the propaganda of the 1530s it came to be reused several times.[11] However, Cromwell apart (and he too on this occasion only), no one seems to have regarded these voices from the past as sufficient justification for the replacement of the pope by the king: to this day, that act of 1533 remains the only one to call for the testimony of historians as the foundations of a political theory. Both the acceptance in 1531 of the royal supremacy by the Convocations and the 1534 act of supremacy[12] in effect ignored the search for theoretical foundations: both simply accept the supremacy as universally known and long since existing. Henry VIII's own position was very uncomplicated and straightforward: he was supreme head of the church as vicar of God and hence by the grace of God. The most impressive treatise in support of this revolution, Stephen Gardiner's *Oratio de vera obedientia* (1535),[13] very elegantly developed this confident claim without trying to justify it in law: mainly directed at the spiritualty and foreign readers, and strictly clericalist, it had no difficulty in swallowing the king's papal position. And Gardiner should be read as mirroring exactly what Henry thought. Apart from having been the king's secretary from 1529 to 1534, he had been deeply involved ever since 1527 in the preparation of the documents for the divorce process; in addition, out of favour since the middle of 1532, he intended his book to help restore him in the king's good grace. Remembering all this, we have here the fullest statement of

[10] It seems to me that John Guy, 'Thomas Cromwell and the intellectual origins of the Henrician Reformation', *Reassessing the Henrician Age*, ed. A. Fox and J. A. Guy (Oxford, 1986), 151–78, does not sufficiently distinguish between a prehistory of ideas and a decision to make a proclaimed reality of them.
[11] G. D. Nicholson, 'The nature and function of historical argument in the Henrician Reformation' (Ph.D. dissertation, University of Cambridge, 1977).
[12] 26 Henry VIII, c. 1.
[13] See *Obedience in Church and State: Three Political Tracts by Stephen Gardiner*, ed. P. Janelle (Cambridge, 1930).

Henry's fundamental convictions. England, he held, was an independent body politic in both its spiritual and secular aspects, so that its ruler combined within himself the offices of king and spiritual head. Such was the will of God, for of course only God could appoint his deputy on earth; no earthly source of power either could or did contribute in any way.

According to this 'high-church' theory, therefore, the royal supremacy rested on the law of God, in precisely the way that the pope had proved the existence of his supremacy, though the king could offer only less persuasive quotation from Scripture (mostly from the Old Testament) than the pope's 'hic est Petrus' and such like. The King simply took over the papal position inasmuch as it concerned his own empire or independent and unitary state. As the act of appeals – rather unnecessarily introducing the evidential labours of historians – pointed out, he thus possessed powers of judicature over both laity and clergy: authorities on both sides derived their powers solely from him. These theoretical expositions raised hardly any problems of either philosophy or theology so long as the right divine extended only to matters spiritual, but behind that monolithic thesis there lurked major practical difficulties which were bound to lead to an ever more manifest conflict between rival legal systems.

These difficulties sprang from the fact that in England *rex solus* (the king in his own person) did not have legislative powers; he could make new law and abolish old only in conjuction with the Lords and Commons in Parliament. It was in this period that it became generally accepted that the king himself formed one of the constituent parts of the Parliament. That principle plainly underlay Christopher St German's detailed explanation of the powers which Parliament could exercise over the church,[14] and it was expressly enunciated by Henry himself in 1542.[15] As a member of the Parliament the king could do things he could not do as a personal ruler. As supreme head (local pope) he was absolute and could issue decrees for matters spiritual; as king he could exercise this fundamental function in the state only as one member of one (sovereign) mixed body. Now it was recognised at once that without the cooperation of Parliament it would be impossible to equip the royal supremacy with practical reality. True, in 1506 the judges had

[14] 'New additions' (1531): see *Doctor and Student*, 317–40. The Parliament is there (p. 317) recognised as consisting of king, Lords and Commons.
[15] *Tudor Constitution*, 277: '. . . the Parliament, wherein we as head and you as members are conjoined and knit together into one body politic'.

laid it down that a secular law (such as an act of Parliament) could not bestow a spiritual jurisdiction upon a layman even if he was king, and Thomas More lost his life because he rejected the act of supremacy precisely on those grounds.[16] This impediment was ignored, or (as in St German's 'New additions') comprehensively eroded: the Reformation constituted a constitutional revolution just because it terminated this limitation upon royal power. For the king needed such secular laws in order to write the divinely granted supremacy into the law of his land. The doctrine behind that supremacy made it a sin against God to deny the king's claims, and that sin could be punished by an ecclesiastical court using the canon law, with excommunication as the ultimate sanction. But the secular head of the church could rest easy only if he was able to prevent subversion or deal with it by means of the punishments available in the common law: the sin had to be defined as a crime over which the courts of the common law exercised jurisdiction. And only parliamentary statute could add to the crimes (treasons and felonies) solely triable there.

The statutes of the Reformation Parliament, as is well known, tried hard to observe the necessary distinctions. None of them ever remotely attempted to ground the supremacy on anything but the ordinance of God, which they accepted as starting point for enacting stated consequences and imposing penalties upon various forms of resistance or disobedience. Since the king was supreme head, it followed that he had powers of taxing the clergy of his church, appointing its bishops, controlling dispensations, and so forth, all of which powers could be defined and protected in the law without ever calling in question the purely divine creation of the king as God's vicar on earth for his dominion. The act of supremacy rode over the problem of the grounds on which Henry rested his supremacy by simply accepting this detail as given: 'Albeit the king's majesty justly and rightfully is and oweth to be supreme head of the Church of England.' Thereafter it proceeded to register that fact for two reasons stated, namely for public awareness of that fact and for 'the increase of virtue in Christ's religion within this realm of England'. Thus the enactment declared that the king and his successors were to be accepted as supreme heads of the church and were to have full power to deal with all 'errors, heresies, abuses, offences, contempts and enormities' correctable by a 'spiritual authority or jurisdiction'. The act did not claim to have created either title or ensuing

---

[16] Ibid., 237.

powers but only to register both.[17] It wished merely to publish the facts, so that all subjects should know their duty. In the same spirit the act of six articles of 1539 rested the king's desire to establish doctrinal uniformity in the realm on his duty as 'by God's law supreme head immediately under Him of this whole Church and Congregation of England'.[18]

Yet that very act also contained hints that the strict separation between the authority given to the king by God and the declaring of certain practical consequences by the authority of Parliament (king, Lords and Commons) would prove increasingly difficult to maintain. The act of supremacy had registered the king's power to control doctrine by the right of his position in the church and by means of his spiritual jurisdiction. The act of six articles took care once again to confine what was done by the authority of Parliament to the creation of penalties enforceable at common law. But the preamble (rightly) noted that the articles of belief there protected had been defined not by the king alone but by his consent as well as the assent of Lords and Commons. The long line of major and unprecedented enactments which had established the theory of the supremacy in the reality of daily lives, and which had helped to extend royal power into a domain hitherto closed to it, had from the first set up a manifest tension within the king's position which the most careful of phrasing could not disguise. His dignity as supreme head he owed to God and God's law; the reality of his powers as supreme head he owed to the common law, enlarged for this purpose by the relevant legislative authority. Thus the supremacy contained within itself a potential strain between two legal systems, a strain which could become dangerous if head and subject were to find themselves differing over the interpretation of the basic principles, or if the exercise of that supremacy were ever to be called in question at law.

All this, of course, was to happen later in the century. But from the first there existed in effect two interpretations of the theory of the supremacy, one high and one low, one theological and the other legal; even though both often enough agreed harmoniously, the possibilities of a conflict could not be ignored. The point was put plainly quite early on by Lord Chancellor Audley, Cromwell's chief assistant in the drafting of

---

[17] 26 Henry VIII, c. 1.
[18] 31 Henry VIII, c. 14. The addition of 'Congregation' to 'Church' deserves more attention than it has received. It meant that this supposedly altogether reactionary act employed both the traditional and the Erasmian translation of *ecclesia*.

those revolutionary statutes, in conversation with Stephen Gardiner. Familiar though the quotation may be, it is worth citing again at length:

"Thou art a good fellow, bishop', quoth he (which was the manner of his familiar speech), 'look at the act of supremacy and there the king's doings be restrained to spiritual jurisdiction; and in another act it is provided that no spiritual law shall have place contrary to a common law or act of Parliament. And this were not', quoth he, 'you bishops would enter in with the king and by means of his supremacy order the laity as ye listed. But we will provide', quoth he, 'that the praemunire shall ever hang over your heads . . .'"[19]

Thus Audley regarded the authority of the (king-in-) Parliament as ultimately superior to that of the king as spiritual head. It is worth noting that it was in effect Audley who created the ambiguities of the act of six articles when he advised Henry to settle the truth of the sacrament of the altar by act of Parliament because no authority in the general opinion exceeded that of that instrument.[20] Thus he held that the law of Parliament (which is the common law) in the last resort defined what free powers the supreme head might exercise. From the first, therefore, Parliament intervened in matters which theoretically lay entirely between God and king. The hidden conflict was accidentally summed up in one of the marginal notes which the translator added to the English version of Gardiner's *De vera obedientia*. That translation, of course, was published when Gardiner, now lord chancellor to Queen Mary, had altogether changed his opinions concerning the supremacy; since the editor meant to cause Gardiner the maximum of political embarrassment his annotations formed a distinctly hostile commentary on the text. Thus, where Gardiner had declared the supremacy to be 'in-existens' (inherent) in the king, the margin carries the explanation 'the king's supremacy by parliament'.[21]

It might be thought that this dispute among the laws manifested itself only in the course of time and especially became serious in the reign of Mary, who meant to divest herself of a title now seen as grounded upon parliamentary statute. However, even under Henry VIII and despite his majestic behaviour, the common law began to attack along the edges of a purely personal supremacy decreed by the law of God. Cromwell revealed his own position in the act concerning Peter's pence and dispensations (1534), for the drafting of which he was responsible.[22]

---

[19] *The Letters of Stephen Gardiner*, ed. J. A. Muller (Cambridge, 1933), 392.
[20] Ibid., 369. [21] Janelle, *Obedience*, 115.
[22] 25 Henry VIII, c. 21; *LP*, VII, 49.

After declaring that England, which recognised the king as supreme head under God, owed obedience only to such laws as had been accepted as there valid by the people 'at their free liberty' and with the king's permission, the act went on:

> It standeth therefore with natural equity and good reason that in all and every such laws human ... your royal majesty, and your Lords spiritual and temporal, and Commons, representing the whole state of your realm in this your most high court of Parliament, have full power and authority ... to abrogate, annul, amplify and diminish ...

Cromwell could hardly have expressed more plainly the principle of an absolute legislative power vested in the tripartite Parliament and extended to all spiritual as well as secular concerns of the 'empire' of England. The theory of the general legislator, here incorporated into a statute, included the assertion that the foundations and the exercise of the ecclesiastical government even belonged, so far as the positive law was concerned, to the Parliament. In this definition Cromwell represented the views of the common lawyers, a sector to which he himself belonged. Though as far as legal practice was concerned the supremacy seems to have mattered only because Parliament had declared resistance to it to amount to treason, the common law had found in Christopher St German a champion who even before the break with Rome aspired to winning for it full control over any other law used in the realm.[23]

Even before the supremacy was fully worked out, signs appeared that the role of the Parliament might offer competition to the role of God. Thus in 1531 an act attended to the pardon which the king in his person and without the Parliament had granted to the clergy because their jurisdiction had allegedly offended against the old statutes of praemunire.[24] The act recited the royal pardon and confirmed it 'by the authority of Parliament', which does not interfere with the original and purely personal action of the king. However, before the enactment there occurs a strange sentence in which Parliament (without any truth or justification) is made to claim more participation than the official doctrine or the facts of the case allowed to it. There we learn that the king had exercised his mercy 'of his mere motion, benignity and liberality, by authority of this his Parliament'. The first act of succession (1534) contained a similar ambiguity or duplicity. It reported that the

---

[23] *The Reports of Sir John Spelman*, ed. J. H. Baker, 2 vols., (Selden Society, 1977–8), I, 57–8; *Christopher St German on Chancery and Statute*, ed. J. A. Guy (Selden Society, 1985), 21. [24] 22 Henry VIII, c. 15.

king's first marriage had been found invalid in the trial before the archbishop of Canterbury (that is, by an action under the canon law); but it then went on to declare 'by authority of Parliament' that the marriage was definitely null and against the law of God.[25] Again and again, the acts contain hints that the endeavour to keep the legal foundation of the supremacy (the law of God) separate from its exercise as defined in the positive law of the realm could not be sustained. The supremacy owed its practical force and therefore its real existence to acts of Parliament, and the drafters of the acts not infrequently, though with an obscurity caused by embarrassment, admitted as much.

The most interesting example of the dilemma arose out of the need to determine what sort of spiritual law was to be used in the schismatic church. On the one hand, the church courts continued as before, except that now they derived their jurisdiction from the royal supreme head; on the other, the canon law of the Universal Church, hitherto also the law of those courts, was held to be papistical and therefore to be rejected.[26] Nevertheless, while there existed ecclesiastical courts they needed an approved ecclesiastical law. In the 1530s some common lawyers, with hesitant support from Cromwell, tried to abolish those rivals and transfer all actions to their own courts, but the bishops, as Audley later put it, entered with the king. Thus the old spiritual jurisdiction remained in existence and, at least down to the outbreak of the civil war, also active.[27] Where, however, could one find a canon law which did not come from Rome and incorporate the papal supremacy? In the spring of 1532 Cromwell provoked in the Commons a general attack which Henry then used to force an equally general submission upon the clergy in their Convocations.[28] This submission was obtained outside the Parliament and without its participation. When the representatives of the clergy signed the submission they accepted two resolutions touching the law of the church: new canons could only be proposed by Convocation and depended for their validity on ratification by the king, while the existing law was to undergo a revision by a royal commission (sixteen laymen and sixteen clerics) so as to cleanse it of all papal traces.

---

[25] 25 Henry VIII, c. 22.

[26] The theory that the medieval church in England possessed its own law and could choose whether to abide by papal decrees – the theory, that is, invented in the Reformation Parliament – was discredited as unhistorical in F. W. Maitland's *Roman Canon Law in the Church of England* (London, 1898).

[27] *Reform and Renewal*; R. A. Houlbrooke, *Church Courts and the People during the English Reformation 1520–1570* (Oxford, 1979).

[28] *Reform and Reformation*: 151–5.

Even in 1532 Cromwell would have preferred a parliamentary victory to one gained by the monarch as *rex solus*, and two years later he managed to get the submission confirmed by statute.[29] Although that confirmation altered nothing in the relations between king and canon law, the normal formula touching the authority of Parliament was to have consequences: once again, however guardedly one brought in Parliament, once in it was bound to assert itself. Setting up that commission underwent years of delay, although a small committee of canonists associated with Cromwell produced as early as 1535 a proposal which turned out to be too general and imprecise for use in the courts.[30] The church itself wished to put an end to uncertainty and petitioned for the promised enquiry. This led in 1536 to a further statute in which the foundations for this reform were drastically changed.[31] While in 1532 the whole matter had been consigned to the personal action of the king, he was now instructed, by the authority of the Parliament, to set up the commission, with the additional provision that his power to do so should endure only for three years from the end of this Parliament. The task thus remained in his hands but he executed it by order of a time-limited statute and not as a free function of his supremacy. The statute also laid down principles for the reform of the canon law which, even though they did not go counter to his own views, yet made him the agent of the Parliament: nothing in the law to be approved was to offend against both the royal prerogative and 'the customs, laws and statutes of the realm'. Beyond any doubt, therefore, the canon law in future was to stand under the control of the common law and not that of the quasi-papal supreme head. The victory of the common law, which had become ever more manifest since 1531, here received official confirmation, but neither the submission of 1532 nor the confirming act of 1534 had made mention of any such thing.

Thus the canon law, to be newly worked over by clerical experts, now became dependent on the approval not only of the supreme head (as the submission had laid down) but more specifically of the king-in-parliament. In practice nothing was to happen for quite some time. The situation grew worse in 1535 when the study of the 'papal' canon law was abolished at both the universities.[32] Soon the dearth of trained

---

[29] 25 Henry VIII, c. 19.

[30] F. D. Logan, 'The Henrician canons', *BIHR*, 47 (1974), 99–103.

[31] 27 Henry VIII, c. 5.

[32] *Documents Illustrative of English Church History*, ed. H. Gee and W. J. Hardy (Oxford, 1896), 269–74.

canonists produced in 1545 a parliamentary licence for civilians to practise in the church courts.[33] Several times also the intended commission was mentioned again in statutes, but no action was taken until 1551. In that year, under the guidance of Cranmer – theologian not lawyer – the commission produced a general code called *Reformatio Legum Ecclesiasticarum*; however, this failed to obtain the necessary ratification in Parliament. In 1571, in the course of a campaign to secure confirmation of the law to be applied in the church courts, this collection was put into print, with John Foxe as editor.[34] Though the campaign had some support in the Commons, it achieved nothing.[35] Now and again, piecemeal reforms of the canon law were attempted by means of royal orders or episcopal decrees, as well as, more drastically, by such acts of Parliament as that of 1540, which liberalised the church's prohibited degrees affecting intended marriages.[36] Only in 1604 after Elizabeth's death, did the church manage to agree to a general code of canon law, though this too never received the approval of Parliament. Nevertheless, it became operable in the ecclesiastical courts, though this had little meaning by this time; before long, those courts in effect ceased their activity, with the exception of testamentary causes, long since subjected to common-law principles of inheritance, which were taken from them only in 1857. Though neither the papal nor the Protestant canon law was ever formally abolished and the courts continued to sit, the common law with the assistance of Parliament had not only subdued the rival system but had effectively demolished it.[37]

Thus the old battle between the canon and common laws came to an end. The politically more ominous dispute concerning the legal foundations of the royal supremacy remained unresolved – hanging in mid-air – during Henry VIII's reign. As we have seen, the original notion of a purely personal power, equal to the papal *potestas*, was soon forced to admit the practical necessity of cooperating with Parliament: the essential charter of the supremacy silently transmuted from an attribute of the *rex solus* to one particular to *rex in parliamento*. Official statements soon came to place the *lex parliamentaria* at least by the side of the *lex*

---

[33] 37 Henry VIII, c. 17.   [34] Houlbrooke, *Church Courts*, 17.
[35] *Parliament*, 99, 208.
[36] Houlbrooke, *Church Courts*, 18; 32 Henry VIII, c. 38.
[37] Cases in the courts continued, and the high commission in particular exercised a serious jurisdiction down to 1641, but the law employed was a form of canonistic custom controlled by common and statute law. [See now R. H. Helmholz, *Roman Canon Law in Reformation England* (Cambridge, 1990).]

divina in explaining the origin of the royal supremacy. While Henry VIII reigned, this concession hardly mattered in practice. That particular supreme head ruled by force of his personality, though his growing trust in the principles maintained by Cromwell (a trust which survived Cromwell's fall) caused him to concede an increasing parliamentary participation in the development of the Church of England. In the most important task that fell to the ruler of the church – the definition of the officially authorised faith and liturgy – Henry used both statutes and personal announcements, a double action possible only because down to 1547 there could be no question of a reform in fundamentals. Even so, it is worthy of note that after 1540 every exercise of the royal power related to uniformity in belief actually rested upon statute, for it was then enacted by the authority of Parliament that the king could, by letters patent, proclaim all changes recommended by the bishops, such patents to be obeyed and observed as though ordained in the act.[38]

After the old king's death the situation altered quickly, and with it the relationship between the personal and parliamentary rule over the church also changed. Though, naturally, no one thought of abolishing or denying the law of God, it became in a manner superfluous. From 1549, only the law of the land, through acts of parliament, determined what kind of church should obey its supreme head. The chief reason for this lay in the decision at last to bring in a proper Reformation, and the reverse decision of Queen Mary to be rid of the Reformation completed a development which Cromwell and his jurists had foreseen and prepared as early as the 1530s.

So far as legislation was concerned, Parliament under Edward VI in the two acts of uniformity (1549, 1552) prescribed by means of successive Books of Common Prayer the only legitimate form of divine service.[39] Both laws derived the universal force of the regulations solely from the authority of the king-in-parliament. The foundations of the English church were built by Parliament in statutes which carried the official liturgies as appendices. The preface of the Prayer Book also based its claim to obedience and exclusive use on parliamentary authority. That the church now existed totally under the Parliament's rule and not only the king's appeared plainly in the fact that the first book, never even submitted to the ecclesiastical authorities, passed after vigorous debates in both Houses of Parliament; the second underwent a similar exper-

---

[38] 32 Henry VIII, c. 26.   [39] 2 & 3 Edward VI, c. 1; 5 & 6 Edward VI, c. 1.

ience, though its details had emerged from long arguments among the theologians.[40]

In 1553 this church built on parliamentary foundations confronted a Catholic queen. Mary, of course, wished to forget and abolish everything that had happened since the opening of the Reformation Parliament, and at first she hoped simply to declare invalid any laws which did not agree with what she regarded as the laws of God. She meant to proclaim from above that any such measures contrary to *the* law had never had any force and therefore also no existence. If she had succeeded, she would have helped the law of God, and with it the canon law of the Universal Church, to an undisputed victory over the law of the land. She found her Privy Council unwilling. For practical reasons, they thought it necessary to observe that principle which, years before, Audley had explained to Gardiner: an act of Parliament could be abrogated only by another such act.[41] In consequence, and very much against her inclination, the queen had after all to turn to the Parliament if she was to rid herself of the incubus of the Reformation and the title she hated. She had to take this step in spite of her own unwavering conviction that God had himself ordained the outcome. The restoration of the papal church in England thus depended quite as completely on the authority of Parliament (and therefore on the authority of the common law) as had the introduction of the Protestant church in her brother's reign.[42] Nor was this a mere formality, as Parliament proved when it delayed the restoration until it had obtained guarantees concerning the secularised church lands. The queen had to come to terms with the fact that what she held to be the truths of the faith had to defer to the legislative authority of the Parliament as well as to the political interests represented in it. Though the exercise of the Protestant religion had become more or less impossible before the passing of the repeal, it could not be punished, nor could the rule of what to her was the only true religion be brought back without an act of Parliament. At the beginning of her reign a good Catholic might have been sentenced to death under the law as it stood, while a manifest heretic would have had to be apologetically set at liberty by any court. The same problem, of course, reappeared on Elizabeth's accession when it was decided to reintroduce the reformed church: the acts of 1559 for supremacy and uniformity in

[40] A. G. Dickens, *The English Reformation* (London, 1964), 218–20, 247–9.
[41] *Gardiner's Letters*, ed. Muller, 369–70.   [42] 1 Mary st. 2, c. 3.

their turn established the Church of England by the authority of Parliament.[43]

I have several times emphasised that the *lex parliamentaria* should not be treated as an independent law; rather it formed the most comprehensive method available for changing the common law by addition, subtraction or piecemeal improvement. The standpoint of the observer determines the view one takes of the outcome of these conflicts of laws. In politics the Parliament won the day: that is to say, the omnipotence of the king-in-parliament became fundamental to law and affairs in England. In matters of the law the common law won a total victory when it subjected the church with its law to itself and incorporated God's decree concerning the vicariate on earth into its own system. This elevated and now virtually unrivalled position received confirmation also in other aspects of the age. In 1533, for instance, Parliament tackled the problem of heresy trials.[44] It did not claim to be able to define heretical beliefs, a duty it continued to leave to the church, except that it expressly exempted attacks on the papacy from this crime against God. We may safely presume that the bill came from the government, and it is probable that Cromwell was behind it. Its terms conferred upon Parliament the task of controlling the conduct of such trials. The act complained of the complexities with which the church had allegedly burdened the pursuit of heretics – complexities which could catch even the wisest and best learned of men unawares. It was declared outrageous that the methods of the church courts left their victims with less chance to prove their innocence than did the law of treason – 'treasons committed to the peril of your most royal majesty upon whose surety dependeth the whole wealth of the realm'.[45] In future, therefore, persons suspected of heresy were to be indicted according to the rules of the common law. Even though this precaution was to be revoked in 1539, the heresy act should nevertheless be regarded as another victory for the common law over its ecclesiastical rival. Even in cases of treason, that law of the land had then not obtained total control; in treason, an accusation, which by the rules of the common law ought to have been effective only if made by presentment or indictment by a grand jury,

[43] 1 Elizabeth I, cc. 1, 2.   [44] 25 Henry VIII, c. 14.

[45] This phrasing, which appears to treat an attack on the king as something much worse thn one on the truth of God's religion, recalls the answer sent by the vice-chancellor of Cambridge in the middle of the nineteenth century to the railway company which proposed to run trains to Cambridge on Sundays. Such a proposal, the promoters learned, was 'unpleasing to Almighty God and offensive to the Vice-Chancellor'.

could still be raised by assertions about general fame or the king's special knowledge. In line with his thinking about heresy trials, Cromwell put an end to such exceptions also in his treason law of 1534, which specified the methods of the common law in charges even of high treason.[46] Of course, since Parliament constituted the ultimate authority over that law, that provision did not eliminate the punishment of treason by acts of attainder without trial – the weapon which Cromwell's enemies employed against him in 1540.

From the 1530s onwards there are thus plenty of signs that the builders of the unitary state meant to erect it, so far as possible, on a monopoly vested in the common law. The possibility that the equity of chancery might become a rival rather than a subordinate assistant to the common law vanished when the latter by statute took over jurisdiction in uses (1536), while the 1540 statute of wills for the first time introduced a common-law jurisdiction over testaments, hitherto exclusively the domain of the church courts. These are just examples of well-known facts – the facts which account for the English law's successful resistance also to propaganda in favour of the civil law of Rome.[47] The elevation of Parliament to legal sovereignty testifies to the determination of the lawyers predominant in Henry VIII's government to equip the common law with a general competence over all legal affairs as well as with an instrument of permanent self-renewal. These ambitions underlay the interesting developments in the native law which for decades had been reforming itself from within, in order to overcome threats of competition by offering litigants a better and safer answer to their problems than was available elsewhere and by different methods.[48] The Reformation Parliament set the seal upon these transformations, and statute took over as the primary means of reform. After 1540, the year in which Cromwell, political architect of that victory, suffered execution, the legislative supremacy and omnipotence of the king-in-parliament remained beyond contesting. Some will call this the end of the Middle Ages and others the beginning of the early modern state, while some, rightly pointing to the medieval prehistory of Parliament and common law upon which Cromwell erected his successful 'revolution', will maintain that the Middle Ages lasted at least until the middle of the nineteenth century. It is true that the law reformers of the Victorian age

---

[46] 26 Henry VIII, c. 13.

[47] See G. R. Elton, *F. W. Maitland* (London, 1985), 79–88.

[48] See the account of these developments in J. H. Baker's Introduction to his edition of *Spelman's Reports* (see n. 23 above).

found themselves still coping with some survivals from the days of Edward I or Edward III, but the bulk of the statutes whose continued effect troubled them belonged to the reigns of Henry VIII and his successors.

In these developments, the battle against the Roman curia and its own *lex communis* played the leading role, if only because here territory was won which previously had been expressly outside the competence of England's *lex communis*, and also because the incorporation of the papal functions in the crown of England might easily have led to a more specifically royal canon law founded on the will of God. Enough people, and they included the king, would have preferred this. The war opened, as we have seen, with a debate concerning only interior problems of the canon law. That stage of the dispute could therefore be settled by the methods and principles of that law, with the king, supported by the theologians and canonists of his realm, simply transferring the papal powers to himself. The support of lay jurists was his also, but on conditions. The traditions of England were not so easily bypassed. Both political calculations, which preferred to involve the realm in the revolution, and the legal necessity to entrust its enforcement to the courts of the common law unexpectedly rendered impossible the first intention to erect the supremacy solely on the abstract laws of God and nature. As Cromwell recognised, only the positive law, valid in court, mattered in the last resort. Thus there resulted the decisive contest of laws, between the *lex ecclesiae* and the *lex terrae*. *Lex terrae* won, and the royal supreme head saw himself compelled to rule his church by the same constitutional methods that already applied to his rule of the commonwealth. Instead of employing the inheritance of Rome in the construction of an absolute monarchy, it became necessary to whittle the papal precedents down until they fitted a monarchy that ruled under the common law. In theory as well as practice, the early Reformation in England produced the sovereignty of the tripartite Parliament and of the law over the making of which it presided.

This transformation thus set the stage for the function and role of Parliament in the reign of Elizabeth I. A unitary realm where one law ruled both monarch and subjects had replaced a community of partly independent orders within one country, looking to various laws for guidance and in which the powers of the crown varied in diverse spheres of action. The maker of this one law, however, was now a mixed body whose decisions stood out by being unappealable and final. This achievement eliminated the possibility, always lurking around during the process of unification, that ultimate power might fall to a single person; however hard some writers, especially from within the clergy and the court, were later to try to elevate the lawful prerogative of the crown into that principle of absolutism which in the subsequent century gained ground all over the European continent, the triumph of the common law and its maker could not be evaded. On the other hand, a sovereign law-making power so organised undoubtedly posed serious difficulties as well as opportunities. The opportunities existed for any interest, indeed any individual, within the realm seeking irrefutable solutions to their problems and desires by operating the legislative machinery of Parliament; the difficulties arose from the fact that such operating called for complex managerial skills and political compromises. The developed institution called the king-in-parliament stood ready to make laws and in consequence received proposals for such laws in numbers which far exceeded anything that the machinery was capable of processing. Thus the history of Parliament became primarily a history of bills and acts, a history which recorded the interchange of internal and external pressures. Much of this remains to be worked out, and much harm has been done by historians who lacked a proper understanding of what lawmaking in that Parliament actually meant.[49] Secondly, the potential embodied in the machinery created a visible and public platform for debating the political, ecclesiastical, economic and social concerns that went to the making of law by means of Parliament. Here, too, superficial views, derived largely from entrenched convictions and an unbalanced assessment of pronouncements issuing from such competing interests, have traditionally distorted the reading of parliamentary, and indeed of national, history. The principle of one law for all, victorious over all rivals and applicable to all aspects of life, may have looked like a striking simplification of what had gone before, but its effect was to complicate the employment and handling of that law and its maker well beyond the experience of the past. It was in the Parliaments of Elizabeth I that the problems now raised as well as the opportunities now offered first came to be a major concern in political life.

[49] I have tried to expound this kind of analysis for the first half of Elizabeth's reign in *Parliament*.

HUMAN RIGHTS AND THE LIBERTIES OF ENGLISHMEN*

This is the age of human rights. Everyone proclaims them; they are listed in various documents; a special court sits at Strasbourg to adjudicate claims based on them; other courts, longer established, allow them to influence their decisions. Progressive opinion in one country after another seeks to promote solemn documents defining them. Portentous bills of rights are the ambition, for instance, of New Zealand liberals and English social democrats. To anyone versed in the lessons of history and the facts of human nature, it will come as no surprise that these alleged rights probably have never been more widely disregarded and broken in every part of the globe, especially in countries which erected new governments upon claims to human rights. Commonly, successful revolutions fighting under the banner of human rights violate every one of these same rights with greater efficiency than the regime they overthrew had done. Thus, there is something disquieting about the constant claims and proclamations of these new governments.

Where and when did the whole notion of human rights actually originate? The term 'human rights' as it is currently used has been used since the end of the Second World War. 'Human rights' replaced an earlier version which spoke of the rights of man. No doubt it will not do today to use language which to certain fanatics will suggest that those rights do not extend to women. Presumably, it is for such reasons that we now resort to a translation of the German usage in which the rights of man were from the first called *Menschenrechte*; that fortunate language happens to possess a generic term for human beings to which feminist linguistics cannot take exception. I sometimes think that the change from the rights of man to human rights has unfortunate implications. Terms are often best analysed by positing their opposites, a test which in this case produces revealingly ominous results. The obvious opposite to the rights of man are the duties of man. The obvious opposite to human rights are inhuman rights. As we shall see, in that shift away from

* [*University of Illinois Law Review* (1990), 329–46.]

matching rights to duties there possibly lies one explanation for much that is unsatisfactory in the whole notion as at present expounded.

We possess a detailed description of that to which we are all entitled in the 'Universal Declaration of Human Rights' issued by the United Nations at the time of its foundation. The list runs to thirty articles, most of which contain several numbered paragraphs. It is a remarkable collection. Some of those rights are simple, plain, and indeed universal. 'Everyone has the right to life, liberty and security of person'; 'no one shall be held in slavery or servitude'; 'no one shall be subjected to torture or to cruel, inhuman or degrading treatment'; 'everyone has the right to own property alone as well as in association with others'. The fact that such noble absolutes make sad reading in the light of what one sees happening in the world today does not diminish the good will that went into the making of them, though it may call forth immediate doubts concerning the understanding of the world displayed in them. We also find articles that go into rather wayward detail. 'Everyone has the right to freedom of movement and residence'; 'everyone has the right to seek and to enjoy in other countries asylum from persecution'; 'everyone has the right to take part in the government of his country'; 'everyone, without any discrimination, has the right to equal pay for equal work'. Here we encounter a not uncharacteristic mixture of innocent good will and hopefulness. A third group seems to reflect peculiar and particular grievances, derived perhaps from bad personal experiences mingled with personal quirks. 'Men and women of full age . . . have the right to marry and to found a family'; and 'everyone charged with a penal offence has the right to be presumed innocent'. A fourth group confers supposed rights which depend so much on prevailing circumstances that guaranteeing them becomes totally impossible. 'Everyone . . . has the right to social security'; 'everyone has the right to a standard of living adequate for the health and well-being of himself and of his family'; 'everyone has the right to education'; 'everyone entitled to a social and international order in which the rights and freedoms set forth in this Declaration can be fully realized'. A *right* to a 'social and international order'? The declarers, anxious to play at being gods, came out looking a bit silly. Article 29 at last introduces the concept of duties: everyone is supposed to be subject only to such limitations as will protect these rights in others. Unfortunately, Article 29 is very imprecise and poorly worded. The possibility of compulsion, even though it underlies the very idea of proposing such far-reaching rights, explicitly occurs only once, in the funniest paragraph of this extraordinary document, namely, the one that

59

deals with education: 'elementary education', it says, 'shall be compulsory'. It does not, by the way, trouble to define what education shall be deemed to be elementary, nor are we told why the freedom to opt out of schooling is the one right barred by this Declaration.

It is not surprising that the drafters of this document (who, by the way, were not endowed with any gift of tongues) wrote under the influence of recent experience – the experience of fascism and the devastating war just ended. It is also plain that parts of the Declaration reflect particular quirks and convictions peculiar to the liberal academics and social scientists of the day – especially Anglo-American ones. The influence of lawyers comes out here and there. Nevertheless, the drafters not only believed themselves to be dealing with eternal verities, even where entitling people of an undefined 'full age' to have children, but also expressly laid claim to such a foundation in the justification with which they introduced the list of rights. Article 1 states categorically: 'All human beings are born free and equal in dignity and rights. They are endowed with reason and conscience and should act towards one another in a spirit of brotherhood.' This is an excellent liberal creed the first sentence of which no sensible person would wish to doubt, while no sensible person of any experience at all can think the second sentence anything but dreamlike. Reason and conscience, so far as I can see, may with a great effort come to develop in those free and equal beings. Insofar as natural endowment goes, greed and selfishness seem to be more evident. The well-meaning definition of a foundation which in so many ways contradicts all the evidence of how men and women really behave to one another illustrates the ancestry of this creed. The preamble of the Declaration explains that the need for the Declaration sprang from the evils committed by man. The Declaration then implicitly denies the existence of evil. It is as though Freud and Jung and Nietzsche, St Paul, St Augustine and Martin Luther had never been.

It is here, in the deliberate avoidance of what we know about human psychology, that one of the more dire consequences of naive expectations may merit consideration. In the years since the Declaration was first drawn up, the enforcement of its dreams has quietly moved location. Originally, the drafters of the Declaration intended that rights should prove enforceable at law, in courts of law. Thus, the framing of the Declaration attracted the self-interest of lawyers. At the time of the drafting of the Declaration there was one country that respected, and even worshipped, lawyers, and in a way the idea of the Declaration worked in this country. In the United States, the campaign for equal civil rights immediately gained the support of the courts and, with astonishing speed, their guidelines became practice. I will not here consider the equally characteristic speed with which absurd exaggerations – promoted by lawyers with a financial interest to serve – made a sad mess of such things as equal opportunity regardless of unequal ability, or of legitimate compensation for losses. It seems to me more interesting to note that the arena of enforcement has steadily moved from the relative certainty and formality of the courts to the unpredictable uncertainties of the press. No country holds journalists in a higher regard, or gives them greater licence, than does the United States of America. We have now acquired a new human right, the right to know, apparently vested in a mystic entity called the people, but which is enforced by a body of men and women who make money out of what is called investigation and publicity. What has gone by the board is the human right to privacy – the right to punch the investigator on the nose till he or she withdraws. The full consequences of this mindless devotion to free information on everything are spreading around the world and have never been evaluated.

The respect extended to journalists is only a particular example of a species of innocence – the refusal to admit mankind's potential for evil. We are back with the simplistic teaching of the eighteenth-century Enlightenment which gave birth to the whole idea of the rights of man. More specifically, we are back with the resounding definitions of those rights first produced in the French and American Revolutions.

One of the earliest pronouncements of the French National Assembly of 1789 declared 'les droits de l'homme et du citoyen' – the rights of man and of the citizen. The assembly called these rights natural, inalienable, and sacred, and it composed them (so it said) 'in the presence and under the auspices of the Supreme Being'. They needed this solemnity because, in actual fact, they could not rest those rights on any demonstrably established or hereditary entitlement. They had to recognise that they were bringing into existence something for which no evidence seemed to exist in the past – a new universal principle. There followed seventeen articles, about half the number thought necessary by the United Nations a century and a half later. One must also admit that the French National Assembly employed a more elegant diction than twentieth-century bureaucracies aspire unto. Of course, the French National Assembly were helped by the fact that they meant to proclaim the general rights of all men (and women) with particular reference to the boundaries of one nation state. Also, the Assembly did not have to legislate for the prevention of the horrors of the 1930s and the 1940s.

Above all, however, the National Assembly avoided pandering to the interfering itch and love of petty detail to be found in the later document. Their concern lay in protecting all citizens against abuses of power by the government of the day, and they thought of those abuses in terms applicable to the recent history of France. These, however, they generalised. The rights of man, they concluded, amounted to four in number: liberty, property, security and resistance to oppression, and they did not mention life. The articles elaborated on these themes. The articles banned arrest and imprisonment except by the proper methods of the law, guaranteed freedom of thought and expression, and based all levies of financial contributions on consent. The Declaration acknow-ledged the need for good order in society and, therefore, accepted the institution of what they called 'a public force' but demanded that this be set up for everybody's good 'and not for the personal benefit of those to whom it is entrusted'. It was to be paid for by everybody according to each person's ability. At least, unlike the men of 1945, those of 1789 did not simply trust to hope or false psychology for the maintenance of the sort of social order that alone can make a reality of any rights proclaimed. If the French National Assembly's document was put together as logically as the first fifteen articles suggest, the ending is revealing. Article 16 would seem to conclude the argument by stating that any society which does not assure the rights of its citizens and separate the powers of rule lacks a constitution. It, therefore, is surprising to find tacked on yet another article containing a defence of private property which (a bit extravagantly) is declared to be inviolable and sacred. It would seem that this is what the constitution really is about.

Less fussy, less verbose, less an accumulation of contributions from various sources, the Declaration of the French National Assembly nevertheless rested on very much the same principles as that proclaimed by the United Nations. We may assume that the French Declaration also identifies the source of those principles, a detail omitted in the secular twentieth century, by claiming the guidance of that Supreme Being whom to have called God would have called up the image of the hated church. According to the first article of the French Declaration, 'men are born and remain free and equal in respect of rights'. The Assembly went on to acknowledge the existence of social distinctions, though the Assembly was aware that after birth total equality ceases. However, the Assembly derived these distinctions not from parentage but from what it called 'utilité commune', public usefulness – distinction by merit. We are not told who decides upon the merit and assigns the distinctions. At the heart of all this philosophising lay Rousseau's social contract by which societies are supposedly created. Once each nation or society is brought into existence they are ruled by a law which is the expression of the general will – more Rousseau. Close to two centuries have made commonplace the principles of a political theory which at the time was at least innovative, perhaps revolutionary, even as those centuries have thoroughly disproved the theoretical underpinnings for the doctrine. It might reassure us that desirable ends can come to be generally accepted, even when they have derived from false, mendacious, or absurd premises. The Declaration of 1789, like its modern successor, assumed an equality among all human beings who were by nature well disposed to each other's rights and had only one duty, namely, to respect the rights of others. It is not difficult to find such principles attractive, or at least it is not difficult until one actually looks at one's fellow beings.

There is no doubt that the French Assembly's sentiments and expression, though formulated under the influence of philosophers, owed a great deal to the principles enunciated by the founding fathers of the United States: the presence in the National Assembly of the Marquis de Lafayette sufficed to make sure of that. In this company, I do not think that I need to go at length into the events that led to the separation of the thirteen colonies from the British Empire, but I should like to take a brief look at the Declaration of Independence of 1776. The thirteen colonies declared that 'a decent respect to the opinion of mankind' required of them a statement of the reasons which led them to cast off the British yoke and establish for themselves that 'equal station to which the laws of nature and of nature's God entitle them . . .'. As the French Assembly did later, the thirteen colonies relied on natural rights and the guidance of a Supreme Being. Before reciting the evil deeds of 'the present King of Great Britain' from whose tyranny they were emancipating themselves, they pronounced those famous words which are drilled into every citizen of the United States: 'We hold these truths to be self-evident: that all men are created equal, that they are endowed by their Creator with certain inalienable rights, that among these are life, liberty and the pursuit of happiness.'

Really, on reflection, these are pretty extraordinary assertions to make. What proof is offered? These truths are 'self-evident', which is to say we know of no positive evidence which we can advance for them. And was it self-evident in a slave-owning society that all men are created equal? If certain rights are inalienable, those rights cannot be discarded by their owners even if they wished to. It does not follow that others cannot take those rights away from them, as they do when they hang thieves or massacre Indians, or when they enslave blacks. It is manifest that we have with this declaration not a considered analysis of human society but a propaganda statement cast in the ringing tones that had become quite familiar a century earlier in a good many pronunciamentos put out during the English Revolution. The tones recall those earlier efforts, but the substance does not because even the Levellers of the 1640s tended to rest their case not on abstract principles but on such things as the proof of God's favour shown in victory over the king's armies. The Declaration of Independence was, I think, the first public document to base itself on unargued propositions taken to be true without needing to be proved.

A word about the pursuit of happiness. I do not exactly know what the drafters of the Declaration had in mind, and this particular right is conspicuously absent from all the descendants of this first pronouncement. The pursuit of happiness would seem to have remained a specifically American ambition – unless the United Nations Declaration supposed that elementary education amounts to a pursuit of happiness. Frankly, I have always felt that this extraordinary phrase casts upon the whole affair a taint of childishness which is hard to understand. Only infants surely can suppose that they have a right to seek always that which will make them happy, regardless of what that supposed happiness may inflict on themselves or on other people. The drug culture and the flower people constituted the apotheosis of that self-evident right to pursue happiness. I hope I am not abusing the hospitality so generously extended to me if I say that to me the recognition that happiness is not a right, nor its pursuit a suitable ambition for any human being, marks the move from adolescence to full adulthood.

Thus, with the Declaration of Independence, the French Declaration, and the United Nations Declaration, we have three sets of people laying down specifications of human rights which they proposed to secure within the political entity over which they could exercise rule or at least influence. The ambition of these declarations is noble, whatever we may think of some of the rights so laboriously worked out. In all three instances, the rights were derived from general and supposedly indisputable principles rather than from any law, precedents, or even visible agreements between parties. The nearest positive foundation for these declarations is the imaginary social contract which supposedly constructed the societies in question. Although not one of the three documents used the language of religion – indeed, they rather laboriously avoided promoting a particular faith – the general ethos behind all of these declarations was Christian in a loose way. The real problems – the problems of the real world – arose, of course, from the need to apply and indeed enforce those rights, and in all three cases reality very quickly cast doubts on the generosity of the statements made. America's founding fathers, as I have already indicated, appeared to possess a somewhat restricted notion of mankind. When they said that all men are created equal, they evidently did not mean all creatures possessed of physical human attributes, and the war and victory which followed upon the Declaration of Independence encouraged no one to safeguard the rights of enemies. But in the United States, long years, changing circumstances, and a constitution possessed of a supreme court, extended those principles well beyond what at one time anyone could have expected to happen, largely by changing the rights of man into civil rights – the rights of citizens enfranchised by their membership of a given political entity. Not all that extension has been an obvious gain in social peace or harmony; some claimants to rights are as absolutist as any kings, and one could wish that courts would employ some gentle restraint in setting rational limits. Nevertheless, it looks as though, in a genuine democracy, one can construct genuine liberties out of assertions to rights.

In late eighteenth-century France, the Declaration, read by many as the opening of a new golden age, fared badly. When Tom Paine, in February 1791, published his book on *The Rights of Man*, he sang praises to the 'rights of man' with passion and joy and with loud contempt for such as Edmund Burke, whose dark forebodings expressed themselves in scepticism. Within a year, thousands had died at the hands of the champions of the rights of man, and more still had lost their property, turning poor Tom Paine into the prototype of purblind liberals who cannot accept the powerlessness of high-flown rhetoric in the face of human passions unleashed. In the wake of the noble principles of 1945 have come horrors inflicted by human beings upon more of their fellow women and men than any preceding age had known. The numbers killed, expropriated, and murdered as a consequence of decolonisation – a worthy practice – greatly exceeded the numbers similarly treated in the far longer period of colonialism. No doubt, Ghengis Khan or Hitler would have tortured and killed as many if they had had the time and the machinery to do so. What has happened since 1945 is a proliferation of Hitlers and Ghengis Khans, many of them marching under the banners of liberation and the rights of man.

However, the United Nations Declaration has not been totally ignored. Both the European Community and the United States have adopted versions of it which can be applied in their courts, and the American version is full of interest. Its thirty-eight articles are ordered under rights and duties, a wise modification. Admittedly, only ten of the articles attend to duties, and they include some remarkable details. Until I prepared this lecture, I did not know – did you? – that 'it is the duty of every person to acquire at least an elementary education'. What happens to a person who refuses to do so, and what is the test of that acquisition? That 'at least' looms threateningly over anyone apprehensive that they may have to acquire even more education. Article 30 actually imports the Fifth Commandment into a list of civil duties: I wonder how many children have been prosecuted in the courts for failing 'to honor their parents always'. It seems to me that in the last three decades a great many children have been guilty of that offence. The good intentions of good people anxious to improve their neighbours do not always get as well heeded as no doubt they should be.

In the United States, however, and in Europe, human and civil rights do obtain some enforcement. Thus, it proved possible, to take two fairly recent examples issuing forth from that extraordinary tribunal at Strasbourg, for a loving mother to save her ill-behaved offspring from getting slapped by a teacher strained beyond bearing, or for another woman to obtain financial compensation for looking after an aged relative. This must come as a great relief to prisoners in dungeons all over the rest of the world from Cuba and Cambodia to Chile and Czechoslovakia, to piles of corpses in Uganda, to people battered into pieces on the West Bank, to those Argentinians who have vanished without trace, to the victims of terrorism in Beirut and Belfast, and to men escaping torture by jumping out of South African windows. And I am far from persuaded that either the United States Supreme Court or the European Court of Human Rights would be able to prevent atrocities of circumstances ever provoked any within the regions they supervise. Ireland, for one, does not offer a story of much hope. I shall be told that in due course, after much labour, 'les droits de l'homme', 'Menschenrechte', human rights, will prevail and will be protected everywhere, but I doubt it.

I doubt it because it seems to me that the whole concept of human rights, as embodied in those declarations, suffers from three fundamental defects. In the first place, it is designed to be of benefit to lawyers and litigants, not to human beings as such. The consequence of this fact is visible even now: trivialisation of rights to satisfy cranks and bring profit to the profession. In the second place, it was a mistake to lay such heavy emphasis on rights while skating over the duties which must surely balance them if there is to be any reality in the system. This false stress has encouraged the antisocial qualities of selfishness and self-righteousness. In the third place, the idea of human rights, however attractive, has always rested on abstract, general, and unproven assumptions – on self-evident truths – many of which are daily disproved in all the corners of the world. For example, in my opinion, women and men are not created equal, except in the simplest sense of being, all of them, the product of sexual intercourse (if we allow that term to embrace creation in a test tube). They manifestly differ, in my opinion, in their bodies, their minds, their intellects, their ambitions, and their feelings – and that is to avoid the highly contentious question of whether there is not a rather notable biological difference also between women and men. And, so differing, they will not behave as equals or treat others as equals. The foundation upon which the whole development of the idea of human rights has rested has always been contrary to manifest fact.

Let me not be misunderstood. I believe in life and liberty, even if I cannot believe in the pursuit of happiness. I even believe in the rights of and to property. I earnestly wish that human rights existed and were respected. What so disturbs me is that the assertion and defence of such rights as nowadays preached will not serve because it erects its much too grandiose and much too interfering structure of doctrine upon the pinhead of an erroneous view of humanity. The protagonists of human rights endeavour to do too much to and about people whom they do not seem to understand. They will inevitably fail in their professed ambition and probably do real harm as well, by fostering expectations that remain unfulfilled, or – worse – by fulfilling the expectations of that considerable part of progressive mankind whose chief thrill lies in inflicting what they think good upon their bewildered and reluctant neighbour.

Is there no better way to protect people against abuse and ill-treatment? At one time, it was widely believed that there was such a way and that this way could be found in the liberties which the law supposedly guaranteed to the subjects of his Britannic Majesty. After all, the first document to speak of rights was drawn up neither at Philadelphia nor at Paris, but at Westminster in 1689 in that bill of rights which rounded off the well-named Glorious and Bloodless Revolution of the previous year when King James II was driven out and replaced by Dutch

William. The document reads: 'An act for declaring the rights and liberties of the subject and settling the succession of the crown', and most of the document attends to the second of these purposes. The rights supposedly secured look very odd after a lengthy diet of declarations concerning the Rights of Man. For one thing, there are only thirteen clauses, which seems a trifle meagre. For another, only six of them can be even remotely identified as liberties of the subject: the right, reserved to Protestants, to possess arms; freedom of election for members of Parliament; free speech in Parliament, challengeable in no other court; no excessive bail, and no cruel or unusual punishments; free and proper selection of juries; and no granting away of men's property before they are tried and convicted. These are very particular points of precise and narrow import, all of them touching the operation of the law of England. The first six clauses declare illegal certain practices allegedly used by the late king's government: suspending laws without parliamentary consent; dispensing persons from the operation of particular laws; setting up a court of ecclesiastical commissioners; non-parliamentary taxation; interfering with people who exercise their right to petition the crown; and maintaining a standing army. As human rights go, these lists would not rank very high in the eyes of enlightened thinkers. On the other hand, the bill does provide what is so clearly missing in the other documents that I have discussed. The bill remembers the need for an established machinery to keep those liberties in good shape and therefore demands frequent meetings of Parliament 'for redress of all grievances'.

We are manifestly in a different world, a world of particular, specific and definable grievances. These grievances arose out of alleged breaches of an existing and ascertainable law. This is rather nicely illustrated by the second clause, which objects to the use of the so-called dispensing power 'as it hath been assumed and exercised of late'. For the power to grant exemption to individuals from the operation of some laws had long been an undoubted attribute of the crown of England. This power was needed to operate the sizeable body of statutory control over various practices in trade and manufacture. Equally well established was the definition that distinguished acts of Parliament that could be dispensed with from those that could not be. The power extended only to *mala prohibita* – acts creating novel offences which in their nature were not offences at all. For instance, there is no law in nature which makes it wrong to export grain out of England, but such a law may be made for some immediate reason, such as the need to keep enough grain to feed the country. If the harvest is good and supply exceeds demand, exports become sensible, yet an act of Parliament stands in the way and, because dearth may again recur, should not be repealed. Therefore, the crown can dispense the exporter by letters patent. Even in 1689, no one wished to destroy this useful instrument of flexibility. What James was charged with was his decision to extend the dispensing power from *mala prohibita* to *mala in se*, things wrong in themselves and not, therefore, made into wrongs only by the statute. This bill of rights was drawn by practitioners of the common law, not by philosophers. It did not rest the so-called rights it listed on innate human qualities but on established precedents, and it made no mention of God or any Supreme Being.

The liberties of subjects (as well as their obligations) were registered in the common law of England, testable in the courts, and protected by the supremacy of that law over all arbitrary executive action. Only statutes made by Parliament (king, Lords and Commons, jointly) could create new law or abrogate old, and the ultimate guarantee of those liberties, therefore, resided in the existence and meeting of the Parliament. Of course, arbitrary action did occur and people broke the law; we are not talking of paradise. The point is that when such things happened, or were complained of, both the instrument of remedy and the means for identifying correct claims were already in existence. Let us note the continuity and concreteness of it all, and the absence of talk about the fundamental rights of man. This bill of rights was, of course, the last in a long list of documents concerned with the rights under the law of English men and women, but it alone originated in a species of revolution which had changed the head of the state. This gave it certain airs absent from earlier declarations which had been in the form of apparently voluntary grants by some king or other. The history of such grants began with the coronation charter issued by Henry I in 1100 and culminated with Magna Carta granted by John in 1215. Magna Carta was reissued, with minor changes, several times, and it was formally confirmed by Edward I and became a foundation-stone of English law after sixteenth-century publishers always printed it as the first item in any collection of the statutes.

By the eighteenth century, the myth of Magna Carta had become rampant. The century of the Enlightenment inducted the Charter into the pantheon of human rights, and commentators, using the new and high-flow language, endowed it with all sorts of principles of universal freedom. Lawyers, who do not commonly think historically, rejoiced in the chance to substitute the grandiose for their more customary preoccupation with pettifoggery. An age which thought that it had finally established true freedom at least in one country on the sure foundation of the law of nature read highly anachronistic principles into the document. All this is well enough known, and more modern historical scholarship has restored sanity, though no one has yet investigated how much damage all that vapour may have done in encouraging the cloudy concepts of the rights of man in countries lacking a Magna Carta. In reality, of course, the Great Charter and similar documents did no more than establish particular limitations upon the powers of the crown over its subjects and provide redress at law for subjects who thought that they had suffered from breaches of those limitations, most of which concerned the danger that the king might be able to rob his vassals unduly by means of the king's feudal rights over their lands. The sixty-three clauses of the original Charter are in form promises by the king that he will not, in the future, extend his rights so as to trespass upon his tenants' particular rights defined in the custom of England. By making these promises and sealing them in the presence of witnesses, the king settled that custom into enacted law. The king will not interfere with the liberties of the Universal Church in England; he will not exact excessive payments from his vassals, who are bound to render a sum called the relief upon inheriting their lands; he assures widows of their rights of dower; he promises not to ruin by over-exploitation lands that come to him temporarily through the custom of wardship; he will observe the chartered freedoms of London; and so forth. The king stated his motives as proper fear of God, for the salvation of his own soul and those of his ancestors and successors, and for the betterment of the realm. In the context of 1215, such phrases signify genuine beliefs and fears, not moral platitudes. Naturally, the document does not refer to the political pressure which baronial revolt had put upon the king, nor to the drafting assistance received from disaffected prelates.

True, at the first opportunity John obtained a papal dispensation which enabled him to cancel his promises. But these ups and downs of politics were not to matter. The Charter was restored in the next reign and remained as a fundamental touchstone of those rights that it defined. Most of its terms make sense only in the kind of society that first produced them, but several of those specific rights, designed for the moment, had within them means of adaptation to changing circumstances. This was especially true of the famous chapters 39 and 40: 'No free man shall be taken or imprisoned or disseised or exiled or in any way destroyed, nor will we go upon him or send upon him, except by the lawful judgment of his peers and by the law of the land', followed by 'to no one will we sell, to no one will we refuse or delay, right or justice'. These very technical terms had a precise and limited meaning in the early thirteenth century, but as society changed they nevertheless continued to stand and expand, so as to become a general guarantee to the right of a proper trial at and by the law. In 1215, they did not guarantee trial by jury, still in its infancy, but even a century later that device, then well established and prevalent, could be read as guaranteed by Magna Carta. The sheer length and adaptability of the Charter leave parts of its in continued effect to the present day. Even now, not all of its clauses have been superseded by repeal or amendment. Rights extorted through highly particular promises appeared in the end to be capable of an over-arching universality.

The reason for this universality is also plain enough. The Charter and its later elaborations rested not on some abstract rights of man but on rights secured by men of standing, rights defined in the law of England, and rights applied by a trained legal profession in the established courts of the land. Its whole character was positive and concrete. Perhaps quite properly, the only part of it capable of abstract construction was chapter 1 with its promise to respect the liberties of the church. Because the papal church did not want to limit itself by definitions, this clause lacked specificity. This clause was to give rise to a great deal of debate partially, at least, because it alone grew out of some principle of faith rather than the facts of legal relationships. By the same token, it was also least able to guarantee anything for long. No wonder that Thomas Cromwell in 1534, engaged upon destroying those liberties, made a note to himself to look up the Great Charter and to see how 'ut libera sit' had got into the document.

However, what sort of protection for stated rights did all of those concrete provisions really offer? Their very framing accepted the principle that in the last resort the king was the fountain of law, though by its phrasing it also underlined the fact that, once declared, this king-made law stood even against kings. Then came the addition of the Parliament to the instruments of government, and by the later four-teenth century it generally was accepted that royal decrees promulgated in Parliament and by its advice ranked above all other forms of lawmaking. Out of this material, the sixteenth century produced a doctrine of legislative sovereignty vested in the joint body called the king-in-Parliament. This development, in effect, undermined the medie-val position which had given to the law an independent status over and against the lawgiver. Though the later Middle Ages made new law at times, they held to a notion of the law existing in the empyrean even before it was discovered and made visible by decree. The danger that the doctrine of sovereignty might weaken the power of the law to protect those who resorted to it did not materialise because the new legislative sovereign was a mixed body in which no one person's voice overrode the rest. Though the monarch could single-handedly prevent law from being made, he could not single-handedly make it. Thus, generally speaking, the common law of England, then and later, well enough sheltered the liberties of the subject. More particularly, the common law protected the rights to a trial solely by recognised rules and the rights of property. In fact, the common law controlled the powers of the king markedly better than did the laws of other European countries. Of course, abuses could still occur, and because most litigation involves two parties, both equally convinced of the justice of their cause, someone usually was bound to feel that the law worked unjustly against her or him. But then, people, and particularly lawyers, really did not seek justice as an abstract principle; they expected to be able to obtain their rights at law, and, if they could prove those rights by the proper legal means, they would so obtain them.

One example will show that that law, though careful of the rights of kings, also took care of people's rights against the monarch. It was an understandable principle of the law that no person could be sued in a court that the person owned (medieval custom regarded all courts as the property of someone, some owner of land, from the king downward, to which the right attached to keep a court for the tenants). The fact that subjects could not be sued in their own courts lies behind the familiar maxim that the king can do no wrong. This did not mean what an innocent mind might read into it: no one supposed that kings, being human, were incapable of committing a wrong. Rather, the maxim meant that, because the king could not be sued in his own courts, and because no remedy lay against him, he technically was unable to do a wrong: no remedy, therefore, no wrong. However, in actual fact kings or their agents could do wrong, legal wrong, as often as not inadvertently and in quite small matters. A drastic remedy like that of 1215, involving the use of force to extort yet another set of promises, manifestly was unsuitable on such occasions. Did the subject go without relief? Certainly not: the law assisted the subject with the procedure known as a petition of right. Suppose a tenant-in-chief died and at the inquest upon the decedent's property held by the county escheator the jury mistakenly declared some part of the inheritance to be held directly of the crown, and suppose that the heir was under age so that the king could claim the heir's rights of wardship and take the property into his possession. While the usual process against dispossessors did not lie against the king, the jury verdict had been false, the king (through his officers) had done wrong. The party offended would then use the method provided to resolve this deadlock. The offended party would enter a petition in Chancery which declared that the party's existing rights had been disregarded and prayed that the king, of his own volition, would restore these rights. If the offended party could prove his or her claim, the rights were so restored. Thus, the law preserved the principle that, where fair dealing demanded it, a remedy should be available, while at the same time preserving the principle that the king could not be restrained by a suit at law. The king's response was termed voluntary, but in actual fact the petition compelled the attorney-general to take the steps necessary for establishing the truth of the matter. I have always thought this to be a most illuminating detail in the medieval common law, whose principles and practice continued in effect, through change and adaptation, into the nineteenth century.

Positive and particular rights at law thus do seem to have some advantages over human rights outlined in documents of muddled composition and justified on grounds so abstract that they are incapable of proof. Also the positive and particular origin of these English liberties did not necessarily confine their operation to what may seem limited and pettifogging details of property and ownership. True, the law of England did not impose universal education (this was later accomplished by statute, but not as a human right) or the equality of the sexes in all sorts of biologically suspect ways, but English law did promote both of these goals by protecting the endowments of schools and the property rights of women, despite English law's refusal to give married women rights against their husbands. English law accomplished these goals through Chancery's equitable manipulations of the law. When every European country and, above all, the Universal Church believed in the use of torture to secure the confessions which were held to be the only safe proof of guilt, the English common law barred torture by the simple device of not allowing confessions so obtained to be pleaded in court at all. And, even while the defenders of the self-evident right of liberty worked their plantations by slaves in whom their property remained protected by their own law, Lord Mansfield, in London, set James Somerset at liberty because the positive law of England knew no such thing as slavery, a condition he declared to be odious. I am not putting forth some starry-eyed nonsense about the glories of the past, its law and its humanity. The law of England could be unjust and its criminal law could be savage – though it too characteristically provided some haphazard means of amelioration such as benefit of clergy and the royal pardon. All I wish to maintain is that the liberties of Englishmen enjoyed an ascertainable certainty, and a protection against executive power which, history has so far proved, is not to be obtained through declarations of human rights.

However, things have changed in the last hundred years or so. The law-generated liberties of Englishmen could last only while the law was regarded in what I have called the medieval manner, as an independent component within the social and political structure of the state. The sixteenth century, which used the law of Parliament to remake the state, temporarily weakened the hold of that doctrine, and the revolutions of the nineteenth century finished off the hold of this doctrine. The vast increase in population, the coming of the industrial state, and the social conscience which wished to remedy the consequences of both, turned the law from a guardian of rights into an instrument of social change. The dread of poverty undermined the sanctity of property, and the powers of government grew enormously. It does not matter which party or which social philosophy happens to control the means available to that power: all of them, willingly or not, find themselves driven to intervene in everybody's life, promoting the hopes of human rights at the expense of the certainty of legal rights. The search for justice then moved from the law courts to socio-economic preaching, from the certainty of legal rights to the vagaries of doing the right thing. When the cohesive society, which had lasted a thousand years, began to break up, the law by which it had lived ceased to be the instrument of stability and satisfaction.

To this unquiet state, our century has added further vast increases in the pressure of people upon available resources, even though in our century these resources have been increased greatly. More importantly, for our present purpose, this century has added the revival of a totally lawless barbarism. We all live in the shadow of the barbarian, whether Hitlerite or Stalinite, who a generation ago proved that, contrary to a general belief, morality lacked all power to maintain itself and that nothing that men can inflict on one another is impossible. All of it happens: it happened then and is still happening in many parts of the world. To this chaos, the liberties founded on law have proved no protection, the more so because these liberties have ceased to speak with conviction for many of the supposed supporters of these liberties. It is no wonder that people unwilling to contemplate total dissolution find the doctrine of human rights so passionately appealing. So passionately appealing that they readily claim these human rights for special groups only. Thus, we are witnessing the development of selective rights which is contributing to the decay of the rights of those humans who do not belong to some chosen sector. The rights of man are broken reeds even in ordered communities. These rights, derived from equality at birth, are disputed by seekers who are after superior rights accruing to people who think themselves handicapped by equality.

In fact, as I hope I have convinced you, the doctrine of human rights rests on no foundation at all except some praiseworthy hope and some weak-minded shutting of eyes to the truths about human beings. It is only since the Enlightenment that doctrinaires have placed their faith in the fundamental goodness of humanity and have ignored humanity's propensity to do evil and inflict suffering. This mindless optimism has done some good: there *have* been liberations. Yet, a doctrine, however attractive and however helpful, which derived from false judgement and blind eyes, cannot forever avoid doing great harm. Take those prophets who for a century or more preached the utopian blessings of socialism. They might have learned something if they had looked more carefully at the selfishnesses, hatreds and killing instincts manifest among their admired inspirers, Marx above all. That agreeable roses will grow on dung heaps applies only in horticulture.

The hopes of those who drew the United Nations' Declaration of Human Rights should have withered within a few years, as they witnessed the beneficiaries of that Declaration use their newly secured rights for the destruction of the rights of others. But, for that recognition to have come and to have worked, very great changes would have had to take place among the makers of opinion. Lamenting evil deeds serves no purpose as long as the mind stays preoccupied with rights. Perhaps the time has come to understand that this endless preoccupation with one's rights is a sign of immaturity and mindlessness. Perhaps the time has come to grow up. Life was never meant to be a pleasure garden. Thumping the tub about rights has filled the earth with selfish children drowning one another in the nearest available lily pond. Unless we remember the two lessons of the past, rights serve only the strong and unscrupulous. One lesson reads: rights grow out of law, not out of philsophical abstractions. The second lesson says: claimants for rights must first earn them by proving themselves capable of understanding and discharging their duties.

52

KING HENRY VII*

Henry VII, the son of Edmund earl of Richmond and the Lady Margaret Beaufort, a few weeks ago and 500 years before that won the battle of Bosworth (on 22 August 1485) and thereby won the crown of England; he then settled down to become king of England. He was twenty-eight years old when he won the crown, and he had twenty-four more years during which he held it. Thus his victory at Bosworth, which was a narrow thing, came effectively halfway through his life. For half his life he worked towards the crown, for much of the time not aware that he was doing so; for half his life he held it and became, in the opinion of many, a new king, a man who really set about making kingship into an effective force again in England.

In the first place I should like to see what Henry VII did to make himself king – what sort of kingship he ran and what inheritance he left to his successor. Henry became king at the end of a muddle of civil wars and disputes which had been going on for the best part of a hundred years, and he had first of all to restore the repute and honour to that position. His predecessors, the Yorkist kings Edward IV and Richard III, had very nearly achieved this but had then fallen short of accomplishing it. Henry therefore had to build up on past memory, a memory which by this time was well out of date, so as to revive the notion that the king of England was the ruler of England, to be obeyed and respected and to provide continuity, peace, order and law. He had plenty of material in that past to draw upon, and in actual fact (let me start from that point) he did nothing new. He did not invent any particular form of government; he did not invent any particular form of political structure; he simply concerned himself with bringing reality back into a kingship which, among the European monarchies of the early and high Middle Ages, had been quite exceptionally powerful, concentrated and successful. This state of affairs was, of course, the result of a conquest: Anglo-Saxon kings did all right, but it took William the Conqueror to make

* Hartwell Jones lecture for 1985 (edited from a taped recording) delivered to the Society in London on 2 October 1985 [*Trans. of the Hon. Society of Cymmrodorion* (1985), 131–45].

sure that kings from that day onwards should be the bosses. This they
have never ceased to be, as anyone will, I think, confirm who watched
on television Princess Margaret entering Toxteth this morning! If we
have a secure institution left in this country, it is not the Parliament and
it is not the Trade Unions; it is still the monarchy.

The first achievement that the new king found it necessary to
consolidate was simply his acceptance as king. The battle of Bosworth
was not the end of the civil wars. It did not look so at the time: the battle
was little regarded and very poorly reported. Its dubious import is at the
moment being much discussed in the literature which has arisen out of
the anniversary. There are even disputes as to where it happened; every
owner of a museum in the neighbourhood of Market Bosworth claims
to be the man who picked up all the bits of the battle's relics around his
particular neighbourhood; there are even arguments between respectable
historians which really are of no significance whatsoever. What happened was that somewhere near Market Bosworth, on 22 August 1485,
Henry, at that point claimant to the throne and earl of Richmond,
managed to kill Richard III, the king in possession, and the throne being
thereby vacant the claimant took it. It took him another decade to make
sure that he was going to retain it.

Henry's queen, daughter to Edward IV, assisted in bringing about on
the public stage of England a reunion of the various factions and parties
which had split the country so badly during the previous thirty or even
sixty years – ever since Henry V had made the bad mistake of dying too
young. By marrying Elizabeth of York, Henry VII gave himself the
chance of surmounting the faction-ridden decline which had become the
political and public character of England.

In this, Henry had a number of specific tasks facing him. In the first
place, he had to restore the honour of monarchy. Perhaps we do not
sufficiently realise, in this twentieth century, the importance of the sheer
concept of honour that ruled behaviour in that highly hierarchic society
500 years ago. By honour they meant an acceptance of respectability,
using a generally approved behaviour, asserting one's claims on those
below, and showing devotion and deference to those above. A king had
to safeguard his honour: it was his duty to do so, and negligence in the
matter only lost respect. That does not mean that he had to be a model
of behaviour (Henry VIII, you may remember, safeguarded his honour
with a great deal of success without ever behaving properly in the whole
of his life). It meant he had to behave like a king. He had to exact

obedience and prevent any scurrilous attacks upon himself. Standing on top of the pyramid he had to be king to all – not only king to some.

Henry VII appears to have recognised this obligation consciously and very effectively. The first thing he did, from the beginning of his reign, was to escape from the scene of faction that had preceded him. The Yorkists – Richard duke of York, who raised the claim to the crown in 1460, his son Edward who became king in 1461 and resumed the crown after a short break a decade later, and his other son Richard III, on whom I hope I shall not have to say too much – had established their rule in England as dominant leaders of a faction. It was all not very different from what happened in nineteenth- and twentieth-century China, where various war-lords set up their rule in one part of the kingdom or another until some other war-lord displaced them. The Edwardian faction was split by the king's own mistake in marrying Elizabeth Woodville (which did not stop him having extra-marital affairs, at which Edward IV, who was Henry VIII's exemplary, excelled): thereby he destroyed the coherence of the faction which had brought him to the throne. When his brother succeeded by usurpation in 1483, he had to rely again on a sectional structure, especially on the northern lords and gentry who supported him, and whom he advanced over the south-erners not keen to accept Richard. It was, of course, this situation that enabled Henry VII in the end to take over. So what we have here is a political system which is extremely labile, extremely unstable, because it is dominated by the advantages given to a sector of the governing order by a king who cannot do without that sector.

Henry VII from the first made it very plain that he was king over all Englishmen. He would not be king to a part of the nation. All his subjects were *his* subjects, and so they remained. You can see this policy evolving right from the start. In securing the crown, Henry VII did not rely on the old Lancastrians or on those Yorkists who happened to have fallen out with Richard. The Stanleys, who won him the battle of Bosworth by not turning up in time or by staying on the sidelines waiting to see how things went (displaying thereby a magnificent grasp of fifteenth-century politics), did no better under him than the Howards whom he restored quickly even though his people had killed the head of the clan, the duke of Norfolk, at Bosworth. Henry liked people to work their way back, but he let them do so very readily. And yet the Stanleys were his mother's people, for the last of the several people that Margaret Beaufort married, from the age of twelve and a half onwards, was

Thomas Stanley, who became earl of Derby. A king compelled to rely on faction would have shown them special favour.

So, in the first place, Henry VII recognised that if he was to hold that throne and maintain it he had to be king of England and not king of some sector or part of the English political nation. As far as I can see, he acted with great consistency and great determination. He was very good about the people who had helped him; he was generous in his immediate rewards; but he did not elevate them above the rest, he did not depend on them. This was an innovation. The last man who had not depended on a faction for the throne of England was Henry V, who had not lived long enough to make much of it. His father had been a faction leader. Richard II had effectively turned into a faction leader. Edward III in his great days had really been the last king of England to occupy the position which Henry VII now had to recreate: and very quickly, with remarkable political skill, he achieved that.

Thus he restored the king's honour – that of a king who was everybody's king, deferred to by all, accepted by all, and whom it was death and dishonour to attack. The ease with which he disposed of the further efforts to dethrone him demonstrates that. Of course, he had advantages. We ought to realise how powerful the English monarchy actually was. If it worked together with the top layers of the English political nation it could never really go wrong. Of course, that was a complicated thing to do. On the one hand you had to keep them with you, using favours, graciousness, court tricks and such like; on the other you had to rule them. They had to be made to accept that they were beneath you, that they were not your equals, that you stood above them, and a young man, suddenly elevated to the throne, would not find this an easy thing to persuade great magnates of. Henry did, by personality and skill, though after an early and quick success he (we are told) found it necessary in the end to employ more positive menaces to keep the great men in order. About this I remain a little doubtful. By giving a working reality to his kingship, and without any threats, he succeeded quite simply in restoring the concept of the English monarchy – that of a king ruling his country from above, by consent, by agreement, by negotiation, by decent dealing, by not upsetting those that can destroy the relationship. You can see the threats to that relationship manifest themselves as far back as Magna Carta, as far forward as the Glorious Revolution of 1688. At the top of the nation stand the king and his immediate inferiors, and they make politics: the peerage and the king. That peerage normally follows the king, but if it finds that it cannot work with him, cannot have any further useful dealings with him, loses its belief in him, it will soon overset and destroy him. This happened to Charles I, I may say, and no better candidate for that fate has been found in our history. Of course, as king you had to be trusted, which was where Charles made his mistake. You had to be firm: when you said a thing you stood by it. You also had to be flexible: no king could survive who was not a politician. All these things Henry VII did. He symbolised his role by that marriage to the Yorkist heiress, even as he consolidated it in the end by suppressing Yorkist claimants; right down to 1497 he was still busy in overcoming what were largely bogus claimants like Perkin Warbeck and Lambert Simnel, and in establishing himself upon the throne: and the bulk of the peerage throughout stayed with him.

The other thing he needed to do was to establish himself in the Concert of Europe. Perhaps an excessive term for the late fifteenth century, but not entirely inappropriate. We are dealing with a community of monarchs. We are dealing with the king of France and the duke of Burgundy, for those were the immediate powers that concerned Henry VII, with the Habsburgs following after. We face here a quite well-developed international system, reaching through Burgundy and Germany into Italy, through France into Spain, and from the reign of the first Tudor onwards increasingly reaching outward into the Baltic and ultimately Russia. This international system called for coexistence and mutual understanding, and Henry VII had to establish his claim in the eyes of his equals, a matter complicated by the fact that women with marriageable prospects survived among the Yorkist claimants. Margaret of Burgundy, who represented what remained of the Yorkist interests, had influence on the continent of Europe and needed constant watching. But Henry won: by about 1492, in just under seven years, he had made himself the only king of England in the eyes of Europe.

So we have a king who has succeeded, by cool and calculated moves, in subduing a nation – a nation, that is, of leaders and bosses, of peers and gentry who had got used to running the show as they pleased. He brought them back to coherence, obedience and cooperation. He had persuaded his fellow monarchs in Europe that he was going to be king of England for quite a long time and that they had better accept this dynasty he was setting up. He had made himself a traditional king by all the old-established tricks and means. There was nothing new about any of this; he had to revive, to reinvigorate, to restore, rather than to invent. One thing he did not do, and this is a point of some interest that somebody might perhaps take a closer look at. I can see nothing 'Machiavellian'

about Henry's policies and practices. We have been taught by generations, even centuries, of scholars that Machiavelli did no more than
describe the normal methods of kingship and rulership, giving coherent
expression to practice observed in fact. There may be some truth in this
if one looks at the peculiarly absurd politics of Italy in the late fifteenth
and early sixteenth centuries. But is there any truth in it if one looks at
the monarchs, the real kings and emperors, of that era? (Was even Louis
XI of France really a pattern of Machiavellian advice?) Like all political
theorists, Machiavelli did not look beyond a narrow range of experience.

I do not think there was anything Machiavellian about Henry VII. He
worked very straightforwardly, very clearly and rather cleanly. But he
worked very determinedly from one basic position – and I want to
emphasise this again, apologising for the repetition – namely that he was
not king of a faction. He was king of England and Wales.

Now, having got himself established as king he needed to maintain the
position: he needed to govern. And here the problems arise which have
given him a bad press in some quarters. Henry VII is accused of being
exceptionally suspicious, exceptionally mean and miserly, and therefore
exceptionally unpleasing on the throne. The truth of this interesting
question has never been agreed and probably will never be established
because as a person Henry VII remains strikingly elusive. It is a problem
of the evidence; we have very little really personal material. We do have
some portraits and a brilliant sculpture by Torrigiani. And a careful
look, I think, should leave us rather impressed. The king was a
reasonably tall and very slender man, sinewy but not massive, his
countenance calm, collected and careful. There is a touch of sardonic
cynicism, which is no wonder. He looks like a man one could bear to
live with – unlike his ghastly son. A man to whom it is possible to talk –
and there is evidence that people did so. His faith was conventional; he
was a good, devout, rather commonplace Christian, which means that
he did not fervently believe in anything but thought he had better look
to his salvation and therefore did all the things the church told him were
necessary. Having secured his crown in this world, he thought he had
better make sure that in the next world he did not chalk up any serious
or dangerous deficits. Hence all those masses for his soul, his patronage of
Observant Franciscans, his alms and all the rest of it – highly conventional, very well meant, respectful. I find no touch of originality in his
thinking or his faith; what does come across is high competence of a
decent kind.

I do think that Henry VII was rather a decent man, which is a surprising thing to conclude about any king of England in the sixteenth century. But we shall never know very much about his personality because there is so little evidence about what went on behind the façade, behind the public face. We have no usable material for the kind of psychological analysis which later monarchs offer us so readily (perhaps too readily), and psycho-historical speculations based on little or no material are an abomination.

Where Henry VII has offended people – I mean historians – is in two respects. In the first place he has offended all those who think that Richard III is a much maligned person. I agree that he was in measure maligned, but he still remains by normal standards of behaviour a fairly nasty piece of work. Shakespeare, building up on Thomas More, did succeed in making him look even worse than he actually was. But, even though we do not have to accept the image of the king presented in the play, we should not think of Richard III as a man of generosity, of kindness or goodness or deep involvement in the fate of the poor – of all the things the Ricardians ascribe to him. In all those respects Henry VII surpassed him. So far, therefore, as criticism of Henry VII projects an attitude of devotion to the last Yorkist we can write it off. However, the other matter to have raised moral doubts arises from his own work, which has been criticised especially on two counts. He is supposed to have taken excessive steps in controlling the upper layers of society when he put them under heavy bonds, with penal obligations in money that he meant to collect. Thus it is alleged that he put illegal burdens on the aristocracy and upper gentry in order to prevent them from defecting. And, secondly, we are assured that in him sheer meanness and greed produced a heavy exploitation of dubious royal rights of the financial kind. There have been some disputes over all these charges. At present, I think, the prevalent view, for instance exemplified in Stanley Chrimes's biography and also in some articles especially by J. R. Lander, maintains that in his latter years the king grew merely miserly, mean and nasty. I am afraid I still hold to the view that this is a serious exaggeration. I certainly think that Henry exacted his rights – those rights to which he was lawfully entitled, and no more. He applied the law, especially against potential law-breakers. Some of this activity was certainly very hard on people. Some of it looks very unfair, even tyrannical, though in most of such cases we can usually track a private quarrel – personal animosities and manoeuvres against their own adversaries by some of the king's advisers who were trading on Henry's unsurprising suspicion of anything that looked devious and a threat to the dynasty. Very often it is not the king who pursues those victims; other people exploit in his name chances offered by the king's service.

Nevertheless, Henry needed money – it assuredly was important to him – because he did not readily have all that much of it. The old story that in the end he left an enormous treasure has been exploded, from which it follows that the king was never in his life overwhelmingly rich. A lack of cash beset all Tudor government because an active royal administration at that time always faced demands well beyond the means at its disposal. The only period of reasonable sufficiency was the first half of Elizabeth I's reign when queen and council, by parsimony, managed to build up a sizeable reserve. No other Tudor monarch ever enjoyed that degree of solvency. Henry VII may have approached that state, but he never possessed the large reserve that people ascribed to him. That story goes back to Francis Bacon, and you want to remember that Francis Bacon, whatever his standing as a philosopher of science, rather lacked propriety and therefore historical trustworthiness. Bacon was one of those unfortunate people whom the Stuarts took seriously while the Tudors could not see much in him; and so he outreached himself in his self-esteem, both in his life and in his claims to the attention of posterity.

I would suggest that Henry's financial claims upon his nation, though they were often stringent and in particular demands could be severe and burdensome, in reality never exceed the minimum of his needs. He could not afford to be in the red or to attempt deficit financing. He could not govern without the means, and much of his government was designed simply to assure the coming in of those means of whose scantness he was necessarily well aware. Hence that exploitation of established rights which no doubt to many will not make him an attractive character. He was not romantic. Romantic kings win affection; unromantic kings win the war.

Thus I rather agree that some of that bonding of his peerage and the like went a bit far, though I doubt whether in virtually all cases Henry ever meant to collect the money. He only meant to put the great men in a position where they could not afford to rebel, and I find it difficult to blame the victor of a civil war for putting his overmighty subjects into such a position. It seems a very sensible thing to do. Therefore I remain on Henry's side when it comes to the extraction of money and the imposition of bonds on those powerful men. On the other hand, the nation did not suffer heavy oppression. It was not in dire financial difficulties because of the king's exactions. The king was taking his rights and taking the last penny to which he was entitled. You may not like that, but you must understand the situation in which he found himself. Unless he prevented conspiracy and rebellion (so rife so recently), and unless he could pay his way, he could not guarantee the continuance of his rule and the rule of his dynasty.

For what Henry VII achieved above all else was the establishment of a dynasty. That was what every king hoped to do. The Yorkists had come near it. Edward IV had produced children. He only needed to live long enough for those children to grow up, and the Yorkists were established on the throne. What killed Edward IV prematurely? Well, so far as we know, it was over-eating, actually a misfortune that can be controlled. Maybe, if Edward IV had valued his position as king (in which role he was good) and his glory as a king and the needs of his country rather more highly than the needs of his belly, we might still be under a Yorkist dynasty and almost certainly we might still obey the rule of Rome (quite a thought). But he seemingly sacrificed the crown and the nation to self-indulgence. Perhaps this is too harsh a judgement. In the fifteenth century, anybody could die with no difficulty at all. But I think that Edward helped his fate along a mite too dramatically. And Richard III, of course, broke up the succession, killed those that could have maintained it, and thereby left the Yorkists naked in the face of the future.

Now the Tudor dynasty actually turned out to be singularly unpro-ductive, genetically speaking. Henry VII was the only member of his dynasty who had a sizeable body of children, though some of them also died very young. Henry VIII, you will remember, had considerable difficulty in finding a successor – I mean, in creating a successor – and all his three children died childless. It is a curious story – fit subject for some dramatist besotted with fate. In those 120 years of Tudor rule there reigned only three generations of monarchs, even though their total number ran to five. And they lasted 125 years altogether only because the last of the Tudors, the great queen (in many ways she was indeed a great queen), had the good sound sense to stay away from doctors, for which reason she lived to be nearly seventy. Those who took medical advice in the sixteenth century died young. I rather think the example is still worth heeding today.

So the Tudors' failure to procreate offered them small prospects for the future, and their endurance through 125 years must be reckoned something of a miracle. However, Henry VII at least produced a sound and solid family. So there was to be material for intermarriage with the

Scots and Spanish monarchies, and briefly under his son with the
monarchy of France as well, not to mention a shortlived eye cast on the
Habsburgs as well. Henry was able to use his offspring in his maintenance
of the dynasty once he had established it. In all respects, therefore, that
mattered Henry VII was a success. He recreated respect for the
monarchy of England; he preserved its honour; he made it accepted in
Europe among his fellow monarchs. By hard work, he gave it a
reasonable financial basis and administrative efficiency. I don't think he
ever took a holiday, and that too I respect. What are holidays for? – only
to let someone else in. On top of all this Henry provided for the
succession; he lived to see grown-up children, though only just. Henry
VIII came to the throne as a minor, by a few months. Kings came out of
their minority at eighteen – girls at fourteen, human beings in general at
twenty-one, but monarchs at eighteen – and young Henry had not quite
got there when his father died. They had to fudge his succession a bit at
that point, though the actual coronation was delayed until the king had
passed that milestone. Well, you just try to keep Henry VIII off the
throne, is all I can say.

Thus Henry VII did everything that a good, solid, monarchic
restoration and its future needed; and what this did in the larger scheme
of things was to bring peace to his country, a measure of order, and a
chance to look with confidence to the future. I do not think that any
king could have done better, or indeed ever did better in the kind of
conditions which prevailed at Henry's accession. Twenty-four years
sufficed for the doing of it – but only just.

So much for what he did once he was king, but of course he lived for
twenty-eight years before that. Was there any kind of preparation for
this success, for this achievement by a person previously very obscure?
For the first fourteen years of his life he lived in Wales. In 1471 he fled
abroad under the aegis of his uncle Jasper. His father, the earl of
Richmond, had died very young. Henry VI, out of respect for this
mother even though in her second marriage she chose a mere Welsh
commoner, created the two sons of Owen Tudor and Catherine de
Valois earls of Richmond and Pembroke, thus accepting the by-blows of
his dynasty into that dynasty's mainstream. Jasper turned out to be the
uncle any sensible nephew really wants. He guarded him, guided him,
ran his politics for him, and ultimately helped him onto the throne.
Behind him, however, stood the person who really mattered in Henry's
life – his mother. The Lady Margaret Beaufort (who became countess of
Derby, having been countess of Richmond, which superior title accord-

ing to the custom she retained to the end of her life) was one of the most remarkable women of that women-ridden Tudor century. Her portrait and her death-mask are known, and although she was not in the least Welsh in blood she looks to me the sort of mother I expect Neil Kinnock had. A very determined lady who was going to see her son through to his success. She was a very devout woman, a very bright and brainy woman, a very formidable woman, and she was really a remarkable conspirator. Once she had got her son on the throne she ran him, being quite dominant at his court for most of the reign. But she knew the rules and showed great respect for her son the king; in their relations with each other, neither ever took a wrong step. The perfection of those relations shines through the little evidence we have, portraying a very loving feeling between mother and son. Without that mother there would have been no Henry VII. Not only did she have to produce him, which she did, but she then also had to organise him and put him on the throne, which she also did, with the assistance of Jasper Tudor, Bishop John Morton, and one or two others.

So Henry VII's career before he became king is very odd indeed. He was brought up in Wales in Pembroke Castle, as a boy effectively ignored and neglected. There was no reason to think that he stood in the line of succession to any practical purpose. Others had better and more immediate claims. His remote cousins of York were running the show. The Lancastrian interest faltered, collapsed. Henry VI was one of the really appalling kings that this country has suffered. A nice enough man, no doubt, when temporarily sane, but a total disaster as a king – for which reason, of course, his good relative Henry VII tried to get him canonised. It is a good way of getting rid of the real memory of people to have then sainted and thus transfer them in the public mind to a politically harmless place. Before Henry Richmond was fourteen there could be no question of his succeeding nor of his claiming the crown. Then he became an outlaw and an exile because of the way the politics of those wars had gone, and he spent some fourteen years in Brittany. Until he went to Bosworth he knew nothing of England. He had never been there. The first time he entered England was when he crossed the border near Shrewsbury and waddled down to Leicester and those parts. Of Wales he had known the neighbourhood of Pembroke, but there is no evidence that he had become acquainted with any other part of that country either. It was a most limited and limiting upbringing. He should in the end have been a small Welsh gentleman; I mean that in respect of power, not of physical size. If ever there was a king of England not prepared for the job it was Henry VII. We do not know, of course, what Jasper told him during their various flights from the Yorkist death-gangs that were pursuing them at intervals. We do not know what he learned at the court of Francis, duke of Brittany, except to keep his counsel and to make certain that he was not sold to the French, as he nearly was. We know very little about those years of near imprisonment, but we see him there in conditions which in no way prepare us for the successful king of England that he became.

However, he had his backing in one particular quarter. I am no historian of Wales, and there are people here tonight who can claim to be such – who really know the Welsh history of that age. I must ask their forgiveness if now I make terrible mistakes. Henry VII was elected by the Welsh bards of the later fifteenth century as the man who would restore the Welsh nation. He was not the first so chosen; there had been a long succession ever since Edward I got the better of Llywelyn. There had been a lot of dreaming about the next Welsh prince who would come and rescue his nation, restoring it to independence, self-respect and power. Now, for some reason, the bards seized on the young earl of Richmond as the latest candidate for this very difficult and highly improbable role, and they backed him in a good deal of poetry for which they were paid when his final attempts to take the crown came in 1483 and 1485. For in 1483 the enterprise failed which in 1485 succeeded. The scene, however, was really set in England. It was the duke of Buckingham's rebellion in 1483 which then nearly got Henry advanced to the crown. It was the activities of the anti-Yorkist factions, organised by his mother and the bishop of Ely, that really put him on the throne in 1485. And therefore, despite the bards, I think it would be wrong to picture him as a Welshman who captured the throne of England.

How Welsh was Henry VII? We do not really know. Later Tudors made no effort to appear Welsh. If you had gone to Elizabeth and said, how nice to meet you, fellow Welshwoman, I think you would not have survived very long. Nor did Henry VIII ever make any point of his Welshry. Henry VII did signal something when he named his eldest son Arthur, but to the English the British king Arthur was not specifically Welsh. Henry VII does not look or act, to my estimation, as a Welshman. We are dealing with Englishmen – English people and an English succession into which the Welsh gentry, the upper gentry of Wales, tied themselves in ways that are not to be described in nationalistic terms. Whatever the bards professed, those people did not think in those mythological ways. If there was anything Welsh about Henry VII,

I fear no one has ever discerned it, nor did he engage in suitably propagandist pretensions. The thing called 'Tudor propaganda' does not in fact exist. It is not the case that after he came to the throne Henry VII organised a propaganda campaign to support his claims and denigrate his enemies. Far from it. If there was propaganda it was put out not by the Tudors but for them, without participation, by such people as Polydore Vergil, Bernard Andreae and the rest who sought favours and fortunes and benefits from the new dynasty; none of this was organised from the centre. The first genuinely organised campaign on behalf of crown policy was that which Thomas Cromwell mounted in the 1530s in support of the break with Rome. And while Henry VII himself took no part, he does appear in his laudators' eyes as a Welshman. Only those bards professed to regard him as a Welsh king.

It is true that in the last campaign for Bosworth he did receive a lot of Welsh support. Rhys ap Thomas came reluctantly and cautiously to offer aid, and it looks as if at Bosworth the biggest part of the claimant's army was indeed Welsh. It was almost certainly a Welshman of common stock who hacked down Richard III, that gallant knight. Welsh armies and Welsh gentry helped Henry as they had assisted his predecessor. Wales had been a reservoir of military force for English kings ever since the end of Edward I's reign. But did those Welsh soldiers and their leaders plan to put a Welshman on the throne? Certainly they hoped to back a winner, but not on behalf of an entity to be called Wales. Here was this unknown young man. He won his battle; he became king of England; he ruled England; he ruled Wales, the Marches of which were by this time in any case in the king's hands. And he ruled as an English king. We have no idea that he ever spoke a word of Welsh, though living all that time at Pembroke he may well have done. The question therefore is whether Wales got anything out of this last candidate advertised by the poets as the great restorer of Wales?

The Welsh did. One of the more interesting aspects of the early sixteenth century – perhaps not yet sufficiently investigated – is the manner in which the Welsh, and especially the Welsh gentry, utilised the restoration of good order under this notionally Welsh king to move into England. A hundred years later the Scots came down with James I and excited an enormous amount of hatred, reprobation, enmity and strife. No one seems ever to have protested about the influx of the Welsh, which is one of the features of the early sixteenth century. The influx strengthened English government, English society, even in many ways English literature and culture, and incidentally it enormously improved the lot of at least the upper ranks in Wales itself. And all without rousing genuine resentment. If you want to understand what the Elizabethans thought of the Welsh, remember Captain Fluellen. Shakespeare is pretty contemptuous of the Irish and rather doubtful about the Scots, but the Welshman is one of the heroes of *Henry V* – on account of his personal qualities.

Yet these migrant Welsh were to record a hidden victory for their nation. Nomenclature plays games with history. The Tudors were not really the Tudors. If they had a family name it was Meredith. By the narrowest squeak England escaped living for 125 years under a Meredith dynasty. And one of the Welshmen who came to Henry VIII's court was a man called Richard Williams whose mother was the sister of Thomas Cromwell. He came to court, he made a career there, and he thought it might be wise, while his uncle's star stood in the ascendant, to adopt that name. And so Richard Williams became Richard Cromwell. It was from him that Cromwells of Huntingdon descended. England not only narrowly escaped a Meredith dynasty; by the merest whisker it did not have a Lord Protector Williams. The bards had won after all.

53

WALES IN PARLIAMENT, 1542–1581*

Though one of the best-known provisions of the so-called Union of Wales with England in 1536 equipped the twelve counties with twenty-four representatives at Westminster, we now know that the first elected members sat only in 1542.[1] Their presence and influence may well have contributed to the very large statute of the next session which at long last attended to the unfinished business of turning the intentions of 1536 into something like a settled order, for that the act incorporated Welsh demands and proposals is clear enough from its contents.[2] Wales thus seemed well placed to share in the expanding use of parliamentary statute for personal, local and national purposes which characterised the years from 1530 onwards; one would expect to find bills promoted by Welsh knights and burgesses as one finds them promoted by other identifiable interests. A study of such bills, so far as the evidence survives, for the first forty years of Welsh participation should therefore prove illuminating, though it can be said from the start that the tally is not impressive, reveals no determined exploitation of the possibilities, and must call in doubt whether an entity to be called Wales had much reality in the middle of the sixteenth century. Wales was never so prominent again in the business of the English Parliament as it had been in the nine years following upon Thomas Cromwell's decision to reduce the region beyond Offa's Dyke to order; nothing like the remarkable sequence of acts beginning with 26 Henry VIII, c. 6 (which created a system of law-enforcement modelled on that of the English shires), and ending with the 1543 Statute of Wales already mentioned, was ever seen again during the century. Those acts, however, testified to government policy, however

* [*Welsh Society and Nationhood*, ed. R. R. Davies et al. (Cardiff, 1984), 108–21.] I am grateful to Professor R. A. Griffiths whose advice most generously enlightened my ignorance.
[1] P. S. Edwards, 'The parliamentary representation of the Welsh boroughs in the mid-sixteenth century', *Bull. Board of Celtic Studies*, 27 (1977), 425–39. The 1536 act set up one knight for every shire but two for Monmouth, and one for every shire town except in Merioneth, deemed to have no such centre.
[2] 34 & 35 Henry VIII,c. 26. For the history of the settlement of Wales, extending from 1534 to 1543, see P. R. Roberts, 'The "Acts of Union" and the Tudor settlement of Wales' (unpublished Ph.D. thesis, University of Cambridge, 1966).

much they may hve been influenced by representations from Welsh interests; we turn to what those Welsh interests did with the opportunities that government had thus prepared for them.[3]

The evidence, as usual in such matters, leaves a good deal to be desired. Before 1547 we have only the Journal of the House of Lords to tell us of bills in the Parliament, and even when thereafter the more informative Journal of the House of Commons is added we rarely get more than a brief description of a bill's purpose, sometimes in terms that leave us baffled. If a bill passed we can study its text, but we rarely know anything about its prehistory or inner history. These are the familiar problems of Tudor parliamentary history, aggravated in this instance by the paucity of private materials surviving from mid-Tudor Wales. Making what we can of this unsatisfactory state of affairs, we may first note that Welsh activity in Parliament was extraordinarily unsystematic: what look like energetic initiatives peter out with distressing regularity. Thus, the first session for which we know of bills in both Houses (1547: 1 Edward VI) was also the session in which most bills touching Wales were promoted: eight in all. Only two more appeared in the remaining five years and four sessions of Edward VI's reign, one in 1549 and another in 1553. In the five sessions of Mary's reign we find only four such bills, three of them in the opening Parliament and none at all after 1554. It looks as though the Marian regime offered little encouragement to Wales. Under Elizabeth activity revived, there being only the surprise meeting of 1572, called to deal with Mary, queen of Scots, which found all Wales unprepared to submit even one bill; in 1566, a very active session altogether, five such appeared. Even so, only sixteen out of the approximately 770 bills and acts before the Parliament in the years 1559– 81 were specifically Welsh bills and acts, and though perhaps one should pay some regard to the rare occasions on which specific reference to Welsh shires was made in general acts, it does not seem that the principality in its recast state found its novel connection with the sovereign legislature of the realm particularly interesting. Alternatively, it discovered that the consequences of the laws made for all the queen's dominions were quite enough to have to live with.

This small harvest of legislative initiatives nevertheless deserves a

[3] For an earlier attempt to investigate more or less this question, see A. H. Dodd, 'Wales's parliamentary apprenticeship (1536–1625)', *Trans. Hon. Soc. Cymmrodorion* (1944 for 1942), 8–72. Dominated by the concepts of the Notestein/Neale school of parliamentary history, Dodd concentrated on men rather than measures; he also made quite a few mistakes and misunderstood aspects of parliamentary procedure.

closer look. Some quite simply dealt with the consequences of the Henrician settlement – loose ends that wanted tying up. The newly arrived representatives of 1542 seem to have discovered that the payment of members' wages, long settled in England, needed sorting out for Wales: so in the next session they obtained an act which constructed a complex contributory system for raising the money – not a system which was to work smoothly. The act started in the Commons, where its history is unknown; it passed the Lords without difficulty.[4] Other consequences of the reorganisation took longer to work out. In the Parliament of 1554–5, the remnant of lords marcher put in a petition to remedy a defect in the first 'Act of Union'. That act had saved the (largely financial) rights of lay lords touching the holding of courts, collection of forfeitures and so forth, but had failed to extend that protection to bishops who happened to have marcher rights or to the heirs of lords in possession in 1536. The statute of 1 & 2 Philip & Mary, c. 15, introduced in the Lords, remedied this defect. Which bishops might be concerned the statute does not tell us, but the fact that Thomas Goldwell, about to bring the pope back to St Asaph, was favourite with both Queen Mary and Cardinal Pole may have significance.[5] Much later still, in 1566, the county of Merioneth woke up to an insult hidden in the 1534 act which had reorganised the trial of crimes in Wales. It accepted that, like the rest of Wales, it might have to see its criminals tried in the nearby English shires, but protested that an accident of drafting had empowered also neighbouring Welsh shires (Caernarvon and Anglesey) to sit upon criminals from Merioneth. The protest produced a soothing Council bill rapidly passed through both Houses, and though all it got was a private act the shire was seemingly satisfied.[6] Since the bill started in the Lords, it would seem that the grievance was presented through a patron there rather than through the knight for the

---

[4] 35 Henry VIII, c. 11 (*SR*, III, 969–70). For the problems of payment, see P. S. Edwards, 'Parliamentary representation'.

[5] *SR*, IV, 262; *LJ*, I, 483, 489 (the first reference being to a 'lord marshall' of Wales, an editorial error). The bill passed the Lords on 3 January 1555 but did not return from the Commons until the 16th, the last day of the session (*CJ*, I, 40–1). Dr Roberts ('Acts of Union', 369–70) refers to the bishops of St David's and Hereford as prelates with marcher interests.

[6] 8 Eliz. I, c. 20 (*SR*, IV, 522), given a chapter number because it was printed in later collections. Its omission from the sessional statute of 1566 defines it as private; its short-formula enacting clause suggests Council initiative (see above, vol. III, no. 34, ii and iv). For the parliamentary history of the act, see *LJ*, I, 657–8, 663; *CJ*, I, 80. Private acts left without a chapter number in *SR* are here referred to by the number inscribed on the Original Acts in the HLRO.

shire. A last afterglow of Henry VIII's reign is found reflected in the act of his son's first Parliament which reversed the attainder of Rhys ap Gruffydd, victim, in 1531, of obscure faction struggles at court.[7] There is nothing unusual about this act, except perhaps the fact that it was the only restitution in blood called for in Wales by the attainders of Henry VIII's bloodstained reign.

A much more immediate and widely felt consequence of the Tudor 'Union' sprang from one of Parliament's foremost purposes – general taxation. Incorporated in the realm, represented in Parliament, Wales had for the first time become liable to the subsidies and fifteenths and tenths regularly voted to the Crown – regularly, that is, in Henry VIII's last years and from 1559 onwards. Until the Union, Wales – old principality and future shire ground – quite properly did not contribute to supply voted in Parliament (no taxation, they no doubt reasoned, without representation). The fact that Wales was still exempt in 1540, together with Ireland and Calais, supports the view that the 1536 act did not constitute a complete reform in itself.[8] In 1543, however, following the completion of the incorporation, Wales dropped from the list of exemptions, and it was also made to pay the last Henrician subsidy, in 1545.[9] Things changed in the less stringent atmosphere of Edward VI's reign. The act for the extraordinary tax of 1549, called the relief, included two provisos added by the Lords which exempted spiritual persons from certain charges and for the first time used the ancient customary payments due in Wales to a new king or prince to postpone the liability of Welsh taxpayers until those 'mises' had been collected.[10] The precedent having been set, the principle reappeared in the next regular subsidy, in 1553. Once again, interestingly enough, it was the Lords and not the taxpayers' proper representatives in the Commons who moved for it, asking the Lower House to substitute their proviso for one (now lost) that had been in the subsidy bill.[11] On this occasion, the (as yet) unpaid relief, held over from 1549, was made the pretext. This curious rolling exemption – no relief because of mises, no subsidy because of the relief – continued for some time. In 1555 the new mises due to Philip and Mary did duty; in 1558, the unpaid subsidy postponed

[7] 1 Edward VI, OA 19, mentioned in the Journal only on the occasion that it returned to the Lords after passage in the Commons (*LJ*, I, 312).

[8] *SR*, III, 824. Calais had had burgesses at Westminster since 1539; its continued exemption probably arose out of its known bankrupt state.

[9] Ibid., 950, 1031.   [10] Ibid., IV, 93.

[11] Ibid., 189, *LJ*, I, 436, *CJ*, I, 24.

by those mises served its turn; and on both occasions the proviso was in the Commons' bill.[12]

The year 1558 brought a new queen with new mises due, but the bill as passed by the Commons (and prepared by the Council) attempted to ignore the by now no doubt 'traditional' rights of the Welsh. Once again it was in the Lords that attention was drawn to the exception, by means of a petition (no names preserved) addressed to that House which, favourably impressed, obtained a statement from the queen that neither subsidy nor mise should be collected in a year in which the other was payable. The necessary proviso appeared in a schedule attached to the 1559 act.[13] For once Elizabeth kept her promise, and the exemption clauses appeared in 1563, 1566 and 1571.[14] Thereafter, however, the view seems to have been taken that old obligations had been discharged, and from 1576 onwards Wales no longer enjoyed freedom from subsidies.[15] Mises next became payable at the accession of James I, but his first subsidy act (1606) only postponed payment by a short period without remitting it altogether.[16] In the most palpable manner imaginable, through their pockets, the inhabitants of Wales joined the realm of England in 1576.

It remains to consider what they tried to make of their membership: what matters did they, or some of them, try to achieve by parliamentary legislation? The bills and acts in question may be divided by content into matters economic, legal reform, and the pursuit of spiritual improvement. The harvest was small in all three respects, but not so small as to be without significance. Wales used Parliament only a little, but it used it.

Like many districts of England, Wales contained its clothmaking interests who hoped to profit from protection by statute. Like their English counterparts, they found the business very frustrating: bills for cloth, clothiers and clothworkers are among the most regular failures in mid-Tudor Parliaments. The Welsh makers of cottons and friezes (cheap and light woollens) put a bill into the Commons in 1547 which never progressed beyond second reading.[17] Discouraged for twelve years, they tried again in Elizabeth's first Parliament (1559) and this time with greater persistence. The bill passed the Commons easily, but the Lords,

---

[12] *SR*, IV, 312, 348.   [13] Ibid., 396; *LJ*, I, 549.
[14] *SR*, IV, 478, 518–19, 581.   [15] E.g. ibid., 651 (1576), 697–8 (1581), etc.
[16] Ibid., 1126.   [17] *CJ*, I, 3.

after three readings in three days, voted it down.[18] In the cutthroat competition between clothmaking districts which doomed one bill after another, this failure at the last hurdle is less surprising than that the bill ever got so far. In 1556, when Welsh woolgrowers hoped to improve their trade with the rest of the realm, they apparently thought to demonstrate a lesson learned by starting in the Upper House; on this occasion the roles were reversed, and the Commons on second reading dashed the bill readily passed by the Lords.[19] Much more obscure is the subject of yet another failure, a bill promoted in 1547 'for the nursing and fostering of children in Wales and divers exactions'. This title – all we have of the bill – makes it impossible to know just what the measure might have achieved. However, it met with success in the Commons who passed it right at the end of the session, so that there was no time left for the Lords even to receive it.[20] The odd thing, quite contrary to more usual practice, is that a bill which had got that far was never brought in again in a later session. P9erhaps it represented a private move by some individual who did not serve in another Parliament. Whoever he was, he may even have got the notion on the spur of the moment, after hearing the two readings given to a bill 'for bringing up poor men's children'; if so, he proved himself something of a novice, for this was the bill *pro forma*, read at the opening of the session, which no one really intended to pass.[21] All this, of course, is conjecture: but why not?

However, four bills of economic import did pass in these forty years. The first of them is in some ways the most interesting – the act of 1544 which empowered a large number of towns in Wales and elsewhere in the realm to override private rights in the interest of rebuilding decayed houses.[22] Such collective acts, evidently promoted by some municipalities and then attracting other interested parties once the bill got going, had been used in 1536 and 1540 to tackle the much complained of urban problems of the day, and the first such measure had probably originated with the towns of the Welsh border country.[23] The 'Union' allowed this sensible movement of reform to cross into Wales itself, though

---

[18] Ibid., 59–60; *EHR*, 28 (1913), 537–8.   [19] *LJ*, I, 642–5; *CJ*, I, 77–8, 81.

[20] ibid., 3–4.

[21] ibid., 1—2. The bill disappeared after a second reading on 24 November; the Welsh bill was read a first time on 15 December.

[22] 35 Henry VIII, c. 4 (*SR*, III, 959–60). It was the Lords who wished to add to the Commons' bill a proviso for the inclusion of Radnor and Presteigne (*LJ*, I, 250); since these towns are listed currently in the text of the act, the Commons seem to have preferred to write it out afresh.

[23] *Reform and Renewal*, 108–9.

whether the powers obtained were ever used is something that local investigation would have to study. Another of Thomas Cromwell's reform measures attracted Welsh attention in 1554 when the powers created by the 1532 statute of sewers were extended to provide protection to the seacoast of Glamorgan against the encroachment of tide-borne sands. A privately promoted bill, it achieved public act status, even though the earl of Shrewsbury, one of the better-known marcher lords, recorded his dissent in the Upper House.[24] Both these acts, in their different ways, testify to opportunities taken to benefit from the new relationship between Wales and the laws made by the Parliament of England.

The other two successful economic measures concern the maintenance of bridges; one of them reflects local conflicts, which we may often suspect lurk behind a bill but are only very occasionally able to unravel. Thus, we have no evidence that the act for the bridge at Chepstow in Monmouthshire caused any problems or roused any concern, but since it implied the possibility of local rates it may well have done.[25] It was a private bill,[26] put up in petitionary form and in the name of 'the greatest part of the inhabitants of South Wales', which professed to remedy an accidental defect in the bridges and highways act of 1531 (22 Henry VIII, c. 5). That act, it was claimed, did not apply to areas then not shired and thus made no provision for the old marcher lordships. Since 1536, however, Chepstow stood in shire ground, and the bill therefore expressly extended the provisions of 1531 to it, placing the responsibility for maintaining Chepstow bridge on Monmouthshire and Gloucestershire jointly. This act, too, started in the Lords and passed both Houses with rapid ease.[27] Of course, it only created powers to levy money for a future contingency, whereas the case stood very differently at Cardiff, where a bridge had actually collapsed and money was needed at once to rebuild it. This led to a prolonged dispute, which has been fully discussed elsewhere,[28] between the town and the shire, each trying to unload the responsibility onto the other.

It appears from the correspondence between the contending parties that a first effort to promote a bill for raising the necessary money was

[24] 1 Mary, stat. 3, c. 11 (*SR*, IV, 235); *CJ*, I, 36; *LJ*, I, 461–2.
[25] 18 Eliz. I, c. 18 (*SR*, IV, 629).   [26] PRO, SP 12/107, fo. 144.
[27] *LJ*, I, 734–6, 742; *CJ*, I, 107–9.
[28] P. Williams, 'Controversy in Elizabethan Glamorgan: the rebuilding of Cardiff bridge', *Morgannwg*, 2 (1958), 38–46. My account is much indebted to this article, and I have provided references only for such points as I have been able to add.

made in 1576, though the silence of both Journals indicates that it never reached even first reading.[29] It looks, therefore, as though the immediate protests from the shire succeeded in stopping proceedings and prevented the town's promoters from handing the bill in. The next four years were filled with acrimonious discussions over the distribution of the costs between town and country, but in 1581 Cardiff (with the support of the knight of the shire, one William Matthew) got its act with surprising ease. Or so would be suggested by the Journals, which record nothing but smooth and rapid progress.[30] A private diarist, who distinguished himself by supposing that Cardiff was in Montgomeryshire,[31] also notes only the readings of the bill, and the original act indicates that no changes were made during passage. However, there survives evidence of frenzied efforts to stop the proceedings. Some twelve months before the Parliament met, but when there was reason to suppose that it would not again be prorogued, the county interests prepared a case against the expected legislation,[32] while on the same day two privy councillors who supported the town (the earl of Pembroke and Sir Henry Sidney) mobilised the sheriff on the other side.[33] When the bill was actually before the Parliament, the protesters moved rather belatedly: they sent out letters of appeal on 24 February 1581, four days after the bill had been ordered to be engrossed after passing its second reading. By then it was rather late for the sort of elaborate statements or points against the town, with detailed (and generally convincing) replies, which survives and which, we may therefore presume, was intended to persuade the Upper House to stop the bill;[34] though not too late for a pompously solemn self-defence by William Matthew, who (rather unconvincingly) asserted that he had been solely moved by the justice of the case.[35] The victory of the town, whose bill compelled the shire to contribute rather more to the rebuilding than an earlier compromise proposal had offered, derived from the fact that it commanded the better interest at court and

[29] Ibid., 39.40.
[30] *CJ*, I, 123, 128, 130–1; *LJ*, II, 43, 45, 46–7. The act is 23 Eliz. I, c. 11 (*SR*, IV, 673–4). A private bill, it achieved printing and thus public act status for no known reason – except perhaps favour; as Dr Williams has shown, the settlement had the backing of the earl of Pembroke.
[31] T. E. Hartley (ed.), *Proceedings in the Parliaments of Elizabeth I* (Leicester, 1981), I, 533, 538.
[32] For some reason, these found their way into the Percy archives at Alnwick: HMC, *Third Report*, App. 47b.
[33] *Cal. State Papers, Dom., 1547–80*, 638.   [34] PRO, SP 12/148, fos. 33–4.
[35] ibid., fos. 35–6.

therefore in the Parliament. One point of interest may be noted: in presenting the case, the town relied heavily on the precedents set in 1576, when not only Chepstow but also Rochester had obtained similar acts for the rebuilding of bridges. Evidently recent precedents, which the 'Union' had made relevant, could override such ancient customary arrangements as those upon which the shire gentry tried to rely.

Wales, in effect, shared the common experience that matters of the law were easier to get through the Parliament than matters of trade, as well as the experience that even in law reform the number of failed bills greatly exceeded those that passed. Two private acts, transferring the county capital in Anglesey from declining Newborough to rising Beaumaris (1549), and arranging for the county days in Cardiganshire to alternate between Aberystwyth and Cardigan (1553), testified to careful local preparation: unless all parties were satisfied, such bills usually got quashed by protests from the unsatisfied.[36] The first bill was a petition put forward by Beaumaris, but once again the Welsh preference for working through the Lords manifested itself, though the Commons added a proviso which the Upper House accepted; this freed Newborough from contributing to the wages of the parliamentary burgess for Anglesey and was obviously obtained by representations from the dethroned shire town.[37]

Four more general bills were introduced in the first Parliament of Edward VI; of these three failed, leaving us with only a brief title to indicate what they may have been about. The Commons gave two readings to a bill 'to avoid the office of ragler in Wales', apparently an attempt to abolish that ancient local officer, the *rhaglaw* or constable of the commote.[38] Of two bills read for a first time on the same day in the Lords, one which in some way meant to reform forest jurisdiction in Wales was committed to the attorney-general and not heard of again; the other – 'for courts to be held in Wales', a title which tells us nothing – slept after being read once.[39] A successful bill, which started in the Commons, remedied a deficiency created by a gap in the Union laws. It dealt with a problem arising out of the processes of the common law – the process known as exigent and outlawry, that is to say, the

---

[36] 2 & 3 Edward VI, OA 54; 1 Mary, stat. 2, OA 23 (not the non-existent 1 Philip & Mary, c. 8, as in Dodd, 'Wales parliamentary apprenticeship', 10, n. 3).

[37] *LJ*, I, 347–8, 351, 353; *CJ*, I, 9–10. For the second bill, only the third reading in the Commons is recorded (ibid., 30); the Lords Journal does not mention it. I am grateful to Mr David Dean for ascertaining the details of 2 & 3 Edward VI, OA 54.

[38] *CJ*, I, 1; see Roberts, 'Acts of Union', 364.

[39] *LJ*, I, 303.

instruments available for getting a recalcitrant defendant into the Westminster courts. Writs of exigent (warning a man to attend), followed, if disobeyed, by a public proclamation making the defaulter an outlaw (and therefore unable to engage in any litigation and in theory deprived of all his movables), were in particular employed against persons accused of felony at the crown's suit, but also against debtors who sought to defraud their creditors. An act of 1512 had tried to ensure that the subject of the exercise became aware of this process against himself by decreeing that proclamation should be made not in the county in which the suit had arisen but in that in which the defendant resided.[40] The legislation for Wales, while creating the necessary shrieval machinery, had failed to remove the pre-Union provision (whereby no such machinery existed) that outlawries in Wales should be proclaimed in the adjoining English shire, an anomaly which the bill of 1547 set itself to remove. It started in the Commons but had no easy passage there. First, it was decided to amalgamate it with a similar bill introduced by Chester, which faced the same problem. The fact that the new bill formed the sole item before the House for one whole sitting day, after which yet another new bill was brought in, proves the occurrence of prolonged debate, much hesitation, and repeated redrafting. The likelihood is that behind these difficulties there lay apprehensions among lords with interests in Wales and the Marches: in the Upper House it was opposed to the last, though in vain, by three prominent marcher lords, including the earls of Arundel and Derby. In the end the Lords added a rather meaningless proviso saving the rights of marcher lords, which the Commons accepted.[41]

Bills of this sort, straightening out differences between England and the newly incorporated parts, evidently stood the best chance of getting through. The principle applies to the act of 1563 which extended a reform of 1544 to Wales, Chester, Lancaster and Durham.[42] That measure had dealt with the not uncommon problem raised at assizes when a jury empanelled by the sheriff upon a precept issued to him by the court either failed to turn up in full or got attenuated by challenges from the parties. In order to avoid trials being protracted by such means, the act authorised the court to complete the jury *de circumstantibus* – that is, from other qualified persons who happened to be present. The bill

---

[40] 4 Henry CIII, c. 4, made permanent by 5 Henry VIII, c. 4.
[41] 1 Edward VI, c. 10; *CJ*, I, 2–3; *LJ*, I, 311–13.
[42] 5 Eliz. I, c. 25: 35 Henry VIII, c. 6, sect. 3.

which extended this useful device to Wales and the rest passed the Commons with ease, was in the Lords given to the chief justice of Common Pleas to revise, and was accepted with the Lords' amendments by the Lower House. Though most of the amendments touched only details of phrasing, it was actually the Lords who added Durham to the bill's beneficiaries.[43] The bishop of Durham, James Pilkington, owner of the franchise affected, was present on the two days that mattered; one would like to know how this earnest prelate took the inclusion of his special charge.

Altogether, the chief problem exercising responsible people in Wales concerned the effectiveness of law enforcement in a region which had only so very recently been provided with the organisation long available in England, and a region, moreover, which everybody – insiders as well as outsiders – regarded as exceptionally lawless. In view of the difficulties which the established English system notoriously encountered in preventing neglect or abuse of the law, the apparent trust in reforming bills for Wales must nevertheless strike one as a trifle naive. Still, earnest men in Wales tried several times. In Edward VI's last Parliament a bill to compel outlaws and fugitives to surrender when proclaimed – a bill, that is, which would give teeth to the act of 1547 – was committed on second reading, understandably enough because such a law must have raised many points of substance and form. The chairman of the committee was an eminent lawyer, Francis Morgan, serjeant at law and later a judge, whose name suggests Welsh connections but who actually sat for Northampton.[44] After revision, the bill again reached second reading but only four days before the dissolution of the Parliament. Since Morgan sat again in the next Parliament (Mary's first),[45] the bill came forward once more, this time to be read once and not heard of again.[46] An attempt to put an end to those potential sources of resistance and lawlessness, the customary popular gatherings known as *commorthas*, also ended after a single reading in 1571.[47] A major effort to reform criminal trials (gaol deliveries and quarter sessions) in Wales actually passed both Houses in 1566, after considerable revision and discussion, only to be vetoed by the queen. Seeing that the bill proposed to terminate the trial of Welsh crimes in adjoining shires, and that during its passage provisos safeguarding the sessions at Shrewsbury and Hereford were added, one

---

[43] *CJ*, I, 64, 66–7; *LJ*, I, 598, 600, 611–12, 615. The Lords' amendments appear on the OA in HLRO.

[44] *Official Return of Members of Parliament* (1878), I, 382.   [45] Ibid., 386.

[46] *CJ*, I, 24–7.   [47] Ibid., 90.

may perhaps conjecture that the government received protests from the Council in the Marches, apprehensive that control might slip from its hands. This caused the Privy Council to block the bill by applying the veto, a device quite common at the time when it was thought that more time for reflection and discussion might resolve difficulties and disagreements.[48] The bill was indeed reintroduced, perhaps altered, in the next session (1571), when it passed the Commons easily. However, governmental doubts evidently remained, for the powerful Lords' committee which took charge of the bill (including, among others, Burghley, Leicester, Bedford and Hunsdon) recommended a conference with the Lower House, which was unfortunately prevented by the closing of the session.[49]

The approach of the next session roused the reformers once more. Advice was received from Sir John Throckmorton, chief justice of Chester,[50] as well as from Richard Price, a Brecknock gentleman, who told Burghley (on 31 January 1576) that he was offering counsel because 'the Parliament going forwards, whatsoever cannot otherwise conveniently, may there be redressed by your wisdom and furtherance'.[51] Price, in fact, produced a fine collection of necessary reforms, some of which called for action by Parliament, though it appears from the comments noted on it that the document did not reach the lord treasurer until after the session of 1576.[52] For in that session an act had passed which followed up a suggestion of Throckmorton's and anticipated one of Price's reforms: evidently the matter was in the air. This was the act appointing a second judge to each of the four circuits in Wales in order to ensure that there should be no lapse in law enforcement or needless delay in the trial of civil suits.[53] To judge by the enacting clause, the bill was drawn up privately, but it was introduced in the Lords, perhaps from Welsh habit but more likely in order to take advantage of the ground prepared beforehand with Burghley; it caused no difficulties.[54] Price had been anxious always to have two experts on the bench, serving in person and not by deputy, though he allowed for the possibility of

---

[48] Ibid., 77–80; *LJ*, I, 660–3.
[49] *CJ*, I, 89–92; *LJ*, I, 695–7. Cf. *Proceedings*, ed. Hartley, I, 252–4.
[50] P. Williams, *The Council in the Marches of Wales under Elizabeth I* (Cardiff, 1958), 263.
[51] H. Ellis (ed.), *Original Letters Illustrative of English History*, 2nd series, III, 42–8.
[52] PRO, SP 12/107, fos. 2–3, 5–33, 43–54, endorsed as coming from 'Mr Price'. Annotations (fo. 13) point out that what Price wanted done had been achieved 'by an act of the late Parliament'.
[53] 18 Eliz. I, c. 8 (*SR*, IV, 618–19).   [54] *LJ*, I, 736, 738, 743; *CJ*, I, 109–11.

illness, when the clerk of assize was to join the bench. The act says nothing on either point, but since justices of assize in England could not in any case appoint deputies to sit for them, explicit provision may have been regarded as superfluous. Anyway, the adviser who went over Price's proposals thought them fully answered by drawing attention to the act just passed. It appears that the reform did not become actual until 1579;[55] when it did, it must have helped to make assizes in Wales more effective for both criminal cases and *nisi prius* actions.

That, however, was the sum total of legal reform – accommodating Wales to English practice in respect of the proclamation of outlawries and the filling up of deficient juries, and giving Welsh circuits two expert judges where one was thought enough in England. Two other bills for Wales pleased the Commons but got shipwrecked in the Lords. One of 1566 wished to set up record offices in every Welsh shire, an excellent proposal, whose failure the historian, not served in such fashion until the 1950s, must deeply regret.[56] Another, of 1579, would have improved the handling of a very common form of land transaction (conveyancing by fine and recovery), probably by better record-keeping at least in Wales; the Lords, who deliberately 'stayed' the bill after reading it only once, decided on a conference with the Lower House, which once again was arranged too late in the session actually to take place. One suspects that the judges raised immediate difficulties, though lacking the bill we cannot even guess what these might have been.[57]

After these sordid, and largely unsuccessful, efforts to exploit the Parliament for profit and advantage, it is some relief to turn to endeavours to promote more spiritual causes – few indeed, but with a much higher incidence of success. In fact, there were three such bills, of which two passed, leading to one further abortive bill for the repeal of one of the successful measures. On 19 December 1547 a bill was introduced (again in the Lords) for the founding of a grammar school at Carmarthen. It was evidently meant to secure the continued existence of the school which Thomas Lloyd, precentor of St David's, had established there four years earlier, and which his death early in September 1547 threatened with closure. Lloyd had hoped to preserve it by provisions in his will, but his executors got entangled with the town authorities, and the money set aside for the school was soon converted to

---

[55] Williams, *Council in the Marches*, 264.   [56] *CJ*, I, 77, 79–80; *LJ*, I, 660–1.
[57] *CJ*, I, 109–11; *LJ*, I, 741–2. When listing the bills left in his hands, the clerk of the Lords included this one among those he described as stayed (PRO, SP 12/107, fo. 190.

other uses. We may guess that the bill was the work of Lloyd's friends, and we may further guess that the introduction in the Lords reflects the lack of enthusiasm for the school encountered in the town. The fact that the bill foundered after only one reading indicates that no one much cared for the preserving of Lloyd's foundation, and Carmarthen had to wait for its school until 1576.[58]

The shire harboured some who cared about spiritual well-being, and in 1559 they got an act which improved their chances of salvation for the parishioners of Abernant.[59] The bill was a private petition, with a handsomely decorated initial letter (in this sort of document, a hallmark of the amateur), from the parishioners themselves. It explained that their existing parish church lay six miles distant from the nearest habitations within the parish, and was in addition too small to accommodate all the congregation. At their own expense, therefore, the parishioners had enlarged a convenient chapel at Cynwyl Elfed, previously annexed to the parish church but much better placed to serve the needs of the parish, and they now asked for an act that would turn this chapel into the parish church. They saved the right of the patron, who was to present to the new church in the same way as he had done to the old. Before the Reformation the living had been in the gift of the Austin priory of St John at Carmarthen, and at the Dissolution the advowson fell to the crown which still held the patronage in the 1550s – a fact which underlines the wisdom of the saving clause.[60] Precautions, however, failed to satisfy everybody: someone, perhaps the patron, tried in 1566 to have this sensible act of 1559 repealed, though he got no further than a single reading in the Lords.[61]

Of greater import was the crown of Welsh parliamentary lobbying in this period, the well-known act of 1563 for a Welsh translation of the Bible and the Prayer Book.[62] Glanmor Williams, who has so well illumined the roles of Richard Davies, bishop of St David's, and William Salesbury, scholar and translator, in this momentous translation,[63] may like to hear a little more about the parliamentary history of this measure, which is not without interest. The bill, clearly the work of

[58] *LJ*, I, 309; Glanmor Williams, 'Thomas Lloyd his Skole: Carmarthen's first Tudor grammar school', *Carms. Antiquary*, 10 (1974), 49–62.
[59] 1 Eliz. I, OA 35.
[60] *Valor Ecclesiasticus*, IV, 410; E. Yardley, *Menevia Sacra*, ed. F. Green (London, 1927), 396.
[61] *LJ*, I, 649. With 2,000 souls the parish was a large one, and the building operations at Cynwyl Elfed must have cost a fair penny.
[62] 5 Eliz. I, c. 28.
[63] Glanmor Williams, *Welsh Reformation Essays* (Cardiff, 1967), 155–205.

its promoters though a professional job, was put into the Commons; the act, though now printed in the *Statutes of the Realm*, was not in the sessional statute and must therefore have been a private one, paying its quite considerable fees to the officers of both Houses. Its relatively slow passage in the Commons, from 22 February to 27 March, reflects the common fortunes of private bills which needed urgent promoting and regular fee-paying if they were to get on, rather than any objections; it was not, for instance, committed. Rather, it looks as though the promoters worked with insufficient zeal, perhaps because the most enthusiastic among them sat in the Lords, or just ran into too much business; certainly this was a very busy session. The bill authorised five bishops (of Hereford, Bangor, St Asaph, St David's and Llandaff) to license a Welsh translation of the Scriptures and the Book of Common Prayer, pleading that the English translation had proved the supreme virtue of a vernacular version in the spiritual life of the nation but that in Wales, 'no small part of the realm', an English Bible served no vernacular purpose. The bishops were to see to it that a Welsh translation was available by 1 March 1565.

In this form the bill reached the Lords, who made some changes.[64] Most of these were verbal, but it was the Upper House who changed the date in the act from 1565 to 1567, a sensible decision seeing that even by that date the translators were able to produce only the Prayer Book and the New Testament, even though Salesbury had translated most of the latter as early as 1551.[65] Furthermore, the Lords added the proviso which is now the last clause of the act and which ensured that not only the Welsh Bible but the English version also should be placed in every parish church in Wales. This proviso maintained that there were people in Wales who could read only English and also hoped that others would find the possibility of comparing the two versions conducive to learning the English tongue. Who was responsible for this piece of English chauvinism? Of the five bishops, Hereford, Bangor and Llandaff did not attend the House at all in this session, and St Asaph was not there on the day that the proviso was read. Only St David's – Richard Davies himself – attended on all the relevant days.[66] He, who worked so much in harness with Salesbury and shared in the work of translation, may well have urged the later and more practical date, but it seems improbable that he, who was so eager to improve and preserve the

---

[64] The OA carries a list of Lords' amendments.
[65] Williams, *Welsh Reformation Essays*, 196–7.   [66] *LJ*, I, 610–13.

Welsh tongue, should also have been behind the less friendly proviso. At any rate, the change of date strongly suggests that Davies had not been consulted in the drafting of the original bill and that Salesbury had been too optimistic.

The real mystery, however, touches the first question of all: why was the act promoted and passed at all? That mystery is deepened by the printing history of the translations called for. The various efforts, dating back to 1537, to provide an English Bible for exhibition in parish churches had never bothered with a statute, such authorisation as seemed necessary being conveyed in royal proclamations.[67] The act in effect did three things. It called for the making of the two translations; it empowered five bishops to act as approvers and therefore licensers; and by omitting all reference to the Bible-printing monopoly held by the queen's printer prepared the way for breaking it. And broken it was, without protest from Richard Jugge and John Cawood, who held the patent at the time. It would appear that Salesbury first came to terms with John Walley, a leading member of the Stationers' Company, who some time in the summer of 1563 paid 4d for a licence to print a Welsh litany (that is, the translation of the Prayer Book).[68] Most likely it was also Walley who, conscious as he was bound to be of the queen's printer's claims, suggested that the two of them should obtain a monopoly patent for printing and selling Welsh translations of the Bible, the Prayer Book and the Book of Homilies; a draft of such a patent was sent to William Cecil for his consideration and approval. The draft took care to mention the bishops' licensing powers created in the act, but it overstepped the mark when it added a monopoly for producing any work of scriptural commentary in Welsh or English. This was a piece of overreaching ambition which would really have harmed Jugge and Cawood, who, one may well suppose, had little interest in printing for the restricted Welsh market; it is quite likely that this was the reason why the patent failed to get approval and never passed the great seal.[69]

---

[67] E.g. it was by proclamation that Thomas Cromwell was given power to approve an English Bible: *TRP*, I, 286–7.

[68] E. Arber (ed.), *A Transcript of the Registers of the Company of Stationers of London* (London, 1875–94), I, 20(9.

[69] The draft is in British Library, Landsdowne MS. 48, fo. 75; it is printed in W. W. Greg, *A Companion to Arber* (Oxford, 1967), 113–14. Greg called it a certified copy of what he took to be a patent issued. Against this view are these facts: no such patent was ever enrolled; there are several signs of unfinished drafting in the document; it lacks the dating clause, one thing that would certainly have been transcribed for a certified copy. The name appended (which Greg correctly identified as that of a clerk of the Signet but wrongly supposed to be the certifier) was that of the man responsible for writing out

Before Salesbury and Davies were ready with their translations, Walley in fact lost interest and wrote off his 4d. The volumes which appeared in 1567 were printed by Henry Denham for Humphrey Toy, who were well enough known London printers and booksellers, Toy paying 3s 4d for entering the Prayer Book in the Stationers' Register but only 12d for the New Testament.[70] Interestingly enough, when a complete Welsh Bible at last became available in 1588, the queen's printer (by this time Christopher Barker's assigns) asserted his patented rights to the production.[71] But it seems that the five bishops failed to do what the act demanded of them; we hear nothing about approval for the 1567 New Testament, whereas the Prayer Book is explicitly stated to have been 'authorised' by the bishop of London, that is, Edmund Grindal. It is to be hoped that he obtained a clean bill from someone capable of checking a Welsh text, but perhaps he contented himself with a reassurance from his brother of St David's, who was so deeply involved in the work of translating.

In a way, this best known and most respectable of all the parliamentary measures promoted for Wales in the years 1542–81 confirms the impression left by its less illustrious companions. An unnecessary act whose provisions were only partially observed just about fits as a symbol for the efforts made by the newly represented region to put its contacts with the legislative institution to use. On the other hand, the act was exceptional in being the only one of all the bills to concern itself with the needs of the true Welsh; the rest really attended to the needs and ambitions of the governing sort, many of whom were surely English or Anglicised enough. Their needs and ambitions as a rule extended to the establishment of a settled order which to the ranks below them must too often have looked like the destruction of old habits and customs.

One further point deserves a summarising comment. We have noted that, except in 1547, the majority of Welsh bills started in the Upper House. When it came to promoting their interests, the Welsh gentry and boroughs looked not to the men they sent to Westminster but to noble

what would have become a Signet warrant to the Privy Seal Office if the queen had approved the application; certified copies of letters patent had to be got from the Chancery. Furthermore, contrary to Greg's printing, the endorsement is not dated. The dorse carried two modern and quite unauthoritative dates – 1563 and 1582, in different hands – but, in view of Walley's action in the Stationers' Register, 1563 may well be a right guess. 1582 is certainly wrong.

[70] Arber, *Stationers' Registers*, I, 336. The books' title-pages confirm the part played by Toy and Denham (Greg, *Companion*, 8), for whom see R. B. McKerrow (ed.), *A Dictionary of Printers and Booksellers . . . 1557–1640* (London, 1910).

[71] Greg, *Companion*, 8.

patrons, more particularly perhaps to the house of Herbert, so influential in Elizabeth's court and Council. It is surely significant that Welsh activity in Parliament stood at its lowest ebb in the reign of Mary, when the earl of Pembroke, having just about managed to survive his prominence under Edward VI, carried least weight at court. If this reliance on noble favour was considered policy, as it very much seems to have been, the 'battle of Cardiff Bridge' shows how well participants understood the position. What use was William Matthew to the shire that had elected him? Like the City, he looked to Pembroke who thus directed both the members of the Lower House concerned in the business. This structure of politics, of course, was by no means peculiar to Wales. The English country gentry carried more weight than the Welsh squirearchy, and English borough interests knew how to push bills through the House of Commons; but in the end favour in high places would do more for a man or an interest than historians of that somewhat overrated House may like to think.

54

PISCATORIAL POLITICS IN THE EARLY PARLIAMENTS OF ELIZABETH I*

In our period State action in economic and social matters can be seen as having four main ends in view: the maintenance of social stability and order; the encouragement and regulation of the internal economy; the encouragement and regulation of overseas trade and shipping; and the raising of revenue.

Thus Donald Coleman sums up a well-known problem and its usual conclusion.[1] His phrasing is cautious: 'state action' must be taken to include the legislation of Parliament, but the possibility that the initiative behind such laws might have come from unofficial quarters is not expressly excluded. Nevertheless, the mention of public order and public revenue does suggest that the author had it in mind here to equate the state with its government. That conviction – that Elizabethan economic legislation originated in official circles and reflected thinking there – is well entrenched in the literature; it goes back at the least to Archdeacon Cunningham, who decided that 'the more we examine the working of the Elizabethan scheme for the administration of economic affairs, the more do we see that the Council was the pivot of the whole system', as initiators and executors.[2] The only person who has dared to question the assumption was F. J. Fisher, though even he in the end resigned himself to the concept of government action, called forth in his view not by sovereign planning but by the haphazard pressures of the market and other circumstances.[3] In any case, he got a firm answer from Lawrence Stone, who, restoring tradition in new clothes, rested his whole case tacitly on the conviction that legislative enactments reflected government policy while failed proposals indicated the defeat of govern-

---

* [*Business Life and Public Policy: Essays in Honour of D. C. Coleman*, ed. N. McKendrick and R. B. Outhwaite. (Cambridge, 1986), 1–20].

[1] D. C. Coleman, *The Economy of England, 1450–1750* (Oxford, 1977), 173–4.

[2] W. Cunningham, *The Growth of English Industry and Commerce*, 6th edn (Cambridge, 1907–10), III, 53. He did not seem to know that most of the regulations he had in mind could only be enforced in the law courts and by actions brought by private informers.

[3] F. J. Fisher, 'Commercial trends and policy in sixteenth-century England', *Economic History Review*, 10 (1940), 95–117.

109

ment intentions by sectional interests in the House of Commons.[4]
General accounts thus returned with relief to the supposition that
manifestations of control and policy arose with 'government', and
conversely that acts of Parliament can be used to find out what
government was about.[5] Yet historians of Parliament are by now quite
well aware that sixteenth-century statutes for problems of the common
weal need by no means have come from monarch and Council. So far,
the history of few such acts has been investigated, though one famous
study, which, trying to distinguish the pressures behind the 1563 Statute
of Artificers, cast much doubt upon the common conviction, apparently
failed to weaken its hold upon the generality. Besides, it may not have
got things quite right, and, this being a case where even a small
discrepancy can throw a general chain of reasoning into confusion, the
simplicities of tradition can re-establish themselves.[6] A look at some
other measure of economic import may therefore help. I have chosen
the 1581 fisheries act, which Ephraim Lipson regarded as an official
attempt 'to stimulate native shipping by forbidding subjects to import
foreign-cured fish'.[7] Is that what it was?

Sixteenth-century England ate a lot of fish, and a relatively large part
of its population made a living out of this fact. When one considers the
place occupied by cod and ling and salted herring in the menus of the
time, it comes as a surprise to find how little serious work has been done
on this theme.[8] Supplying England with the fish it needed, especially in
Lent and on other fast-days, involved the despatch of regular annual fleets

[4] L. Stone, 'State control in sixteenth-century England', *Economic History Review*, 17 (1947), 103–20. Abandoning the traditional view, according to which regulations aimed to forward prosperity, Stone claimed to have learned from the war just past that Tudor governments controlled the economy for reasons of national security.
[5] E.g. L. A. Clarkson, *The Pre-Industrial Economy in England 1500–1750* (New York, 1972), ch. 6.
[6] S. T. Bindoff, 'The making of the Statute of Artificers', in S. T. Bindoff, J. Hurstfield and C. H. Williams (eds.), *English Government and Society* (London, 1961), 56–94. According to Bindoff, (p. 72), sect. 33, which exempted Norwich and London, did not enter the bill until at a very late stage of its passage through the Commons; yet, discussing the bill three weeks before the Parliament even met, the city council of York saw that clause included in it: *York Civic Records*, ed. A. Raine, VI (1948), 50. [See now *Parliament*, 263–7.]
[7] E. Lipson, *The Economic History of England*, 6th edn (London, 1956), III, 119.
[8] For a general introduction – no more – see A. R. Michell, 'The European fisheries in early modern history', *The Cambridge Economic History of Europe*, V, 134–84. A very few points of direct relevance, as well as interesting details about the physiognomy and ecology of the herring, are found in J. T. Jenkins, *The Herring and the Herring Fisheries* (London, 1927).

to the Iceland fishing grounds; it involved following the shoals of cod and herring as each year they travelled south from Scotland to the German Bight; it involved hundreds of small vessels exploiting the inshore fisheries off the English east coast from the mouth of the Tyne to the mouth of the Thames; it involved acquiring large quantities of salt, which the more distant voyagers had to carry with them while the close-in fishermen stacked it on shore to deal with the catch unloaded there. It was widely, and correctly, thought that the safety of the realm, depending as it did on the maintenance of a large body of experienced seamen, called for a healthy fishing industry as a training ground for mariners. By the middle of the sixteenth century, English fishermen were retreating before the advancing enterprise of the Dutch, equipped with their superior vessels (the cod and herring busses), large enough to hold great quantities of fish salted on board – a considerable economy in the trade. From this grew an ever-increasing reliance on Dutch fish, bought up in the Netherlands by English merchants – especially the members of the London Fishmongers' Company – who could undersell English fisher-men increasingly forced back upon the scattered and uneconomic operations of individuals fishing the inshore grounds. There was a crisis in English fishing, and the Protestant dislike of popish fast-days did not help. And as many thought, there was a resulting crisis in the supply of experienced manpower to sail English ships and guard the island.

Thus, even before war forced the needs of the navy and of shipping upon government, the Elizabethan Parliaments several times concerned themselves with the protection and promotion of English seafaring interests. The legislation, proposed or enacted, pursued two separate but connected lines of thought: it tried to restrict English seaborne trade to native vessels, mariners and owners, and it tried to protect English fishermen against foreign competition. Most of what was done owed little to any initiatives by queen or Council; instead, the acts testified to concern and agitation on the part of private interests. Since these interests included rivals as well as cooperators, the prehistory, passage and later fortunes of the statutes were never straightforward, as in particular the act of 1581 (23 Eliz. I, c. 7) well illustrates. Its history throws much light on the manner in which economic pressure groups used the legislative power of Parliament.

The sessions between the queen's accession and 1581 provided a sort of run-up to the manoeuvres of the latter year. The act of 1559 (1 Eliz. I, c. 13) – to judge by its enacting clause, the only one of all these measures to stem from the Council[9] – tried to consolidate earlier legislation for the limitation of imports to English-owned vessels; ineffective from the first and limited to a trial period, it was not continued in 1571 and seems to have lapsed.[10] Markedly more important was the so-called great navigation act of 1563 (5 Eliz. I, c. 5), a comprehensive measure initiated privately in the Commons and much enlarged in the course of passage. It dealt with both the main concerns of all this legislation. Touching fisheries, it freed Englishmen from various constraints and from the payment of customs, but (for reasons which have not so far become apparent) expressly excluded Hull from these benefits;[11] it also contained the notorious clause promoted by William Cecil which made Wednesdays into fish-days – a clause which led to one of the few divisions recorded for these Parliaments.[12] A bill to repeal 'Cecil's fast', which probably reflected religious opposition rather than economic concerns, was introduced in the Lords in the next session but got no further than a first reading; the same fate befell efforts in the Commons to modify the ban on foreign fish imports and to protect the annual herring fair at Great Yarmouth in Norfolk, efforts which unquestionably involved commercial considerations.[13]

This is the first positive appearance in the story of the special herring interests represented by Yarmouth, and they gathered strength from then on.[14] Though the 1563 act was not due for renewal until the first dissolution of a Parliament after Michaelmas 1574 (it therefore called for action in the Parliament summoned in 1572 which after the session of 1581 petered out in repeated prorogations), the 1571 Parliament passed an act renewing and slightly amending it; the amendments all served the interests of the herring fishery. The time-limitation clause of this act took it out of the struggles over parliamentary recontinuation: after an initial

[9] See above, vol. III, no., 34, iv.
[10] The act was to endure for five years from the end of the 1559 when the expiring laws continuance bill (whose text is unknown) lapsed in the Lower House. The successful continuance act of 1571 (13 Eliz. I, c. 25) does not mention this navigation act.
[11] Sec. 3, which tried to balance this adverse discrimination against Hull by permitting the town to retain the tolls assigned to it under a repealed act of Henry VIII.
[12] *CJ*, I, 58: the clause passed by 179 votes to 97.
[13] *LJ*, I, 6, 56: *CJ*, I, 77, 80.
[14] For the Yarmouth fishery see Robert Tittler, 'The English fishing industry in the sixteenth century: the case of Yarmouth', *Albion* 9 (1977), 40–60. This article has nothing to say about the parliamentary transactions investigated here; it is also somewhat in conflict with A. R. Michell, 'The port and town of Great Yarmouth and its economic and social relationships with its neighbours on both sides of the seas, 1550–1714; (Ph.D. dissertation, University of Cambridge, 1978).

time limit of six years, its further existence was thereafter to be at the queen's pleasure. Somebody in the Lords, confused as well he might be by these complexities, secured a first reading for a formal continuance bill in the session of 1576, but the law officers very likely drew his attention to the superfluity of his bill, of which no more was heard.[15] In fact, throughout the seventies the fishing interests of such outports as Yarmouth seem to have been in the ascendant. In 1571 they beat off a more determined effort to repeal the Wednesday fast, the bill passing the Commons but lapsing in the Upper House;[16] and in 1572 a bill hostile to Yarmouth was talked down on introduction, not being read even a first time.[17] Intended to permit the free sale of fish by all Englishmen to all comers except the queen's enemies, it was put up by men of Suffolk and eventually demolished by one of the burgesses for Yarmouth – unquestionably William Grice, a man (as we shall see) of importance in this story. Yarmouth, he claimed, needed its special privileges in order to be able to maintain its harbour, a duty which in the last few years had allegedly cost it some £12,000.[18] Besides, Yarmouth paid a fee farm of £50 to the queen in exchange for the privilege, and another £50 a year towards the upkeep of the fishing wharf. These claims to dedicated and expensive excellence prevailed, and Grice won the day.

As a matter of fact, the men of Suffolk seem on this occasion to have stepped out of line, for the next parliamentary session witnessed a most remarkable display of solidarity on the part of the coastwise fishing interests, a display which also shows how sophisticated the practice of lobbying the Parliament had become. A few days before the end of the session, perhaps in support of that superfluous renewal bill already mentioned, the seaports of England presented a certificate underlining the beneficent effects of the 1563 act, whose fishing clauses, they maintained, had saved English shipping from disastrous decline: 'If the said law should no longer endure it would be in manner as utter decrying of all the whole fishermen within this realm.' This certificate was signed on behalf of twenty-eight ports (plus others unnamed) running round the east and south coasts from Newcastle to Devon, and including not only Yarmouth but also several Suffolk towns. Signed on their behalf, or

---

[15] *LJ*, I, 745.   [16] *CJ*, I, 89.90; *LJ*, I, 690.
[17] The bill is not noted in *CJ*; we know of it from Thomas Cromwell's 'Diary' (*Proceedings [in the Parliaments of Elizabeth I, I, 1559–1581]*, ed. T. E. Hartley (Leicester, 1981), 363).
[18] The figure may well be correct: in the half-century after 1549, harbour repairs at Yarmouth ran up a bill for £31,873 14s 4d (Tittler, 'English fishing industry', 55).

so the document maintains; the actual signatures reveal something rather different about the lobby which promoted this appeal.[19]

Twenty-two men put their names to it, of whom three cannot be made out. The tally included eleven sitting members of the Commons, one ex-member and one man who later got elected to Parliament, four persons described as masters (that is, of the queen's ships), one man from Dover (John Lucas – not a burgess in any Parliament), and one man about whom nothing relevant can be discovered (Richard Foxlyffe). Of the burgesses, five actually represented fishing ports, all of them on the east coast: Sir Henry Gates (Scarborough), William Grice (Great Yarmouth), Charles Calthorpe (Eye), Edmund Grimston and Thomas Seckford (Ipswich). Three not directly involved but all influential men in East Anglia added their names in support of their Yarmouth and Ipswich colleagues. Henry Woodhouse, knight for the shire of Norfolk, was vice-admiral for both Norfolk and Suffolk as well as Lord Keeper Bacon's son-in-law. One of the lord keeper's sons, Nathaniel, who sat for Tavistock in 1576, was to prove his standing in the shire by getting elected for it in the next Parliament. And Robert Wingfield, though resident at Peterborough, which he represented, belonged to the powerful Suffolk clan of that name. The really impressive signatories head and end the list. At the top stood William Wynter, the leading professional seaman in the House; although he sat for the land-bound Duchy borough of Clitheroe, his real interests here came through, and he was a splendid recruit for the campaign. At the tail there appeared two of the Council's most influential men of business in the Commons: Thomas Wilson (Lincoln), secretary of state, and Thomas Norton (London), the famous and ever-active Parliament-man. Norton revealed something about his character by adding the words 'to the latter part' to his signature: apparently he did not wish it thought that he supported the opening statement about a recent increase in the number of sizeable fishing vessels, a detail of which he could hardly have known from personal experience. The two people who sat in other Parliaments were Wynter's son Edward (1584) and William Holstock, an official of the navy, who had represented Rochester in the previous House. A striking

---

[19] PRO, SP 12/107, fos. 170–1. The named places are: Newcastle, Hartlepool, Whitby, Scarborough, Lynn, Blakeney, Yarmouth, Lowestoft, Goole (out of order), Dunwich, Aldeborough, Orford, Harwich, Colchester, Eye, Margate, Ramsgate, Broadstairs, Sandwich, Dover, Folkestone, Hyde, Rye, Hastings, Brighton, Portsmouth, Exmouth, Burport – a roll-call of fishing towns. All details concerning members of the Commons are taken from P. Hasler (ed.), *History of Parliament: The House of Commons 1558–1603*, 3 vols. (London, 1982).

mixture of fishermen's representatives, local men not technically connected with the ports involved, and expert mariners drawn from outside the House, the group attracted the sponsorship of the outstanding naval pundit of the day and the support of two powerful government-men in the House. The many ports on whose behalf they professed to speak could be content with such unsolicited representation, but, while the list of places put forward included all the English seacoast except the west, from the Bristol Channel to Cumberland (no fishing interests there), the signatories reveal that the campaign originated in Norfolk and Suffolk: with the herring interests.

Meanwhile these matters had also attracted the attention of one of those learned propagandists and promoters who, one sometimes feels, abounded in Elizabethan England, and whose writings have been too often treated as plain statements of the truth, especially about matters economic. Robert Hitchcock, described by the *Dictionary of National Biography* as 'a military writer', became an enthusiastic convert to the patriotic virtues of fishing, both near to home and on the Newfoundland banks. He wished to copy the Dutch in building seagoing vessels of a large capacity, and he drew up plans which, he claimed, would augment the number of English seamen by 6,000 and corner the world's fish supply for England. In order to achieve this he proposed to set up a national organisation based on eight leading fishing centres and financed by a loan of £80,000 raised from these ports – London, Yarmouth, Hull, Newcastle, Chatham, Bristol, Exeter and Southampton: the profits of the trade, he argued, would soon cover these initial costs and maintain the scheme thereafter.[20] Hitchcock's enthusiasm inspired John Dee, ever willing to dream dreams and capable of outdoing anybody in the production of impracticable fantasies: in 1577 he published a proposal for a standing royal navy which would patrol the English fishing grounds in order to keep out foreigners. Dee singled out the Yarmouth herring fishery, allegedly so damaged by the Dutch that Norfolk and Suffolk had only some 140 ships left, all of them too small to support the ancient annual voyages to the Iceland fisheries. He envisaged a navy organised in six squadrons – one each to watch off the shores of Ireland and Scotland, one 'to intercept or understand all privy conspiracies by sea to be communicated', a fourth to be (apparently) permanently at sea against possible sudden attacks from abroad, another to control foreign fisher-

---

[20] Robert Hitchcock, *A Politic Plat* (1581: *STC* 13531); reprinted in E. Arber, *An English Garner* (London, 1897), II, 133–68. How well did he know the industry? Were Exeter and Southampton at all prominent in fishing and the trade in fish?

men, and a last one to clear home waters of pirates. The last in particular would be such a service to foreign princes that they would eagerly seek England's friendship: 'what liberal presents and foreign contributions in hand will duly follow thereof, who cannot imagine?' Who indeed? Unfortunately he concluded only with a confident 'dictum sapienti sat esto'; what was needed was rather his skill in the occult sciences.[21]

Hitchcock did not confine the dissemination of his notions to written memorials. As he tells it, he arranged a dinner at Westminster, a few days before the end of the 1576 session, to which he invited 'the burgesses of almost all the stately port towns of England and Wales'.[22] He read a summary of his programme to them and fired them with his own enthusiasm. Speaker Bell, burgess of King's Lynn, declared that 'a Parliament hath been called for less cause', and others offered to get their towns to equip suitable fishing fleets without national assistance. Others admittedly scoffed. It would be sensible, they said, to send off such armadas with crews drawn from the dregs of the people; if they were lost, as was likely to happen, 'it is but the riddance of a number of idle and evil disposed people'. Such sceptics, said Hitchcock, would soon change their minds when they saw the benefit in wealth and employment that his programme would bring. Indeed, these burgesses of the Parliament had not been the first to learn of Hitchcock's ideas. In 1573 he had sent a copy of his memorial to the queen and a year later another to the earl of Leicester; during the 1576 session, twelve 'counsellors of the law and other men of great credit' had received copies, and one of them, Thomas Digges, had tried to raise the matter in the Commons – gaining great credit and a promise that, since the 1576 session was nearly at an end, the issue should be properly investigated in the next session.[23] Digges did not forget this promise, and in order to help him Hitchcock got his pamphlet printed as soon as it was known that the Parliament would reassemble in January 1581.

The first days of that session (which began on the 23rd) were preoccupied with attempts by extreme men in the Commons to set up a

---

[21] John Dee, *General and Rare Memorials* (1577: *STC* 6459); reprinted as *The Petty Navy Royal* in Arber, *English Garner*, II, 61–70. The anonymous advocate of reform, cited by Dee, was Hitchcock (ibid., 65 and note).

[22] Arber, *English Garner*, II, 167–8. Though the dates fit, it seems unlikely that the round-robin certificate mentioned above was produced at this meeting: the names of the signatories do not support such a conclusion, and the subject-matter also differs.

[23] Hitchcock speaks of Leonard Digges, who never sat in Parliament; Leonard's son Thomas, however, did – for Wallingford (Berks.), as a Leicester client. Clearly the agitation roped in more than burgesses for port towns.

public fast – a thing sufficiently displeasing to the queen to hold up business.[24] Since the Wednesday fast, which she also disliked, stemmed from a navigation act, one might have supposed that Digges would take the opportunity to revive the discussion of fishery, and he did so on the 30th, with a speech which would appear to have rehearsed the arguments of Hitchcock's *Plitic Plat*.[25] Having listened to an exhortation which promised a stronger navy, larger army, employment for the workless and general economic improvement for the realm, all by means of a great and purpose-built fishing fleet, the Commons next day appointed all the privy councillors in the House as a committee to consider the possibilities; all members 'acquainted with that matter of plot [plat] and advice' – that is, all who had read Hitchcock – were urged to attend on the committee and press their points. A fair start, one might think, for a determined pressure group, but in fact also the end of the line for the propagandists: there is nothing to show that the committee ever met, and it certainly never reported any outcome of possible deliberations. For while Digges and his few enthusiasts were trying to persuade the realm to arm and re-edify itself by means of fishing around Newfoundland and Iceland, preaching national unity against interloping (and better equipped) foreigners, it soon became apparent that the reality of fishing involved violent clashes between different English interests, more particularly a dispute in which the fishermen of Norfolk (and other parts) confronted the importers of foreign-caught fish and especially the London Fishmongers' Company. A related complication arose from the quarrel between the latter and the London butchers, who were accused of supplying meat on days supposedly set aside for the eating of fish.

The several interests involved submitted their memorials to the Parliament, for it seems likely that an undated petition of the Fishmongers belongs to this agitation.[26] In it they complained that repeated proclamations against the eating of meat in Lent and encouraging the eating of fish as a way to maintain English shipping had quite failed to stop people from preferring meat – the butchers flourished and the fishmongers decayed. Their fish 'watered [washed] for the market rests upon our hands unsold'. Complaints to the lord mayor had elicited answers 'with so little hope of reformation that we are forced to make

[24] J. E. Neale, *Elizabeth I and her Parliaments 1559–1581* (London, 1953), 378–82.
[25] *CJ*, I, 121. It is interesting to note that Thomas Cromwell's 'Diary' passes this over in silence; he was interested only in the bills read that day.
[26] PRO, SP 12/177, fos. 173–4.

great complaint to this high court of Parliament'. They asked that the butchers licensed to sell meat to persons for health reasons exempt from the Lenten regulations should be stopped from public selling during that time; the names of those licensed were listed but the petitioners knew that at least a hundred more practised their unlicensed trade in the suburbs. What was needed was 'a most plain and very penal law'. Quite probably the Fishmongers had a good case: it does not look as though the standard annual proclamations against supplying meat in Lent had had much effect,[27] while as late as 1600 a proclamation tried to enforce the Wednesday fast of the 1563 act in terms which suggest comprehensive non-observance.[28]

The Fishmongers received very qualified support from the wardens and assistants of Trinity House, Deptford, who, in addition to certifying on the eve of the debate that navigation acts were successfully increasing England's fishing fleet,[29] also submitted a list of proposals for the intended act of Parliament.[30] They agreed that the fish–day clause of the 1563 act was not being properly observed (except, they said diplomatically, at the queen's court and in her navy), and they asked for stiffer penalties; they approved of the clause in an act of 1566 (8 Eliz. I, c. 13) which empowered them to license seamen to work Thames wherries between voyages and asked (superfluously, since it was not time-limited) that it be continued; but they also attacked the practices of London's dealers in fish. Especially they complained of the merchants' willingness to buy up 'putrified' Scottish fish at Lynn and Harwich, selling it for Iceland cod after washing and drying it, as well as of the Fishmongers' restrictive practices which confined the trade in imported fish to selected members of their Company even when other fishmongers were willing to buy. However, the real opposition to the London interests came from 'the coastmen with the consents of the masters of her Majesty's navy' (a revival, it would seem, of the pressure group of 1576), in a petition 'for the increase of navigation'.[31] This paper revealed the violent resentment felt in the outports and among practising fishermen against the London merchants. The petitioners wanted free trade in fish for all Englishmen,

---

[27] Not all those annual proclamations survive but those that do show that from 1561 onwards their terms remained unchanged: they had become a formula (*TRP*, II, nos. 477, 489, 592, 600, 604, 638 – down to 1581). From 1577 the Council regularly and in vain added detailed regulations of its own (F. A. Youngs, *The Proclamations of the Tudor Queens* (Cambridge, 1976), 123–5).

[28] *TRP*, no. 800.   [29] PRO, SP 12/147, fos. 55–6 (26 January 1581).

[30] Ibid., fos. 190–4.   [31] Ibid., fos. 188–9.

with customs duties paid only by such foreigners as bought from them, and they wished a stop to be put to the practices of merchants and fishmongers who bought up catches in the Low Countries for import into England, in rivalry with what the native fishermen had to offer. In addition they asked that alien importers of salted herring and other fish should pay double customs and be compelled to land their cargo at one or two appointed places where it could be effectively inspected for 'goodness and sweetness' before being sold.

It seems likely that this last paper (the foundation of the act to be passed this session) was promoted by the leaders of the 'coastmen', the fishing interests of Yarmouth: its terms are plainly reflected in the bill which we know originated with that town. As its Assembly recorded later, the new statute of navigation 'hath been obtained by special and great costs of this town'.[32] Yarmouth, in fact, on the very day that the Parliament opened instructed two of its leading townsmen to ride to London in order to convey to the town's burgesses in the House the instructions previously agreed upon, 'concerning the causes and estate of this town, and whatsoever they shall do therein the house [i.e. the Assembly] shall allow'.[33] Whatever the men of Yarmouth may have felt or said at the dinner organised five years before by Robert Hitchcock, they now mobilised their influence for the promotion of a narrowly self-interested bill in Parliament and forgot about the prospects of a great navy to protect the expansion of English fishing all over the northern Atlantic. Most surprisingly, they made no attempt to capitalise on Digges's initiative in the Commons: instead of presenting their case to the committee of privy councillors, their representatives in Parliament saw to the introduction of a suitable measure in the House of Lords, where that bill was read a first time on 16 February.[34]

The likely reason for this manoeuvre throws light on the realities of Elizabethan parliamentary life – so very different from the picture of an ascendant Commons presented by Neale and his school.[35] Although Yarmouth professed much civic pride and enjoyed oligarchic government by its own burgesses, it had usually been willing to allow its high

---

[32] Norwich Record Office (henceforth NRO). Yarmouth Assembly Books, IV, fo. 22v. I owe all references to this source to Mr David Dean to whom I am grateful for permission to cite it.
[33] Ibid., fo. 18v.   [34] *LJ*, II, 34.
[35] The following analysis rests on the facts collected in Hasler, *The House of Commons 1558–1603*, I, 211–12, and II, 226; the interpretation is my own.

steward to direct its choice of members for the Parliament. After the execution of the fourth duke of Norfolk in 1572, that office fell to the earl of Leicester, and in 1581 the two burgesses for Yarmouth were both his clients. One of them, Edward Bacon, a younger son of Lord Keeper Sir Nicholas Bacon, owed his choice at a by-election in 1576 to the earl whose influence overcame the desire of a majority of the electors to elect a strictly local man. But Bacon, a notable absentee from the Commons, mattered little; it was his fellow member, William Grice, who really watched over the interests of the constituency. Grice, also a client of Leicester's, occupied an ideally suitable position: a member of the Yarmouth corporation, he could be called a local man, but in reality he practised as an attorney in London and in that capacity had all the right legal and parliamentary contacts. In particular he knew that influential Parliament-man, Thomas Norton, the most active draftsman of bills in the 1581 session when, according to his own testimony, he worked mostly in cahoots with the Privy Council.[36] Both of them had been among the men who signed the memorial of 1576, and later in the year they cooperated on Yarmouth's behalf in the quarrel with Hull which sprang from the fisheries act of 1581;[37] both men also sat on the two Commons committees appointed during the passage of that act. Yet, despite this influential contact in the House of Commons, Grice put his bill into the Upper House, nor – to judge from the enacting clause – had Norton or any other Council draftsman anything to do with its composition. Rather than commit his concerns to the overworked and inefficient Lower House, Grice apparently utilised his connection with Leicester – who, it will be remembered, had been solicited by Hitchcock years before and may well have had a more than casual concern for England's navigation. If in this way Grice hoped to secure a rapid passage for his bill he was reasonably successful, though a mysterious ten days' delay between the second reading on 22 February and a further second reading with an order to engross on 2 March suggests that the Lords found themselves lobbied by interests hostile to the coastmen-fishers and thus hesitated a while before proceeding with the bill. However, by 4 March they had passed it and sent it to the Commons.[38]

We do not know the terms of the bill as first read in the Lords; all that survives is the engrossed version passed by that House and amended in

[36] See M. A. R. Graves, 'Thomas Norton, the Parliament man: An Elizabethan MP, 1559–1581', *HJ*, 23 (1980), 17–35.
[37] NRO, Yarmouth Assembly Books, IV, fo. 26v.
[38] *LJ*, II, 36, 40, 43.

the Commons.[39] Its preamble denounces the 'merchants and fish-mongers of divers places of this realm' (read London) for their willing-ness to buy great quantities of fish caught by foreigners. Not only is the fish inferior to what Englishmen bring home from their Iceland voyages, but the practice moreover results in the export of much money and the impoverishment of the realm. In addition to these 'unnatural dealings', the eating of meat 'on the accustomed and usual fish days' has caused a crisis in English shipping; more than 200 vessels – 'good and serviceable ships' – have had to drop out of the Iceland fisheries, and a great many seamen fit for the defence of the realm in time of war have been lost. The preamble thus reflects both the grievances of the fishermen of England and the national concerns of the propagandists, but (as the body of the act showed) it was the former that mattered. The remedies proposed were embodied in three clauses and two provisos, and since the three clauses came straight from the memorial of the 'coastmen' it may be conjectured that they constituted the original bill, the provisos being added during the hold-up over the second reading as a result of further representations received in the House.

The main clauses prohibited, under penalties of forfeiture, all import of foreign fish by natives acting in person or through agents: such imports were reserved to aliens who in addition to the normal duties were to pay sums equal to any impositions levied on English ships in their own home ports. Provided that the foreigners importing their fish into England paid all the customs due, English shipowners were permitted to carry such cargoes. That is to say, the original bill simply aimed to stop the flooding of the home market with fish bought abroad, in part by barring Englishmen from trading in it at all and in part by rendering such fish much more expensive than English catches, but it allowed English vessels a share in the carrying trade so long as the higher costs fell on the foreigner. The two provisos did not touch this core of the measure. The first gave the act some very necessary teeth by providing penalties for attempts at deceitful evasions, that is to say, those standard practices of bogus manifests and pretended ownership which so regularly defeated all efforts to protect English trade against foreign competition: natives stood to incur fines of £200 for every breach of the law, while aliens committing frauds would forfeit their shops as well as their cargoes if these on inspection were declared unfit for sale. Since nobody would wish to be saddled with forfeited loads of rotten fish, this last provision

[39] OA in HLRO.

must be read as an ominous opening for chicanery: it must have been dangerously easy to acquire good fish for free after a word with the inspector. The other proviso, however, broke ranks and conceded a point to the London Fishmongers: it totally prohibited the sale of meat in Lent by any butcher, poulterer or victualler. It seems likely that the acceptance of this additional clause (also, we conjecture, added during the passage of the bill) caused the reference to meat-eating on fish-days to be inserted in the preamble. In a manner quite familiar from the histories of bills in Elizabethan Parliaments, a straightforward measure promoted by one identifiable interest was amalgamated with a different though cognate issue raised by quite another.

In this form the bill reached the Commons, on 1 March;[40] it was read a first time that afternoon, for in expectation of an early prorogation or dissolution the House at that time also sat after dinner in order to get as many bills through as possible.[41] Even so, the bill did not turn up again until the 15th, but in view of the pressure of unfinished bills it would be rash to assume that this delay reflected organised opposition to it. In any case, the interval was not entirely wasted. When the bill came up for second reading it was accompanied by three provisos presented to the House which were read twice on the same day and thus incorporated in the bill. Quite evidently, these provisos dealt with various doubts or reservations felt after the first reading and thus made passage easier.

One exempted all fish imported from Iceland, Scotland and Newfoundland, with their adjoining seas, as well as fish taken and salted anywhere by the queen's natural subjects. On the face of it this might be thought a wrecking clause; that it proved acceptable to the promoters confirms that all along the real purpose of the bill lay in the protection of the one fishery not included in the exception. Thanks to this proviso the act in effect safeguarded the North Sea herring grounds and banned only supplies obtained in the Low Countries. The second proviso weakened the act further by permitting everybody (including presumably Dutchmen and London Fishmongers) at present engaged in the import of staple fish and ling 'for the better furnishing of this realm withal' to continue to operate for three years after the end of the session. Though time-limited,

[40] The diary entry (*Proceedings*, 542) defines the contents of the bill at first reading in the Commons as 'restraining the buying of any salt fish or salt herring from beyond the sea, and buying it of any strangers, and against the killing of any flesh between Shrovetide and the Tuesday before Easter, and against the selling of flesh to any not having license to eat'. [41] *CJ*, I, 131.

this marked a notable concession to precisely the people whom the bill had meant to bar altogether from the trade; and it also recognised some virtue in the merchants' standard argument that English fishermen could not supply all the fish the country needed.[42] From these facts it may be inferred that the proviso originated with the London interests; it too may well have proved acceptable to Yarmouth because it remained silent on the topic of herrings, the trade in which continued to be ruled by the main clauses of the act. (Herrings were not 'staple fish'.) The last proviso, on the other hand, constituted a frontal assault on the London Fishmongers (though it took care to speak also of other like bodies, none being involved) by declaring void any ordinance they had made or would hereafter make to inhibit trade in fish within the realm; for every breach of the statute, offenders were to be fined the prohibitive sum of £100. Thus when the bill was committed after second reading it had been quite noticeably narrowed in its effect but also explicitly turned against the London Company, which would lose control not only over outsiders but even over its own members.

The timely production of these provisos left the committee with little to do, and most of its amendments concerned minor drafting points.[43] But the committee did one drastic thing: it deleted the clause against the killing and selling of meat in Lent. Thus the proviso added in the Lords in response to the Fishmongers' memorial went out again, leaving the bill with no joy at all for this much disliked privileged body. When, however, the bill was reported on the 17th and read a third time, further problems arose and it was recommitted; we do not know what held it up or was done to it now (nothing significant, to judge by the Original Act), but on the following day it finally passed the Lower House.[44] The Lords accepted all the changes made and read the amended bill three times on the 18th, the last day of the session;[45] at the assent, the Speaker especially singled it out with two other bills as worthy achievements of the session, which at least demonstrates that its hesitant and disputed passage had not gone unnoticed.[46] However worthy, it really had caused quite considerable difficulties especially in the Commons, a fact which indicates that Grice had been wise to start it in the Lords, though even there there had been hesitations. In the end, Yarmouth got the essence of what it wanted, at the cost of relinquishing any larger purpose

[42] See below, p. 128.
[43] A paper schedule of amendments made in committee is attached to the OA.
[44] *CJ*, I, 134, 136.   [45] *LJ*, II, 53.   [46] *Proceedings*, 546.

or national interest in the act. Its grandiloquent title – 'For the increase of mariners and for the maintenance of navigation' – better described the ambitions set out in the preamble than the import of the much amended enactment. A more accurate title would have been 'For the protection of the east coast fisheries and against the Fishmongers' Company of London'.

A little more may be learned from a look at the two committees that reviewed the bill. The ordinary bill committee appointed on second reading consisted of fifteen members, and it says something about the bill that not one of them was a privy councillor. The most likely explanation is that the government wanted to keep clear of the conflict of interests involved in the measure. Instead, the chair was taken by Owen Hopton, lieutenant of the Tower and knight of the shire for Middlesex, and it may not be without significance that round about this time he was involved in a rather prolonged dispute with the City of London.[47] Grice and Bacon, burgesses for Yarmouth, naturally sat on the committee, as did other representatives of port towns: Edward Lewknor (New Shoreham, Sussex), John Cowper (Steyning, Sussex), Edward Grimston (Ipswich, Suffolk), Charles Calthorpe (Eye, Suffolk), John Shirley (Lewes, Sussex). Two Londoners were included but cannot be regarded as intended balances in the interest of the merchants: both Thomas Aldersey and Thomas Norton were regular and active committee-men in all the Parliaments they sat in, as were two otherwise rather surprising members – Sir Thomas Sempole (Lincs.) and Robert Newdigate (Berwick). Sir Thomas Scott (Kent) may be thought to have had an interest, but Thomas Onley (Brackley, Northants.) and Giles Estcourte (Salisbury, Wilts.) must be regarded as makeweights. The two Suffolk men well balanced the self-interest of Yarmouth, and the presence of three men from Sussex reminds one of the deep involvement which that shire had with the cod fisheries at Scarborough and the herring fishery at Yarmouth.[48] The committee thus presented quite a typical mixture of members of the Commons directly interested in the bill, active men of business experienced in committee work and usually employed during a session in supervising the efficient management of bills, and a handful of extras who were there to make up numbers and gain experience. An office-holder of modest distinction made a reasonable figurehead.

[47] *Calendar of State Papers Domestic, 1581–90* (1865), 83.
[48] C. E. Brent, 'Urban employment and population in Sussex between 1550 and 1660', *Sussex Archaeological Collections*, 113 (1975), 35–50.

However, it is notorious that members appointed to committees did not by any means attend with assiduity – the chief reason for the constant increase in the size of committees. Here the second body becomes of interest. Appointed only two days after the first, it contained only four of the fifteen members of its predecessor – Sempole, Aldersey, Grice and Norton: three men of business and one interested party. It is a reasonable guess that they were the committee members who actually attended on the 15th, or at any rate had on that occasion done the real work. To them were added five new men: Sir Walter Mildmay, chancellor of the Exchequer and privy councillor; Sir Henry Radcliffe, who sat for Portsmouth, a town concerned with navigation; and three more of the experienced men of business – Francis Alford (Reading, Berks.), Robert Wroth (Middlesex), and Thomas Cromwell, the diarist, a resident of King's Lynn though he sat for Bodmin in Cornwall. The accident that the bill necessitated the appointment of two committees within three days thus enables us to see something of the manner in which such bodies were selected and went about their work. Since Hopton's committee had (apparently) left raw edges in its drafting, it seems to have been thought wiser to get that influential man, Mildmay, to preside on the second occasion; but the work would really seem to have been done by Grice, burgess for the promoters, and his friend Norton, with the assistance of other 'men of business'. Aldersey belonged to the Haberdashers' Company and Norton to the Grocers', so that the Fishmongers had no representative and apparently no friend on either committee. It is no wonder that Yarmouth got what it wanted, despite the clear signs that opposition to its plans existed in both Houses.

The act thus unquestionably favoured the interests of those engaged in sea fishing and went counter to those of men engaged in the buying and selling of foreign fish. Despite its origin in the Lords, it owed absolutely nothing to any initiative from the government, who did not even bother to put a privy councillor on the bill committee, and it did nothing for larger policy or the active promotion of English industry and trade. Its most surprising feature remains to be mentioned: it carried no limitation in time. As we have seen, earlier navigation acts all included clauses designed to bring them up for reconsideration at some fixed point in the future, and this was particularly the case with the much more important statute of 1563. Great Yarmouth, on the other hand, meant to hide behind a permanent act, so that any persons attacked or affected by it would have to promote a full-scale repeal if they were to recover the ground lost. An attempt had, in fact, been made in the Lords to prevent so total a victory for one side. Among Burghley's papers there survives a draft proviso which, arguing that the act might not turn out so useful to the common weal as its promoters claimed, meant to appoint a committee on whose advice the queen could by proclamation suspend it.[49] The projected committee can only be called crazy: six spiritual and six temporal peers, one knight for every shire, and one citizen or burgess for any one constituency in every shire. Such a body could never have been assembled, and it is no wonder that the idea got no further than Burghley's files, but its existence demonstrates that someone felt apprehensive about the effect of the act. Why no one saw to the addition of that familiar device, a time-limitation clause, must remain a puzzle; by putting the issue before the whole of a future Parliament, it would have achieved much more readily what, it seems, this select body of parliamentarians was intended to do.

Was the act successful? To judge from the fortunes of the Yarmouth herring industry in the fifty years after 1581, legislation proved as helpless as in such matters of commerce and industry it usually was.[50] Perhaps this disappointing result sprang from inadequate enforcement, and someone might look into the history of the various conflicting interests as well as at the king's remembrancer's memoranda rolls in the Exchequer after 1581, for that is where any action brought under the penal clauses of the act would have had to be initiated. The results are not likely to be impressive: esoteric penal legislation in economic matters tended in this period to sit silent upon the statute book. What is certain is that Yarmouth's parliamentary triumph did not silence its adversaries for long. Immediately after the session, the town decided to recoup some of the costs incurred over the bill: 'for that the same is to the benefit of the whole coast', it was resolved to send an emissary up and down the shores of Norfolk and Suffolk to acquaint neighbours with this splendid act and 'see if they will extend any benevolence towards the charges aforesaid'.[51] So far as the evidence goes, Yarmouth merely learned the advantages of getting your money in advance. At least two rival ports started suits to limit the benefits obtained by Yarmouth. With Hull, it

---

[49] PRO, SP 12/147, fo. 197.

[50] Tittler ('English fishing industry', 52) speaks of stagnation or decline, Michell ('Port and town of Great Yarmouth', 27, 37–8) more convincingly argues that Yarmouth was prosperous in the reign of Elizabeth, with a flourishing fishing industry backing up notable developments in maritime trade. Either way, the statute made little or no difference.

[51] NRO, Yarmouth Assembly Books, IV, fo. 22v.

would appear, the town came to some sort of terms quite quickly;[52] the dispute with Lowestoft dragged on.[53]

The interest most affected did not allow the grass (or seaweed) to grow long under its feet. By early October 1581, Yarmouth had to take steps to resist the counter-agitation of the Fishmongers' Company. A member of the town oligarchy was despatched to London to agree action with Norton and Grice, still looking after Yarmouth's interests, after coordinating things with the London agent for the smaller ports of Norfolk (Blakeney and Wells).[54] They had reason to act, for the Fishmongers had put forward a memorial to the Council which constituted a comprehensive denunciation of the act and a demand for its rescission.[55] It therefore looks as though the Company may have been caught by surprise in the 1581 session, and it is not beyond the parliamentary possibilities that such surprise could be engineered more readily by introducing a bill into the Lords rather than the Commons. At any rate, the Fishmongers now turned up, after the event, with the kind of powerful arguments that would surely have influenced opinion decisively in one House or the other.

As they saw it, Parliament had been persuaded to pass the act by statements which looked plausible enough so long as they were not questioned. (A familiar line to take: but why then had they not been questioned in Parliament?) It was alleged that English fishmongers, for private gain, brought in inferior foreign fish. But (the inferior apart) this was a longstanding practice, at its height when the English Iceland voyages were still going strong; without it, fish supplies would prove insufficient and prices be driven up. Indeed, that was exactly what had happened since the passing of the act, thus fulfilling the real ambitions of 'the coastmen, the solicitors and procurers of this law ... for their own private lucre and gain'. People now ate meat on fish-days because it was cheaper; and Flemish fish could cure this, being as good as but much cheaper than what could be got from Iceland. That English merchants buying foreign fish had to export money for this purpose was simply untrue: it was well known that they either exported trade goods or used the exchange. (Accusing an adversary of denuding the realm of specie in return for unwanted imports had been a standard tactic for a century or more.) Nor was it the case that these foreign imports were driving out

[52] Ibid., fos. 26v, 27v, 34vc.   [53] This is being investigated by Mr Dean.
[54] NRO Yarmouth Assembly Books, IV, fo. 32v.
[55] PRO, SP 12/148, fos. 127–33.

native supplies caught by native labour: English fishermen had never been able to satisfy the needs of the realm, whereas now (thanks, one presumes, to section 1 of the act) they were in fact selling a lot of their catch especially of Yarmouth herring to customers abroad – engaging in a trade profitable to themselves and leaving England short of fish. The Fishmongers forcefully questioned the assertion that 'unnatural dealings' and failure to observe fish-days had cut the Iceland fleet by 200 ships; they doubted whether there had ever been as many as that engaged in the trade, but if there existed as many as that or more they would easily sell all they caught. In their view the decline of the Iceland fishery arose from quite other causes: to judge from the fact that ships regularly returned from there with small catches and much of their salt unused, the grounds were being fished out, and in any case English fishermen had decided that inshore fishing with small boats was both safer and more profitable. There was also the fact that general trading into various countries had so much grown in recent times that shipowners preferred to use their vessels 'to traffic from place to place for a good hire and freight, which is certain unto them, than to venture upon these casual Iceland voyages, not knowing whether they shall lose or win thereby'.

The document contains less self-contradiction than such papers usually do, and its major points sound convincing enough. English trade had expanded without shipbuilding keeping pace, so that there were fewer seagoing fishing vessels available. Even supposing, however, that the reasons advanced by the coastmen had more substance, the Fishmongers argued that the statute passed could not be expected to mend matters. English merchants who had employed English ships to export English manufacturers and had used fish as a return cargo were now forbidden this sensible practice (did foreigners really like fish-scented English cloth?). Alien merchants had jumped at the chance of taking over. 'It hath never before been seen . . . in any common weal that any subject hath been forbidden to bring in any victual, and strangers permitted': a good point.

However, while the Fishmongers could legitimately and successfully controvert the economic arguments of their adversaries, they had to resort to more highflown and woolly assertions when they turned to the true nub of their grievance. That cursed act had declared their Company's ordinances void – as we have seen, in a proviso added by the Commons. Perhaps the Fishmongers had at first been willing to let the act pass without any very energetic protest, believing it to be of little import or effect; and this thrust to the heart came too late for them to mount a campaign in the Parliament. In their view, the clause had had disastrous consequences. 'It is well known that a multitude living without government grown to disorder and abuse,' they said; and since the act the common weal had promptly suffered from ill-ordered persons' dealings whose chief effect had been to push up the price of all fish. 'Wherefore we pray ... that we may have liberty to put in execution only amongst ourselves such ancient orders as have been confirmed unto us according to the law and long time used, liked and allowed of to be good and wholesome for the common weal.' Let all members of the good Company 'brought and trained up in the buying and bringing in of fish' once more import the necessary victual from anywhere, provided 'it be in English bottoms', paying the old duties and customs to her Majesty, 'the statute aforesaid notwithstanding'.

The argument that freeing the trade from restrictions had increased prices supposes the existence of large numbers of Englishmen from outside London competing for the available stocks or unusual self-restraint by the Londoners in the days of their monopoly. Neither point seems very probable at first sight. Nevertheless, the Fishmongers' general case had real merit; as we have seen, not everybody believed that Yarmouth herring merited advantages which hindered much fishing and the trade in fish elsewhere. However, the offending act stood unlimited in time and more was therefore needed to overthrow it than would have been required if it had had to come up for renewal at some fixed point in the future. This memorial, in fact, was the opening shot in a long campaign of agitation, with bills in Parliament and such like, which cannot here be pursued. It was only in the Parliament of 1597 that Yarmouth's victory of 1581 was apparently reversed, and even then most of that victory survived. The act of 39 Eliz. I, c. 10, repealed the earlier statute as ineffective: English suppliers had not been able to satisfy England's need for fish and only foreigners had benefited. So the Fishmongers had said from the first, and it is probable that they were right. However, the repealing act went on to re-enact the bulk of what it had just wiped off the book. The only part of the 1581 act to disappear was its first clause, which permitted free trade in fish by all Englishmen but prohibited the import of foreign fish by English merchants. All the rest, including the voiding of the Company's ordinances, came back by the other door. It was only when this act, now time-limited, was considered for the expiring laws continuance act of the next Parliament (43 Eliz. I, c. 9) that the Fishmongers secured the removal of that offensive provision – incidentally proving how much easier it was to amend an act needing renewal than to repeal a permanent act in all the details objected to. What was left of the Yarmouth fisheries act of 1581 after the session of 1601 was, thus, a law which generally penalised aliens engaged in the fish trade with England but kept the trade open provided English vessels were used – a true navigation act of the kind to which that title is commonly given.

The efforts of Yarmouth and its associated coastal ports around the shores of England to exploit fish and fish-days for their sectional interests thus in effect foundered, but they did so less on the superior strength of their opponents, the London merchants, than on their inability to serve the needs of the realm. Meanwhile, the Dutch took the herring in English waters and sold it back to the English.

55

ENGLISH NATIONAL SELF-CONSCIOUSNESS AND THE PARLIAMENT IN THE SIXTEENTH CENTURY*

The English people early acquired a high degree of national self-consciousness – if by this term we mean an awareness of their own identity and their difference from other nations. Geography helped, in two quite different ways which on the face of it one might have thought contradictory. The boundaries of an island identified themselves with a precision that was lacking in the rest of Europe – a part of the medieval world in which apparent frontiers served rather to mingle the members of adjacent kingdoms and separate them from their own hinterlands, creating a dark area of marches in which national self-identification retreated before a common consciousness resting on a difference shared along the border. In England, the fact that there existed one such march right into the sixteenth century happened to increase the national feelings of the people. The march against Scotland displayed many of the characteristics of such frontier belts as they were found, for instance, in the Iberian peninsula (Moors and Christians confronting each other but growing like each other in the course of time), or along the eastern edge of the Holy Roman Empire. Along the Anglo-Scottish border, too, a broad strip of territory extending south and north stood apart from both England and Scotland away from the march; and here also common experience and private relations across the supposed divide brought into existence a marcher people of both English and Scots who were more clearly marked by these experiences and relations than by their supposed English and Scottish nationhoods. Yet on the English side at least the fact of Englishness was also never forgotten. The English of the northern marches regarded the Scots not only as fellow marchers but also – and even more so – as visible enemies, men of another kind: as enemies, that is to say, whose existence made the inhabitants of the English march more conscious of being English. For the English living away from the march, in vastly the greater part of the realm, the Scots were, of course, nothing but enemies, thus providing within the boundaries of an island

---

* [*Nationalismus in vorindustrieller Zeit*, ed. O. Dann (Munich, 1986), 73–81.] This is a reconstruction, from memory, of an address that was originally delivered without a script. I hope this fact will excuse my failure to provide a full apparatus of notes.

so well defined by the sea one further ingredient necessary for national self-consciousness – the presence of another body of people, habitually hostile, opposing whom meant identifying more consciously with your own kind on a national scale.

One chief reason why the normal conditions of a marcher existence did not, even along the border, overrule adherence to the English nation lay in the precocious development of the English monarchy. The realm cohered more definitely than any other medieval unit of comparable size because of the policy of kings. The kings of Wessex had managed to establish a nation-wide rule even before the separation from Scotland became manifest, and the Danish conquerors of the eleventh century inherited something like a territorial unit. Above all, the Norman Conquest led to an energetic and persistent assertion of royal authority throughout the kingdom, and this authority extended, with qualifications, even over the border lands of north and west. Peculiar circumstances produced an exceptionally early diffusion of one culture – one set of national reference points – throughout England. The Conquest left the country populated by three peoples – English, Norman and Welsh – who spoke different languages and lived by different popular traditions and laws. Establishing royal rule in such conditions meant creating and asserting a common identity overbearing all disparities; more particularly, it meant asserting one king's law for the whole realm over all local custom (an end achieved to a surprising degree by the beginning of the thirteenth century); and this endeavour was quite consciously pursued by the post-Conquest monarchy, certainly from the middle of the twelfth century. A hundred years later, the ruling order represented an amalgamation of Norman and Anglo-Saxon elements which spoke of itself as the community of England and thought in national terms.[1]

At this point, however, the English kingdom still faced the existence of a separate Welsh principality within what were becoming its natural frontiers. Thus Edward I's conquest and absorption of this Celtic remnant opened the door to the typically English king-centred attitudes for penetration into Wales, and by the sixteenth century this interpenetration had gone a long way towards wiping out a Welsh self-consciousness, especially among the gentry which some centuries before had been strong. The so-called Union of England and Wales, codified in the statutes of 1536 and 1543, was indeed based on a programme of reform put forward in Wales itself and accepted by the administration of

[1] M. T. Clanchy, *England and its Rulers 1066–1272* (London, 1983) provides an excellent summary of these developments. See especially ch. 10.

Thomas Cromwell. As for the specifically English consciousness of national identity, this achieved consolidation in the Hundred Years War with France. Even by the middle of the fourteenth century the language spoken by high and low alike was English – no longer Anglo-Saxon or Norman French, but a product descended from both. The age of Chaucer is an unmistakably English age, however much court and chivalry still looked to the international models presented by the Valois monarchs and their knights.[2] As so often, fighting an enemy did not necessarily mean breaking all cultural ties, but it did mean fighting as conscious Englishmen. No doubt, the long struggle with France started as a family dispute over an inheritance, but, as is the habit with such quarrels among relatives if only they last long enough, it set up a confrontation between two resolutely hostile parties (in this case nations), a confrontation filled with distrust and dislike that still have life in them to the present day.

By the sixteenth century, therefore, the English *were* a nation and conscious of the fact. There are some subtle implications in the scene in Shakespeare's *Henry V* in which three captains (English, Scottish and Welsh) tease their Irish companion. 'I think, look you, under your correction', says Captain Fluellen to Captain Macmorris, 'there is not many of your nation', only to be interrupted by a storming outburst: 'Of my nation! What ish my nation?', and so forth. A people divided into warring septs and clans, only in part subjected to what the English regarded as a civilised form of government, could not claim nationhood or national identity, and Macmorris understood that he was being charged with lacking the outward aspect of a cultural development that made his companions more advanced than himself. As a matter of fact, by Shakespeare's time the Welsh also were hardly a genuine nation any more, though it was in the age of Elizabeth that Welsh self-consciousness began to be recreated by a group of humanist intellectuals, especially George Owen, a Herder *devant ses jours*. The notion, so often asserted, that the Tudor dynasty itself made propagandist use of its supposed Welsh origin is not, to my knowledge, borne out by any evidence: a few poets' devices late in the century hardly support the case, and I shudder to think what Elizabeth would have said if someone had called her Welsh to her face! In reality, the national self-consciousness of England included Wales, a fact made apparent by the statutory union of the 1530s and well illustrated by the lack of resentment with which the sizeable

2 See Janet Coleman, 'English culture in the fourteenth century', in *Chaucer and the Italian Trecento*, ed. Piero Boitani (Cambridge, 1983), 33–63.

influx in the early sixteenth century of Welshman seeking to better themselves in the king's court and government was accepted by the English proper. When a century later the Scots similarly flooded down from the north in the entourage of the first Stuart king of England, they caused the most violent hostility and provoked xenophobic feelings that lasted into the nineteenth century. England and Wales were one kingdom with one national self-consciousness; Scotland was such another, and James I never got anywhere near success with his very sensible proposals for a union of the two kingdoms.

The Scots were not the only victims of xenophobia. Predictably, English self-consciousness expressed itself most clearly, indeed most stridently, in hostility to and contempt for other nations. Pride of nationhood easily turned to chauvinism, as the Spanish attendants of Philip of Burgundy and Castile discovered quickly enough when their master, by marrying Mary Tudor, briefly became king of England. The streets of London witnessed frequent clashes in which blood was shed and two manifestations of stubborn pride fed on one another. Englishmen, whether they had travelled abroad or never left home, thought themselves superior to other nations – or at least, in moments of unwonted humility, as vastly more fortunate. They had plenty of meat to eat, whereas the French and Italians had to make do with 'grass' or 'herbs' – vegetables and salads. They knew peace and plenty, whereas abroad there reigned lawless war and penury. They lived under the law; other nations were ruled by tyranny. Even critics unwittingly repeated such assessments: thus Richard Morison explained in 1536 that the English were notoriously idle and unwilling to work because the demi-paradise they inhabited rendered unnecessary those constant and painful exertions by which other people had to earn a living. No doubt one can find similar national chauvinism elsewhere: it seems improbable that the French sense of superiority, so dominant in the seventeenth and eighteenth centuries, should not have been present already in the sixteenth. Nor should it be forgotten that Englishmen of taste and intellect looked abroad for their inspiration – to Italy, to Burgundy, to Erasmus, to Calvin's Geneva. Nevertheless, a peculiarly fortified kind of self-awareness, at times deteriorating into smug contentment, pervaded the thoughts on national identity even among the more distinguished members of the nation. A very real truth about English feelings in the sixteenth century was summed up somewhat innocently in the famous marginal note found in John Aylmer's *An Harborowe for Faithful and True Subjects* (1559): 'God is English'.

Yet there is another side to the story. Englishmen talked readily about being English and proud of it; yet the pull upon their deeds, allegiances and feelings seemed often to be exercised by a territory much smaller than the whole realm. No wonder that quite a few historians will emphasise a different image: to them it seems clear that this apparent consciousness of nationhood covered – and covered thinly – a powerful localism that would seem to make nonsense of the concept of one nation. When men, we are reminded, spoke of their country they meant their county. Most people's horizons did not in practice extend to the limits of the kingdom: they lived in and for a shire, a borough, a village, a manor; and for most of them the realities of social and political existence occurred within these narrower confines. The gentry, and even very often the aristocracy, played out their faction-ridden quarrels for ambition and aggrandisement within their counties: it was there that they wished to shine and rule. Among the lower orders, a man could be a foreigner without having crossed the Channel to come to England; it was enough if he stemmed from another county, sometimes from a neighbouring village. How can we be sure that the men of Lancashire and Kent, of Devon and Durham thought of themselves as members of one nation? An example often cited is that of Cornwall, whose levies rebelled in 1497 at least in part because they regarded a demand for their services against the Scots in the far north an irrelevant intrusion upon their affairs. Or there are the Pilgrims of Grace, who in 1536 demonstrated (so it is held) the separateness of the whole north of England from the larger and hated south. Localism has become quite a growth industry in English historical studies; the investigation of this or that shire is reckoned to be the best way to get at social realities and to demolish allegedly anachronistic ideas of 'one nation'.

While I do not doubt the importance of the local scene, I have to say that I cannot agree with the conclusion which denies the existence of a national stage. There is plenty of evidence that even people of lowly status wished to hear the national news and to know what was going on in the greater world beyond the bounds of the realm, especially if such events seemed to threaten the whole kingdom. Troubles on the Scottish border made the news in Norfolk, and rumours of French or Spanish fleets approaching the Solent stirred apprehensions in Yorkshire. As regards those Cornishmen of 1497, it has always seemed to me a strange expression of local separatism that manifests itself in a warlike march across all southern England, to the outskirts of London. In fact, recent work shows that the rising was organised by a remnant of the Yorkist faction seeking to reconquer the crown: it was far more than just an outburst of Cornishness. Similarly, the Pilgrimage of Grace really originated in a policy devised in London, by a defeated court faction, though it exploited local hostilities to the centre.[3] The error lies in supposing that localism positively excluded the larger sense of nationhood. People were quite capable of thinking of themselves as members of the English nation who also had particular local allegiances and concerns. Nevertheless, I agree that those local allegiances and concerns could at times be strong enough to override the attractions of the centre and thus disrupt the outward appearance of one nation conscious of its single nationhood. National consciousness required embodiment in working institutions in order to acquire enduring reality.

Two such institutions in fact existed and did the necessary work: the crown and the Parliament. The house of Tudor fulfilled the monarchic function very successfully, both in outward show and in inner reality. Henry VIII is still the one king of England whom just about every inhabitant of the kingdom would recognise without difficulty, and Elizabeth remains Gloriana to this day. More important, perhaps, was the deliberate decision made by Henry VII and followed by his descendants to be king of all his people and not the leader of a faction among them. The Yorkist recovery of royal authority had been much weakened by the failure of both Edward IV and Richard III to shed their dependence on that faction of the ruling order that had enabled them to win the crown. Edward IV by his marriage split the Yorkist faction and set up Richard's usurpation; Richard III brought his northern supporters south and favoured them there so extravagantly that he created a counterfaction for Henry Tudor. Thus Henry started as a faction leader, too, but from the day he triumphed at the battle of Bosworth he set himself to widen his support and reabsorb all factional interests in a single allegiance to the crown. He was to be ruler, and father, of all Englishmen – often a stern father but never the servant of some part of them whom he would advance at the expense of others. For the rest of the century, factions often provided the structure of politics, but they did so as the monarchs' instruments and not as their captors.

That the monarchy should provide a focus of national sentiment and a way of overcoming the splintering effects of local or personal allegiances causes no surprise: the Tudor kings simply resumed the role which

---

[3] For the new explanation of the Cornish rebellion see Ian Arthurson, '1497 and the Western rebellion' (unpublished Ph.D. thesis, Keele University, 1981); for the northern rising see G. R. Elton, 'Politics and the Pilgrimage of Grace', above, vol III, no. 36.

kingship had worked out for itself from Alfred to Edward III. And at first sight Parliament also fits the part well enough. After all, Parliament supposedly represented the coming together of all parts of the realm, on special and specially important occasions: this had been its function from the first beginnings of the institution. As Tudor writers never tired repeating, in the Parliament everybody was present in his own person or by proxy (deputy), a fact upon which rested the claims to obedience vested in its edicts (statutes). What Parliament did had every man's consent, or so the constitutional convention went. Indeed, the sixteenth century gave signs of recognising this 'uniting' function with exceptional clarity as hitherto unrepresented parts of the realm received the right to elect members to the House of Commons. This right was extended to Calais in 1536, to Wales in the same year with representatives first appearing in 1542, and to the old palatinate of Chester in 1542, whose first members turned up in 1545. Even the town of Tournai, in France, temporarily possessed by England early in Henry VIII's reign, sent representatives in 1513, so as to underline the principle that lands of the English crown should all come to the Parliaments called by the kings of England. In the end only the episcopal franchise of Durham remained outside the system (until 1833), not, I think for any very positive or meaningful reason but only because under the old order no principle ever existed without some exception to call it in question among tidy-minded historians. There just arose no occasion for summoning Durham to a Parliament (its bishop, of course, sat in the House of Lords) – whereas members were granted to Calais during a general overhaul of its government and organisation, to Wales in the course of turning the principality into a part of the normal shire structure, and to Cheshire because some influential people there did not want to be left out. Ireland, of course, had its own Parliament, a fact which neatly symbolised its separateness – a lordship under the English king but no part of the crown of England, and from 1541 a second kingdom vested in the king of England. It seems likely that Thomas Cromwell entertained hopes of abolishing the Dublin Parliament and incorporating the second island in the one unitary state, which was his constitutional concept, but like most Englishmen throughout history he, too, failed to make a success of his Irish policy.

Thus the Parliament at Westminster certainly signified the unity of the realm and nation of England, but it needs to be shown that the sign and symbol actually worked in overcoming localism and sectionalism, so as to give substance to a national self-consciousness. It must be said that hitherto dominant views of the Parliament in the sixteenth and seventeenth centuries do not really lend support to such an interpretation. After all, it has been customary to regard Parliament, and especially the House of Commons, as the opponent of monarchy (that symbol of the nation), as the counterweight to the king's rule, the embodiment of all sorts of divisions within the people. Some, content to accept the kings as the embodiment of nationhood, have read Parliament as representing purely sectional interests detrimental to a sense of nationhood. Other historians have emphasised the fact that elections reflected local power and the battles of local factions; people, we learn, came to Parliament to serve specifically sectional interests. Whether the members of the Commons regarded themselves as the champions of the localities, or as the guardians of alleged liberties against royal encroachment, they would in either case have taken away from a common feeling of that English identity that looked to the monarchy as its symbol. Thus, while kings called Parliaments in order to bring the whole nation together in one place, the outcome seemed to show that instead they thereby encouraged entrenched feelings of local identity and sectional self-interest. Did the Parliament in fact offer an inducement to men from Devon and from Yorkshire to think of themselves as all one people?

I must here ask leave to interpose a brief summary of the present state of parliamentary studies. This is necessary because widely familiar and seemingly well founded views have quite recently been just about totally overthrown by a new look at what happened – and indeed a first proper look at the sources. The interpretation of such scholars of the last generation as Sir John Neale and Wallace Notestein – an interpretation which in essentials continued a tradition of historical perversions first put forward by the victorious parties of the seventeenth century – have quite amazingly collapsed before the more scholarly and dispassionate investigations of the last ten or fifteen years. This may sound like no more than promotion of self at the expense of scholars no longer with us, but in fact it has come to be accepted as the replacement of legend by something much nearer the truth. The news has not yet spread widely outside the Anglo-Saxon community (and encounters resistance in that hotbed of reactionary prejudice, the United States), for which reason it needs to be announced on every possible occasion! It also, however, bears on the theme of this paper.[4]

---

[4] A comparison of the section on Parliament in the first (1960) and second (1982) editions of *Tudor Constitution* will best show the transformation in understanding that has happened to this topic. The second edition also lists the relevant writings that have so far

The old view regarded king and Parliament as separate and commonly counterpoised aspects of the constitutional framework as well as the political scene: we remember Otto Hintze's famous definition of the *Ständestaat* in which ruler and assembly balance each other, a definition quite disastrously misleading at least so far as England is concerned. The old view neglected the House of Lords, which it regarded as a mere tool in the monarch's hands, and it concentrated attention on the alleged rise to pre-eminence of the House of Commons as the political instrument of opposition to the crown. All this, of course, was supposed to explain the events from 1640 onwards when two sets of people somewhat misleadingly termed king and Parliament came to clash in a civil war – an explanation which has turned out to be so inadequate that some of us wonder whether there really was a civil war since its famous causes have all disappeared. That old view was so much taken for granted – it seemed so obviously right – that its foundations were never tested or even argued: one simply knew that Parliament (that is, the Commons) mattered and functioned correctly when it came into conflict with the crown over issues of principle. Those conflicts had to arise from basic differences concerning the constitution and be fuelled by religious division. Such comfortably ancient views have had a hard time when it began to be seen that legitimate debate did not equal conflict, and (worse) that apparent occasions of battles between king and Commons really reflected rival lines of policy and interest pursued inside the king's government. As soon as people began to question the unconscious assumptions underlying the old convictions and to give proper attention to evidence that had been either ignored or manifestly tailored to a purpose, that whole structure vanished like the shadow it was.

Let me summarise the main results that have led to the demolition of this old view and to such drastic rethinking.

(1) From at least the 1530s the king was regarded as a member (the head) of the Parliament which structurally included him. He should not be seen standing outside and over against it: if there was conflict or even disagreement, it took place within one institution, one arena of political debate, and not between separate elements of the constitution.

(2) It follows that Parliament was in fact a part of the king's government. This should always have been obvious since only a royal summons could bring Parliament into existence, and only the mistaken concentration on expressions of protest ever obscured a fact which

appeared; but see especially G. R. Elton, 'Parliament in the sixteenth century: functions and fortunes', above, vol. III, no. 35.

remains central to the English Parliament from its early days to the present: like other courts and departments of the state's machinery, it is in the first place an instrument of the crown used in the government of the realm.

(3) The House of Lords mattered greatly. Not only did it contain the recognised social superiors of the members who sat in the Lower House but it played a far more weighty political role. Much of the work of the institution was done there, and the Lords generally led even in all those advances of procedure which had been misinterpreted as the means by which the Commons supposedly acquired independence and power.

(4) Leadership in the House of Commons belonged to what one may call the official element – Speaker, privy councillors, and other members whom we have learned to call the men of business. Far too much importance had been assigned to occasional protesters like Peter Wentworth, whom the House ignored or silenced. Looked at more closely, all those so-called oppositions and their arguments turned into legitimate debate over means rather than ends; supposed leaders of opposition turned into privy councillors continuing the disagreements of the Council Board, or into men anxious to impress their usefulness on the government, that is to say into careerists who quite often achieved their ambitions in this way. The Elizabethan classic case is that of Thomas Norton, whom Neale regarded as the champion of a Puritan opposition but who in fact, as he himself once stated, worked throughout in the interests of queen and Council to promote official policies.

(5) The primary concern of Parliament – the reason for which it was called and the work demanded of it by monarch and nation alike – was not political but legislative: it authorised taxation and it made laws. This function it could exercise only if all disputes ended in sufficient harmony to secure the consent of all three partners, and the operations of Parliament were therefore governed not by confrontation but by managerial devices designed to produce such consent. Differences of opinion, which of course existed, represented not conflict but the hammering out of agreement.

On this occasion I obviously cannot work out these points and all their implications, but in any case, surely, on reflection they cease to be especially surprising. Why should anyone either summon or attend a Parliament unless holding it would prove useful? And usefulness implied sufficient agreement to secure productive results. Trouble-makers, so far as they existed, got their usual reward: sighs of impatience at all that wasting of time, or, if they persisted, verbal slaps which freed the road to getting on with business. Parliament was the occasion when people brought problems and needs (technically called grievances, a term which has caused much misunderstanding) from the localities to the centre and tried to get them solved and satisfied. If the issues were general enough to have a political implication, the Parliament would find itself discussing politics (as for instance the problem of Mary Stuart in 1572, or the Union of England and Scotland in 1606), and such discussion would be useful to the government who, generally speaking, raised them in the first place. Such discussions fulfilled a purpose similar to the granting of taxes in Parliament: they informed the nation of the problems confronting government, and they solicited its agreement in what was being done. Insofar as Parliament acted as a political institution it did so because from the crown's point of view it was politically more sensible, indeed more successful, to proceed by debate and managerial tactics than by order and edict. Manifestly, therefore, this kind of Parliament – involving all the governing sort in the business of ruling – fulfilled the role of a national instrument overcoming particularism, and it fulfilled it very well.

However, the chief function of this institution touched the making of laws. That is what people wanted from it, whether we are looking at the Privy Council anxious to obtain an extension of the treason law, at leatherworkers anxious to protect their interests against shoemakers, or at the town of Ipswich anxious to take powers to pave its streets. The range of legislative concerns was enormous; historians have done harm by their inclination to set up hierarchies of importance in the laws passed. Acts of great national significance often took up markedly less parliamentary time than arguments over an enclosure bill or over a bill transferring the seat of the local assizes from one town in the shire to another; and from the point of view of the people involved in Parliament, more particularly those charged with getting business forward, the length of time taken signified more than a possible historical impact in a measure. The number of proposals seeking promotion and passage was large. In the first half of Elizabeth's reign parliamentary sessions averaged about ten weeks in length. Each session saw something like 110 bills put into one House or the other of which an average of about 35 succeeded in passing. Failure to do so could arise from many causes, but lack of time stood high among them. However diligently the hard-core of members who troubled to attend actually worked, the queen's preference for short sessions killed more bills than did disputes over them, high-minded or self-interested.

Still, it was a respectable harvest, of a very mixed sort. Here it is important to realise that acts of Parliament were of two kinds – either public or private. Public acts were those printed at the end of a session; private acts remained unprinted. The two kinds differed in other, highly technical, ways: thus private acts could not be alleged in a law-suit without the production of a copy bought from the clerk of the House of Lords and certified by him, and private bills paid fees to the officers of both Houses during passage which were not exacted on public bills. Private bills and acts were thus a significant source of income to the clerical staff of Parliament. But the two kinds of acts in no way differed in authority. Both were made by the supreme legislature of the realm, received the assent of Commons, Lords and king, and could not be altered or repealed except by another act of Parliament. Both were thus equally the work of Parliament in the fullest sense of that phrase. But on this occasion private acts deserve special attention. They are, it seems, a peculiarity of the English Parliament, being unknown, for instance, even in the Parliaments of Ireland and Scotland with their lawmaking powers. They served the purposes of a locality or an individual: in 1607 the Speaker laid it down that for a bill to be private it must not affect more than three counties. Legislation by private act enabled a guild to govern itself, protected monopolistic interest in trade or manufacture, empowered a municipality or a county to levy money needed for such local purposes as the building of bridges, the repair of houses, the setting up of schools, or the paving of streets. Private acts also settled problems in the affairs of individuals: they naturalised children born to English parents living abroad, they repealed attainders that affected the rights of persons descended from an executed traitor, they confirmed deals in property, they secured the jointures of wives and widows, they protected inventions and they clarified last wills and testaments. Legislation by private bill and act decanted the affairs of the localities into one central reservoir.

Thus, while taxation and public legislation generally speaking involved the men coming up from the country in the affairs of the nation, private matters of very particular concern similarly travelled up to London, there to be scrutinised and legitimated by a national institution – incidentally an institution which, with the judges in the Upper House and many lawyers in the Lower, contained large numbers of experts in the kind of problems raised. By making laws for the whole realm that demanded obedience from the whole realm, Parliament testified to the existence of a single nation, membership of which overrode sectional or local attachments. By making laws for sectional or local interests, Parliament directed these potentially separatist and disruptive concerns towards an instrument of government of which all the members of the nation were deemed to be part. And so that national self-consciousness of sixteenth-century Englishmen, loudly enough voiced in speech and writing, found practical entrenchment not only in the monarch and his glory but also in the Parliament and the laws it made for all.

56

THOMAS MORE AND
THOMAS CROMWELL*

There is little need to justify a public discourse on Thomas Cromwell; there is a certain amount of need to justify yet another one on Thomas More. Most of us have by now recovered from the searing experiences of his 500-year anniversary – which had to run for two years because an error occurred in the entry of the man's birthdate, thereby proving right from the beginning of his life that he was ambiguous and mysterious and incomprehensible. To talk about these two men jointly, however, needs perhaps a word of justification. Why should one? What is it really that puts them side by side into a context? I think it is not unfair nowadays, after the work that has been done in the last fifty years or so, to regard them in a way as the two poles of the earlier Reformation era; two men whose experience, personalities and contributions mark out the range of possibilities and of the actions, as well as the sufferings, that the age included. And it is in those terms that I would like to discuss them today: first, as representers, if you like, of the two really different possible lines, and second, but more particularly, as individuals, to see whether they are in any way representative of anything except themselves.

The first problem that one faces in this discourse, therefore, is the question of how well we know either Thomas More or Thomas Cromwell. Both pose certain problems in very different ways in this respect. More appears to be the best documented individual of the sixteenth century, excepting just possibly Queen Elizabeth. We have biographies, we have his letters (or some part of his letters), we have his writings, and so forth. Now, what we have is the traditional picture of More, which was in fact created after his death. If you want to understand the biography of Thomas More, the first thing you have to grasp is that the conventional More was deliberately put together in the 1550s by More's family, in readiness for the canonisation which they thought would soon be coming – though it was then delayed by nearly four hundred years.

* [*Reformation, Humanism, and 'Revolution'*, ed. G. Schochet (Washington, 1990), 95–110.] This unscripted address is printed as delivered [in 1985], with a few minor amendments. 'Alistair' refers to Alistair Fox; 'John' refers to John Guy.

Roper's very influential *Life*, originally conveyed through Harpsfield but ultimately printed in the nineteenth century by itself, is a long-distance memory, selected and informed by a particular state of mind. Harpsfield, of course, more so than the rest of the biographers of the day – whose purpose has to be understood before they can be interpreted – really based himself upon this particular treatise with the addition of dubious family memories, invented anecdotes and suchlike. What seems to support the Roper tradition are the two famous letters of Erasmus, one to Hutten, one to Faber, respectively in 1519 and in 1532, in which Erasmus describes his friend and close acquaintance to two people who didn't know him. More precisely, one didn't know him at all and the other knew him only as a writer. These seem to confirm Roper's picture of More as a great and good man, never in a fume, kindly to everybody, fond of monkeys. (I've never quite understood why the hero worshippers of More don't go further into the detail of his menagerie and arboretum, which he set up at Chelsea.) That is the hero of the tradition which finally culminates in R. W. Chambers's disastrous biography, in Robert Bolt's more disastrous play, and in Margaret Durer's biographical enterprise. (Those of you who have had occasion to read it will know better.)

So the More figure that we have always been presented with is deliberately and artificially created. This is very important to remember. The created More may nevertheless be a true one. But it is one which historians have had to accept at second hand from people who had an end to pursue, who were not trying to write history, but who were trying to prepare for a canonization. It is their anticipatory 'Saints' Lives', those early books, which have so greatly influenced the later ones.

I don't know how many of you have recently re-read Chambers. It is quite extraordinary to read it now, to think that in 1935 this was regarded as a really major biography. Chambers, of course, suffered from one particular fervour – weakness, I suppose – or lack – for which he is not really responsible. He was not an historian. He was a professor of English at the University College and got his history from J. E. Neale. This is a combination of disasters which is very difficult to get over.

Now, we have some means of controlling this artificial More, to see whether they got him right or not; we have, for instance, his writings. They were never properly analysed until Alistair's book came out. Alistair really tried for once to take the whole corpus into account and to make sense of it, which is why so many of the traditionalists have found that book unacceptable. More's correspondence also has its uses. Indeed, it is very useful and some of it is clearly perfectly easily used. But then, some of the most important of More's letters do not survive in manuscript. The famous ones from the Tower, if not addressed to Henry VIII or Cromwell, were addressed to the family and survived only in the printing that the family produced in the 1550s; we do not know what the family did to them. Indeed, we do not even know whether they had them. Margaret Roper died in 1544. (Well, it was always believed she died in 1544, but about two years ago I received a very curious book, from a lady whose name I have forgotten now, which was full of a careful argument, according to which Shakespeare's sonnets in fact represent an epistolary exchange between Sir Thomas and his daughter Margaret. Therein, Margaret did not die in 1544, but lived on under the name of Alexander Alesius, usually moved in drag, and finished up by writing the first version of *Hamlet*. I acknowledged the receipt of this book. The letter that accompanied it said – I had to agree – that if she was right, history would have to be rewritten. I wrote back and said that that was certainly true, but that there were certain difficulties. And I cited a few; I hastened to add that she had more work to do. That was fortunately the last of that one. I only cite this fascinating story to show how madness can prevail even amongst great ones. I would warn you not to get yourselves involved with Baconians.) But Margaret died in 1544. If her husband, William Roper, kept the letters, which is very likely, then no doubt he used them. To be certain of those letters, we really have very little to go on except internal evidence: tone, voice, style and suchlike.

This, however, is a position of relative superabundance and a great deal more preferable to the position touching Thomas Cromwell. For Cromwell we have no evidence at all, really, except the evidence of public action. We do have, of course, some comments of the time, the attack by Reginald Pole, in *De Unitate* and the *Apologia* to Charles V, things of that kind, and a few remarks from the generality preserved in this or that state paper. From his own pen, however, we have only correspondence of an official kind or public life kind, drafts of acts, and things of that sort. He has to be reconstructed, therefore, from his deeds, which is not actually the most satisfactory way of getting at the psychology of a person or the reality of a person. Action may well reflect a man, but if you try to reconstruct a man from his actions only you are liable to be influenced by the accidents of that action. It is a very difficult thing to do. One reason why I haven't done what I have always been asked to do, which is to write a biography of Cromwell, is that he is not biographable. We know absolutely nothing about him until he was about thirty-five. Even without Freud, one would regard the first ten years as important in a person's development. And after that we have only this very limited light. We could be right about Cromwell's work, but a biography would be an absurdity.

So we start off, in comparing these two people, with very different backgrounds of fact and information. Neither is easy or straightforward, in different ways: too much about More, and some of it known to have been manufactured for a reason; far too little about Cromwell. There are two terrible brief sentences in the record of the early sixteenth century. One occurs in Archdeacon Harpsfield's *Life of More*. He is speaking of Antonio Bonvisi, a Genoese merchant resident in London, who knew, as he tells us, both More and Cromwell very well; he had told Harpsfield many interesting stories of these two men, but 'that is not to our present purpose'. You will understand from this story why the Middle Ages doubted whether archdeacons actually could be saved. The other one occurs in Sanuto's diaries, when the Venetian ambassador to London returns to Venice in 1535 and makes his report. Everything is fairly carefully recorded. One sentence reads: '... and then the said Master Orator spoke about the said Lord Cromwell'. Period. There has been a conspiracy to keep Cromwell in obscurity and darkness; this is the challenge that made me seize upon the manifest factor of his importance in the record and do something about it. But whenever one gets near the personality, where one might have heard something really illustrative, the curtain falls.

Well, leaving aside these difficulties – or, rather, remembering them in the following attempt to make something of these two people – let us first look at the fact that the similarities in their lives and careers are really rather striking. Cromwell and More knew one another well before the troubles of the thirties. They were both Londoners, if you allow a man who was born in Putney to be essentially a Londoner in due course. They were both lawyers (well, I think you could say they were). And both in their lives and work expressed a spectacular and manifest concern with the state of the commonweal and its need for reform. One thing that separates them very clearly is social class. More came from the ranks of the prosperous London bourgeoisie, from a legal family (I don't know who it was who persuaded Erasmus that the English aristocracy were all descended from lawyers, but evidently the Mores were proud of their legal ancestry). He had a straightforward educational career, especially at Oxford and Lincoln's Inn (leaving out the four idiot years during which he tried to stay in the Carthusian monastery). He had a very easy, prosperous, straightforward career upward in his profession as a lawyer and judge; he finished as lord chancellor of England, which, after all, was and still is in a way the top job in terms of repute and then in terms of money as well. I won't go over the grounds again for persuading you that More wasn't so indifferent to worldly wealth as his admirers have suggested. He certainly wasn't enriching himself overwhelmingly, but he was doing all right. That estate at Chelsea was a comfortable, happy, well-organised household.

Cromwell was the son of a man who was best described as perhaps an alehouse keeper, perhaps a woolworker, but apparently also a drunkard. But fathers' drunkennesses do not need to be visited upon sons' heads. For reasons that remain obscure, Cromwell spent a part of his early life in travels in Europe, which took him as far as Italy. It is said that he served in the Imperial Army in Italy. By 1514 he turned up in Antwerp; before that he was found in Rome; and he got into mercantile activities. He obviously had no kind of a start in life, not that secure and comfortable kind of start that we find with More. Indeed, in the twentieth century, with its passion for equality and its dislike of the elite, Cromwell ought to be a much admired character compared with that middle-class character, More. Thereafter, he made his own career as well by hard work as, evidently, by brains, by attaching himself to Wolsey at a very early date, much earlier than used to be supposed. Cromwell picked Wolsey out as the man of the future (or else Wolsey picked Cromwell out as the man of the future), certainly by about 1514 and probably even earlier. Cromwell then became a man-of-all-work to Wolsey. But how he acquired some understanding of the law, we do not know. His admission to Gray's Inn in 1524 was probably a matter of honour rather than a piece of training. Incidentally, this in itself is a kind of symbol of the future. Lincoln's Inn remained for a long time a hotbed of popery. It was only Burghley who in the end cleaned it up and made the lawyers conform. It was More's family, actually, it was the Ropers, who kept it on the straight and narrow path. Gray's Inn was the inn of the reformed lawyers. So you get even in this particular detail, wherein these two were connected, a foretaste of the future. And, of course, Cromwell finally made his career in the royal service, which we needn't go into now.

Cromwell worked his way up from nowhere, and More worked his way steadily along the top reaches, but in the end they met on the same level. The similarities are, therefore, not uninteresting. We have people who both, in many ways, have ultimately the same background and training, especially the background of the City of London. But More is the natural Londoner; Cromwell is the immigrant Londoner – immigrant not only in fact, but in spirit. More is the obvious lawyer, the common lawyer of full training and so forth, who makes a profitable career in the law. Roper tells us he was making £400 a year at the law before he took office under the crown. If that is true, then he must have been an extremely rich lawyer, because, according to Ives's latest calculations about what a lawyer could make in this time, he got at least twice as much as the norm. Now I wouldn't pin Roper down to a figure like that, but that is what he says. Those are the similarities.

Now, if we were to try to identify what it is that really ultimately forms the mind, the character, the personality of Thomas More, we might begin with the idea that he was a humanist. Yes, of course, he was a humanist – until a certain day. I think he ceased to be a humanist in any very real sense about 1521, when he started getting worried about the Lutherans. And to think of him as a man still concerned with reform of a humanistic kind or with the study of good letters and suchlike thereafter strikes me as unconvincing. I have come to the conclusion, assisted, I would say, by Alistair's book, that More's humanism was, like so much else about him, rather adolescent. It was something he grew out of. He played with good letters, and he was good at it, and he enjoyed it. He saw the virtue of an education along these lines, but I don't think he was ever serious in the way that Erasmus or Erasmus's real followers were, that Vives was, or even those humanists who served the Emperor Charles V in his court were, and so on. It is probably saying too much to suggest that it was a game for him; it was a bit more than that. But it was a phase that he got over. I am sure his father was very pleased when he did get over it, and said, 'Oh well, the boy is out of that phase at least.' And after that, his humanism seems to me to be of little relevance to his behaviour, his beliefs, or his reactions.

What really seems to be dominant in Thomas More is a deeply passionate, though entirely practical and unmystical, religiosity: an appreciation of the fate of man, that impossible challenge of Christianity which speaks of a merciful God and experiences nothing but a merciless life. And this was one of More's major concerns throughout his career, throughout his life. How can you retain the love of God when all you get in return is disaster, destruction, disease and death? You cope with it, as we know he did in the end, greatly assisted by imprisonment in the Tower. But, to me at least, it is the only really continuous and enduring

149

strand in his thinking and his intellectual and moral makeup. It is not the Christianity of the twentieth century or of the nineteenth century. It is very much a late medieval Christianity, in which hell is probably the dominant element. It should never be forgotten about More that he could not ever surrender on the issue of the royal supremacy as long as he believed that to do so would mean burning in hell for all eternity. And I wish you to visualise this as a reality. This is not a metaphor. This is real: eternal pains for the ultimate sin. This is what More was facing and what he lasted out, hoping to die in the Tower before they could actually inflict anything further on him. But, unless you grasp that, you get More entirely wrong. He was not a liberal humanist; he was not John Paul II. He was a late medieval, very conventional believer in all the essentials.

As a theologian, he was late starting; it was only in the twenties that he began to equip himself with theological training. He did pretty well considering the time he had. Though it would be absurd to compare him with Luther as a theologian, or with Melancthon, or even certainly, I think, with Erasmus, nevertheless he had a quick mind. He was a good study, as they say in the law, and he picked up a great deal of the straightforward, conventional theology of the later Middle Ages without much difficulty. But it is that kind of Christianity we are talking about in which the other world is the only thing that matters. This world has no reality. Life after death is governed by behaviour in this life which is a preparation for it, nothing else, and which must therefore be filled with good and righteous conduct. It is not a moral issue but an issue of beliefs. It is not a matter of being good to people, kind to people, or patting dogs on the head. It is a question of not committing a sin which leaves you in hell for all eternity. That religion, I think, is the essence of Thomas More, and, as you know, in my opinion, his standard in these matters was very largely arrived at from his consciousness of original sin, because he had not been able to follow the call to abandon the flesh. I have said this before and I have described More as a sex maniac, but this is exaggerating a little. Certainly, though, he was obsessed with it.

Now, if we turn to Thomas Cromwell, well, there, of course, we face the problem that we don't know enough about him. Nevertheless, if one goes by what we do know about him and can learn about him, he appears to have been shaped by his experience; more so than More in many ways, whose mind was essentially formed by that failure to enter the Charterhouse. Thomas Cromwell's whole being was that of a public man, a man of action in public affairs. If he really did carry a pike at the battle of wherever it was (I have forgotten now which battle it was supposed to have been), it would have been very typical, I think. He was a man who translated experience into action, action into experience. He did things. He didn't only think about them. He did them, though, with a very practical and very decisive and clear-cut mind. Cutting of corners came easily to him, as did speed of action.

All of this grows out of the experience of a young man barely out of his boyhood, drifting about an alien continent, acquiring the languages. He certainly spoke Italian and some French and he could understand Latin, but, I think, when Richard Morison tried him on Greek, that was a bit too much. He acquired an understanding of the European scene in which he was reasonably exceptional even amongst the English diplomats because he had seen it from the bottom up. He hadn't gone to the courts. He had gone into the company houses and, perhaps, into the field of battle; he had been learning it from below. That seems to me to have been an important element in his formation. He transmuted these experiences into the activities that made him so useful to Wolsey and later to Henry VIII.

He wasn't – and this is where the tradition, of course, goes wrong – he wasn't simply an agent or a competent, able executor of other people's ideas. I would no longer stand quite by the picture I presented thirty years and some ago, in which Cromwell is the *éminence grise* of everything. I now think that he was the *éminence grise* of about 98 per cent. But even that is exaggerated a little. What he did have, it seems clear to me, was an intellectualising mind. That is to say that when faced with tasks he was not content with a simple, practical answer to this or that which produced an immediate solution to a problem, got it out of the way for the moment, got the fire buried under a pile of other fires, or that sort of thing. He searched out the fundamentals of issues and questions and attempted to provide a fundamentally based solution for them.

He had a powerfully twentieth-century mind in one respect: he liked statistical information. He would have loved a minicomputer. He would have been at home with a word processor. (All of which are things, and I must emphasise it, that are not reflected in me. I do not have a minicomputer. I do not want to use a word processor, and those who have maintained either that I created Cromwell in my own image or that I am in fact Cromwell reincarnate, are proved wrong by this very fact.) Cromwell was a systematiser of information and used that systematised information for the production of fundamentally based solutions to problems.

And then, in this respect, he was fairly unusual even amongst sixteenth-century statesmen: he pursued the solution that he had arrived at with an extraordinary tenacity in the face of all sorts of difficulties, which of course was in the end the cause of his fall. He could have abandoned some of his policies if he had wanted to and could have saved his life after 1539. But, once convinced of a particular line, he pursued it with every kind of determination. He was not in fact nearly as pragmatic as people have supposed. I have sometimes regretted that he wasn't, that he did have his ideals and principles, and that he did serve these ideals and principles even unto death.

In that respect he was very much like More, even though the principles and convictions and causes and ideals were different. They were both determined men who did not give up. The main difference in this respect was that Cromwell's not giving up meant action in the state, and More's not giving up in the end, for reasons I will come back to in a moment, meant not giving way on his own behalf. As far as the state of the realm was concerned, More's basic principle seems to me to have been the law – the law as it was, the law as it stood, the law modified by equitable principles and considerations, but not really a law that was dynamic and reformable – whilst Cromwell manifestly had a very powerful belief in the power of Parliament to create new law and thereby to alter the conditions in which men lived and worked and suffered in the realm of England.

There is a kind of static quality about More's attitude to public life, whereas Cromwell's is powerfully dynamic. This goes together again with More's form of religion, which is in a sense very static. More was not an innovator. People seem to think that More owned a great original mind in affairs and in everything. The one original thing he really did was to produce writings in which a kind of poetic originality expressed itself. This is certainly the case of *Utopia*, in which there is nothing really original in the substance, but a great deal of poetic originality in the exposition and in the penumbra that builds around that mysterious and infuriating book which More was deliberately creating by means of this penumbra. He was not original in his theology; anything but. He was not original in his scholarship; compared with Erasmus, he was nowhere. His was essentially, and I am not saying this as a term of abuse, an unoriginal mind. Not a copycat, but an unoriginal mind, a mind that was content with things as they were.

Now, with Cromwell we have the opposite. More – you may, if you like, psychologise on this – was a man who had a comfortable early life and so didn't need to think about change. A man who experienced Cromwell's early life would like to improve things, if only for himself, but in the process also for others. Cromwell was, therefore, potentially a revolutionary, if by revolutionary we mean someone who wishes to change the structure and the effect, in toto and in detail, of the given commonweal in which he happens to work. More's reaction to all problems was 'stare super vias antiquas'. Cromwell's was 'What's the best line for the way forward' – there is no Latin tag to match. So they were men of very similar concerns with totally different reactions to those concerns.

Cromwell's religion remains in many ways difficult to pinpoint, and people will continue to vary upon this. I would say only that his own statement, which was recorded by some Lutheran envoys when he spoke to them, was that he would be inclined to think in their way, if other things were equal, but that as the world now stood, he would believe even as his master the king believed. It is a typical Cromwell joke, but with a lot of truth in it. That incident showed that Cromwell as well as More had a sense of humour, but that it differed from More's in one respect. All mankind may in certain respects be divided into the prurient and the Puritan. More was prurient; Cromwell was a Puritan. Cromwell violently objected to *risqué* jokes; More loved them. I am not going to ask you to decide between the two of them here and now, in case you give yourselves away.

But Cromwell's and More's reactions to the possibilities that life offered seem to me to be profoundly in contradistinction. They were, in other words, built to be people who would clash. They were bound to be in conflict. If there had been happier times, if the thing hadn't been quite as it was, More would, of course, have continued as lord chancellor and been one of the great statesmen of the age: Wolsey, Gattinara, More, Cardinal Pole perhaps, and so on and so forth. Cromwell would probably have continued as a very useful but ineffective man, because it needed a break with Rome and it needed Henry VIII's great change of tack to open the door to his revolutionary temperament. But as it was, of course, things went otherwise.

In normal times, the two of them could have agreed. They played bowls together in Rastell's garden. Back in an earlier time, they could still have played bowls for a little while or had a drink together, and Thomas Cromwell would have looked down his nose at some of the jokes that More would have made at the time. But I think probably More might have regarded Cromwell as a bit dull. They respected one another, incidentally, right to the end; and Cromwell never wanted More's death, if only because it was a disastrously bad move – a typical Henry VIII move. Henry VIII was the biggest procrastinator around; but he had, like all the Tudors, violent rushes of blood to the head. He lost control at fairly frequent intervals, as indeed did his daughters. We don't know too much about the son, but Edward VI would, I think, have been much the worst of the Tudors had he lived. England has been blessed in the death of its sovereigns.

With that rush of blood to the head, More was condemned. But that wasn't Cromwell's intention at all. As for his religion, the innovation suited him; he had no love for priests. He was, if you like, an anticlerical, a term that would need a lot of discussing. He disliked especially the snuffing pride of them, according to Edward Hall. He was fairly contemptuous of bishops. He saw through the pretences of the late medieval church, the contradictions of much of its behaviour and much of its preaching. He was not inclined, like More, to return to the Middle Ages or to enter a monastery, but rather to cope with the fact that the church had diverged so far from the alleged intentions of its founder, by becoming some kind of copy of the founder in a monastic institution. Instead, he found the Protestant proposal, if you like, to desecularise the world, actually to spiritualise the world. I think that was probably Luther's real purpose. Cromwell found that attractive, which is to say that he believed in God, he had a faith. It was not over-ardent. It did not dictate all his actions, but it was there quite strongly. He was not an atheist. He couldn't be. Nobody at the time really could be, if you supposed that the universe existed. If it existed, it must have come into existence somehow; and until natural science came to the aid, a creator was a necessary precondition. Cromwell was a Christian, but I think he was the sort of Christian that one could live with. I don't think More was.

Now, as regards their respective work in the state and in the commonwealth, I don't think I need to elaborate here. I just want to summarise. All I have said about their characters and purposes seems to me to be borne out by what happened. More had a long career in public life. The upshot of his rising through offices, earning good money, and probably exercising more influence as an adviser around the king than we know (because that would not have got into the record), was that he stood well with King Henry. This was not only because the king liked his amusing conversation, which was amusing, as Roper tells us, to the point where More pretended to be more stupid than he was in order to get home once in a while. No, Henry liked and respected him. This is why he came to hate him so much after. But yet, whatever influence he had seems to have been fairly slight. The policies that so far as we know he wished to pursue – peace abroad and attacks on heresy at home – were not the policies of Cardinal Wolsey and did not ever make themselves felt in time. So, while it was a long career, there wasn't really much to show for it in the end. It is true that in the short time he had as a judge in the Chancery he did a good deal of work to anchor the developments which were largely Wolsey's own, as John Guy has shown. But then he spent two and a half very frustrating years desperately trying to fight politics within the Council and outside it in print, to arrest the rapid run down the slope towards the schism with Rome, which was from his point of view the last and total disaster.

In other words, at the time when he should have been most powerful he was a leader of opposition – a leader of opposition against an overwhelming, powerful flood on the other side. He scored some successes. He held things up for a while. But it was not a role for which he was very naturally qualified, nor was it a role which would have satisfied him. And he was very glad to get out of it in those last years when he devoted himself to his private salvation, as he would explain, in certain action and deed. He did not do so quite as quickly as he said he did, because at first the old Adam continued to gyrate around. More was a man of considerable passion. He was not a quiet man. He was a man who exploded on surprising occasions. His attack on Dorp, for instance, rather distressed Erasmus. He belonged to that not unfamiliar type who is not as good a scholar as perhaps he should be and, therefore, is very, very touchy indeed on the subject of possible defects in his scholarship, or in the scholarship, in this case, of his friend. I could cite you examples, but I won't trouble with that.

Cromwell, on the other hand, had a career which was shorter in years, but which was one of immense activity, positive activity, creative activity. This is not to say that you have to like what he created, just that it was very creative indeed and was cut short, very suddenly, prematurely, in the middle of a large programme of further reform. Cromwell, the reforming mind, got his opportunity, certainly from 1533 on, or perhaps even a little earlier, and took it with both hands. So far as I can see, it was Cromwell's plan – there was a plan. He was a man who looked ahead. In the first place, he needed to create that unitary state which would give England an inner dynamic under the crown and under the law which could then lead to improvement and development in both church and state, religion and matters social. This meant what we normally call the Henrician Reformation: a break from Rome, the setting up of the royal supremacy, and the gradual subjection of that supremacy to a parliamentary supremacy. This last included the king. It called for the enforcement of that new state upon a realm which needed to accept the political transformation before there could be any prospect of a genuine reformation – call it what you will – a change in the nature of the religion that the country practised. This took a long time, but in fact even Cromwell got somewhere with it in his short ascendancy.

Besides getting that straight, Cromwell united the realm in various other ways – the incorporation of Wales and his attempts to incorporate Ireland. He was neither the first nor the last English statesman who found that success was relatively easy everywhere except in Ireland. Some of that arises simply from the existence of St George's Channel, I may say. Do not please project Daniel O'Connell and everything that came thereafter back into the sixteenth century. In any case, having got his unitary state and having got a dynamically powerful social structure with a weapon which could express purpose – a weapon of attack, the Parliament with its lawmaking powers properly organised – Cromwell then attempted to promote various reforms, most of which had been expected or wanted by other people, too. He collected anybody's proposals, some silly, some good; some he worked up, some he could do nothing with, some he would do nothing with; some were sensible, some were hopeless – no reform regime has yet succeeded in choosing only sensible reform. For instance, the attempt to enforce price fixing in the sixteenth century was obviously idiotic, but he persisted with it. And he wished then to roll forward with programmes of this kind of reform. In 1540 he was cut off, and the reform hadn't got very far. I have myself no doubt whatsoever, however, that the programme was in existence, that it was there in Cromwell's mind and in the minds of the group he had got around himself, and that the king had very little to do with it, if anything. The evidence that Cromwell did many things without the king's knowledge, ahead of the king's state of mind, does not need reciting, because it was the cause of his death. I won't say he would still be alive today had he not done that, but he would have lived out a natural span of probably another twenty years. That would have been a very interesting phenomenon, actually.

So as far as the work is concerned, these two who were so alike were finally very different, in the sense that More could not do very much, as it turned out. Cromwell could start a great deal, but the only thing he did finish was the creation of that single realm of England under the crown, the law and the Parliament. Now, if we look at the effect of these two people, I think a very interesting difference arises. Cromwell was obviously, immediately, very effective. What he started became the essential character of the English state and commonwealth, certainly down to the civil war and, in some ways, down to the nineteenth century. I am not thinking just of such things as administrative reform, but of the notions of an active commonwealth, repairing itself, reforming itself, mending what is wrong in the realm, in the state of the poor, in the state of the rich, in the state of the wicked, in the state of the good. I am thinking of a constantly socially active commonweal, which you find in the reign of Elizabeth, which you find attempted very strongly by Charles I, which is there in the Restoration period, and which is right through the eighteenth century a principle upon which government is conducted, although not often very effectively. All of this really goes back to those Reformation-era plans that we associate with Thomas Cromwell. In a way, if you want to be quite extravagant, Cromwell was the first architect of the welfare state. And if you know my views on this subject, you would agree that this is a concession from someone who respects Cromwell.

More had no immediate effect at all. In England, he was almost immediately forgotten. Very occasionally we get reports that show that his death had caused some anger and anguish in the realm. The Pilgrimage of Grace was certainly linked with the destruction of Thomas More. But there is no great outburst of rage or anything like that – nothing like, for instance, what happened over the executions during Mary's reign. He doesn't appear to have been read all that much in his time. *Utopia* was not translated into English until 1551. By the reign of Elizabeth it is, however, a rather well-known book, so much so that John Foxe, who didn't like More, can make fun of it. The play of *Sir Thomas More* is something that I wish the Moreans would explain to me. It's a daft play; it's not much good. It's an anecdotal play. It enshrines a memory of Thomas More as the great friend of the people and a wise and witty man. In fact, his own jokes are a great deal better than those of the play, which are absolutely dreadful. Perhaps you can suggest somebody who might like to follow this up.

Then again, because of the Roper family, the life of More was almost processed. You know, there are people who think that Bacon wrote not only Shakespeare, but all the poetry down to Tennyson. They believe that in order not to overwhelm his own age with it all, he left it to his disciples, the Rosicrucians, with instructions that left them to dole out things that eventually became ascribed to Herbert, to Wordsworth and Shelley and Byron, and all the rest of them. And you can prove all of it, I assure you. Well, it looks almost as though the Morean revival proceeded in that way, leaving a series of apparently independent biographies to be trotted out at regular intervals, repeating one another, Cressacre More and all the rest of them. So by the eighteenth century, More was back; it was especially Dr Johnson who preferred More and the old ways to the new ways. Nevertheless, it was really the second stage of the More revival that brought him into his present fame and that was the work of the opposite movement. It was the attack on the Reformation which began with the Tractarians that concentrated the mind on More.

There is a curious seesaw in the reputation of More and John Foxe: when More is up, Foxe is down, and vice versa. And until about the 1830s, on the whole Foxe was up and More was down. Foxe was believed; More, it was thought, was capable of perverting truth here and there. That switched, and from the work of S. R. Maitland onwards and other Tractarian products of the age, when the Church of England, or some of it, wished to return to the Mother Church, More became a hero, Foxe became decried. In actual balance, when it comes to a controversy, Foxe is more reliable than More; More did distort the truth. He was capable of lying, knowingly lying, I mean. He was certainly capable of colouring to quite a degree what he said. So was Foxe, though his lies are few and his colourings are more frequent, and he was a very much better historical researcher than More was. He put a lot more trouble into it, and he knew how to do it as well. He was not at all bad. He should have entered all of those discussions of Tudor historiography which concentrate on tedious people like Samuel Daniel, Holinshed, and which leave Foxe aside. The Lord knows why, and He isn't telling.

So from about the middle of the last century, More has been a figure of greatness in the history of England. His effect, therefore, is long distance. What that effect has been – well, insofar as it has produced a market in Moreana, it has been rather sad. Insofar as it has produced a very powerful series of studies of this man, of his ideas, his notions, his personality and so on, it is nothing but good. Though (if they will shut their ears for a moment) it is my considered view that until we had Alistair's and John's books, we were living in an aura of hagiography, of little virtue in the twentieth century. In other words, it is not unfair to say that the canonisation of 1935 is entirely accurate. More is now a saint, that is to say, he is not an historical character. And it is as a saint that he plays his current role, and that is a role he will continue to play.

The historical More is another story; he was in effect a failure. Now why was he a failure? This is the point. He was a man of great ability and a great mind. He was a failure because the times were against him. More cannot be understood unless you grasp that he came at the end of an age. Within ten years of Wolsey's fall, the world had changed to a quite fantastic degree. The 1520s and the 1540s are two different worlds, what with the Reformation; what with the progress of Charles V; what with the Turks; what with the splintering of that community of Christendom which, though More much exaggerated its existence, had some reality; what with the disappearance of that simple-minded community of scholars who never recognised reality when it hit them in the face, the Erasmians and their like. With all that gone and so altered, a world had come to an end – a world that in some ways goes back at least to the days of Innocent III. Of course, I am not saying that there has ever been a period in which no change occurred. But in this period the whole of the Middle Ages had vanished. What trailed thereafter trailed along by the sufferance of the new. And More belonged to that old world. In everything that really mattered, he was part of it. If you like, it is not unfair to say, he was a kind of last great creation of it. But the new world in all its detail was one that he could not cope with. Had he not had his religion, which made him so medieval, perhaps he could have. Although he was not an adaptable man, perhaps he could have. But, in view of the fact that his religion was what most manifestly had come to an end, it is not surprising to find that his life and his career in the end were empty – if not empty, at least very far from full and effective.

Cromwell, by a curious accident of nature at the very same time, was the very man for whom the new world was right, to whom the new world gave his chance, the man who could utilise, exploit, and promote what this new world was beginning to look like. The fact that the old world trailed its trailers, its spider's web, across the future – that was one reason why he died. He got caught by what was left of the old. And, of course, much of it was left for quite a long time, even till the present day in some respects.

Nevertheless, what makes these two people so very, very interesting is that they exemplify the clash of these two worlds, the dying and the being born, to such an extraordinary degree. If you want a judgement in the last resort, I, for one reason above all, will opt for Cromwell and his world. Both were men concerned about humanity as it lived on earth, and one of them was concerned very much about humanity as it lived after death. Both, however, had their vision of society, and More gave us a picture of it in *Utopia* as well as in other examples. It seems to me that there was no prospect in More's world of anything opening. The doors and windows were shut, the curtains drawn. That society had no prospect of freedom or even variety. It would have been constrained and constricted under a much more severe, more censorious, more affected because purer, spiritual control. That was the kind of church that More wanted. I am not saying that Cromwell was the kind of man who loved liberty. All I am saying is that the society that Cromwell stood at the birth of was the only one that in the end could provide us with the liberty which we are now defending.

[The works alluded to are: A. Fox, *Thomas More, History and Providence* (Oxford, 1982); E. W. Ives, *The Common Lawyers of Pre-Reformation England* (Cambridge, 1983); J. A. Guy, *The Public Career of Sir Thomas More* (Brighton, 1980).]

57

LANCELOT ANDREWES*

Four hundred years ago, the fellows of Pembroke College in Cambridge elected a new master. Their choice fell upon their treasurer, Lancelot Andrewes, only thirty-one years old but already highly regarded as a scholar and theologian. Newly elected, the master took off from Cambridge to pursue a highly successful career in the church, obtaining several livings in London and becoming dean of Westminster, a real plum and a very influential position. Only when, in 1606, he made it to the bench of bishops (his first see was that of Chichester) did he resign the mastership. Not that absentee masters were a new thing at Pembroke. From 1507 to 1519, the office had been held by Richard Foxe, bishop of Winchester and till 1516 keeper of the privy seal – one of the really active ministers of both Henry VII and Henry VIII. That quintessential Oxford man, founder of Corpus Christi College there, was presumably picked by the fellows of Pembroke as the right man to carry weight in high quarters, and it may be suspected that the unlikelihood of his turning up at the College added to his attractiveness. So far as we know, he never showed his face in Cambridge. In this respect, Andrewes did better – or, depending on what the fellowship had had in mind, worse. It would seem that he made a point during his mastership of regularly putting in at least one annual appearance, to attend the audit and to keep an eye on new admissions. However, this touch of modest concern did not alter the fundamental fact: the master of Pembroke lived in London, followed there the calling of a scholar and a divine, and once James I had succeeded Elizabeth on the throne made himself well known at court. His usefulness to the College no doubt increased as he gained friends and enlarged his acquaintance in the centres of influence, but it would be interesting to know how Pembroke operated in the master's absence.

In the thirty-seven years that followed upon his departure from Cambridge, Andrewes certainly made a name for himself. So far his life had been fairly typical for a scholar in the sixteenth century. Born in 1555, in the reign of Queen Mary, son to one described as a seafaring

* [*Pembroke College Cambridge Society, Annual Gazette*, 64 (1990), 22–35.]

man who seems to have leant to the new religion, he started his earthly existence with a mystery: how, living in Barking, did he acquire that aristocratic baptismal name? Did his mother spend the winter evenings reading Sir Thomas Mallory? Young Lancelot however, from the first made for the pen rather than the sword. He went to school at Merchant Taylors where he benefited from the instruction of Richard Mulcaster, the foremost schoolmaster of his day. His promise was evidently discerned quite early, and in 1571, sixteen years old, he came up to Pembroke, which he soon enough persuaded of his quality. More particularly, he proved to be a linguist of exceptional skill: he really enjoyed languages. The commentators have come to doubt the truth of the story that he commanded twelve or more of them, and it would indeed be difficult to compose such a tally. But that, apart from a perfect command of Latin and Greek, he knew Hebrew very well and was not ill-versed in Chaldaean is certain enough, and he made sure of acquiring also modern languages like French and Italian. We need not doubt his right to be thought an exceptionally learned young man, a fact first made publicly manifest when barely thirty old he proceeded to the degree of BD with a Latin thesis on usury, a practice which he rather delicately justified up to a point – 'etiam', as he said, 'lege humana permissa'. His moderate stance in this academic exercise is worth noting: in the 1580s, most Cambridge divines of ambition and renown were more likely to thump some tub or other. However, men of peace and moderation were more likely to attract official approval, and Andrewes's move into the great world should therefore cause no surprise. He was the sort of man who in his day was cut out for a career that would end on the episcopal bench.

Most of the Jacobean bishops, though commonly quite good scholars, really excelled at politics and administration; what set Andrewes apart were his special qualities as a teacher and a spiritual guide. Outwardly, it must be said, he fitted the part of the courtier. His handsome face, with its friendly smile and its elegant little beard, suited the court of James I excellently well, and it was said that the awe of his presence restrained the king's normal tendency to frivolity. I must say that I am sorry to hear this and do not altogether believe it: it would take more than a solemn face around the corner to stop King James from jesting. Perhaps Andrewes put a curb on James's frequent and crude prurience. It is certainly plain that the king liked and respected the bishop but quite clearly did not judge him to be a man of affairs, and those who expected Andrewes to succeed Richard Bancroft at Canterbury in 1610 were more disappointed than he himself, content to move on to Ely and Winchester, seems to have been. Nevertheless, Andrewes was widely reckoned to command influence. He acquired quite a reputation as a preacher at court and became a privy councillor; yet doubt must affect one's estimate of him in both these roles.

Was he indeed, as tradition has often asserted, an outstanding preacher? Owen Chadwick tells us that soon after his death he began to be cited as an example of awfulness.[1] Volumes survive of his sermons to show the reason why; in retrospect, what is mysterious is his reputation during his life. But in such matters tastes do alter. Not that everybody fell for his style. He was accused of lacking life in his method, and the champions of John Donne's thunders did not think much of Andrewes's tinkles. Richard Baxter thought that he only played with holy things, and James himself remarked that he merely toyed with the details of Scripture – 'here's a pretty thing, and here's a pretty thing, like the monkey with the diamonds'. But that is not altogether fair: Andrewes meant to use the pulpit for an edifying exposition of the faith. To judge by the edited text, he tended to preach in the manner of a philologist, taking words apart and seeking a sequence of meanings in them, and this at a time when fashion and passion were calling forth thunderously revivalist sermons not only in city churches but at the royal court too. Some people felt that if only they stuck it out they would in the end get spiritual nourishment from Andrewes's playing with texts, and it would appear that his personality – his genuine charm – endowed his discourse with weight and respect. As a presence he could awe; on the page he became awful. His other chief legacy are the prayers – in Latin, Greek and Hebrew – that he composed and committed to print. Whether one likes that sort of thing depends on one's own relation to piety, but it needs to be understood that Andrewes's subtle, overdone and often macaronic expression of man's relations to God suited his age. We should not allow our lack of comprehension for all that filigree work to prevent us from understanding his place in his own time.

Indeed, rather surprisingly, it has proved possible for some people in our century to respond to his call. Thus T. S. Eliot expressed great admiration for the way in which Andrewes 'squeezed' the words of the text until they yielded 'a full juice of meaning which we would never have supposed any word to possess'. That is to say, Andrewes's manner

---

[1] Owen Chadwick, *Clerical Anglicanism and Lancelot Andrewes* (2nd Southwell Lecture, 1986).

suited the taste of an Anglo-Catholic ex-poet, who in his own work liked to put words through a wringer; and unlike his admirer, Andrewes possessed that multilingual equipment which endowed words with pregnant layers of meaning. Though he preached and prayed in the guise of a philologist, he meant to illumine the road to faith, and his lamps, throwing a bit of light here and a bit of light there, helped some to see who wanted to. At least he avoided the bogus appeal of deep-throated passion.

In a way, therefore, these productions, which at the time constituted his claim to fame, were surprisingly time-bound, but this is not true of the ultimate achievement of Andrewes the scholar. His reputation as a Hebraist came conveniently to hand together with his renown at court when the new translation of the Bible was taken in hand early in James I's reign, and he chaired the committee responsible for the greater part of the Old Testament, from Genesis to the Second Book of Kings. Most of the really troublesome problems facing the translators arose in that sector, with complex questions arising over words of dark meaning in Hebrew that needed the highly sophisticated guidance of such medieval Jewish commentators as Rashi and Kimchi, names mysterious to us but familiar to Andrewes who had studied them. He possessed a copy of the works of Maimonides, a name still known amongst us present-day heathens. Andrewes was able to display his scholarship to much advantage both in the English text of the Authorised Version and even better in the marginal notes setting out alternative possibilities,[2] and generations have had grounds to be grateful to the man who would squeeze every word until he had extracted unsuspected juices of meaning. It is, of course, a commonplace to give thanks for the fact that the Authorised Version came to be made at a time when the English language had reached one of its peaks of flexible beauty, but we should not forget the individual practitioner in our respect for a generation's skilful ease. Andrewes (amongst others) demonstrated what a classical education could do for a writer of English, even as the New English Bible testifies to the fact that a solid scholarly grounding in no way guarantees an ability to write good English.

As a courtier and councillor, on the other hand, Andrewes fails to convince. Either he never really understood the world of politics, or he understood it well enough to stay on the sidelines. It has been noticed

---

[2] For all this see G. Lloyd Jones, *The Discovery of Hebrew in Tudor England: A Third Language* (London, 1983), esp. 147.9.

that he never went abroad or even left England for Scotland; possessed of large numbers of friends and correspondents on the continent, he yet knew nothing of the world beyond the Channel at first hand.[3] As a member of the king's Privy Council – by no means yet a merely honorary position – he assiduously avoided the opportunities for influence and plotting which such other bishops as George Abbott or William Laud took with both hands. Tradition has it that when he did turn up at the Council Table he asked whether any of the business in hand touched the church, and that if none did he left again, saying 'I will be gone'.[4] He could be amazingly absent-minded, to a degree that argues indifference to the company within which he was moving: thus in November 1616, John Chamberlain, the letter-writer, attending one of his sermons at court, was astonished to hear the preacher pray solemnly for Prince Henry, four years dead, 'without' (as he put it) 'recalling himself'.[5] Andrewes's refusal to play the part of a bishop–politician and accept the leading role for which both his views and his place seemed to cast him exasperated Richard Montague, falsely charged with popish views by bigoted Puritans. Montague needed friends and knew that the bishop of Ely was on his side, but he waited in vain for the desired intervention. He was the more disappointed because his hopes had been raised. In May 1625 he received *evangelia* (good news) of 'our Gamaliel' (the great teacher – his name for Andrewes) who 'now if ever hath occasion to put home . . . that the Church may have cause to thank him; . . . I hope he will . . . As he sayth well, if I have written Popery himself hath. But *manum super os* . . . till I hear further from you, as I hope I shall shortly'. Four days later his informant, young John Cosin, had indeed written, but most discouragingly: our Gamaliel had still not opened his mouth. Indeed, he never did, thus forgoing the chance that he might 'do that good for which God will reward him and all posterity thank him'.[6] Andrewes simply was not the sort of man to put himself at the head of a faction in the church, but we should not ascribe this to pusillanimity. Unlike Montague, and very much unlike Laud or Cosin, he simply was a scholar and not a political animal. From this fact arose the air of ambiguity, of indeterminacy, that tends even now to surround him. However, one must wonder whether he was correctly placed as a

[3] F. Higham, *Lancelot Andrewes* (London, 1952).
[4] D. Lloyd, *State-Worthies*, ed. Charles Whitworth (London, 1766), II, 347.
[5] *The Chamberlain Letters: A Selection*, ed. Elizabeth M. Thomson (London, 1965), 78.
[6] *The Correspondence of John Cosin, DD*, ed. G. Ornsby, Part I, Surtees Society, 52 (1869), 70, 90; the second letter, misplaced in the edition, should come first.

bishop in the Jacobean church. I have found no evidence or argument to show that this unquestionably famous man of high learning and high principles left any real impression on any of the three dioceses over which he presided for altogether twenty-one years.

Thus the truth would appear to be that Andrewes always remained what he had been at the beginning of his career – a passionate scholar and a dedicated pedagogue. At times he looks to have been the quintessential Cambridge tutor, always willing to give time and attention to his pupils; to the end of his life, the most sympathetic notices of him emphasise his readiness to listen and to instruct. The office of dean of Westminster he held in his late forties, by the standards of his time well past middle age, and an office moreover that opened the door to public fame and political influence. Yet what was remembered about his tenure of it was the trouble he took with the boys of Westminster School. He stood in for any absent teachers; he frowned on the conventional methods of punishment; he devoted much time and effort to making scholars out of the material provided. Like so many teachers, then and now, he manifestly wished to reproduce his own pursuit of learning among the next generation. But what made this dean quite exceptional – for which reason the fact was carefully recorded – were his activities outside the class-room: it was he who organised holiday excursions for the boys and marched at the head of the mob, the destination being (so it appears) distant Chiswick, then of course a country village. From this story, as from a good many others told about him, the man's essential kind-heartedness shines out.

A preacher, a man of prayer, a teacher and a friend: but even all that does not complete the public figure of Lancelot Andrewes. As the conventions of learning required then, as they still require today, he wrote books – books of theological argument and controversy. And this raises the ultimate question about him, perhaps the only one that matters in any endeavour to assess his place in history. Andrewes lived and worked in an age of intensive controversy, of continuous warfare conducted in the cause of the Prince of Peace – an age when experts professed to battle for the souls of unfortunate victims persuaded that eternal salvation was available to those correctly instructed and more particularly to those willing to hunt out and destroy fellow human beings who had fallen into the hands of rival purveyors of the necessary specifics. The history of Christianity is a history of principled per-secution, inside and outside the faith, but even so the lifetime of Lancelot Andrewes displayed a special excellence at this game, as single-minded predestinarians, convinced of their unrevocable righteousness, assured themselves of election by damning lost souls in every corner. This was the time when what came to be called Puritanism was forming its battle-lines, pouring boiling oil not only on papist idolatry but also on everything else that to them smelled of half-heartedness. It should be remembered that they were not against sin, original or otherwise; had it not been for the omnipresence of sin they would have had to fold their unemployed hands. What they were against were sinners who differed from themselves in the definition of sin. Not for the first time or the last, the air was thick with the voices of men (and women) who armed themselves against doubt by building walls of total and smug self-assurance. They knew the will of God, and they could soon show to unbelievers what God meant to do to them. What else is hell for? It is no wonder that in a less Christian age the devotees of Calvinist election have turned to Marxism – to another religion which offers to the faithful both the certainties of victory and the opportunity to smash those who would raise doubts. Where, in all this mêlée, stood Lancelot Andrewes?

Though Patrick Collinson seemed at one time to think that in his young days Andrewes should be called a Puritan,[7] I can find no evidence to support this, except perhaps the insufficient supposition that in Elizabeth's reign Pembroke College favoured advanced Protestant opinion. All the evidence we have indicates that Andrewes was always inclined to moderation and unwilling to accept the simplicities of the extremists. In consequence, he has of course been claimed for what is called the Arminian camp – that mysterious entity which evades proper definition because it was really invented by Puritan controversialists of the seventeenth century and is too readily wheeled into the firing line by some modern historians. Nicholas Tyacke, the leading chronicler of Jacobean anti-Calvinism, invariably hangs that label around Andrewes's neck, but since he offers no really usable definition of that term (except that it meant opposing extreme predestinarianism, a position open to several forms of belief) such labelling really brings us no nearer to Andrewes's fundamental position in the strife among Protestants.[8] Hugh Trevor-Roper with equal determination, in the course of his battle of revenge against Peterhouse, makes Andrewes a leader of the Arminian faction, but he does offer a description of sorts: to him all anti-Calvinist thinking in the reformed churches of Europe is directly

---

[7] P. Collinson, *The Elizabethan Puritan Movement* (London, 1967), 455.
[8] N. Tyacke, *Anti-Calvinists: The Rise of English Arminianism c. 1590–1640* (Oxford, 1987).

descended from the teaching of Erasmus.[9] Unfortunately I cannot find
that those English Arminians self-consciously referred themselves to
Erasmus, and it seems that Trevor-Roper elected him for that role
because he once defended free will against Martin Luther's version of
predestination. Indeed, somewhat surprisingly Erasmus, whose *Paraph-
rases* were certainly used in the teaching of religion in England, is absent
from Andrewes's library catalogue. However, so are other works that he
demonstrated he had read when he cited them in his own writings;
Erasmus he does not cite. As for Arminius, chosen by the Puritans to
identify the enemy, that Dutch theologian died in 1609, though his views
were not formally condemned and therefore made current knowledge
until 1618; his opposition to Calvinism was shared by men who (like
Montague) had formed their opinions long before they had heard of
him. The name, though useful to their enemies especially in the days of
William Laud, is not useful to us, who also remember that Laud for one
rejected the appellation. I would suggest that the anti-Calvinist tradition
within the Church of England long preceded these Jacobean follies and
should not be traced to the supposed influence of that very worthy
Dutch theologian; it should be tracked back to a set of convictions that
dominated that church before Calvinism, in the course of Elizabeth's
reign, won its victory in the universities and in many pulpits without
ever winning over the hearts and minds of the majority of English men
and women, and which re-emerged as the central position of that church
after the Restoration. Even the historians who have recently begun to
cast doubt on the idea that England ever became a Protestant nation
might feel less certain of their assessment if they had not accepted the
misleading identification of Tudor Protestantism with an ascendant form
of Calvinism. I think it is a little strange that more attention is nowadays
paid to the Lambeth Articles of 1595, which were never formally
accepted as a definition of faith, than to the Thirty-nine Articles of 1563,
enacted by Parliament in 1571: the Lambeth Articles do indeed house
the pure milk of double predestination, but the Thirty-Nine do not.

It is certain that Andrewes rejected double predestination, but that
does not make him an Arminian: it makes him a main-line English
Protestant and what later ages were to call an Anglican. He went so far
on one occasion as to say that 'God would have all men saved',[10] a

[9] H. R. Trevor-Roper, *Catholics, Anglicans and Puritans: Seventeenth Century Essays*
(London, 1987), esp. 44–8.
[10] Cited in H. C. Porter, *Reformation and Reaction in Tudor Cambridge* (Cambridge, 1958),
396.

devastating heresy in the ears of all who believed, with Beza and his like, in the immutable supralapsarian decree, and he avoided touching on predestination in all the many sermons that are preserved. When the battle over the issue conducted at the 1618 Synod of Dort (which he, a leading theologian of the day, was not sent to attend) compelled him to take some sort of a stand on the issue, he resorted to the escape route originally devised by Calvin himself: people who claimed to know 'God's secret decrees' presumed to know that which must be outside human knowledge; such mysteries should not and cannot be probed.[11] He had, in fact, always held to the view that 'we are not curiously to enquire and search out God's secret will touching reprobation or election', which meant ruling out the main plank of rigorous Puritanism.[12] Indeed, he was not even altogether sound on the issue of salvation by faith alone; on one occasion he asserted that 'we hold good works necessary to salvation and that faith without them saveth not'.[13] But, though such views could give support to those who saw here adherence to the rags of popery, it was in fact a sound enough Protestant position going back to Luther and Zwingli, who had regarded works as necessary evidence of God's bestowal of grace. Yet in other ways Andrewes endorsed the high moral tone characteristic of the Protestantism of his day: 'The promises of our religion', he asserted, 'are not worldly pleasures, as other religions do promise, but contrary', and he welcomed the destruction of images, those devices of the devil.[14] He stood with those who wished to reform the Church, but had no ambitions to restructure it altogether: 'we are', he said memorably, 'renovators and not innovators'.[15] Does it help to call any of this moderation Arminian, especially since the contents of Arminianism have invariably been left vague, or Erasmian when Erasmus is never mentioned? Anti-Calvinist, yes: Andrewes, of whom Thomas Fuller once said that 'his masterpiece was in comforting wounded consciences', was much too compassionate a man to rest content with the fire and brimstone of the true Calvinists. It is worth notice that in this he resembled John Foxe, the martyrologist, who long before Arminius was heard of decided that the Calvinists offered no help to bruised souls.[16]

Yet here is a strange thing: this man who engaged at great length in

---

[11] Tyacke, *Anti-Calvinists*, 103.   [12] Porter, *Reformation and Reaction*, 396.
[13] *Andrewes Works*, ed. J. P. Wilson and J. Bliss, 11 vols. (London, 1841–54), XI, 29.
[14] Ibid., II, 55; V, 6.   [15] Ibid., III, 26.
[16] See my remarks in 'Luther in England', below, no. 61, pp. 237–9.

theological controversy never once wrote anything explicitly against Calvinism or Puritanism. At least, nothing survives, though it is possible that he once composed a piece for Archbishop Whitgift that may have tended that way when he was apparently asked to clarify where he stood to full-blooded Calvinism. By 1617 he could not think what had become of that exercise, remembering only that he had given a copy to Richard Hooker, who despite a promise to return it never did so.[17] The form of Christianity against which Andrewes plied his learned pen and the printer's craft was Roman Catholicism, and his chief adversary was that outstanding Catholic champion, Cardinal Bellarmine. No one has lately shown much interest in those writings – the biographers concentrate on the sermons – and I do not propose to pursue such esoteric themes today. But it should be noted that if – as William Laud's enemies continuously claimed – Arminianism formed a half-way house on the road to Rome, Lancelot Andrewes clearly did not qualify for the appellation at all. He argued, and argued fiercely and at length, with the representatives of the popery of his day. By way of a footnote we may note that even in his relations with the Church of Rome he managed to retain a touch of his favourite stance, namely toleration. As he once put it, 'to prefer a better thing is not to condemn a thing': he did not believe that the only alternative to white was outright black.[18] In 1579, only twenty-two years old, he put his signature to a petition to permit the safe return of John Hopkinson of Grub Street in the city of London, who, seduced by papists, had fled abroad. Hopkinson, an expert in Hebrew, Chaldaean, Syriac and Greek, had been giving private tuition to Andrewes before deserting his country and his wife.[19] It is not known whether the appeal succeeded.

Thus Andrewes was neither a Puritan (a type hard enough to define) nor an Arminian (merely a term of refined abuse); he was a member of the Church of England, given to moderation and the middle way. He believed in the innate virtue of the church to which he belonged, holding that it was a catholic church and nearer to that of the Apostles than was the Church of Rome: England, he maintained, had been cleansed of the 'filth of history'.[20] Perhaps it is not surprising that the member of that church with whom his name has sometimes been associated is his good friend Richard Hooker, though Hooker conducted just that war against

---

[17] *Chamberlain Letters*, 229.

[18] See Trevor A. Owen, *Lancelot Andrewes* (London, 1981), 38.

[19] *Calendar State Papers Domestic*, I, 627.   [20] Owen, *Lancelot Andrewes*, 36.

Puritanism in which Andrewes refused to embroil himself. Once again, I am at a loss to see how we can link those two men as leaders of a faction, though they both possessed an even temper and a sense of moderation, unusual gifts in the age of Whitgift, Perkins and Robert Parsons. However, there is a father of the Anglican church, comparison with whom proves much more enlightening, and since 1989 is also the 500th anniversary of his birth I am glad I feel compelled to turn our minds towards him. That man was Thomas Cranmer, the first archbishop and in many ways the major inspiration of the Church of England. I might add that both Cranmer and Andrewes appear in that extraordinary list of post-Reformation saints inserted into the Alternative Prayer Book, but since that list also includes such victims of the Reformation as Thomas More and John Fisher, not to mention John Bunyan and King Charles I, it should be plain that it is not shared experiences and beliefs that qualify for inclusion there.

Over the centuries, Cranmer has attracted much condemnation from scholars (never faced with his dilemmas) for being supposedly undecided and too willing to change his mind, but I think we can benefit from the turmoil of our own time in order better to understand the behaviour and speech of a man who could not rest content with brutal simplicities and opened himself to guidance from people he respected. In the end, of course, Cranmer knew where he stood, and, since where he stood was the stake, the contempt expressed by armchair critics devoted to intellectual certainties itself deserves only contempt. It would be more appropriate to put the searchlight on the central concept that governed his vision of the church, even as it determined the thinking of his principal ally in the English Reformation, Thomas Cromwell. Both believed that the church needed reforming, and both were moved by spiritual dissatisfaction, even though to Cromwell the practical problems of creating a political entity capable of comprising and nourishing the sort of church he wanted mattered as much as did questions of religion. And both desired a church intent on keeping the peace. Reform inevitably called forth conflict and confrontation, but Cromwell demanded, and Cranmer supplied, a main line between the extremes, a *via media* in all the unavoidable disputes. Cranmer's gradual adoption of reformed doctrines – at first mainly Lutheran, later influenced by Zwingli and Bucer, but at all times idiosyncratically English and informed by a native tradition of a moral free will in man – lay behind what was to become the most obvious hallmark of the reformed Church of England: a traditional and 'catholic' structure welded to a moderately

Protestant body of beliefs. The fact that the Thirty-Nine Articles can be accepted, as well as in part be doubted, by just about every form of Protestant in English history owes a good deal to the politics of the middle of the sixteenth century, but it owes more to the temper – the careful modesty and modest care – which marked its first archbishop. The essence of the Anglican reality lies in the absence of fanaticism regularly denounced by the more ardent and more half-witted spirits as merely Laodicean. That was the note that Cranmer struck at the start of it all. And insofar as Cromwell and Cranmer respected Erasmus (as they did), Trevor-Roper may even be said to have a point, though it should be stressed that neither of those two progenitors thought of building an Erasmian church or laboured in service to his ideas.

Thus it was within this Cranmerian tradition that Andrewes really operated. He was unusually well aware of the origins of his church and in one of his writings against Rome expressly referred to the collection of learned opinions concerning Henry VIII's case for his first divorce, in order to demonstrate that the world at large approved of that king's doings.[21] He cites there the Latin version of that propaganda tract, not the English translation published in the following year (1531); but in any case he was, so far as I know, the only scholar of his day to have profitably read that well-doctored justification of Henry's proceedings. Andrewes knew whence he came, and he did not think he had descended from Arminius. Nor did he represent a merely partisan stream within the Church of England. The line that came from Cranmer and to which he hewed was the lifeline used by the most genuine and most enduring aspects of that church, as the settlement after 1661 was to prove. Once the neo-Calvinist accretions upon Cranmer's building had been separated off into the camps of Dissent, the Church of England – Protestant but moderate, episcopalian but subject to the state, built upon the middle way and a readiness to tolerate diversity – emerged to testify to the completion of that form of the Reformation which characterised England. And, though that dominant note had become muted behind the ferocities of Calvinist predestination, Andrewes testifies to the fact that it had never quite vanished or indeed lost influence and adherence. Furthermore, his conviction that it represented the Catholic tradition much better than did the Church of Rome of his day had a lot to be said for it: once the Council of Trent had tightened things up in the papal church, only that of England still resembled the

---

[21] *Tortura Torti* (*Works*, XI), 444–5.

medieval ancestor who had managed to provide a number of mansions in the house of the Father in whom it professed to believe.

As we might expect, Andrewes's collection of books – which in due course came to his College – reflected his ecumenical attitudes.[22] It is an impressive list, which in its length alone supports the awe inspired by his learning as well as the sense of his welcoming humanity. Some rather surprising gaps may be the result of losses or inadequate cataloguing. One might have expected that the opponent of Bellarmine would have possessed his adversary's works, but they are not there. Nor do we find the leading patristic writings – Ambrose, Augustine, Jerome, Origen and so forth – and other materials used by the man who superintended the translation of large parts of the Old Testament. He does not seem to have acquired books as a matter of course when they came out: there is no sign of Bacon's *Advancement of Learning* (1605) or James I's *Collected Works* (1616). But, on the other hand, he spread himself across the field. Thus we find there Bede's *History*, published at Cologne in 1537, Bodin's *De Republica* in the printing of 1586, a copy of Luther's translation of the Bible (did Andrewes read German?), and perhaps more surprisingly the works of Geoffrey Chaucer (1561). The collection reflects rather more the tastes of an omnivorous general reader than the working library of a professional. Among the authors he acquired were Demosthenes, Froissart, Hooker, Hackluyt, Hus, Marsiglio of Padua, Fynes Morison, Otto of Freising, reflecting a very wide range of interests. Andrewes acquainted himself with those who opposed the English Reformation; he owned several of Thomas More's attacks on the reformers (but not *Utopia*) and Reginald Pole's denunciation of Henry VIII (*De Unitate*, in the Strassburg edition of 1555). The most surprising section of the collection comprised matters of the law. Perhaps one might have expected a learned cleric to own Justinian's *Codex Iuris*, but four volumes of Edward Coke's *Reports* (in Law French) and several of the sessional printings of acts of Parliament throw a very different light. (It is possible that those statutes constitute perks of his appointment to the Privy Council.) Andrewes even possessed a copy of the Scottish statutes from James I to James VI, in the 1597 edition. To judge by his bookshelves, Andrewes had the widest interests but employed them thoughtfully. It would be really interesting to know what he made of Copernicus's work on planetary motion, or of Gilbert's treatise on the magnet. We no longer believe that an interest in the natural sciences

---

[22] D. D. C. Chambers, 'A catalogue of the library of Bishop Lancelot Andrewes (1555–1626), *Transactions of the Cambridge Bibliographic Society*, 5, (1969–71), 99–121.

testified to Puritan beliefs, but it would be nice to know what this so-called Arminian wished to learn about such things. On the other hand, I do not know that the progress of science left any deposit in Andrewes's own writings; and, as I have said, he does not seem to have bothered with the mystical pragmatism of the man chosen by posterity as the father of the natural sciences. Indeed, we seem to have no evidence of any contact between the bishop of Ely and Lord Chancellor Bacon.

In the end, Andrewes left his library to his old College, to which he also bequeathed a valuable living and £1,000 to establish an additional fellowship. Though for most of his adult life his connections with Pembroke were pretty tenuous, he had not forgotten his origins there and he testified to his grateful memory in the way that best pleases a Cambridge College. And there was much truth about this deathbed recollection. When all is said, Lancelot Andrewes – bishop, courtier, leading member of his embattled church – was above all a man of a learning and a teacher, and thus we remember him today.

58

PERSECUTION AND TOLERATION IN THE ENGLISH REFORMATION*

The century of the Reformation, in England as elsewhere, sharpened all conflicts and augmented persecution. As the unity of Christendom broke up, the rival parties acquired that sort of confidence in their own righteousness that encourages men to put one another to death for conscience sake; an era of moderation and tolerance gave way to one of ever more savage repression. To the openminded willingness which characterised the humanism of Erasmus and More as well as the Rome of Leo X there succeeded the bigotry typical of Carafa, Calvin, Knox and the English Puritans; only the gradual evaporation of such passions, produced by each side's inability to triumph totally, produced a weariness with religious strife which made the return of mutual sufferance possible. That, at least, is the received story. Historians of toleration, as for instance Jordan and Lecler,[1] firmly described the history of persecution in this way. Jordan identified six developments which led to its decline in sixteenth-century England: a growing political strength among dissident sects, the impossibility of preventing splintering and preserving uniformity, the needs of trade which overrode religious hostility, experience of travel, the failure to suppress dissident publications, and finally a growing scepticism which denied the claims to exclusive truth advanced by this or that faction.[2] In other words, only two things moved men, once they had fallen away from the generosity of the pre-Reformation era, to substitute an uneasy toleration for a vigorous persecution: the external pressures of experience and the decline of religious fervour. By implication, men of power called for repression and only those who could not hope to win favoured toleration, until general exhaustion set in. It is a convincing enough picture, and much evidence no doubt supports it. But it is a picture – a general and rather schematic panorama which makes little allowance for

---

* [*Studies in Church History*, 21 (1984), 163–87.]

[1] W. K. Jordan, *The Development of Religious Toleration in England from the Beginning of the English Reformation to the Death of Queen Elizabeth* (London, 1932); J. Lecler, *Toleration and the Reformation*, 2 vols. (London, 1960).

[2] Jordan, *Toleration*, 20–3.

the real opinions of individuals. On this occasion I should like to test it by looking at the attitudes of two highly articulate sixteenth-century Englishmen – Thomas More, humanist and loyal son of the Universal Church, and John Foxe, humanist and faithful protestant. Both, we know, were men of sensitivity and sense. How did they stand to the problem of persecution?

It may be thought that Thomas More deserves a rest: has not enough been said about, for and against (mostly for) him? He is, however, really rather central to this discussion. A major figure in that humanist and Erasmian movement in church and society whose influence (political and intellectual) can fairly be traced in all sorts of places through the remainder of the century, he was a believing Christian who before the Reformation had offered reasoned criticism of his church, then came to dread the Reformation, and as lord chancellor was in a position exceptional for an intellectual of having to apply his convictions in practice. Of course, he was not a 'typical' Erasmian if only because such a thing could hardly exist among those individualists whom only loose ties of shared ideals and occasional friendship held together. With respect to the treatment of heresy he may have been even less typical because he chose to stand forth as its chief opponent, to a degree that bewildered even those Erasmians who continued to adhere to the old church. Even in (mistakenly) defending him against a charge of imprisoning suspects, Erasmus was obliged to admit that More 'hates those seditious teachings which are now so tragically shaking our world; that is something he has never disguised or wished should remain secret'. Indeed, Erasmus added in an aside which the overactive community of More-scholars has chosen to ignore, 'he is so firm in his piety that if there is to be any tilting of the balance even a tiny bit he must be said to be closer to superstition than to impiousness'.[3] In the mouth of that chief foe to 'superstition' – the form which official Christianity had taken in the later Middle Ages – that assessment, uttered as late as 1532, is distinctly critical. Sir Thomas, it seems, had long before this made it plain to Erasmus that the problem of heresy – toleration or persecution – stood at the centre of his thought; and since the two men never met and rarely corresponded after 1521 his position had evidently become solid well before he started combating the Lutherans. And his devotion to the existing church was such that to

---

[3] *Erasmi Epistolae*, ed. P. S. Allen, X, 137: 'Odit ille seditiosa dogmata, quibus nunc misere concutitur orbis. Hoc ille non dissimulat, nec cupit esse clam; sic addictus pietati vt, si in alterutram partem aliquantulum inclinet momentum, superstitioni quam impietati vicinior esse videatur'.

176

the prince of humanists it seemed appropriate to speak in terms which accused his old associate of betraying the central tenet of Christian humanism.

That More contemplated diversity in religion and the problems it posed even before Luther's irruption is, of course, well known, as are the apparent tensions between the attitude he adopted in *Utopia* and his behaviour towards Tyndale and the rest. With a breathtaking boldness which elevates a *non sequitur* to the status of an explanatory epigram – the sort of boldness which marks More's devotees – R. W. Chambers jumped the gulf by saying that 'it is precisely More's tolerance that makes him, on true Utopian principles, intolerant of the Reformation'. He went on to allege that More's fury against heretics derived from his conviction that 'all religious experience is sacred': his inner beliefs were offended by the heretics only because they attacked the worship of saints and such-like practices.[4] Quite apart from the fact that More's objections to Luther and Tyndale went vastly deeper than that, we may note that Chambers does not explain why More was always so scathing about the religious experiences described by heretics. Bland and smug, this remains the level of reflection at which More-idolaters treat a very delicate problem: and it will not do. We have More's word – endless thousands of words – to testify to his belief in persecution; indeed, it has been shown that he practised it precisely by the definition of it that he himself set up in the *Dialogue of Comfort*.[5] I do not propose to go over all that ground again. 'Odit ille seditiosa dogmata' and made no bones about it: why should we, in our post-Enlightenment squeamishness, deny his convictions and their consequences when he himself wished to make them public? But questions remain. What sort of toleration did the humanist More believe in, and what did the persecution of heretics mean to the More who preferred to appear leaning to superstition rather than impiety?

On the face of it, religious toleration prevails in Utopia. 'They count it among their most ancient principles that no one should ever suffer harm for his religion'.[6] Utopus had introduced this regulation

[4] R. W. Chambers, *Thomas More* (London, 1935), 252–3.

[5] Leland Miles, 'Persecution and the *Dialogue of Comfort*: a fresh look at the charges against Thomas More', *Journal of British Studies*, 5 (1965), 19–30.

[6] *Utopia*, 218/29–30: 'Siquidem hoc inter antiquissima instituta numerant, ne sua cuiquam religio fraudi sit'. All citations from More's works are from the Yale edition of *The Complete Works of St Thomas More*. Quotations for *Utopia* are given in my own translation, and where necessary I have repunctuated the Latin; throughout this paper I have modernised the spelling of English quotations.

not only for the sake of peace, which he recognised would be totally ruined by constant wrangling and implacable hatred, but also because he decided that this rule would best serve the cause of religion itself. He would not venture rashly to lay down the law, feeling uncertain whether God would not prefer to have varied and manifold forms of worship, inspiring different people differently.[7]

This reflects the humanist conviction that, while Christianity represented God's only truth, Jews and Moslems – and possibly other heathens – must be allowed to regard their religion as also permitted by God, especially if they have not had the chance to learn about the Christian revelation. We find this species of tolerance also, for instance, in Thomas Starkey, whose Lupset cited 'the opinion of great wise men' to support the view that obedience to the law of nature and their own civil ordinances would save Jews, Saracens, Turks and Moors – though he added that he would have to leave it to 'the secret judgement of God' whether 'it be so or not'.[8] This special concession to other established confessions can be found granted occasionally through the rest of the century; it deserves a little better than it gets in the grudging comment of Father Surtz, who seems anxious to save More from any charge of relativism or from being thought to agree with God's preference for variety in his worship.[9]

Not pausing to wonder what Utopus would have thought of the constant wrangling and implacable hatred that fills More's *Confutation of Tyndale*, we note that to all appearance religious intolerance was absent from the kingdom he founded. However, there were limits. In the first place, More spoke of Christianity as though it was a single, agreed and perfect doctrine: he says not one word about heresy. Secondly, Utopian toleration knows bounds. There everybody is entitled to try to convert others to his own beliefs, but only if he confines himself to quiet and moderate argument. If, finding persuasion unsuccessful, he descends to reckless verbal attacks or attempts to use actual force, he becomes liable to the ultimate Utopian punishments – exile or enslavement.[10] In view

---

[7] Ibid., 220/7–12: 'Haec Vtopus instituit non respectu pacis modo, quam assiduo certamine atque inexpiabili odio funditus uidet euerti, sed quod arbitratus est, uti sic decerneretur, ipsius etiam religionis interesse, de qua nihil est ausus temere definire, uelut incertum habens, an uarium ac multiplicem expetens cultum deus aliud inspiret alij [sic: ?alios].'

[8] Thomas Lupset, *The Dialogue between Pole and Lupset*, ed. K. Burton (London, 1948), 34–5.

[9] *Utopia*, 521.   [10] Ibid., 220/3–7.

of the vocabulary which More was to acquire in his polemics, we may note that the laws of Utopus specifically condemned intemperate abuse. Utopus, we are told, dreaded the civil strife which such disagreements bring about and in particular held that verbal or physical violence was much more likely to promote the victory of a false faith: for he expected that in the course of time rational thought would discover that true religion in expectation of which he decreed toleration, and which would then be formally established. Utopian tolerance represented a holding action and presupposed the existence of a single true religion; it did not admit the right of several religions, each held to be true by their followers, to exist side by side once the real truth of God's will had become known. Thus in the last resort there was toleration in Utopia only so long as it had not turned Christian. Even so, as Christian attitudes to rival faiths went, More's Utopian fiction had some eirenic virtue.

In due course, More was to discover that it had become impossible to speak of a single Christian faith, and if in 1516 he had been honest he would even then have admitted and considered the problems of heresy and schism; if he had done so, it seems unlikely that he would ever have been thought of as essentially a man of toleration. Once he confronted heresy he had to explain his new-found violence: he did so by taking the line that Luther and his followers could not be tolerated because their noise led to civil strife and they promoted their cause by violent attacks on the existing order. Reading More's controversial writings, it is hard to believe that even if Luther had cooed as any sucking-dove More would have granted him the right to deviate from orthodoxy. However, he used the reservations contained in Utopus' scheme of things as a handy bridge to the other shore where he could forget about the possibility that God might prefer variety in his worship or that all the truth was not yet known. Submitting himself totally to the authority of the church, he could become a persecutor. In view of his use of those Utopian limitations, his account of behaviour which was not tolerated there deserves a glance. One unfortunate man, converted by Hythloday and displaying all the zeal of the new believer, exceeded the properties in his efforts to persuade fellow Utopians to turn Christian. In his anger he called all other religions profane, accused their followers of blasphemy and sacrilege, and assured them that the fires of Hell were waiting for them; for which reason he was tried and condemned to exile, not (we are told) because he expressed such contempt for their religion but because he was stirring up riots – though we are not told that anyone in fact rioted.[11] Zeal of this kind was frowned upon, but it had to be of the kind that condemned other believers outright; moreover, both cause and agent of the man's punishment belonged to the civil sphere. It is thus fairly clear that, given the right reactions and carefully defined allegations, Utopian toleration did not inhibit the persecution of heretics: thus More prophetically guarded his later apparent change of mind. But he did not change it because he held, with Utopus, that all forms of worship must be tolerated so long as they do not cause tumults. He persecuted heresy not (as Chambers suggested) because he treated denunciations of harmless pilgrimages as offences against the multiplicity of worship, but because he saw in it a threat to that only truth which in Utopia still needed discovery.

From about 1521, More discovered himself involved in the realities of religious strife; the speculations of *Utopia* ceased to be adequate for his purposes. At first he certainly tried to adhere to the proposition that heretics must be persecuted because they pursue their ends in violent ways which disturb the people. Killing them is a surgical form of social therapy.[12] They always started it: Augustine turned to repression only after the Donatists had resorted to violence, and the English statute under which heretics were burned resulted from Oldcastle's (Lord Cobham's) rebellion. Similarly he justified the current severity against heretics by charging them with savagery: it was 'the violent cruelty first used by the heretics themselves against good catholic folk' that forced princes to suppress them by fire and the sword, 'for preservation not of the faith only but also of the peace among their people'. More's allegations of heretical violence are very tendentious. In the *Dialogue against Heresies* he blamed the Sack of Rome on the Lutherans and ignored the part played by good Catholic Spaniards, and in the *Confutation* he offered the German peasants' war as a characteristic consequence of heresy;[13] yet he must have known that the onset of persecution preceded both events. In any case, he provided no proof for the connection between those disturbances and the Reformation but confined himself to emotional outcries and loud resentment at the language used by the Lutherans against the church. Reading his own violence, one feels inclined to remind him that the Utopian preacher was exiled for overstepping the mark in advocating orthodoxy. No doubt More believed that the revolting peasants of 1525 would have remained at peace had it not been

---

[11] Ibid., 218/21–9.   [12] *Dialogue against Heresies*, 406–10.
[13] Ibid., 370–2; *Confutation of Tyndale*, 482–3.

for Luther, and he may have believed Augustine's charges against the Donatists. No honest lawyer, however, should have argued that the Lancastrian heresy acts resulted from a rising of 1414 when (as he must have known) the most important of them was passed in 1401. In short, the links with Utopian principles represented by his attempts to justify persecution by the need to maintain peace in society against violent disruption are spurious; they hide convictions about the treatment of dissidents which are anchored in a genuinely persecuting temperament.

For soon More forgot that heretics caused trouble by annoying people in their settled ways and pursued them because they were only too likely to win people over. That he came to advocate the killing of heretics as a worthy end in itself emerges disconcertingly from the unbridled violence and savage concept with which he referred to them. As he said in 1534, when debating with St German: let the adversary prove that a number of heretics consigned to the fire had suffered any wrong 'but if it were that they were burned no sooner'.[14] He persecuted worse than the orthodox bishops, as when he lambasted Thomas Hitton, a heretic apparently burned upon first conviction, as 'the devil's stinking martyr'; even Foxe's account makes it plain that his interrogators gave Hitton every chance to escape the stake but were defeated by his characteristic exalted stubbornness.[15] More would no doubt have regretted any such misplaced charity, as he did in other cases. He resented the royal pardon given to Robert Barnes and disapproved of the relative tolerance shown to James Bainham, who nearly managed to get one too; and he never once expressed any doubt about the practice of burning men alive. His profession that the clergy burned no one but merely handed the convicted and excommunicated heretic over to the secular arm must be read in the light of his admission that the law left that arm no option but to burn the man.[16] The mixture of lip-smacking and evasiveness in all these diatribes against individuals becomes truly nasty.

It is, in fact, idle to pretend that More's references to particular victims of the persecution have any humanity left in them. Take the case of John Tewkesbury, a wandering preacher and colporteur, in whose apprehension and trial More played an active part. In December 1531 Tewkesbury was burned as a relapsed heretic, and Tyndale expressed joy over his steadfastness at the stake. (I am not saying that More's opponents were particularly attractive either, but on the virtue of true martyrdom

[14] *Apology*, 94.   [15] *Confutation*, 13–17; *AM*, VIII, 712–15.
[16] *Confutation*, 10–11; 17–18; *Dialogue against Heresies*, 410; *Apology*, 92–4.

they were all, of course agreed. They differed only over who could claim the crown.) Confronted with this joy, More could see no reason for it, unless Tyndale 'reckoned it for a great glory that the man did abide still by the stake when he was fast bound to it'. This thoroughly unfeeling remark was made about a man who had borne his awful death bravely; it was followed by allegations that Tewkesbury refrained from recanting only because he knew that his relapse made this pointless – allegations supported by the testimony of 'one James', apparently a fellow prisoner.[17] This particular passage is interesting not only because it shows up More's attitudes and his polemical methods, but more especially because he here drops the only other 'humane' argument in favour of burning heretics that he at times advances. This is that an abjured offender who, having relapsed, is yet burned is thereby saved from changing (perjuring himself) once more: the fire destroys the body but comes nicely in time to save the soul. Thus we find More condescendingly content over an unnamed heretic who was captured with Tyndale's books on him.

and both burned together, with more profit unto his soul than had been haply to have lived longer and after died in his bed. For in what mind he should then have died our lord knoweth, whereas now we know well he died a good Christian man.[18]

This apparently comforting notion underlies his several accounts of Thomas Bylney's fate – accounts in which he was mainly concerned to prove that the heretic had recanted at the last and thereby saved his soul, even as he died at the stake.[19] After all the abuse he had heaped on Bylney, his trust that God will accept the heretic's revocation of his heresies as part-payment for 'the poor man's purgatory' can only be called unctuous. Moreover, in order to be able to maintain that recanting when being burned at the stake was better than risking a relapse into heresy during the rest of one's life, he deliberately falsified the truth of Bylney's death by ignoring or decrying the solid testimony that no such recantation had taken place.[20]

In sum, then: More believed in persecution rather than toleration, and in respect of Christian heretics he almost certainly did so before he encountered Luther. Such toleration as he permitted in Utopia could

---

[17] *Confutation*, 21.   [18] Ibid., 359.

[19] E.g., *Dialogue against Heresies*, 255–8; *Confutation*, 23–5.

[20] J. F. Davis, 'The trials of Thomas Bylney and the English Reformation', *HJ*, 24 (1981), 775–90.

easily be converted into repression on grounds to be judged by the ruling
magistrate alone and was so converted by himself from 1521 onwards.
When he came to face the reality of the problem he not only himself
assisted in the repression of heresy but in his writings proclaimed a
consistent and relentless defence of persecution. The justifications which
he provided for drastic action were no doubt sincerely felt but he
supported them with such manifest deviations from the truth and
wrapped them up in such volubly violent language that his real feelings
are not obscured. He hated those seditious teachings and he was doing all
he could to root them out by violence. We shall later say a word about
the possible explanation behind this extreme reaction; for the present let
it be noted that before heresy became rampant or successful in England
the Christian humanist who as lord chancellor presided over English
justice believed in persecution.

The second writer under consideration here, another man who had
much to say about the dilemma of tolerating or persecuting dissent, is
John Foxe. Foxe found it necessary to involve himself with More,
especially because the chief attack on the first edition of the *Book of
Martyrs* came from Nicholas Harpsfield, a leading member of the group
who in Mary's reign had set about constructing Sir Thomas's posthumous fame in preparation for the canonisation they sought to obtain
from Rome.[21] The chief occasion for tangling with More, quite
understandably, arose for Foxe in Bylney's case.[22] After telling the story
as he in his turn saw it, he went on:

But here now cometh in sir Thomas More, trumping in our way with his
painted card, and would needs take up this Thomas Bilney from us, and make
him a convert after his sect. Thus these coated cards, though they could not by
plain Scriptures convince him, being alive; yet now, after his death, by false play
they will make him theirs, whether he will or no. This sir Thomas More, in his
railing preface before his book against Tyndale, doth challenge Bilney to his
catholic church . . . And how is this proved? By three or four mighty arguments,
as big as mill-posts, fetched out of Utopia, from whence thou must know,
reader, can come no fictions, but all fine poetry.

Here he makes a valid point against More, which applies not only to
Bylney's case but to most of More's polemical writing: 'With the like
authority as he affirmeth, I may deny the same, unless he brought better
demonstration for his assertion than he doth, having no more for himself

[21] Harpsfield appears in *AM* under the pseudonym of Mr Cope.
[22] *AM*, IV, 643–52.

than his own αυτοσ εφη'. As he admits, he comes close to trading vituperation with More – with 'this vein of yours, which so extremely raileth and fareth against the poor martyrs and servants of Christ'. So he stops himself: 'But because Mr More is gone and dead, I will cease any further to insult upon him, lest I may seem to occur the same vice of his, 'in mordendo mortuos'. However, he needs to combat More's books 'which be not yet dead, but remain alive to the hurt of many': he must do battle with More's 'book-disciples', that is to say, especially Harpsfield. It should be said that when Foxe rather contemptuously pushed aside those who held that More invariably spoke the truth – that More who 'hath cracked his credit so often and may almost be bankrupt' – he taught a needed lesson to modern scholars.

In this exchange Foxe did rather well, not so much in his arguments concerning Bylney (though he had the right of that) as in his temper. Where More ever rages, Foxe is rarely found uttering any real abuse, though he can speak very sharply about popery. That Foxe always inclined to the search for peace is well enough known, and those who have studied him have seen him expressly as a proponent of toleration. I think that in essence they were right, and I may refer myself to that work of others which I do not mean to rehearse here at length.[23] Of Foxe's eirenic temperament and preference for mildness there should be no doubt – John Foxe who even in Luther could see only the bringer of spiritual solace, the balm to 'the poor mourning souls of the afflicted'.[24] In all the disputes among the reformers themselves, Foxe always took the side of peace, preaching moderation and conciliation: in the Vestiarian controversy, the dispute between Whitgift and Cartwright, the usual eucharistic debates.[25] On this last issue he could speak in terms which to the committed must have sounded dangerously close to indifference. Thus when commending Luther's *Commentary on Galatians* to the reader he admitted that Luther's teaching on the Lord's Supper might upset some, seeing that it differed a little from Zwingli's views; however, he added, it differs much more from the views of the papists – so let us not fret over so trifling a difference.[26] One soon comes to recognise the tone of moderate reason – here applied to the issues which in 1529 caused the irreconcilable breach between Luther and Zwingli! – as Foxe's character-

---

[23] J. F. Mozley, *John Foxe and his Book* (London, 1940), 35–6, 54–5, 86–9; V. N. Olsen, *John Foxe and the Elizabethan Church* (Berkeley, 1973), ch. VI.

[24] Foxe's introduction to *Special and Chosen Sermons of D. Martin Luther* (London, 1578: STC 16993).?

[25] Olsen, *Foxe*, 203.

[26] Foxe's introduction to Luther's *Commentary on Galatians* (London, 1575: STC 16965).

istic note. In the age of Elizabeth, when railing was still much more common than sweet reason, Foxe must be regarded as unusual in his manner, and even as More's violence had distressed Erasmus so Foxe's mildness puzzled some of his friends. When early in 1558 he expostulated with John Knox about the vehemence of *The First Blast of the Trumpet* – and thus did so while the regiment of women still included only papists – Knox admitted that he himself had begun to have some doubts; however, he wrote, 'to me it is enough to say that black is not white, and man's tyranny and foolishness is not God's perfect ordinance'.[27] Foxe lacked this kind of brutally simple certainty, and the lack made him tolerant. For the chronicler of man's inhumanity to dissenters this is no doubt a comprehensible, as it is certainly a satisfactory, state of mind.

However, while there is no need to prove again that Foxe believed in toleration rather than persecution, it is still necessary to establish what exactly toleration meant to him and where its limits lay. He habitually used opprobrious terms for the Church of Rome, but I know of no evidence that he advocated persecuting it. No conforming English Protestant in the reign of Elizabeth ever called popery heretical; the term was reserved for protestant deviation and especially for sectarian dissent. Thus the question of applying the treatment prescribed for heretics – burning at the stake – could not arise over papists, however much a man might profess to abominate the teachings of Rome. Insofar as the papists were regarded as secular enemies, as potential or actual traitors, the Elizabethan treason laws appointed secular penalties for them, and there is no reason at all to doubt that Foxe accepted the right of the magistrate to use such weapons. Yet even in this sphere he remained true to his principles, pleading repeatedly for judicious mercy rather than copying the murderous cruelty (as he saw it) of the adversary. Especially he interceded for Edmund Campion, at a time when even Elizabeth had ceased to believe that Catholic machinations could be overlooked.[28]

There was thus some high degree of consistency in Foxe's belief in toleration, though it had its limits. Interestingly enough, he drew the line at the Jews to whom (as we have seen) the humanists of the previous generation had even allowed a chance of salvation provided they obeyed their own law. For those who in his view had killed Christ, Foxe held out no hope: God of necessity must root them out. What else remained possible 'after that he was once revealed unto them for whose cause only

[27] BL, Harl. MS 416, fo. 70.   [28] Mozley, *Foxe*, 90–1; Olsen, *Foxe*, 212.

all the commonwealth of the Jews was instituted and erected?' And he decried the Jewish pride in ancestry, for it should incline them to Christ rather than away from him:

What may be thought of Christ himself, whom we do worship? In whom if you require who was his father, he came not indeed from man but descended from God. But if you demand of his mother: he is on his mother's side a Jew born . . . an issue of the same seed that you are . . . Why do you hate and revile your own kinsman?

He chose the baptism of a Jewish convert to preach this mixture of prejudice, naivety and appeal to better judgement.[29] It is not without interest that such sentiments distinguished him quite clearly from the characteristically deferential line taken by Puritans over the Old Testament and Judaism in general.

Of Jews, who could do him and the realm no harm, he demanded conversion; from papists he expected only persecution but for them he favoured as much mercy as might be feasible. The crux of the present question touches the treatment he advocated for heretics, for those whom all the major Christian denominations – Catholic or Protestant – abominated and persecuted. He had to consider the problem all the time, of course, as he collected and wrote up his story of martyrdom through the ages, and in his book he consistently and predictably denounced persecution. Nor did he do so only for martyrdoms of the distant past or suffered by those whom he regarded as the founders of his own church, but also in the cases of men and women whom he himself thought heretical. He had no sympathy with anti-Trinitarians like Joan Bocher, but nevertheless regretted that she was burned. As is well known, his faith in toleration was positively tested in 1575 when five Dutch Anabaptists were arrested and sentenced to be burned for heresy. Foxe intervened with two powerful letters, in Latin, addressed respectively to queen and Privy Council.[30] As for Anabaptists, he declared himself utterly opposed to their tenets and wished them converted to a better faith; yet that did not seem to him to justify the sentence. He pointed out that England was really very free of such excesses (which in 1575 was true enough) and therefore had no cause to use violence against these small groups of immigrants: it would be much better to prevent

[29] John Foxe, *De Oliua Euangelica: Sermon Preached at the Baptism of a Certain Jew* (London, 1578: *STC* 11236), sigs. B.iii^v, C.vij.

[30] The letter to the queen is printed as App. X to Townsend's 'life of Foxe' prefaced to the standard edition of *AM* (I, [27–8]); for the letter to the council see BL, Harl. MS 417, fo. 101v.

them coming in the first place. However, as he told the queen, to consign to the fire the living bodies of men whose error arose rather from blindness of judgement than wilful wickedness struck him as very hard and more reminiscent of the Roman example than of Protestant custom. 'Vitae hominum, ipse homo quum sum, faveo': I am for men's lives, being a man myself. Indeed, he went on, though such feelings might look foolish, he could not even pass a slaughter-house without grieving at the thought of what was happening to the cattle there: had not God in his mercy forbidden the use of such beasts as sacrifices at his altar? So, while he agreed that Anabaptists could not just be left to themselves, since they were heretics and liable to spread dangerous doctrines, he wanted to see them dealt with by other means than the stake. At this point he weakened somewhat: his other possible means included not only prison and branding but also the gallows. What above else he wanted to avoid was a rekindling of the 'pyres and fires' of Smithfield, but (as he put it to the Council) if prudence demanded that an examples be made 'non desunt, opinor, alia supplicionum pharmaca'. However, he hoped that death was not required and asked for a month or two in which to work on those deluded Dutch deviationists; it might prove possible to save them yet. As a punishment, if they remained obdurate, he clearly preferred exile – oddly enough, the Utopian punishment for religious offenders – but was prepared to accept execution if that could be carried out by means less cruel than burning. 'Vitae faveo' – subject to the reservation 'nisi statuendum de iis exemplum iudicet prudentia'.

Foxe's special horror of the fires of Smithfield (understandable in the historian of the Marian persecution) comes out further in a legal argument he put into his letter to the Council. Had the state, he asked, in fact any right to burn anyone? If the Council were relying on the act of Henry IV (he meant *de heretico comburendo*: 2 Henry VI c. 15), he wished to point out that the alleged statute had no force since it lacked the assent of the Commons 'without which any promulgation of an act of Parliament is invalid'. He reminded the Council that he had proved the point in his book 'ex publicis et authenticis huius regni archivis'; what he called 'your printed volumes of statutes' he alleged embodied a false and mendacious view 'inserted by the cunning and sophistical malice of the papists'. It would therefore be very wrong to rekindle the fires of Smithfield, long since extinguished by the queen, through a Council decree which lacked the necessary authority of the law of the realm. Foxe may have thought that he had good legal opinion behind him, and he had himself looked up the roll of Parliament for 2 Henry IV.

However, in these historical researches Foxe unfortunately fell victim to an error which more sophisticated historians have at times repeated since: he failed to allow for the drastic changes in the structure, records and standing of Parliament, and especially of the Commons as a necessary part of it, which, culminating in the proceedings of the Reformation Parliament, had produced the 'modern' instutition familiar to Elizabethans. By the tests of his own day, the act of 1401 did indeed bear an incomplete and insufficient enacting clause but what was vouched in it fulfilled all the conditions of legal validity applicable at the time of its making.[31] Nevertheless, Foxe was right in thinking that in 1575 there existed no statutory authority for burning heretics handed over by the spiritual arm: the three relevant statutes (5 Richard II c. 5, 2 Henry IV c. 15, 2 Henry V c. 7), having all been revived by 1 & 2 Philip & Mary c. 6 after their repeal in 1547, had again been repealed in the first Parliament of Elizabeth (1 Eliz. I c. 1, sect. 6). However, though Foxe secured a reprieve of several weeks during which he and others tried in vain to dissuade the Anabaptists from their tenets, two of them were thereafter burned; one more having died in prison, the remaining two were let go. If the council issued a writ *de haeretico comburendo* they did so without legal authority; but the treatment by the judiciary of repealed or expired statutes remains an unexplored and mysterious territory.

Burnings for heresy grew exceedingly rare after 1558, and the fate of those two Dutchmen for that very reason made a stir. While it gave Foxe a chance to proclaim his genuine belief in toleration, it also showed that his views were not typical of his generation – rather less typical than More's had been of his, if we may judge by the use of the stake during his years in high office. Foxe, we must note, professed his views even after his side had won and controlled the machinery of repression, thus giving some sort of a lie to More's jibe that Tyndale would soon talk differently

---

[31] For Foxe's research see *AM*, III, 400. In the statute of 2 Henry IV none of the chapters stated an authority for this legislation; as was the custom, this was given at the head of the statute and covered all the acts contained in it. According to the formula used, the king had ordained the laws following at the prayer of the Commons and with the assent of the magnates and other lords. However, as Foxe discovered, with respect to c. 15 (the heresy act) the formula somewhat misstated the case, though no papistical malice was involved and legal validity remained unaffected. This chapter was in effect enacted in response to a request from the English clergy, who begged the lay power to assist in the extermination of heresy; in reply the king 'de consensu Magnatum et aliorum Procerum Regni' ordained certain heads of measures (including the duty of the secular arm to burn a relapsed heretic handed over by the church) which were duly drawn up (probably by the judges) as an act and thus incorporated in the statute engrossed at the end of the session and in due course included in the printed volumes (*Rotuli Parliamentorum*, III, 466–7).

about persecution if once he were in a position to dispense rather than to receive.[32] No such double standard, it would seem, for Foxe. Faced with the first threats of division in the church, More called for the stake. Faced with his own church, so lately emerged from the Marian persecution, now under heavy attack from Rome and possibly endangered by the growth of further schismatic sects, Foxe pleaded for Campion and Anabaptists alike. However, have we here anything more than a difference between two people?

There can be no question that that difference existed and mattered. More, the public figure, civil servant, judge, the confidant of kings; Foxe, a rather private man who never rose above a canonry at Salisbury and had no place at the queen's court. There were nearly forty years between them, which fact (as we shall see) perhaps mattered most. The one thing that unites them is that they owed their fame to their pens, but even as authors these products of a humanist education differed markedly. Foxe, as we have noted, found *Utopia* worth a sneer; on the other hand, Foxe's way of conducting religious controversy by means of an historical narrative turned out to be both more attractive and more effective than More's production of strictly polemical effusions. It is odd to see how their reputations for trustworthiness have see-sawed together. Until the middle of the nineteenth century More was widely understood to have twisted the evidence a bit when attacking Protestants, while Foxe was treated as gospel-truth; today most people seem to take More on trust while convinced that Foxe was quite capable of saying whatever suited his book. The earlier assessment was in fact nearer the truth and is beginning to creep back. In a variety of ways, the two men form a pair of contrasts.

The main contrast, however, lies in the psychology of their characters. Foxe's objection to persecution sprang less from calculation or reasoned

---

[32] *Confutation*, 789–91. The passage offers a fair example of More's polemical methods. First he constructs an imaginative and very tendentious case out of Tyndale's lament that the elect have always been persecuted, in such a way that Tyndale is made to appear ready to endorse persecution when it suits him. Next he speaks of thieves, heretics and murderers (a carefully arranged threesome) persecuting the Catholics in Switzerland and Saxony, calling up visions of killings for which he has no evidence: even the well-biased modern commentary (ibid., 1663) can speak only of severe restrictions on Catholic worship – and even that is an exaggeration at this point. More then clinches his case with one of his merry tales; about a lady who would have a man who committed adultery with his wife's maid 'hanged by the neck upon the nearest bough', but when asked what should happen to a woman who did likewise with her husband's man-servant answered that yes, the lady did wrong and should have a good talking-to. Neatly done, and in this case clever enough controversy, but a long way from being honest.

princple, and least of all from a weariness with theological debate: he was and always remained an ardent Protestant. Rather it reflected an ingrained passion for peace, conciliation and, as he put it, life. To the man who grieved over the fate of bullocks in the shambles nothing seems to have justified the shedding of blood, not even the cause of his faith. This point needs stressing, for it makes Foxe very exceptional even among those who were beginning to think some degree of toleration preferable to principled persecution. More similarly stands at an extreme of the spectrum and his passionate advocacy of forcible repression arose, as I have suggested before this, from a profound apprehension of the evils caused by disobedience to the church, the only protection for man's hope of order on this earth and salvation in the hereafter; and this apprehension in turn arose from a personal consciousness of man's helpless sinfulness which only the obedience exacted by the church could prevent from destroying those two necessary conditions.[33] Moreover, as he proved at the end of his life, More had a contempt for man's fear of death and pain; death to him was a release which opened the door to eternal life. I cannot see that More would ever have said, 'vitae faveo'. Exceptional in the strength of their divergent convictions, the tolerator and the persecutor embody the two possible answers to the problems raised by the Reformation in terms so stark as to be illuminating.

There was, however, one further difference between them, and a look at it takes the whole question beyond the purely personal issues. They had had very different experiences of persecution, mainly because one was born later than the other. When More attacked heresy and demanded its elimination by violence he was the man in the driving seat; his experience of persecution was that of the policeman. The story of his raid on the house of that respected London worthy, John Petyt, whom he rightly but in vain suspected of having a copy of Tyndale's New Testament, forms a splendid illustration of police methods through the ages and in any biography of More (though not here) deserves the place which has been denied to it.[34] I do not know that More ever actually witnessed a man being burned alive for the sake of his faith, though both his deeds (in pursuing heretics and their books) and his words should have been enough to allow his powerful imagination to work on the consequences for those he caught or denounced. However, he really

---

[33] See my 'The Real Thomas More?', above, vol. III, no. 45.

[34] *Narratives of the Days of the Reformation*, ed. J. G. Nichols (Camden Society, 1859), 25–7. Foxe did not use the story in *AM*, but its truth was vouched for by Petyt's wife, herself involved in it.

knew persecution only from the outside, and it is notorious that as his own tribulations grew upon him he lost his passion for persecution, not because he dreaded what might happen to himself but because he came to see its irrelevance to the truths of religion or the realities of salvation.[35] Foxe probably also never attended at a burning, but he had been an exile – a victim of persecution – and the men and women who died in the fires of Smithfield included acquaintances or friends. In a very real sense, he knew what he was talking about. Thus one result of the history of religious strife was that people came to experience persecution in reality; it jumped off the page into their lives. Of course, many reacted with a more bitter passion and a desire for revenge, but, as Foxe showed, one could also come to recoil from it, and, as Foxe also showed, it was not only those who grew sceptical about the religious issues fought over who took that line. Are there, therefore, any signs that a preference for toleration spread more widely than the mind of John Foxe as the truths about persecution became manifest?

There were very few burnings in the reign of Elizabeth, but it is, we know, notorious that the regime pursued many of its enemies to the death. The famous debate between William Cecil and William Allen merits another look.[36] Cecil – Lord Burghley – published his defence of *The Execution of Justice in England* in 1583; in the following year Allen replied with his *True, Sincere and Modest Defence of English Catholics*. At issue stood the persecution of the Catholic missionaries in England which had been going on for about half a dozen years. Cecil maintained that the enemies of the realm were being dealt with not 'upon question of religion, but justly, by order of laws, openly condemned as traitors'; the priests were executed not under any new laws invented for their case 'either for religion or against the pope's supremacy' but under the old and fundamental treason law of 1351.[37] (This was for instance true of Campion.) Against this Allen, intent on showing that the persecution was not political but religious, at length cited the new treason legislation of 1571 and 1581 (and soon 1584 as well) which by stages made it treason in itself to be a Catholic priest, especially a Jesuit, working in England. The indignation which he and his party regularly expressed over this identification of religion with treason should perhaps be assessed against

[35] This is the message of More's *Dialogue of Comfort*.
[36] The works in question are most readily available in Robert Kingdon's edition in the series 'Folger Documents of Tudor and Stuart Civilization' (Ithaca, NY, 1965); I shall use it here.
[37] Ed. Kingdon, 7.8.

Robert Persons's proposal that the first law to be passed in an England restored to Rome should make it treason to advocate any change in the 'Catholic Roman faith'.[38] Cecil contrasted the 'mild' policy of Elizabeth's government with Mary's treatment of Protestants; Allen retorted that those doings had been 'commendable and lawful'. What he meant was that if the treason act of 1351 entitled Elizabeth to execute Catholics, the heresy acts of 1401 and 1414 entitled Mary to burn Protestants. Allen struck a particularly unpleasing note when he insisted that Mary did more worthily because she chose victims of no account while Elizabeth's included quite a few persons of standing, an argument which involved degrading Cranmer by calling him names; this kind of snobbery was not commonplace at the time (as Foxe sufficiently proved) and became the prerogative of the Catholic polemicists.

Both sides indeed expended much time – Cecil markedly less than Allen – in good sixteenth-century abuse of the adversary, and Allen's tract abounded with atrocity stories about the ill-treatment of priests and the horrors of execution for treason – in which he was right, even though he exaggerated the suffiently disgusting truth. At heart, the two tracts pursued the familiar but pointless debate over the justice of deeds legitimised by statutes designed to defend respective views of public safety; they provided an unedifying commentary on Thomas Cromwell's penetrating remark to Thomas More at More's second interrogation. As Cromwell pointed out, execution for treason at the king's behest left a man quite as dead as burning for heresy at the pope's command; if one was entitled to inflict death by the law of his church, why not the other by the law of his realm?[39] The only suitable modern comment must deplore equally the fate of heretics burned and of traitors hanged, drawn and quartered.

However, in the course of the exchange the disputants did touch upon the topic of toleration. Cecil made heavy play with the fact that many subjects of the English crown 'differ in some opinions of religion from the Church of England': yet so long as they remain loyal to the queen they will suffer neither persecution for treason nor have their consciences searched 'for their contrary opinions that savour not of treason'.[40] He pointed out that even the Marian bishops who in 1559 had refused to conform and had 'maintained the Pope's authority against the laws of

[38] Robert Parsons, *Memoriall for the Intended Reformation of England*, ed. Edward Gee (London, 1690), 105.
[39] *The Correspondence of Sir Thomas More*, ed. E. F. Rogers (Princeton, 1947), 557–8.
[40] Ed. Kingdon, 9–12.

the realm' had never been put on trial, being left in comfortable seclusion in private houses. In this, by the way, he exaggerated very little. Allen riposted that the only reason why Catholics had to be persecuted under the treason acts arose from the state of the law. 'You have purposely repealed . . . all former laws of the realm for burning heretics, which smelleth of something that I need not here express' – a comment either mystifying or unpleasant. Since therefore the English church at present possessed no definition of heresy, it was compelled to persecute religion under the guise of treason.[41] Although he here scored a point of sorts, he really had the worse of the argument. The official doctrine of the English church simply did not then or ever regard Roman Catholicism as heretical; because of the bull of deposition of 1570 and the papacy's avowed intent to see the bull executed, it branded the Roman faith as politically dangerous. It was not accident or some temporary insufficiency in the law which provoked trials for treason instead of heresy against the priests. Later, however, Allen picked up Cecil's hint that co-existence (a species of toleration) was possible. If English Catholics, he said, 'might have obtained any piece of that liberty which catholics enjoy in Germany, Switzerland or other places among protestants', he would not complain.[42] How sincere was he in asking for the kind of co-existence which, as he put it, would have made it possible to practise the Catholic religion in England without resort to seminaries abroad and agitation from there? He certainly exaggerated the freedom permitted to Catholic worship in German Protestant territories after the settlement of 1555 had divided the region into mutually exclusive religious havens. Moreover, no Swiss or German ruler was threatened with deprivation by papal edict. Allen's positive point comes out later. If England's rulers refused to return to Rome – and he suggested that only fear of losing face prevented them – they should still consider the error made in refusing liberty of conscience to Catholics, 'being far the greater and more respective part of the realm'.[43] Toleration was asked for only as a preliminary stage to re-conversion.

And that, indeed, remained the position taken up by the English Catholic propagandists to the end of the reign.[44] From first to last they insisted that their religion was being persecuted in England for religion's

---

[41] Ibid., 94.   [42] Ibid., 261–2.   [43] Ibid., 265.
[44] For all this see T. H. Clanchy, *Papist Pamphleteers* (Chicago, 1964), ch. 6: 'Persecution and Toleration'.

sake and denounced the English government's allegations of treason as false. In 1580, Robert Parsons went back to Thomas More by allowing the exercise of their religion to Jews and Turks but not to heretics.[45] When he, as it has been expressed, tried 'to put a reasoned moral case' for toleration,[46] he developed the theme of the inviolability of the individual conscience, though he first of all eliminated the conscience of heretics (as More had done) on the grounds that they had been given the chance of professing the truth and had expressly and deliberately rejected it. I think he also misunderstood what conscience meant to More, who had always avoided giving it that tinge of personal judgement. However, this kind of tolerance would simply allow Catholics to practise in England and leave them free to treat Protestants as intolerable heretics the minute they got their chance; it was never meant to replace the real aim – total victory for Rome in England. At moments when Allen and Parsons thought the omens truly propitious for the triumph of Rome they dropped all talk of even such tendentious toleration; and as late as 1596, when a Spanish victory seemed increasingly improbable, Parsons returned to asking for toleration only as a convenient means for the promotion of the re-establishment of Catholic orthodoxy in England.[47]

Parsons' own words are worth attention here. His real position on toleration comes out very clearly in two pieces he wrote on either side of the year 1600, as the prospects of victory waxed and waned. In 1607 he published a reply to the Protestant propagandist Thomas Morton which had been in the making for several years.[48] As the title-page declared, the book meant to demonstrate 'that it is not impossible for subjects of different religions (especially catholics and protestants) to live together in dutiful obedience and subjection, under the government of his Majesty of Great Britain'. However, in 1596 he had put up a blueprint for the restructuring of England after a Catholic victory, a secret scheme which remained unpublished until 1690 when it was put into print in order to show what the country would have suffered if James II had won.[49] In chapter 4 Parsons discussed the treatment of three categories of subjects – Catholics, schismatics (that is, 'close or weak Catholics' who had sought peace in outward conformity), and heretics (that is, all Protestants). Obviously, the first group would take over the running of the country.

---

[45] Ibid., 145–6. [46] Ibid., 143. [47] Ibid., 148.51.
[48] *A Treatise Tending to Mitigation towards Catholic Subjects in England ...* (St Omer, 1607: STC 19417).
[49] *Memoriall*, esp. 29–34.

The second would by stages and after careful investigation be allowed back into the ruling order. As for the 'enemies, or obstinate heretics', they should at first be treated gently and have a chance to mend their ways. However, 'this toleration be only with such as live quietly and are desirous to be informed of the truth, and do not teach and preach or such to infect others'. What he advocated was 'a certain connivance or toleration of magistrates only for a certain time'. He very urgently did not wish to be misunderstood. He was not saying that Catholics and Protestants could live together peacefully within a Catholic state:

> Yet I do give notice that my meaning is not in any way to persuade hereby that liberty of religion, to live how a man will, should be permitted to any person in any Christian commonwealth, for any cause or respect whatsoever: from which I am so far off in my judgement and affection as I think no one thing to be so dangerous, dishonourable or more offensive to Almighty God in the world than that any prince should permit the Ark of Israel and Dagon, God and the Devil, to stand and be honoured together, within his realm or country.

For Parsons, toleration was only a tactic; persecution became essential if persuasion failed; and, as I said earlier, he wished to make it high treason in the secular law to speak against the faith of the Church of Rome.

One cannot imagine Parsons interceding for a prisoner of the Inquisition in Spain as Foxe did for Campion. There is really no good sign that the position of Catholic spokesmen ever really changed in the sixteenth century from that taken up by More: there being but the one church, heresy must be extinguished, and if this can be done only by violence let violence be used, whether it be the violence of the stake or the violence of armed invasion (followed, presumably, by the use of the stake). So acceptable toleration meant only provision of protection for the Catholic faction in its endeavour to restore its exclusive rule which would once more enable it to repress the Protestants whom it continued to regard as heretics. I am not, of course, saying that this view prevailed among the English Catholic laity, who better understood reality, but it formed, I maintain, the unchanging teaching of its spiritual leaders. More, living while the Catholic hierarchy was still in the saddle, had not been tempted to permit even so much toleration. On the other side, the Protestant case that such persecution as there was (more than enough of it) arose strictly from political perils and simply represented the right of the state to protect itself against subversion misleadingly ignored the religious passions which drove many individuals into persecuting with the weapons of the state an enemy hated as the servant of Antichrist. On the other hand, down at least to the early 1580s it represented official policy quite correctly. Even thereafter, when refusal to come to church would ruin a man and being a priest sufficed to bring him to the scaffold, it still remained true that these measures embodied not a strictly religious persecution but fear for what might happen to the outward uniformity thought essential for the survival of the English state without civil war. As we have seen, when the English government confronted what they themselves regarded as heretics – people who had offended in religion – they used the old instrument of the stake, even though in law they probably had no right to do so. The Elizabethan persecution of Catholics really sprang from secular and political motives, even though, pressed by panic, the age extended the definition of the supposed threat in a deplorably categoric fashion. But in respect of religion, their attitude did not preclude genuine toleration for varieties of faith, whereas the attitude of the Catholics did. Everybody, of course, drew the line against those 'heresies' which stirred up the common people, everybody except Foxe – against true sectaries, though they too were not usually burned at the stake in England as they would have been in Madrid.

As J. W. Allen demonstrated long ago, budding ideas of toleration can be found among Elizabethan Protestants, but they are (Foxe excepted) half-hearted and hesitant, so much so that Hooker, whom one would have expected to pronounce on the subject, avoids it with studious deliberation.[50] All that can be said for them is that they left doors open for the co-existence of more than one Christian faith in one community; they did not advocate it or ask the state to cease persecuting. Altogether, however, the thinkers we have considered do not really bear out the 'model' of persecution and toleration which I suggested at the start is pretty generally accepted. A leading member of the supposedly tolerant Christian humanist movement immediately set standards of persecuting determination which were never surpassed and rarely matched. Such signs of toleration as can be seen appearing had little to do with Jordan's six criteria: dissident sects grew no stronger though Elizabethan attacks on them were markedly less ferocious than those of Henry VIII or Mary had been; uniformity remained the ideal preached; trade and travel (dubious points) worked both ways and in the main encouraged each side to think more self-righteously of itself; censorship kept the threat of the printing press at bay; and an inclination towards tolerance grew among believers as much as among sceptics. It has not, of course, been

[50] J. W. Allen, *Political Thought in the Sixteenth Century* (London, 1928), 231–46.

196

possible to survey the whole field thoroughly, and further research may restore Jordan's scheme, but the test cases of More and Foxe have suggested that individual character and experience had more to do with any moves towards or away from toleration than the general developments alleged which could as easily harden attitudes as they could alter them.

Nevertheless, I should like to suggest one large thought on this whole subject which goes well beyond the confines of the sixteenth century. In the last two generations or so, it has become habitual among historians to react rather violently against the excessive use of self-satisfaction and self-congratulation that prevailed among our nineteenth-century predecessors. The glorious reign of Queen Elizabeth, the virtue and mildness of her rule, have been thrust out (among other things) from our history books; much new sympathy has at the same time replaced ancient bigotry about the Church of Rome. Even though one concomitant effect has been a curious collapse of Protestant confidence beyond what the case requires, much of this revision is wholly admirable – a move towards balance and truth. But the reaction against a blind admiration for the Reformation has also deprived us of one once familiar notion, and perhaps it is right that one who adheres to neither side in the wars of religion, or indeed to any form of the Christian faith, should remind you of it. I am glad to be able to cite approvingly the opinion of Charles and Katherine George with whom I otherwise find myself so often in disagreement. 'English Protestantism', they wrote, having cited William Perkins to show that by 1600 that branch of the faith could consider it possible that the true church might appear in various guises, 'provided in the very nature of its logic a greater scope for the development and the acceptance of ceremonial, institutional, and even doctrinal variations than did Roman Catholicism'; but, they went on to say, it did not provide 'a conscious and general programme of religious toleration'.[51] To that last reservation John Foxe formed an exception. In general, however, that century did not, and in the clash of passionate convictions perhaps could not, really achieve a truly tolerant position. To that extent it is true that only the passing of passions, perhaps the growth of a sceptical indifference, could permanently guarantee the end of persecution for religion's sake. But there are flowers and there are seeds. It was in the age of religious passions that the implications of the great schism made themselves first known. As the possibility of reunion

[51] C. H. and K. George, *The Protestant Mind of the English Reformation* (Princeton, 1961), 376–7, 380–1.

receded, true Christians of one kind came to see, by painful stages, that provided they were left alone by others they had better leave others alone too – a lesson seemingly never learned by the Catholics of that era. The powerful voices raised for true tolerance belonged to the helpless – to the likes of Michael Servetus, Michael Sattler, Caspar von Schwenckfeld. The stiller voices worked within the Church of England, among men for whom toleration was not a first condition of survival but increasingly a dictate of humanity. They observed variety and came to see true piety in various outward guises. So long as the Church of Rome adhered to its determination to rule all Christians, only Protestantism offered a hope of an end to persecution.

59

AUSEINANDERSETZUNG UND ZUSAMMENARBEIT ZWISCHEN RENAISSANCE UND REFORMATION IN ENGLAND*

Zunächst muß man definieren, denn beide Begriffe – Renaissance und Reformation – sind in der englischen Geschichte nicht eindeutig. Handelt es sich bei der Reformation ursprünglich um den Bruch mit dem Papst unter Heinrich VIII. oder um die vorübergehende Einführung des Protestantismus unter Eduard VI. oder um die scheinbar endgültige Bekehrung zum Protestantismus von 1559? Ein paar Historiker behaupten sogar, der Protestantismus habe selbst in der zweiten Hälfte des 16. Jahrhunderts noch keinen sicheren Sieg erreicht: Erst durch den Bürgerkrieg im folgenden Jahrhundert sei sein Fortdauern garantiert worden. Diese Ansicht halte ich für etwas bedenklich, obwohl gewiß die Weiterentwicklung der englischen Kirche nach 1559 neue Probleme im Verhältnis zur Renaissance aufwarf. Nur die Königin Elisabeth blieb bei der Ansicht, die Supremats- und Uniformitätsakte ihres ersten Parlaments hätten die Umwälzung beendet. Heute betont man (m. E. zu einseitig) den langsamen und mehrfach unterbrochenen Fortschritt des Protestantismus im Volke. Jedenfalls ist es klar, daß man nicht von einer einzigen Reformation reden kann, die sich in direkter Linie von der Ausschaltung des Papstes zur calvinistischen Kirche der 90er Jahre entwickelte. Dazu kommt noch die Einsicht der jüngsten Forschung, die

---

* [*Renaissance, Reformation: Gegensätze und Gemeinsamkeiten*, hrsg. v. A. Buck (Wolfenbüttel, 1984), 217–25.] Dieser Vortrag wurde ohne Manuskript gehalten und sollte auf Tonband aufgenommen werden. Da dies mißglückte, habe ich ihn aus dem Gedächtnis rekonstruiert. Ich möchte aber die ursprüngliche Idee beibehalten. Es war ein Vortrag und kein mit einem wissenschaftlichen Apparat ausgestatteter Aufsatz. Daher bleibt es bei dieser einzigen Anmerkung. Ich möchte sie auch dazu benützen, auf ein paar neuere Abhandlungen hinzuweisen, die, abgesehen von meinen eigenen Arbeiten, hier meine Ausführungen beeinflußt haben: P. Collinson *Archbishop Grindal 1519–1583* (London, 1979); Ders.: 'English Puritanism' Historical Association Pamphlet (1983); H. M. Colvin u. a., *The History of the King's Works*. Bd. IV/2 (London, 1982); J. F. Davis, *Heresy and Reformation in the South-East of England, 1520–1559* (London, 1983); C. Haigh, 'The Recent Historiography of the English Reformation', in *HJ*, 25 (1982), 995–1007; P. Lake, *Moderate Puritanism and the Elizabethan Church* (Cambridge, 1982); N. Tyacke, 'Puritanism, Arminianism and Counter-Revolution', in *The Origins of the English Civil War*, hrsg. v. C. Russell (London, 1973).

den nicht unwichtigen Einfluß der einheimischen, vorlutherischen Häresie der Lollarden wiederentdeckt hat. Man muß also drei separate Stadien bis zum Triumph der Reformation berücksichtigen und danach auch die weitere Geschichte der Kirche bis zur Restauration der Monarchie im Jahre 1660, die in der Entwicklung des englischen Protestantismus eine wahre Zäsur darstellt. Bei diesem komplizierten Vorgang wirkte natürlich das Zusammentreffen mit der Renaissance recht verschiedenartig. Im vorliegenden Rahmen kann ich all dies nur in großen Zügen und daher auch etwas oberflächlich erklären.

Eine Definition der englischen Renaissance macht noch größere Schwierigkeiten. Obwohl besonders Kunst- und Literaturhistoriker oft von einer englischen Renaissance sprechen, läßt sich nicht leicht feststellen, was damit gemeint sei. Nur über eins soll man sich aber einig sein: Der Begriff 'englische Renaissance' muß auf solche Erscheinungen beschränkt werden, die von der wahren, europäischen Renaissance abzuleiten sind. Andere Veränderungen und Vorgänge, die zufällig zur gleichen Zeit aber nur auf englischem Boden auftraten, gehören nicht dazu. Insofern es eine englische Renaissance gab, ist sie die englische Version der europäischen Renaissance. Die Wiederentdeckung der Antike vollzog sich bekanntlich in zwei Bereichen; Einerseits in Italien, wo es sich um Entwicklungen in der Kunst (vor allem in der Malerei und der Architektur des Quattrocento) und die Wirkung von Dichtern und Denkern in der Literatur und der Philosophie handelte, andererseits in dem nördlichen Humanismus, insbesondere in dem von Erasmus eingeleiteten christlichen Humanismus, der durch Vermittlung von Thomas More auch in England Einfluß gewann.

Das Quattrocento und die Dichtung lassen sich leicht aus dieser Diskussion eliminieren. Die englische Architektur des Reformationszeialters hatte mit kontinentalen Entwicklungen einen so geringen Zusammenhang, daß man von einem wirklichen Einfluß nicht reden kann. Gebaut wurde viel. Heinrich VIII., der 13 Häuser und Paläste ererbte, hinterließ über 50, die fast alle während seiner Regierungszeit neu errichtet oder gründlich umgebaut worden waren, und zwar in einem aus der eigenen Tradition stammenden Stile. Obwohl seine Nachfolger mehr damit beschäftigt waren, die teuren Spielzeuge wieder loszuwerden, hielten auch sie die italienischen Vorbilder fern. Adlige, bürgerliche und ländliche Bauten blieben ebenfalls von der Renaissance unberührt. Die Malerei des 16. Jahrhunderts – fast ausschließlich Porträtmalerei – war in England hauptsächlich auf ausländische Maler angewiesen; die einheimische Entwicklung der Miniaturen inspirierte sich noch an der mittelalterlichen Manuskripttradition. Obwohl manche künstlerischen Produkte (besonders Wandteppiche) aus dem Ausland eingeführt wurden, blieb der Geschmack bis ins frühe 17. Jahrhundert nach europäischen Begriffen recht altmodisch. Jedenfalls kreuzten sich Kunst und Reformation niemals.

Im Schrifttum findet man allerdings Einflüsse aus der Renaissance. Besonders verhalf das Beispiel von Petrarca, Boccaccio und ihren Nachfolgern der englischen Dichtung zu einer, nach der Verkalkung der Chaucer-Tradition sehr notwendigen Erneuerung. Doch kann man die Dichter der Zeit mit der Reformation nicht in eine bedeutungsvolle Verbindung bringen – weder als Anhänger noch als Gegner. Die ersten erfolgreichen Schüler der Renaissance waren der der Reformation zuneigende Thomas Wyatt und der der alten Religion treu gebliebene Graf von Surrey[1]; und in ihrer Dichtung spielte ihre Stellung zur Reformation keine Rolle. Die Blütezeit unter Elisabeth scheint noch niemand einer religionsbedingten Kritik unterzogen zu haben – aus guten Gründen, denn der Zusammenhang scheint bestenfalls minimal zu sein. Shakespeare haben bigotte Katholiken für sich in Anspruch genommen, weil er sehr oft Hinweise auf den alten Glauben einfließen läßt; doch trifft das genauso zu wie die Behauptung, nur ein Lordkanzler hätte so viel von den Rechtssachen verstehen können wie der Verfasser der Shakespeareschen Stücke. Wenn bei Shakespeare Bettelmönche, Marienverehrung, Heiligenkultus und dergleichen vorkommen, beweist das nur, daß er seinen Quellen treu blieb und sich darauf verlassen konnte, die Zuhörerschaft würde diese 'altmodischen' Anspielungen noch immer ohne Zögern begreifen. Der italienische Neuplatonismus, besonders der des Giovanni Pico di Mirandola, beeinflußte Thomas More; doch lehnte More die Reformation aus Gründen ab, die damit nichts zu tun hatten und aus einer viel früheren Theologie herstammten. So wird deutlich, daß in England Quattrocento und Reformation nicht auf dem gleichen Geleise fuhren: Man würde vergebliche nach Auseinandersetzung oder Zusammenarbeit suchen.

Wenden wir uns zum Humanismus. Hier erkennt man sofort einen eindeutigen Zusammenhang, schon deshalb, weil für Erasmus und seine Gefolgschaft die Kirche und der Glauben in der Mitte ihrer Gedankenwelt standen. Den Humanismus zu definieren, versuche ich nicht: Wie schon mehrmals in diesem Kolloquium festgestellt wurde, ist dies ebenso schwierig wie es andererseits klar ist, daß es etwas gegeben hat, das diesen

---

[1] [Wrong: Surrey leant towards the Reformation.]

Namen verdient. Hier kommt es hauptsächlich auf den Humanismus als eine Studienmethode an, als ein wissenschaftliches System. In England entnahm man der erasmischen Lehre sehr schnell ein besonderes Gedankengut, nämlich die Pädagogik. Der andere Aspekt des Vorbildes, die originäre Forschung in Theologie und Wissenschaft, war viel wirksamer auf dem Kontinent als auf der Insel, wo man jedoch das Schulwesen energisch nach humanistischem Muster ausbaute und umgestaltete. Die Lateinschule übernahm sofort die Führung in der Erziehung und behielt sie auch fast unangefochten bis ins 20. Jahrhundert in einem erstaunlich langwierigen, oft auch langweiligen Prozeß. Nur in Engalnd, glaube ich, verfaßten Schulkinder noch in den 30er Jahren unseres Jahrhunderts lateinische Übersetzungen aus der Muttersprache. Diese Schulung hat bedeutsame soziale und historiographische Folgen gehabt. Im letzten Jahrhundert kritisierten die Anhänger Humboldts die englischen Universitäten besonders deswegen, weil sie bloße Fortsetzungen der Schulen wären. Erst seit dem zweiten Weltkrieg ist es wichtiger geworden zu wissen, an welcher Universität jemand studiert hat als an welcher Schule. Nur in England wurden und blieben Schuldirektoren wohlbekannte Figuren in der allgemeinen Lebensgeschichte, während von den Gelehrten nur Spezialisten gehört hatten. Für unsere Zwecke liegt die Bedeutung dieser einseitigen Entwicklung des erasmischen Erbes darin, daß von der Mitte des 16. Jahrhunderts an alle Bildung zunächst an den Schulen, bald auch an den Universitäten, von den christlich-humanistischen Prinzipien beherrscht wurde. Die Generation, die die endgültige Aufnahme der Reformation vollzog, war humanistisch erzogen. Seit dieser Zeit ist also der Zusammenhang unbezweifelbar. Doch auch die Frühreformation konnte dem Rencontre mit dem Humanismus nicht entgehen. Hier also liegt unser Thema: Die Auseinandersetzung und Zusammenarbeit zwischen Renaissance und Reformation läuft in England auf die Begegnung zwischen dem christlichen Humanismus und den verschiedenen Stadien des anwachsenden Protestantismus hinaus.

Obwohl der Bruch mit Rom unter Heinrich VIII. hauptsächlich aus politischen und dynastischen Ursachen erfolgte, stand auch die Religion von Anfang an zur Debatte, besonders da der Streit mit dem Papst schnell zu einem dauernden Schisma führte und den reformierenden Absichten Cromwells und Cranmers die Türe öffnete. Bekanntlich stießen diese Vorgänge gerade bei den angeblichen Führern des englischen Humanismus auf entschlossenen Widerstand. Die Hinrichtung von Thomas More und John Fisher scheint zu beweisen, daß es hier zwischen Reformation und Renaissance zu einer überaus scharfen Auseinandersetzung gekommen ist. Dieses traditionelle Urteil wird heute als nicht mehr so überzeugend angesehen. Fisher war immer mehr Theologe als Humanist gewesen; in seinen Streitschriften gegen Luther und dann auch gegen Heinrichs VIII. Ehescheidungsprozeß tritt er eher als spätmittelalterlicher Scholastiker auf. Bei ihm war also der Humanismus nur eine modische Tünche gewesen. Ob More ungefähr nach 1528 überhaupt noch ein Humanist genannt werden kann, ist die Frage, trotz der Behauptungen seiner vielen Verehrer, zu denen ich nicht gehöre. Von da an schrieb er ja nur noch polemische Schriften gegen die Ketzer, die eine erstaunliche Abhängigkeit von der Scholastik, dazu besonders von Augustin verraten. Er war ein ebenso eifriger Schüler dieses Kirchenvaters wie Luther, und seine Einschätzung des menschlichen Potentials nach dem Sündenfall ist genauso pessimistisch wie die des Reformators. Nur zogen beide sehr verschiedene Schlüsse aus denselben Prämissen. Während Luther die Lösung der Probleme der sündigen Menschheit in der freien Gnade Gottes entdeckte und daher zu den Begriffen 'sola fide' und 'sola scriptura' kommen konnte, versteifte sich der Jurist More fast verzweifelt auf eine Institution, die 'sola ecclesia', der allein die Verwaltung der Gnadenmittel zustand. Beide gingen von der Theologie des Paulus und des Augustin aus – der Weg des einen führte zur Revolution, der des anderen zur Tradition zurück. Das humanistische Schlagwort 'homo mensura' war für More und Fisher ebenso unannehmbar wie für Luther. Letzten Endes waren sie alle keine Humanisten. Dazu kam noch, daß More und Fisher an den Kampf mit den einheimischen Ketzern gewöhnt waren, mit deren Lehre sie sofort die neue, aus Deutschland eingeführte Häresie verwechselten. Die vorherige Erfahrung verursachte bei ihnen eine viel härtere Einstellung, als man sie z. B. bei Erasmus vorfindet.

Daher hatte der Widerstand dieser untypischen Humanisten gegen die Reformation nichts mit ihrem Humanismus zu tun, sondern ging aus Beweggründen hervor, die eigentlich als antihumanistisch bezeichnet werden sollten. Es ist ein Irrtum, diese Männer als echte Vertreter der humanistischen Weltanschauung zu betrachten, und dieser Irrtum hat lange Zeit die Tatsache verschleiert, daß die jüngere Humanistengeneration sofort die Reformation willkommen hieß und alle Stufen ihrer Weiterentwicklung enthusiastisch unterstützte. Sowohl die Gruppe von Universitätsgelehrten, die sich um Cromwell scharte, als auch die Bischöfe, die er und Cranmer zur Einsetzung erkoren, waren deutlich humanistisch gefärbt. Das gilt für begeisterte Reformatoren wie Robert Barnes, einen persönlichen Freund Luthers, oder Hugh Latimer, den erfolgreichsten Prediger der englischen Frühreformation; es gilt auch für Cromwells begabtesten Propagandisten, Richard Morison, und auch für den besten Philosophen dieser Bewegung, Thomas Starkey, der zu früh starb, um sich zum Protestantismus zu bekennen.

Als dann nach der Reaktion der 40er Jahre die echte religiöse Reformation unter dem Protektor Somerset eingeführt wurde, konnte sie sich nicht nur auf die aus dem Ausland herangezogenen Theologen wie Martin Bucer oder Peter Martyr verlassen, sondern auch auf einheimische Vertreter, sowohl Laien als Kleriker, die alle in ihrer Gedankenwelt Erasmus viel näher standen als Luther. Dies war ja einer der Gründe, warum die englische Reformation mehr nach Zürich als nach Sachsen blickte. Die führenden Humanisten der Zeit – Männer wie Sir John Cheke oder Sir Thomas Smith, die hervorragendsten englischen Kenner des Griechischen – waren alle Protestanten. Widerstand sammelte sich weiterhin um solche Vertreter der älteren Theologie und besonders des alten Kirchenrechtes wie Stephen Gardiner, der seine Wissenschaft zu einer Zeit erworben hatte, als die Universitäten vom Humanismus noch unberührt gewesen waren. Prinzipiell ist es also eindeutig, daß jede Stufe der Reformation von Anfang an bis zum Tode Eduards VI. in Zusammenarbeit mit der einzigen in England vorzufindenen Manifestation der Renaissance, d. h. dem Humanismus, verlief.

Nach 1553 änderte sich die Lage. Von da an gab es wenige Gebildete im Lande, die sich dem Einfluß des Humanismus in den Schulen und Universitäten hätten entziehen können, so daß Vertreter der Renaissance auf beiden Seiten begegnen. Daß die Gegenreformation ebenso humanistisch eingestellt sein konnte wie die aus der Schweiz vordringende Reformation, ist ja bekannt; man denke nur an das Schulwesen der Jesuiten. Die Wiederherstellung der römischen Kirche in England unter Königin Maria wurde von einem führenden europäischen Humanisten älteren Gepräges begleitet, dem Kardinal Reginald Pole, der die letzten zwanzig Jahre in Italien verbracht hatte. Und obwohl die nächsten Reformatoren Englands wie z. B. Matthew Parker und Edmund Grindal sich zum Humanismus bekannten, trifft das natürlich auch auf Oxforder Gelehrte wie Edmund Campion und William Allen zu, die am katholischen Glauben festhielten. Beide Seiten waren humanistisch erzogen und benützten bei ihrem Studium und in ihren Schriften humanistische Methoden. Die Suche nach einer Verbindung zwischen Reformation und Renaissance wird eigentlich bedeutungslos; man könnte fast annehmen, die hier gestellte Frage sei mit der Gründung der englischen Staatskirche im Jahre 1559 als beendet anzusehen.

Es wäre richtig, das Stadium einer offensichtlichen und bemerkenswerten Zusammenarbeit hier abzuschließen, denn nach 1559 bahnte sich eine erste wirkliche Auseinandersetzung zwischen dem protestantischen Glauben der englischen Reformation und der humanistischen Bildung der englischen Protestanten an. Eine solche Auseinandersetzung trat bei ihren katholischen Landsleuten und humanistischen Kollegen aus guten Gründen nicht zu Tage: Die erneuerte Kirche von Rom, die sich von Augustin Thomas von Aquino zugewandt hatte, hatte sich dem Humanismus in gewissen Grundzügen angepaßt, die dem Protestantismus Schwierigkeiten machten. Zunächst hatten diese Schwierigkeiten allerdings wenig mit der Dogmenlehre und noch weniger mit der Ekklesiologie zu tun. Sie veranlaßten niemanden, sich von dem zunehmend calvinistischen Glauben der anglikanischen Kirche abzuwenden oder den Ekel vor der päpstlichen Kirche zu überwinden, obwohl sie dazu beitrugen, daß noch vor der Jahrhundertwende hie und da Zweifel an der Reformation auftraten, die dann im nächsten Jahrhundert gewichtige Folgen haben sollten.

Das Problem enstand aus der Spannung zwischen den Anthropologien des Protestantismus und des Humanismus. Auf diese Reibungsmöglichkeit ist ja auch schon mehrmals während dieses Kolloquiums hingewiesen worden, besonders in dem Referat von Herrn Buck. Etwas vereinfachend kann man die Spannung aus der Auseinandersetzung zwischen Luther und Erasmus über den menschlichen Willen ableiten. Eine Weltanschauung – die Überzeugung, der Mensch sei hilflos sündig – die der angebliche Vertreter der humanistischen Tradition More und der angeblich antihumanistische Revolutionär Luther geteilt hatten, ohne deshalb ihre Feindschaft zu überwinden, bereitete jetzt den Erben des von dem Humanismus begünstigten Protestantismus auch in England unerwartete Schwierigkeiten. Die überspitzte Prädestinationslehre des entwickelten Calvinismus ließ dem Menschen keine Chance zur eigenen Besserung: Ohne die Gnade Gottes, die er nicht beeinflussen konnte, blieb er ein rettungsloser Sünder, und ob ihm die Gnade gewährt wurde, war durch das Gebot Gottes schon vor der Schöpfung festgelegt worden. (Die englischen Calvinisten waren 'Supralapisten': Nach ihrer Lehre gehörte der erste Sündenfall auch zum Plane Gottes). Hingegen hatte sich der christliche Humanismus erasmischer Art immer durch eine optimistische Einschätzung der Kräfte, die dem Menschen zur Selbsthilfe verliehen worden waren, ausgezeichnet, wie schon das *Enchiridion* von

Erasmus klarmacht. In der Frühzeit der Reformation war es selbst für die, die den freien Willen und die guten Werke ablehnten, möglich gewesen, an einen Rest des guten Prinzips im sündigen Menschen zu glauben, besonders, da die englischen Theologen sich bisher mehr mit den ethischen und sozialen Hoffnungen der Reformation befaßt hatten als mit den raffinierten Punkten der Dogmatik.

Die jüngere Generation hingegen stand unter dem Einfluß überzeugter Calvinisten. Hier treffen wir die Leute, die man Puritaner nennt, obwohl der Name heute jede feste Definition verloren hat und von der Forschung nur mit Zurückhaltung angewendet wird. Ihre humanistische Grundausbildung schenkte ihnen ein Vertrauen in den Menschen; jedoch ihre theologische Weiterbildung verneinte dies ausdrücklich. Die Spannung ist deutlich und würde sich dokumentieren lassen, wenn dazu Zeit wäre. Für die nachdenklicheren Kleriker entstand sie besonders dann, wenn die Karriere sie aus den Universitäten, wo es ja nur um Theorie und Spitzfindigkeit ging, ins Pfarramt führte. Wie konnte man es einer einfachen Laiengemeinde in einem Dorfe beibringen, daß die meisten von ihnen ohne ihre eigene Schuld und ohne irgendeine Möglichkeit, ihrem Schicksal zu entgehen, zum ewigen Tode verurteilt wären? Wie konnte man die Gemeinde zu einem besseren und frömmeren Leben ermahnen, wenn man behaupten mußte, selbst ein anständiges Leben trage zum eigenen Heil nichts bei? Man kann sich den inneren Zwiespalt bei den sanftmütigeren, aber doch puritanischen Geistlichen vorstellen, die ihren ehrlichen Glauben mit ihrer ebenso ehrlichen Menschenliebe nicht in Einklang zu bringen vermochten. Ein unkomplizierter Fanatiker wie John Knox brauchte sich hier keine Sorgen zu machen. Ein Calvinist seiner Art schöpfte Freude aus der Überzeugung, als wahrer Erwählter stehe er vor einer im allgemeinen von Gott zurückgewiesenen Menge. Andererseits ist es kein Wunder, daß ein so um die Seelen bekümmerter Pfarrer wie John Foxe, der Martyrologe, bei Luther den Trost suchte und fand, den ihm Calvin nicht anbot.

In den 80er Jahren trat daher auf den Universitäten – selbst in dem überwältigend puritanischen Cambridge – bei ein paar Theologen die Neigung auf, die strenge Logik des Calvinismus zu mildern. Man spricht heute von einer vorarminianischen Bewegung, der z. B. Peter Baro und Lancelot Andrewes angehörten und die auch bei Richard Hooker Spuren hinterließ. Die adiaphoristische Einstellung, die der Anglikanismus von Anfang an freudig begrüßt hatte, konnte auch immer noch ein wenig ausgedehnt werden, aber für gute Puritaner – überzeugte Calvinisten – ging dies denn doch etwas zu weit. Bis dahin hatte es zwischen ihnen und den konformen Protestanten eigentlich keine theologischen Streitpunkte gegeben. Die Puritaner griffen nur Äußerlichkeiten an wie z. B. das Knien bei dem Abendmahl oder den Ringwechsel bei der Hochzeit, Zeremonien, die ihnen nicht reformiert genug vorkamen. Nur einige wenige, rasch unterdrückte Extremisten beabsichtigten, die bischöfliche Kirche mit ihrem königlichen Oberhaupt in eine presbyterianische Organisation umzuwandeln. Doch die anthropologischen Zweifel führten zu einem Streit über die Grundlagen des Glaubens, der die Kirche entzweizubrechen drohte. Der Friedensversuch der sogenannten Bündnistheologie ('covenant theology'), die man einst von Heinrich Bullinger übernommen hatte und nun zur Grundlage einer Versöhnung im englischen Calvinismus auszubauen versuchte, da sie dem Menschen bei der Erlösung eine etwas aktivere Rolle zuzusprechen schien, empörte die strengen Puritaner und war für die 'arminianisch' Gesinnten unzureichend.

Daß es erst während des Bürgerkrieges und auch dann nur zeitweise zu einem vollständigen Bruch kam, verdankte der Anglikanismus seinem mittelalterlichen Erbe. Bekanntlich verbindet ja die englische Staatskirche eine katholische Organisation mit einem protestantischen Glauben. Diese Organisation hat man auch als Begründung für die von Anfang an betonte Behauptung herangezogen, die Kirche von England sei eine katholische Kirche und stamme in ununterbrochener Erbfolge von der primitiven Kirche ab. Wie man das auch beurteilt, sie war wirklich in einer Beziehung der spätmittelalterlichen lateinischen Kirche ähnlicher als alle anderen Kirchen, die aus den Wirren des 16. Jahrhunderts hervorginnge. Sie behielt die Fähigkeit bei, Strömungen verschiedener und sogar einander gegensätzlicher Art in sich aufzunehmen. Selbst die katholische Kirche ging ja aus dem Tridentinum viel exklusiver hervor, als sie es vor der Reformation gewesen war. Hingegen konnte der anglikanische Protestantismus Variationen dulden, die anderswo nicht unter einem Dach untergebracht werden konnten. Seine Glaubensformel – die 39 Artikel – ist so weit gefaßt, daß wohl nur der Türke und der Teufel sie nicht hätten unterschreiben können. (Die Artikel wenden sich mehr gegen das Täufertum als gegen den Katholizismus). Gerade diese Versöhnlichkeit it dafür verantwortlich, daß wir heute solche Schwierigkeiten mit dem elisabethanischen Puritanismus haben: Es handelt sich eben nicht um deutlich verschiedene Differenzen oder gar Sekten, sondern um Schattierungen innerhalb eines umfassenden Staatskirchentums. Nur keinen öffentlichen Skandal wollte man riskieren. Solange die Pfarrer die vom Gesetz lizensierte Liturgie benützten und die vorgeschriebenen Priestergewänder trugen, konnten sie sogar recht verschiedenartig predigen. Selbst die Königin mußte manchmal kritische puritanische Predigten über sich ergehen lassen.

Daher machte der Anglikanismus es möglich, mit der Zeit den rauhen Calvinismus abzuschleifen, so daß der humanistische Bestandteil seiner Grundlagen erhalten werden konnte. Der Arminianismus des Erzbischofs Laud verusachte nur deshalb so viel Empörung, weil er der Kirche auch in der Theologie eine monolithische Einheit aufzwingen wollte – also gegen eins ihrer Grundprinzipien verstieß. Infolgedessen wurden die staatskirchlichen Puritaner zu verfolgten Sektierern. Die Verschärfung der Verhältnisse führte auch sofort zu der Suche nach einer Vermittlung. Von den 1630er Jahren ab findet man z. B. bei der Versammlung schöner Seelen in Great Tew oder bei den sogenannten Cambridger Platonisten Friedensbewegungen, die die Strenge des Protestantismus mittels der Milde des Humanismus menschlich annehmbarer machen wollten. Nach dem Trauma des Bürgerkrieges sah man sich nur widerwillig dazu gezwungen, die äußere Uniformität aufzugeben. Doch ermöglichte der Rückzug der unbeugsamen Gewissen in das Gefilde der geduldeten Dissenter den Neubau einer umfassenden Kirche mit einem gemäßigt protestantischen Glauben, in dem das humanistische Erbe auch Platz finden konnte. Gewiß steckte dahinter die Gefahr des Deismus oder doch wenigstens eines lauen und erastischen Glaubens (Latitudinarianism); gewiß kam es von Zeit zu Zeit zu weiteren Rissen im Gebäude, wie z. B. bei der Abtrennung der Methodisten. Dennoch sollte man die Geschicklichkeit einer Kirche anerkennen, die einen wahren Humanismus mit erinem wahren Protestantismus zu verbinden verstand und damit der viel größeren Gefahr der Engstirnigkeit und des Menschenhasses entging. In der 1660 restaurierten anglikanischen Kirche versöhnten sich Reformation und Renaissance wieder so, wie sie es bei der Gründung dieser Kirche gewesen waren.

60

HUMANISM IN ENGLAND*

I

Overwhelmed as at present we are by students of humanism in Tudor England – by art historians, literary historians, ordinary historians – we fail to remember how relatively recent that outburst is.[1] Until the 1940s, Frederic Seebohm's barnacle-encrusted study, first published in the year of the Second Reform Bill,[2] was still being cited as not only authoritative but actually dominant; even in 1959 the second edition of Conyers Read's bibliography did not include a section specifically on this topic. Instead it scattered relevant material among such headings as 'Ecclesiastical history – general' or 'Education'.[3] By 1968, the situation had changed sufficiently for Mortimer Levine to devote a section of his bibliography to intellectual history; this accommodated most of the proper studies, by then much increased in number.[4] Until the war, two convictions governed inherited wisdom. One was that English humanism should be approached from Italian origins; the other believed that its career ended with the defeat of the papal church in England. The first notion produced an interest in such lesser figures as William Grocyn and Thomas Linacre, generally rather overrated as pioneers; the second resulted from a devout belief in John Fisher and Thomas More as the greatest lights of English humanism, a belief much encouraged by the canonisations of 1935. In his extraordinarily influential biography of More, R. W. Chambers linked both streams: he emphasised More's

---

* [*The Impact of Humanism on Western Europe*, ed. A. Goodman and A. MacKay (London, 1990), 259–78.]

[1] This chapter does not pretend to exhaustive coverage; of necessity it will deal with the main developments only.

[2] F. Seebohm, *The Oxford Reformers* (London, 1867; revised edn, 1869).

[3] Conyers Read (ed.), *Bibliography of British History: Tudor Period 1485–1603* (2nd edn, Oxford, 1959). The works listed under general church history (pp. 173–4) included a good deal on humanism, most of it remarkably venerable. The appearance of W. G. Zeeveld's book (n. 8, below) in the general political section suggests that the compilers read only its title.

[4] M. Levine (ed.), *Bibliographical Handbooks: Tudor England 1485–1603* (Cambridge, 1968), 92–100. Here, too, religion usurped part of the relevant publications.

derivation from Ficino and Pico, and he decreed that with the death of his hero humanism had died in England.[5] Erasmus was not forgotten, but he tended to appear as the pupil of Colet and associate of More. Seebohm's inclusion of him among, of all things, the Oxford reformers set a scene: he was, so to speak, absorbed into the English manifestation of humanism, a step behind the tragic victims of Henry VIII, whose disappearance closed a glorious chapter in the nation's intellectual life and initiated the dark days of Protestant bigotry.

A new era in the study of humanism opened in the later 1940s. One of the innovators was Denys Hay, whose work on Polydore Vergil, begun in 1937, reinforced the tendency to look towards Italy but reached a different level altogether of scholarship and insight.[6] His splendid edition of that part of Vergil's *Anglica Historia* that dealt with the reign of Henry VII had shown him that the Roman Catholic tradition of humanism in England ignored far too many other influences of a strictly secular sort.[7] His Vergil emerged not just as a papal collector who happened to dislike Wolsey and kept a chronicle, but as a highly productive man of learning and of influence, a man who shared the concerns of Erasmus, though he lacked the Dutchman's originality. Hay thus drew attention to the density of humanist activity in England; he got behind the front men and taught us to look also at the second rank. The same lesson was taught, even more effectively, by Gordon Zeeveld's study of a group of young English scholars gathered around Reginald Pole at Padua.[8] Zeeveld's innovations, seemingly unsuspected by himself, proved powerful. In the first place, he demonstrated what no one in this field of research had previously grasped: for humanist writings, evidence in print alone does not suffice and the historian must also look at treatises left in manuscript. This recognition greatly enlarged the available material as well as the company of humanists to be studied. Secondly, Zeeveld opened up the possibility that intellectuals might have exercised a direct influence on national policies. And thirdly, without remarking on it, he helped to put an end to the Chambers doctrine according to which English humanism died in 1535. This point

[5] R. W. Chambers, *Thomas More* (London, 1935). Read, in one of his absurd annotations (see his no. 481) called the book 'scholarly but partisan'. In fact, its partisanship gained strength from sizeable defects in scholarship.

[6] D. Hay, *Polydore Vergil: Renaissance Historian and Man of Letters* (Oxford, 1952).

[7] Denys Hay (ed.), *The Anglica Historia of Polydore Vergil AD 1485–1537*, Royal Hist. Soc., Camden 3rd series 74 (1950).

[8] W. Gordon Zeeveld, *Foundations of Tudor Policy* (Cambridge, Mass., 1948).

had previously been made by Douglas Bush,[9] but his voice had failed to drown the popish message.

Since the early 1950s, studies of humanism in England have in the main followed four different lines of enquiry. The bulk of the work has concerned itself with particular individuals – men of learning and men of affairs. Out of these investigations there came by stages the realisation that among the foremost characterstics of English humanism was the ambition to apply the results of learning to the service of social amelioration. Later there arose unexpected doubts about the old hero figures in this landscape whose right to be counted humanists became less certain than it had been. Lastly, very recently, the supposed 'Erasmian' coherence of the movement in England has been questioned. I propose now to track these four different groups of writings, though, of course, I recognise that they must not be thought strictly delimited one from another. Perhaps, then, we shall be able to see where at present we stand and where we should go from here. Despite the flood I mentioned, there is certainly no cause to think that the chase is over.

II

The great figures of the earlier analysis have received further attention. John Fisher has not had much of it because his share in the resistance to Henry VIII's first divorce has shut out an investigation of his purely scholarly work, but the large compendium put together by Edward Surtz will at least prove a good starting point for future scholars.[10] The book comprises a fairly detailed analysis of Fisher's many writings and tends to demonstrate that, thanks to the Lutheran Reformation which roused him to a passionate defence of the existing order, he should chiefly be regarded as a traditional theologian. It was in that guise that he impressed his contemporaries in Europe. However, he also fulfilled some of the conditions of the humanist stereotype, especially in his support for the study of Greek and Hebrew and in his services to education. His involvement with Cambridge, of which he was chancellor for thirty-one years (1504–35), where he presided over two Colleges (Michaelhouse and Queens'), and where he became instrumental in the founding of two more (Christ's and St John's), constitutes his best claim to the title of humanist. A little conference held there to commemorate his death

[9] D. Bush, 'Tudor humanism and Henry VIII', *University of Toronto Quarterly*, 7 (1938), 162–77.
[10] E. Surtz, SJ, *the Works and Days of John Fisher* (Cambridge, Mass., 1967).

very properly concentrated on that aspect of his life and never got around to the issues that came to terminate his life.

As Surtz showed, in 1535 the European face of Fisher easily outshone that of Thomas More, but it did not take long for their standing to be reversed. Nor has More retired from the champion's place. On the contrary, the last thirty-five years have raised him ever higher, thanks especially to two very different enterprises. Founded and dominated by the Abbé Germain Marc'hadour at Angers, a gathering of the devout calling themselves 'Amici Thomae Mori' have been keeping the laurels green by means of a journal. *Moreana* contains an extraordinary mix of matters (I cherish the memory of a set of verses entitled 'A posthumous poem by St Thomas More'), but in more recent years it has also published a number of sensible articles and reviews. Since both Marc'hadour and his company started from the fixed position that More was a saint of the church and therefore beyond criticism, *Moreana*, adding much detail, has not greatly developed our knowledge of the man; more particularly, it has hampered the study of his humanism because his criticism of the church has had to be played down.

The other enterprise also sprang from feelings of piety but produced vastly more substantial results. This is the great edition of More's *Complete Works*, published by the Yale University Press. It was initiated by Richard Sylvester, who until his sadly premature death in 1978 remained its general editor and driving force.[11] Most of the fifteen volumes so far published do not throw light on More the humanist because the bulk of his own massive production was directed elsewhere (against heretics and concerning the after-life), but three books do contribute, being in fact the essence of his claim to the humanist accolade. More's cooperation with Erasmus in producing translations of Lucian throws the clearest light on his endeavour to train himself as a humanist scholar;[12] his incomplete but immensely influential account of Richard III displays an idiosyncratic but also humanist ambition to write a new kind of history;[13] and *Utopia* remains, of course, his chief claim to fame in that role.[14] The great edition has stimulated much work on the man, some of it in the introduction to those volumes, some in separate

---

[11] *The Complete Works of St Thomas More* (hereafter *CW*), ed. Richard Sylvester et al. (New Haven, Conn., 1963–). It now appears that financial problems will after all prevent this edition from being complete, but the things to be omitted are indeed of little significance.

[12] *Translations of Lucian*, ed. Craig R. Thompson (*CW* 3/I, 1974).

[13] *The History of King Richard III*, ed. Richard Sylvester (*CW* 2, 1963).

[14] *Utopia*, ed. J. H. Hexter and E. Surtz (*CW* 4, 1965).

books, and more in articles, of which two useful collections have
appeared. The first contributes little to More the humanist, being more
concerned with his activities as a public figure and with his last
transformation into a budding saint;[15] the other assembles a gathering of
very varying quality in which a number of pieces analyse mostly
linguistic problems arising from More's humanist works.[16] The notable
edition of his letters also, of course, includes material bearing on his
notions of scholarship and learning, especially his rebuff to Oxford's
traditionalists and his battle with Martin van Dorp, who had dared to
decry Erasmus.[17]

More's history of Richard III has not attracted as much study as one
might hope, especially if the production of the king's self-appointed
champions is ignored which usually confines itself to abuse of Sir
Thomas. A sensible assessment of the book as a piece of history is found
in Charles Ross's recent biography of the king.[18] Ross refuses to go all
the way with Alison Hanham's cheerful conclusion that More was really
composing 'a satirical drama'; 'To adopt her arguments *in toto*', he says
with unwonted severity, 'tends to lead to the conclusion that More did
not believe a word of what he was writing'.[19] Even if it did – and I think
the stricture exaggerated – one may ask, why not? Hanham offered a
more convincing reconstruction of More's mode of composition than
did Sylvester in the introduction to his edition, and she displayed greater
independence in the face of More than is usual; and she made a strong
case for her views. There is indeed much dramatic construction, much
stage-play 'modo Italiano et modo Moreano', which is where its link
with More the humanist shows much more clearly than in some
conventionally high-minded denunciation of tyranny. The evil of
tyranny was a general humanist *topos*, no doubt, but when More tackled
it he did so with his usual searching irony and with a verve which turned
the conventionally abstract into a positive human experience.[20]

However, More the humanist was above all the author of *Utopia*, and
the battles of scholars continue to rage around that book. *Utopia* from

[15] *St Thomas More: Action and Contemplation*, ed. Richard Sylvester (New Haven, Conn., 1972).
[16] *Essential Articles for the Study of Thomas More*, ed. R. S. Sylvester and G. P. Marc'hadour (Hamden, Conn., 1977).
[17] *The Correspondence of Sir Thomas More*, ed. E. F. Rogers (Princeton, 1947).
[18] C. Ross, *Richard III* (London, 1981), xxvi–xxxi.
[19] Ibid., xxvii, n. 22; A. Hanham, *Richard III and the Early Historians 1483–1535* (Oxford, 1975), ch. 7.
[20] D. B. Fenlon, 'Thomas More and tyranny', *Journal of Ecclesiastical History*, 32 (1981), 453–76, makes some interesting points in the course of too pious an argument.

the date of publication has always offered to every reader that which he sought in it. The great debate was reopened by J. H. Hexter who in a slender book of 171 small pages and a big essay of 151 large pages laid out four propositions, the first three of which have rightly never been contradicted.[21] He firmly disposed of various earlier attempts to read *Utopia* as either a tract for modern times (socialism and democracy before their day) or a medieval song of praise for the life monastic; he worked out the history of its composition, showing that the description of the island with its ideal society preceded the writing of the framework in Book I; he drew attention to what he called 'the Dialogue of Counsel', the separate argument concerning the scholar's role in public life, which concludes the first book; and he developed his theory of More as 'the first modern radical'.[22] He saw More as a strictly Christian humanist but held that to its author Utopia, a country which had ordered its existence without ever receiving the gospel message, even so represented the true Christian way of life which More positively wished to bring into existence.

This last part of the interpretation has led to much argument. Though Quentin Skinner expressed himself as fully convinced,[23] Dermot Fenlon seized on the suggestion that by inventing a truly Christian commonwealth for the non-existent island of Nowhere More meant to express a strong criticism of the half-hearted and pussyfooting views of other Christian humanists, especially Erasmus. While they expected to create a good Christian society on earth without calling for any revolutionary transformation, More – so Fenlon argued – wished to show them that on earth there was no hope of their ambitions being realised.[24] Hexter held that More believed Utopia to be not only the right ideal but also obtainable if the necessary effort – that marginally modern revolution – were but faced; Fenlon reversed this by arguing that More outlined what indeed he regarded as the ideal society in order

[21] J. H. Hexter, *More's Utopia: The Biography of an Idea* (Princeton, 1952); and the introduction to *CW* 4 (above, n. 4).
[22] J. H. Hexter, 'Thomas More: on the margins of modernity', *Journal of British Studies*, 1/1 (1961), 20–37.
[23] See his review of *CW* 4 in *Past and Present*, 38 (1967), 153–68. Hexter's interpretation lies at the heart of Skinner's assessment in his *Foundations of Modern Political Thought* (Cambridge, 1978), I, 255–62. Stop-Press: Professor Skinner has now revoked his agreement with Hexter in his latest contribution to the debate on *Utopia* – see his 'Sir Thomas More's *Utopia* and the language of renaissance humanism', *The Languages of Political Theory in Early-Modern Europe*, ed. A. Pagden (Cambridge, 1987), 123–57.
[24] D. B. Fenlon, 'England and Europe: *Utopia* and its aftermath', *TRHS* 5th series, 25 (1975), 115–35. I in effect accepted that interpretation in *Reform and Reformation*, 42–6.

to demonstrate its unattainability. However, the latest review of the work on which More's reputation as a great figure among humanists must rest has rather tended to return to an earlier and less sophisticated tradition. Brendan Bradshaw enabled himself to take this journey into the past by rejecting all efforts to solve the mysteries of the book by calling in aid More's ironic temper: he asks us to take More's words at their ostensible meaning.[25] In his view, therefore, More did believe in the virtues of the structure which he had created for Utopia – in the community of property, the precisely ordered existence, the political hierarchy, the deference to age, and all the rest – but by introducing the conversion of the islanders at the end he expressly denied that their commonwealth had been a Christian one. As regards More's judgement as to the practicality of such propositions, Bradshaw rejected both Hexter's More, looking for revolution, and Fenlon's, putting forth a pessimistic denunciation of idealistic dreams. Bradshaw reads the fictitious More's argument with Hythloday, the man who has actually been to Utopia, as an attack on the uncompromising absolutism found in Plato (whose views Hythloday is used to represent) – the absolutism of all or nothing. Better acquainted with real life and circumstances, More was willing to accept piecemeal and halfway answers. He neither sought revolution nor despaired of betterment; convinced that reform was both necessary and possible, he allowed that service to the common weal must involve statecraft and diplomacy and compromise which will secure that available measure of reform which is better than none.

There is something basically agreeable about Bradshaw's interpretation, but it does not really stand up. Like others before him, he takes More to express his opinion straightforwardly where it suits the thesis but to hide it where it would confuse the thesis. More is made to switch his irony on and off: once again, the reader sees what he wants in that infuriatingly ambiguous book. I have to admit that to me all recent commentators have seemed rather overawed by the reputation of author and book and thus seek profundities not of More's making.[26] Did More expect that his little book, started as a *jeu d'esprit* among friends and not intended for publication, would be taken to sum up his inmost feelings on human society, the state and the ways of God? As his *Richard III* proved, he liked to write fiction with a message, and *Utopia* is his

---

[25] B. Bradshaw, 'More on Utopia', *HJ*, 24 (1981), 1–26.

[26] My short life of More, above, vol. III, no. 45, represents my previously most recent and most considered assessment. I apologise for drawing attention to a piece in a foreign language: it was written for a German collection.

masterpiece in that genre. More also loved to make pointed jokes, and *Utopia* is full of them. So it certainly deserves some of its fame: it lovingly presents a splendid invention, swiftly and elegantly worked out with spirit and manifest delight. It made More famous on the continent of Europe, where nothing like it had been seen; there it was rapidly reprinted several times. In England, on the other hand, where people had heard this kind of criticism made before, it seems to have had no noticeable impact until Ralph Robinson published his translation in 1551, and until the growth of the More cult tended to be regarded for what it was – fiction. John Foxe disparagingly called it poetry. Nowadays it regularly receives praise for its supposedly penetrating and original analysis of contemporary life especially in England. This praise ignores the fact that More's analysis very unoriginally concentrated on the standard complaints of the day, regularly mentioned, for instance, in the preambles to acts of Parliament. He adds memorable formulations: More was a writer of genius, but a modestly interesting thinker. Everybody remembers the sheep devouring men; nobody bothers to recall the acts against depopulating enclosure which had long since made the point – and which, incidentally, mistook the causes of agrarian unrest. Social critics from William Langland to Edmund Dudley had thought as deeply on these matters as Thomas More. Unlike him, they had not been able to think of a cure, but it must be said that the Utopian arrangements which More prescribed deserve rather more adverse criticism than they have received. More's recipe involved putting mankind into universal strait-jackets. His island commonwealth lacks genuine liberty because men, being sinful (greedy and proud), will always pervert liberty into licence. It also happens to lack all privacy and would not have pleased the More who found the peace of the monk's cell in prison, twenty years later. In Utopia, a reasonably good life is offered to all in exchange for submission to a stringent system and constant supervision. That the system has some attractive features, such as restricted working hours and the absence of serfdom, is true enough; every restrictive regime has always paraded such minor bonuses as sprats which draw the mackerel of independence into the net.[27]

Every reading of *Utopia* ultimately comes up against the question

[27] Others have recognised the totalitarian aspect of *Utopia* but seem more willing than I am to allow More his little foibles. See J. H. Hexter, 'Utopia and Geneva', *Action and Conviction in Early Modern Europe*, ed. T. K. Rabb and J. E. Seigel (Princeton, 1969); J. Colin Davis, *Utopia and the Ideal Society: A Study of English Utopian Writing 1516–1700* (Cambridge, 1981), ch. 2.

whether More really meant us to believe what he said. Irony pervades the book – the kind of irony which leaves its import very unclear. Did More think community of property ideal (as Hythloday makes out), or absurd (as Morus objects)? Did he approve the Utopians' pleasure in sexual intercourse or their contemptuous jokes at its expense? Did this essentially conventional Christian really think that a truly pious life could be lived without knowledge of the gospel? And how can we even put such questions to an author who gives his philosopher and guide, Hythlodaeus, a name which translates as either the enemy of nonsense or the purveyor of nonsense?

Nevertheless, the student of humanism has to make up his mind on at least some of these puzzles. For myself, I now reckon that More did think Utopia an ideal society in the double sense that life cannot be better ordered on earth, and that it was unrealisable in actual fact. I agree with Bradshaw that More wished to help improve the condition of earthly commonwealths and for that purpose accepted the need to come to terms with the facts of life at the courts of princes. I agree with Fenlon that More liked to show to his fellow humanists that scholarly vapouring about reform was as pointless as all refusals to compromise on abstract principles. I agree with no one when I maintain that quite enough ink has been wasted on *Utopia*. More meant to amuse, shock and bewilder, all of which he achieved; but he would have been greatly surprised by all those solemn debates about his meaning that still continue.

Naturally enough, no other humanist has attracted as much attention as Thomas More. Among those well known to an earlier generation of scholars, Thomas Elyot already stood assured of his position as a writer on political thought, thanks to the rather outdated discussion provided by H. H. S. Croft in his edition of Elyot's *Governor*.[28] In the new wave of humanist studies, a much better account of the man was offered by Stanford Lehmberg, who also reviewed his very varied writings;[29] shortly afterwards, John M. Major, analysing Elyot's production, some-what predictably raised him on a pedestal as a Platonic thinker – a moralist and educator, of real and original influence on his age.[30] It would meet the case better to treat him (as Lehmberg hints he was) as a prolific populariser with occasional ideas largely produced by what Elyot, in jaundiced moods, regarded as undeserved ill fortune. Alistair Fox has

[28] Thomas Elyot, *The Boke Named the Gouernour*, ed. H. H. S. Croft (London, 1883), with a biographical introduction.
[29] S. E. Lehmberg, *Sir Thomas Elyot, Tudor Humanist* (Austin, Tex., 1960).
[30] J. M. Major, *Sir Thomas Elyot and Renaissance Humanism* (Lincoln, Nebr., 1964).

picked on two short pieces written in the 1530s in protest against the collapse of his career in the king's service as his most original and revealing writings.[31]

Pursuing individuals: Zeeveld's signpost pointing to Padua has not gone unnoticed. Too little has so far been done about Reginald Pole himself, a personality so ambiguous that he might almost have been invented by Thomas More. The brief study by William Schenk is commonplace about the man's thought, while the important work of Dermot Fenlon concentrates on Pole's participation in the reforming movement within the Church of Rome in Italy.[32] There is a *terra nova* waiting to be explored. It looks as though Thomas Mayer will be the one to travel there, having already succeeded in altering our view of Pole's companion, Thomas Starkey. Mayer has reconsidered the dating and purpose of Starkey's manuscript treatise on government; he concluded that it was written before Starkey had any idea about seeking service with Henry VIII, that he meant it for the instruction of Pole above all, and that, so far from being a premature constitutionalist, Starkey wished to set up the kind of aristocratic control over monarchy which some fifteenth-century noblemen had hoped to erect.[33] Among lesser figures one might notice Roger Ascham, who has attracted a careful new biography with little new to say.[34]

Is there anything to hold all these thinkers together? The one umbrella that floats above them is held there by a conviction which – to judge by his work on Polydore Vergil – must have somewhat surprised Denys Hay. Increasingly we have been taught to distance English humanists from their once universal Italian ancestry and to seek the unifying principle in the role and influence of Erasmus – *supra omnes et omnium praelector*. In 1965 there appeared a book which gave comprehensive expression to this growing conviction: James McConica's study of three generations of scholars, and indeed of public figures, who were all said to owe their world of ideas to Erasmus and no one else.[35] McConica deserved full appreciation for helping to demonstrate that the age of the

---

[31] A. Fox, 'Sir Thomas Elyot and the Humanist Dilemma', *Reassessing the Henrician Age*, ed. A. Fox and J. A. Guy (Oxford, 1986), ch. 3.

[32] W. Schenk, *Reginald Pole, Cardinal of England* (London, 1950); D. B. Fenlon, *Heresy and Obedience in Tridentine Italy: Cardinal Pole and the Counter Reformation* (Cambridge, 1972).

[33] T. F. Mayer, 'Faction and Ideology: Thomas Starkey's *Dialogue*', *HJ*, 28 (1985), 1–25.

[34] L. V. Ryan, *Roger Ascham* (Stanford, 1963).

[35] J. K. McConica, *English Humanists and Reformation Politics under Henry VIII and Edward VI* (Oxford, 1965); see my review in *HJ*, 10 (1967), 137–8.

early Reformation in England witnessed a major and principled manifestation of general reformist thinking; here he added weight to the
argument that English humanism not only survived the year 1535 but
mattered far more after the disappearance of Fisher and More than
before. On the other hand, as we shall see, the thesis of a lasting and
protean Erasmianism does not fit the facts; these had to be placed under a
distorting glass to create that image. Nevertheless, for some decades the
rule of Erasmus endured. With an exception: every herd has to have its
maverick. In this case, the part was played by Stephen Gardiner, whom
earlier scholars never treated as a humanist at all. As a lawyer, and as a
champion of a discredited pronunciation of Greek, he seemed to have
nothing to do with the 'new learning'. Thus Peter Donaldson's specula-
tive but to me convincing identification of Gardiner as a careful student
of Machiavelli came as something of a shock to those who could not
suppose that a champion of the old religion would go to that source for
his ideas.[36]

III

Rather more interesting than this continued conventional study of
individuals (always excepting Thomas More) is another development
which derived from Zeeveld's look at the role of humanist thinkers in
the practical planning of reform. The recognition that English humanists,
unlike their continental colleagues, tended to agree with Morus rather
than Hythlodaeus in bringing their minds to the service of the common
weal was not, of course, entirely new, though previously historians had
mainly investigated the ideas and activities of educators. After all, the
founding of St Paul's school formed Colet's chief claim to membership
of the humanist circle. Though F. Caspari's book claimed to be
concerned with what he called the social order, it was really about the
educational programmes (education of the ruling elite) put forward by a
diverse body of writers, from Erasmus, More and Starkey to Sidney and
Spenser; even at the date of its appearance it carried a rather old-
fashioned look.[37] More comprehensive analyses of the penetration of
humanist concepts into schools, universities and private tutorships were
supplied by Joan Simon and Kenneth Charlton, who at any rate

---

[36] P. S. Donaldson (ed.), *A Machiavellian Treatise by Stephen Gardiner* (Cambridge, 1975);
for doubts about the ascription see Fenlon's review in *HJ*, 19 (1976), 1019–23.
[37] F. Caspari, *Humanism and the Social Order in Tudor England* (Chicago, 1954).

established the far-reaching changes that came to permeate English education in the course of this century.[38]

However, a novel recognition of a practically active humanism arose from the pursuit of scholars not into schoolrooms but into government service. Naturally enough, since he was the most eminent humanist to make this move, Thomas More has been set up as the presiding deity of this enterprise, but this theory errs. More entered Henry VIII's service in 1517 and stayed there for fifteen years;[39] small wonder that his claque expected the author of *Utopia* to put at least some of his reforming notions into practice.[40] However, the supposed evidence is illusory. Scarisbrick ascribed to More a detailed programme of projected reforms which I had identified with the circle of Thomas Cromwell,[41] and we have both turned out to be wrong. The paper came from Christopher St German, the foremost legal writer of the day; it entered history and effect through being submitted to Cromwell and had nothing whatsoever to do with More.[42] A most thorough investigation of More's career in the king's service has been unable to discover any genuine reforming activity; even in his court of Chancery he at best consolidated and systematised the innovations introduced by Cardinal Wolsey.[43] On the other hand, St German's emergence as a planner of reform is very important. A man close to seventy when he began to show himself in that role in the 1520s, he cannot at all be accommodated under the humanist umbrella and is therefore a very necessary reminder that the humanists participated in a general movement for reform rather than inspired it.

As Zeeveld had discovered, the urge to help the community to a better living came from the second generation of English humanists, many of whom, for the same reason, also sought reform in church and religion. He singled out Thomas Starkey, Richard Morison and Richard

---

[38] J. Simon, *Education and Society in Tudor England* (Cambridge, 1966); K. Charlton, *Education in Renaissance England* (London, 1965). W. T. Costello, *The Scholastic Curriculum at Early Seventeenth-Century Cambridge* (Cambridge, Mass., 1958) attempts to deny the influence of humanism, but he misleads because the innate scholasticism of theological study, with which he was concerned, is by no means the whole of Tudor education.

[39] G. R. Elton, 'Thomas More Councillor', above, vol. I, no. 7.

[40] J. J. Scarisbrick, 'Thomas More: the King's Good Servant', *Thought*, 52 (1977) 249–68.

[41] *Reform and Renewal*, 71–5.

[42] J. A. Guy (ed.), *Christopher St German on Chancery and Statute* (Selden Society, 1985), 62–3, 127–35. See also Guy's further essays on St German in *Reassessing* (above, n. 31), chs. 5, 6, 8.

[43] J. A. Guy, *The Public Career of Sir Thomas More* (Brighton, 1980).

Taverner, all of whom were promoted into service by Thomas Cromwell. Indeed, the pull offering its chance to the push originated with the
man who, it was later remembered, 'loved not the men who pedanti-
cally boasted their reading, but that rationally made use of it',[44] a
memory well supported by a personal archive full of reform proposals
some of which he found the time to promote.[45] Typically, in that
atmosphere redolent of humanism, Cromwell took a serious interest in
educational reform; in fact, he seems deliberately to have looked for
servants of the state among university graduates, adapting the earlier
reliance on a trained clergy to the needs of a lay-governed state. Out of
this policy came the careers of men like William Cecil. At the same time,
university dons increasingly offered their learning for employment in
affairs, the outstanding examples being Sir John Cheke and Sir Thomas
Smith. Known at one time mainly as 'Erasmians' seeking to promote
classical studies at Cambridge, they have more recently emerged as
leaders of an unsystematic movement of social and political reform that
rested on humanist principles. Smith, regius professor of laws at
Cambridge and principal secretary to both the duke of Somerset and
Queen Elizabeth, has some right to the champion's title: his analysis of
the economic problems of mid-century England represents a level of
insight and understanding not matched again for the best part of a
century.[46] Arthur Ferguson's wide-ranging survey of what was less a
movement than a general intellectual and political fashion, though short
on the practical effects of it all, satisfactorily established this socially
involved face of English humanism.[47] Even so, he was too ready to
engrave the features of Erasmus and More on that face.

IV

The discovery of post-Reformation humanism has, perhaps not surprisingly, been accompanied by growing doubts about their pre-Reforma-

[44] D. Lloyd, *State-Worthies* (new ed., 1766), I, 78.
[45] The reform activities of Cromwell and his circle form the theme of my *Reform and
Renewal*. See also my 'The Political Creed of Thomas Cromwell' and 'Reform by
Statute: Thomas Starkey's *Dialogue* and Thomas Cromwell's Policy', above, vol. II, nos.
31 and 32.
[46] M. Dewar, *Sir Thomas Smith: A Tudor Intellectual in Office* (London, 1964); M. Dewar
(ed.), *A Discourse of the Commonwealth of this Realm of England* (Charlottesville, 1969).
On the other hand, the reformers of Edward VI's reign, none of them humanists, have
been shown up as legendary in my 'Reform and the "Commonwealth-men" of Edward
VI's Reign', above, vol. III, no. 38.
[47] A. B. Ferguson, *The Articulate Citizen and the English Renaissance* (Durham, NC, 1965).

tion predecessors. This has particularly affected our views of the great
pillars of the past. No one questions the description as humanists of such
less influential persons as William Grocyn, teacher of Greek, or Richard
Pace, civil servant and diplomatist.[48] The standing of Colet, Fisher and
even More is less secure.

In part, of course, such debates depend on a definition of humanism,
Christian or otherwise, and one quickly becomes aware how slippery
that term is.[49] Criticism of the church, for instance, was not confined to
humanists, nor even was devotion to the classics, often enough found in
the so-called Middle Ages.[50] Certainly, humanists insisted on the
purification of Latin as well as the study of Greek and the introduction of
Hebrew to a degree not found before: above all, they were philologists
rather than philosophers. They broke with the investigative techniques
of the scholastic tradition, replacing logic by rhetoric and the syllogism
by the dialogue. In all Erasmus's vast output, perhaps the most typical
production – the one that only a humanist would write – is his textbook
on style, *De Copia Verborum*. Thus humanists can up to a point be
identified by their principles as students and teachers: humanism was
above all an educational movement. However, there is surely one
characteristic a man had to display in order to join the club: he must
think *humaniter* and believe in a human ability to control human fate.
Not all of them need to have fully subscribed to the slogan, 'homo
mensura'; it was possible to doubt that man is the measure of all things
and to allow for the work of God's grace in men nevertheless endowed
with free will. What no one properly to be called a humanist could
adhere to was an Augustinian belief in the total and helpless depravity of
fallen man, or to Lutheran solafideism, or to a clericalist view by which a
priesthood acted as the sole channel of grace, or to a total denial of free
enquiry. Measured against these principles, the membership of that
established trio does become questionable, especially when all are ranked
under the Erasmian banner. For it remains correct to regard Erasmus,
who fulfilled all the conditions, as the prototype and leader.

[48] Pace has recently, a bit surprisingly, entered into the discussion: Fox, *Reassessing* (n. 31),
41–.3.
[49] For a sensible discussion see ibid., 31–2, 34–5, where the best use of the term is made to
rest on the techniques of study and exposition.
[50] Differences from the Renaissance are emphasised in R. W. Southern, 'Medieval
Humanism', *Medieval Humanism and Other Studies* (Oxford, 1970), 29–60; they are
regarded as less clear-cut by R. Thomson, 'John of Salisbury and William of
Malmesbury: Currents of Twelfth-Century Humanism', *The World of John of Salisbury*,
ed. Michael Wilks (Oxford, 1984), 117–25.

Erasmus several times acknowledged his debt to John Colet, from whom he learned methods of enquiry and discourse, though the most recent review of that relationship demonstrates that any similarity of thought was confined to Erasmus's earliest writings.[51] Colet also displayed his credentials when he created in St Paul's School an example of reformed teaching centred upon the classics and the return to the sources. Nevertheless, it is difficult to call a man a humanist without very severe qualifications who held the lowest opinion of fallen mankind, demanded full submission to the canon law, wished to educate only the clergy, and preached the superior virtue of the clerical estate provided it returned to primitive asceticism.[52] As has been said, his 'whole career was a protest against worldliness', and he showed really quite insufficient interest in the reform of the laity to make the grade.[53] Certainly he resisted scholasticism and knew his Plato and Plotinus, but the distinctly humanist Colet of tradition owed his character to Erasmus's description which, as was usual with that scholar, pictured the assessor far more than the assessed.[54] Much the same doubtful verdict must be passed on John Fisher. He too enjoyed the friendship of Erasmus and proved himself a convinced progressive in matters of education, though even in these his successor as chancellor of Cambridge, Thomas Cromwell, possibly did more to promote a humanist reign in the university. Fisher, of course, like Colet, was primarily a theologian – the only notable theologian on the English bench of bishops in his time. And here the two great campaigns of his life – against Luther and against Henry VIII's first divorce – proved him to be a committed adherent of tradition and of Thomas Aquinas (whom Colet disliked). Fisher wrote his Latin treatises in the manner of the past; he evaded the innovations in discourse and presentation which we rightly associate with humanism. He was a man of great and varied learning, a man of principle and purpose, but being a friend of Erasmus and More is not sufficient proof of his attachment to

[51] P. I. Kaufman, 'John Colet and Erasmus' *Enchiridion*', *Church History*, 46 (1977), 296–312.
[52] H. C. Porter, 'The Gloomy Dean and the Law: John Colet, 1466–1519', *Essays in Modern Church History* (Ft. Sykes), ed. G. V. Bennett and J. D. Walsh (London, 1966), 18–43.
[53] P. I. Kaufman, 'John Colet's *Opus de sacramentis* and Clerical Anti-Clericalism: The Limitation of "Ordinary Wayes"', *Journal of British Studies*, 22/1 (1982), 1–22.
[54] J. B. Trapp 'John Colet and the *Hierarchies* of the PS-Dionysius', *Religion and Humanism* (Studies in Church History, 17, ed. K. Robbins; Oxford, 1981), 127–48. Colet's use of the ancients is investigated in Leland Miles, *John Colet and the Platonic Tradition* (1962), but the author's attachment to Rome has produced a book in the medieval style, calling for an exegete or glossator.

humanism, which must at the least be reckoned intermittent and in the last part of his life invisible. He calls for more work.[55]

On More, on the other hand, the work has been plentiful, quite apart from the debates about *Utopia* already outlined. The trouble started, I think, when I found myself growing doubtful whether hagiography had a place in history and asked some impertinent questions about that supposedly humanist scholar who gave so much of his time to routine employments in the king's service where he promoted no reforms, who displayed such a tendency for disputing the human power for good, and who became such an exceptionally determined persecutor of heretics.[56] I showed cause why we should not simply trust one of the chief foundations of the inherited image of More, namely William Roper's notes assembled twenty years after his father-in-law's death and designed to smooth the path towards canonisation. And, somewhat embarrassingly, I drew attention to More's manifest preoccupation with matters sexual, on which Erasmus had actually remarked only to be ignored down the ages. More, like Luther, preferred Augustine to all other Fathers of the Church; More, again like Luther, believed man to be totally depraved as a consequence of the Fall. True, unlike Luther he tried to rescue free will, though not (I still think) altogether convincingly.[57] His chief difference from the reformer, however, lay in his unswerving allegiance to the Church Universal to which he ascribed a total authority well out of step with normal humanist principles. I pointed out that the traditional and humanist More appeared to be constructed exclusively out of what he did and wrote before about 1521; the image-makers had ignored the next twelve years of his life and the bulk of his writings. To me it thus became doubtful whether More could be called a humanist after the time that he turned his mind solely to the defence of the church and the demolition of heresy.

Since I first entered my comprehensive *caveat*, two large and important books have appeared which express similar doubts, though possibly

---

[55] The problems emerge from Surtz's study (above, n. 10) which takes Fisher's humanism for granted but tends to reveal the difficulties of believing in its existence.

[56] See above, nos. 7, 8, 45, 58, and Reviews (c).

[57] See e.g. *Confutation of Tyndale* (*CW*, 8, 1973), 502–3, where More refutes Tyndale's Lutheran doctrine of God's unsolicited grace by calling it absurd that men should be compelled to 'sit even still and do nothing toward it'. The Lutheran doctrine does not stop men from seeking grace but denies that such a manoeuvre will persuade God to grant it, a point which is not met in More's display of angry irony. More seemingly did believe in grace bestowed freely and not bought by works, but I do not see that he ever succeeded in resolving the incompatibility of predestination by God's decree with human free will. Not that he has been alone in this.

in more measured tones. Alistair Fox was the first scholar to use the whole corpus of More's writings in an attempt to understand the man and his intellectual development.[58] While professing a greater respect for More's personality and thinking than I had done, he came to much the same conclusions on More's inner psychology (the psychology of a man exceptionally conscious of the fact of evil in this world) and also held that the onset of the Reformation terminated More's humanist phase. Instead, his diagnosis put before us a More who tried to reconcile a belief in God's goodness with the evidence of misery in a world created by God. In the end, More came to treat human history as a sequence of temptations to desert an all-demanding God who, however, would reward humble obedience and unquestioning submission with salvation at the last. Nothing very humanist about that. Even more critical of More the humanist is the large biography by Richard Marius, the only member of the Yale team to have resisted saint-worship.[59] Marius, who had won his spurs by a brilliantly convincing analysis of More's faith in the authority of the church,[60] added one further, rather crucial, item to the question of More's humanism when he disproved the ancient legend of an exceptionally close and long-enduring friendship between More and Erasmus. So far as real evidence goes, it now looks as though relations between the two men were really intense only in about the three years surrounding the production of *Utopia* (about which Erasmus was as hesitant as More was about his friend's *Praise of Folly*); after 1521, the signs of a growing distance are really clear enough. Not that they quarrelled, but they went their different ways, so that it will not do to make More's humanism depend solely on a likemindedness with Erasmus. In the end, Erasmus's first reaction to More's ultimate fate not only lacked true sorrow but also indicated that in his view More had long left the fold. 'I wish he had never dabbled in so perilous a business and left theology to the theologians', was all that the prince of scholars could find to say about his supposed bosom friend.[61] Though it is true that a week later he had collected himself sufficiently to lament more convincingly,[62] it is plain enough that in Erasmus's opinion More had ceased to be one of the gang.

[58] A. Fox, *Thomas More: History and Providence* (Oxford, 1982).
[59] R. Marius, *Thomas More: A Biography* (New York, 1984).
[60] In his contribution to the introduction to the *CW* edition of the *Confutation*, III, 1271–363.
[61] 'Utinam periculoso negocio se nunquam admiscuisset, et causam theologicam cessisset theologis' (*Opus Epistolarum Des. Erasmi Roterodami*, ed. P. S. Allen, XI, 216).
[62] Ibid., 221: 'In Moro mihi videor extinctus.'

The most recent attempts to restore More firmly to the ranks of the humanists either concentrate , once again, exclusively on *Utopia* (already discussed) or sound a trifle bewildered. Craig Thompson decided that 'as a humanist More was essentially Erasmian', a verdict which, of course, highlights Marius's subsequent critique of the later More. When their relations can be shown to be less than those of David and Jonathan, Thompson rather feebly sees only 'minor matters of imperfect sympathies and misunderstandings'. And while acknowledging David Knowles's remark about More changing through life as all men change, he concluded that the continued quality of his writing proves him to have remained a humanist to the end.[63] That does seem a weak last resort – not to mention that it calls for a charitable assessment of the style of most of More's anti-heretical writings. I rather share C. S. Lewis's low opinion of the literary quality of More's controversial works, the *Dialogue Concerning Heresies* alone excepted.[64] However, this is unquestionably a debate that has not yet ended.

v

This is where quite a short while ago the story terminated and the matter could be left to rest. We might be arguing about this and that, but we were essentially agreed that a group of learned men who acknowledged Erasmus as their leader thought and wrote in early Tudor England about the issues, and in the manner, appropriate to humanists. But about a year ago a rather formidable cat from New Zealand landed among the cooing pigeons. Having firmly put Thomas More in his place, Alistair Fox next found himself very dissatisfied with an analysis which treated English humanism as a single 'movement' any participant in which shared the fundamental convictions and the outlook on the world entertained by all the rest. Thus, in two short essays, he broke up the scene and put forward a new interpretation which still awaits development in the fires of debate.[65] To Fox it has become plain that English humanism

[63] C. R. Thompson, 'The Humanism of More reappraised', *Thought*, 52 (1977), 233–48; D. Knowles, *The Historian and Character* (Cambridge, 1963), 7. Thompson was sufficiently ambiguous for Fox to read him as saying that in the Tower More *had* ceased to be a humanist (*Reassessing*, 10). But I think that Thompson meant to apply this only to the last devotional works.

[64] *English Literature in the Sixteenth Century, Excluding Drama* (Oxford, 1954), 174. The somewhat critical assessment in Rainer Pineas, *Thomas More and Tudor Polemics* (Bloomington, 1968) has found little favour with the More brigade.

[65] 'Facts and fallacies: interpreting English humanism' and 'English humanism and the body politic' in *Reassessing* (above, n. 31), 9–51.

constituted 'a multifarious phenomenon'. Multifarious but not totally fragmented: he finds a key in the different uses to which different men wished to put their learning outside the mere cause of learning. They shared a respect for the revival of classical literature: thus his ignorance of it eliminates St German from the ranks. They also shared a conviction that their philosophy carried implications for the betterment of men's condition, especially for men charged with the exercise of government. But where Caspari (n. 37) reduced all problems of 'social order' to a general programme for educating the ruling elite, while McConica (n. 35) lumped all ideas together under the title of Erasmianism, Fox saw the need for fundamental distinctions.

In effect, Fox identified three possible reactions to the demands the world made upon the scholar. Erasmus held to the rather naive view that an exposure to good letters and moral maxims would suffice to bring about a better common weal. He was the Hythloday of reality, determined upon absolutes which had to be spelt out and maintained in perfection, even if in consequence the good world could exist only in the imagination. Erasmus is thus described as a pessimist since the ends of his optimistic dreams could never achieve reality, but I would think it more pointful to term him an opti-pessimist because experience seems never to have persuaded him out of his ethereal position. More differed from his friend, whose innocence he criticised in *Utopia*, by an explicit pessimism based upon his despair of mankind; he understood that comprehensive or fundamental reform was out of the question and resigned himself to piecemeal reform (or in practice none). The third choice available to the humanist escaped 'from both the Erasmian and Morean pessimism' by positively tackling the problems of society – of taking action on the basis of remedies worked out by reason and experience. The prototype of this 'optimistic' stance, Fox argues, was Thomas Starkey, and the humanism that prevailed in England from the 1530s onwards opted mainly for this kind of participation in government. More (this is an addition of mine to the thesis) had no real disciples until Utopian writers like Harrington picked up some of his message in the next century. The only true Erasmian among English humanists (this *is* Fox) was Thomas Elyot, who shared both the master's belief in the power of learned instruction and his total ineffectualness in practice. One question now to be pursued concerns possibly later Erasmians, that is, humanists distinguishable from the likes of Thomas Starkey and Thomas Smith, but even at first sight, before the review of the whole scene by means of this analysis has progressed further, the underlying ideas carry a great deal of conviction.

They seem especially convincing because Fox throws in one insight that he has not yet had a chance of following up. Recognising the strain to which the Lutheran explosion exposed a generation of thinkers whose anthropology had always tended to be superficially hopeful, he notes that 'there was always, therefore, an incipient fracture in the Christian-humanist synthesis'.[66] The Christian view of man as sinful and corrupt could not really be reconciled to the humanist hopes that men could and would help themselves to a better life. Theocentric Christianity and humanocentric humanism could form an alliance only by ignoring the abyss between them. The Reformation brutally acquainted Erasmus with those facts of life that he would not admit destroyed his constructs, while with equal brutality it demonstrated how right More had been in his ingrained pessimism about the role of good letters in a fallen world. Luther in effect rendered Erasmus irrelevant, and More, who seemed to see this, discarded his earlier humanism in order to fight for that form of Christianity which to him constituted the sole hope of salvation. The third set of humanists for the time being found it possible to maintain their cheerful belief in Thomas Cromwell and the virtue of secular action; most of them, though not Thomas Starkey, regarded the new faith as congruent because it demolished the barrier between the service of God and the service of man. But – and here we part company with Fox – this new synthesis could only be temporary. It did well in Cromwell's decade when the power of the state encouraged the practical participation of the humanist scholar. And though the example was to be fitfully followed later, the ways began to show signs of a new parting. The failure in government of Thomas Smith differed from that of Thomas Elyot only in that the latter, guided by Cromwell, accepted his relegation to the study, whereas the former never quite understood why he had got no further as a statesman.

The fundamental trouble lay in the fact that the reformed religion, as it was preached in the sixteenth century, in its essence rejected the teachings of the humanists. The humanists had won their sole victory when they conquered the territory specifically reserved to education, for even there it proved easier for Thomist Jesuits than for Calvinists to absorb the new form of classical education. From the 1550s onwards, no Englishman who passed through the hands of teachers escaped a system

---

[66] Ibid., 30.

built on the return to the ancient authors and a training of the mind in the techniques of rhetoric and literature. With this went a respect for man's potential which continued to serve practical statesmen engaged in facing the problems of society – such men as William Cecil. But if the educated scholar opted for the service of God – especially, if he entered the clerical profession – he found himself compelled to a view of man as totally sinful and totally dependent on God's unpredictable grace. Double predestination marches ill with any form of humanism. Though Calvin himself could cope with his humanist training by relegating everything not consonant with it to the realm of God's mysteries which it is not the function of reason to examine, others proved less relaxed; the reformed religion that sprang from him set up manifest and often intolerable tensions within the minds of men educated by the humanists and committed to a predestinarian faith. In the end, it was the second that gave way and largely disappeared in its stringent form; by about 1660, at any rate, the main part of thinking Christians among Englishmen had insensibly surrendered to the triumph of the humanist view of the world.[67]

---

[67] For a first attempt to set out the problem see above, no. 59. There are some interesting pointers in R. M. Douglas, 'Talent and vocation in humanist and protestant thought', *Action and Conviction* (above, n. 27), 261–98.

61

LUTHER IN ENGLAND*

Es ist ja nicht unbekannt, daß die englischen Protestanten Martin Luther weniger studiert haben und ihm weniger zu verdanken hatten als anderen Reformatoren. Auch die Ursachen dieser Tatsache hat man schon erklärt – den Streit mit Heinrich VIII., dessen jäher Angriff auf Luther es später schwierig machte, die englische Reformation dem Wittenberger Vorbild anzupassen, und die gemeinsamen Interessen besonders am Humanismus, die die Engländer nach Straßburg, Zürich und letzten Endes Genf lockten.[1] Zweifellos hat ein gewisser Abstand auch bis zur jüngsten Zeit weiterbestanden, selbst wenn sich der Hintergrund oft verändert hat. Trotzdem kann man jedoch auch die englische Reformation und ihre Weiterentwicklung nicht ganz ohne Luther und dessen Einfluß verstehen; es lohnt schon, seine etwas unklaren Spuren durch die Jahrhunderte hindurch zu verfolgen.

Von Anfang an besteht freilich ein heuristisches Problem: wie belegt man den Einfluß eines Mannes, der so viel geschrieben hat, und dessen Werke oft nur geheim gelesen werden konnten? Englische Theologen haben ganz gewiß manche von Luthers Schriften gelesen, solange sie lateinisch geschrieben waren, und wahrscheinlich kam das schon vor 1520 öfter vor, als wir beweisen können. Dabei haben sie natürlich von ihm gelernt, obwohl man vor dem Problem steht, daß sich Luthers Einfluß oft nur schwer von der einheimischen Häresie der Lollarden unterscheiden läßt. Daß Erzbischof Cranmer recht luthertreu wurde und es auch trotz seiner Ehrfurcht für Bullinger und Bucer geblieben ist, erscheint mir deutlich schon darin, daß er nach Luthers Tod von allen deutschen Kollegen Melanchthon am meisten bevorzugte und es sehr bedauerte, daß es ihm nicht gelang, den Verwalter von Luthers Erbe nach England zu ziehen. Gerade in der englischen Frühreformation dominierten echte Lutheraner, besonders William Tyndale, dessen Schriften man jetzt eifrig und nicht ohne Erfolg nach Spuren eigener Originalität untersucht, und Robert Barnes, ein Diener Thomas Cromwells und Doktor Martins guter Freund, dessen Hinrichtung im Jahre

* [*Luther in der Neuzeit*, hrsg. v. B.Moeller (Gütersloh, 1983), 121–34.]
[1] Above, vol. III, no. 43.

1540 Luther tief erschüttert hat, wie es sein wahrhaft gefühlsreicher Nachruf beweist. Tyndale und Barnes, wie auch ein paar andere jüngere Theologen der Zeit, waren schon wahre Lutheraner, und nicht nur in dem Sinne, in dem jede abwegige Neigung irgendwelcher Art in den 1530er Jahren mit diesem Titel wie mit einem Schimpfwort belastet wurde. Und Einfluß auf den Fortgang der Politik hatten sie auch, wie es die Zehn Artikel von 1536 mit ihren reformatorischen Anklängen und die allerdings erfolglosen Verhandlungen mit den Schmalkaldenern 1536 und 1538 genügend deutlich machen. All dies ist wohlbekannt. Am Anfang seiner Reformation, und trotz der unerbittlichen Feindschaft des Königs,[2] suchte auch England nach Belehrung und Unterstützung bei Luther und seinen Parteigängern.

Tyndale, der nach 1524 niemals wieder nach England kam, starb 1536 und Barnes 1540, beide auf dem Scheiterhaufen; der vielversprechende John Frith war schon 1533 auf dieselbe Art umgekommen, ein Opfer der Verfolgung, die Thomas More veranstaltet hatte und die dessen Verehrer leider zu Unrecht verleugnet haben. Über die weiteren Märtyrer im Dienste derselben Sache kann man viel bei John Foxe lesen – etwas mehr sogar, als ihrer wirklichen Bedeutung zukommt. Aber vereinzelte Leute solcher Art erlauben, selbst wenn sie ein paar führende Politiker anziehen konnten, doch noch keinen Schluß auf weiten Einfluß; hat das Volk, haben selbst die Geistlichen mehr im Allgemeinen etwas von Luther gewußt? Hie und da findet man Bemerkungen über den Wittenberger Revolutionär, die aber den Eindruck erwecken müssen, daß Luther eher ein Symbol, ein Name ohne Inhalt, war. Zum Inhalt hätte man letzten Endes nur dadurch Zugang finden können, daß man Luther selbst zu lesen bemüht war: Jeder breitere Einfluß müßte aus seinen Büchern herzuleiten sein, und zwar soweit diese in der Muttersprache zugänglich wurden. So möchte ich also bei diesem Anlaß einmal untersuchen, wie und wann Luther mittels Übersetzungen und Kommentaren vor das englische Volke getreten ist. Da im 16. Jahrhundert nur sehr wenige Engländer Deutsch verstanden und nur die Gebildeten seine lateinischen Schriften lesen konnten, war eine ausgedehnte Vergegenwärtigung Luthers in England nur mit Hilfe englischer Versionen möglich.[3]

Auf den englischen Universitäten hat man Luther beinahe von Anfang an im Original gelesen. In jedem Geschichtsbuch kommt die Gruppe vor, die sich in Cambridge in den zwanziger Jahren versammelte und die

[2] Vgl. Erwin Doernberg, *Henry VIII and Luther* (London, 1961).
[3] Ich zitiere die englischen Titel etwas abgekürzt und in modernisierter Orthographie in den Anmerkungen, mit Hinweis auf *STC*.

'kleines Deutschland' genannt wurde, aber auch im konservativen Oxford fand man die gefährlichen Werke selbst nach dem Verbot, das der Kardinal Wolsey 1521 durch eine öffentliche Bücherverbrennung energisch unterstrichen hatte. Der damalige Erzbischof von Canterbury, William Warham, der auch Kanzler der Universität war, schrieb im März 1521 mit großer Sorge an Wolsey, es sei erschütternd zu sehen, 'wie begierig diese unsteten Leute und besonders die unerfahrene Jugend neuen Ideen zufällt, auch wenn sie noch so verpestet sind – wie eifrig umarmen solche Menschen gerade die Dinge, deren Benutzung ihre Vorgesetzten ihnen zu ihrem eigenen Wohl verboten haben'.[4] Beschwerden dieser Art kommen einem wohlbekannt vor, und wie gewöhnlich hatten die Unterdrückungsversuche nur begrenzten Erfolg. Noch sieben Jahre später hat man einfache Priester gefangen gesetzt, die einzelne Schriften Luthers besaßen und dafür leiden mußten, und im Jahre 1531, als die Verfolgung durch die Behörden einen Höhepunkt erreichte, suchte Thomas Cromwell (damals noch nicht Minister) in Antwerpen nach einem neuen Buch des großen Mannes, allerdings ohne Erfolg, da zu der Zeit nur ein einziges Exemplar die Stadt erreicht hatte.[5] Das Augsburger Bekenntnis hingegen, hieß es, sei vorhanden und solle Cromwell sofort zugeschickt werden.

Von Übersetzungen jedoch hört man um diese Zeit recht wenig. Vor 1540 kann ich nur ein knappes Halbdutzend festsellen. Anonym wurde ungefähr 1529 Luthers Kommentar zum siebten Kapitel des 1. Korintherbriefes veröffentlicht, als Anhang zu dem Buch des Erasmus über das Studium der Schrift, und zwar 'in Marburg bei Hans Luft', eine falsche Angabe, hinter der wohl Tyndale steckte.[6] Selbst in der Periode von Cromwells Vorherrschaft, als ziemlich viele reformatorische Schriften ins Englische übersetzt wurden, hörte man wenig von Luther, zumal in etwaigen Übersetzungen sein Name nicht genannt werden durfte. Auch wenn vielleicht mancher Student dem Beispiel eines gewissen Thomas Paynell gefolgt sein mag, der privat für sich ein Werk von Luther ins Englische übertrug[7] – zum Druck kamen nur ganz wenige solche Arbeiten. Cromwells guter Freund Miles Coverdale veröffentlichte Bearbeitungen von Luthers Auslegungen des 23. Psalms (1537) und des

---

[4] *Original Letters*, hrsg. v. H. Ellis, 3. Reihe I, 239–42.

[5] *LP*, IV, 4396; V, 303.

[6] *An Exhortation to the Diligent Study of Scripture [with] An Exposition into the Seventh Chapter of the First Epistle to the Corinthians* (?1529: *STC* 10493).

[7] J. K. McConica, *English Humanists and Reformation Politics* (Oxford, 1965).

Magnifcat (1538).[8] Diese Werke hatten theologische Anziehungskraft. Interessanter sind vielleicht zwei von Luthers Streitschriften, die man übersetzt, aber anonym herausbrachte – wütende Angriffe auf den Papst und die päpstliche Kirche. Diese dienten schon eher der Politik des Königs oder jedenfalls derjenigen Cromwells, und ihre englischen Titel deuten an, wozu man Luther verwenden wollte: 'Ein von einem großen Gelehrten gemachtes Buch über den neuen Abgott und den alten Teufel' (1534) und 'Hier folgt eine richtige Abhandlung über die guten Werke' (1538).[9] Das sogenannte Testament Martin Luthers dagegen, auf englisch geschrieben und 1543 angeblich in Wesel (das heißt, geheim in England) gedruckt, hat wenig mit Luther zu tun, zeigt jedoch den propagandistischen Nutzen, den man aus seinem Namen schöpfen zu können glaubte.[10] Indirekt konnte man ihn allerdings leichter lesen, besonders da More in seinen Streitschriften gegen Tyndale und Barnes die Werke der Gegner immer ausführlich zitierte; was aber seine eigenen Bücher betraf, blieb das Verbot Heinrichs VIII. in Kraft.

Wie zu erwarten war, änderte sich die Lage nach dem Tode des Königs, der ja nur ein paar Monate nach Luther starb. Zunächst übersetzte der berühmte und berüchtigte Propagandist John Bale den von Justus Jonas, Michael Coelius und Johann Aurifaber zusammengestellten Bericht über Luthers Ende bereits ganz kurz nach dem Erscheinen des deutschen Buches. Zu seinem Band fügte Bale auch die Grabreden Melanchthons und Bugenhagens hinzu und ein angeblich vom Kurfürsten Johann Friedrich verfaßtes Gebet.[11] Offensichtlich wollte er Luthers erbauliches Ende bekannt machen, um einerseits dem Gerücht, der Teufel habe den Ketzer geholt, den Weg abzuschneiden, und andererseits den Boden für die künftige Wiederbelebung der Verbindung mit Wittenberg vorzubereiten. Heinrich VIII. war damals noch am Leben, und das Buch wurde auf einer Geheimpresse gedruckt. Kurze Zeit danach erschien ein zügelloser Angriff auf die papistische Messe 'mit einer Predigt hinzugetan von dem berühmten und würdig im Gedächtnis

8 *A Very Excellent and Sweet Exposition upon the Two & Twentieth [recte 23rd] Psalm (STC* 16999); *An Exposition upon the Song of the Blessed Virgin Mary Called Magnificat (STC* 16979.9).
9 *A Book Made by a Certain Great Clerk against the New Idol and the Old Devil (STC* 16962); *Hereafter Ensueth a Proper Treatise of Good Works (STC* 16988).
10 *The Last Will and Last Confession of Martin Luther's Faith (STC* 16984). Für den Weseler Druckvermerk vgl. D. M. Loades, 'The Press under the Early Tudors', *Transactions of the Cambridge Bibliographical Society,* 4 (1964), 29–50, besonders 33.
11 *The True History of the Christian Departing of Martin Luther (STC* 14717).

gebliebenen Dr. Martin Luther'.[12] Dieses Buch ist also erst nach Luthers
Tod erschienen und wahrscheinlich bereits unter Eduard VI., doch blieb
der Übersetzer noch anonym, und der Drucker versteckte sich hinter
einem Spitznamen – Hans Hitprick, d. h. einer, dessen Pfeil die Scheibe
getroffen hat. In der Vorrede wird behauptet, die jüngst erschienene
Geschichte Englands von Polydorus Vergilius habe die Abscheulichkei-
ten des Papstes unterstützt, was diese Widerlegung notwendig mache –
eine etwas merkwürdige Anklage, die jedoch immerhin das Veröffentli-
chungsjahr des Buches auf 1547 festlegt.[13]

Als dann die Reformation unter Eduard VI. in Gang kam, konnte
man sich endlich auch öffentlich zu Luther bekennen. Verschiedene
seiner Schriften wurden jetzt *cum privilegio* vor das englische Publikum
gebracht, von denen einige besonders genannt zu werden verdienen, weil
sie die Absichten der der Reformation Zugeneigten gut illustrieren. 'Die
Hauptartikel des christlichen Glaubens' (1548) sammelten verschiedene
Bekenntnistexte aus Luthers Feder oder solche, die ihm zugeschrieben
wurden und die zur Grundlage für eine wahre protestantische Reformation dienen sollten.[14] Weiteren Stoff fand man in Luthers Predigten,
von denen zwei – über Jeremia 23 und über die Engel – übersetzt
wurden.[15] Weiterhin übertrug der im Glauben etwas wankelmütige
Richard Argentine, ein Schulmeister zu Ipswich, eine Predigt Luthers
über Johannes Kapitel 20, allerdings weniger, weil sie die wahre Kirche
betraf, als wegen der dort vertretenen Überzeugung, daß Lehrer und
Pastoren bessere Bezahlung verdienten.[16] Endlich übersetzte man, um
die Reformation populär zu machen, aus dem Deutschen das recht
chauvinistische Büchlein 'Der bösen Weiber Zuchtschul' und fügte
Luthers Predigt über die Ehe hinzu.[17] Luthers wichtigste und berühm-
teste Schriften blieben freilich weiterhin unübersetzt.

Doch wurde Luther noch einmal während dieser tumultuösen Zeit

---

[12] *The Disclosing of the Canon of the Popish Mass, with a Sermon Annexed unto it of the Famous Clerk of Worthy Memory, Dr Martin Luther* (?1547: STC 17627).
[13] Es handelte sich um die 1546 erschienenen englischen Kurzfassungen von Polydore Vergil (STC 24654–6). Gegen Ende Mai 1547 hatte Stephen Gardiner das Buch gesehen (*The Letters of Stephen Gardiner*, hrsg. v. J. A. Muller (Cambridge, 1933), 277).
[14] *The Chief and Principal Articles of the Christian Faith* (1548: STC 16964).
[15] *A Faithful and Godly Exposition of the Kingdom of Christ; A Fruitful Sermon of the Most Evangelical Writer Martin Luther, Made of the Angels* (1548: STC 16982, 16983). Laut W. Clebsch (*Harvard Theological Review*, 56 (1963), 75–86) war der Übersetzer der letzten Predigt John Foxe.
[16] *A Right Notable Sermon Made upon the 20th Chapter of John* (1548: STC 16992).
[17] *The Virtuous Schoolhouse of Ungracious Women* (1548: STC 21826.6). Der Neudruck von 1581, unter dem Titel, *A Watchword for Wilful Women*, hat das Buch allgemeiner bekannt gemacht.

nützlich. Im Mai 1554 erschien eine englische Fassung seiner 'Warnung an seine lieben Deutschen', ohne daß allerdings sein Name erwähnt wurde: er wurde nur als 'ein gewisser wahrer Pastor und Prophet' beschrieben.[18] Die Absicht war recht eindeutig. Luthers warnende Worte hatten sich gegen die Gefahr einer spanischen Eroberung Deutschlands unter Karl V. gerichtet. Der unbekannte Übersetzer, der sich hinter dem Namen Eusebius Pamphilus versteckte, wollte nun gegen die Heirat der Königin Maria mit Karls V. Sohn, Philipp von Burgund, protestieren. Er nannte Luther 'einen so wertvollen Propheten, wie es ihn seit der Zeit der Apostel kaum gegeben hat'; hätte England seinesgleichen bessen, dann hätte Gott Eduard VI. vielleicht am Leben erhalten und die Unterwerfung Englands 'unter die scheußlichste und gottloseste Nation auf Erden' verhindert. Das Buch gab vor, *cum privilegio* zu erscheinen, allerdings nicht mit dem normalen königlichen Privileg, sondern mit einem, das 'der Allmächtigste Gott, der König von Himmel und Erde', gewährt habe. All dieser Wagemut erklärt sich daraus, daß trotz des Kolophons, das von Greenwich und einem gewissen Conrad Freeman spricht, das Werk in Wahrheit bei Froschauer in Zürich gedruckt worden ist. Es gehört also zu den Propagandaarbeiten der damaligen protestantischen Exulanten.[19] So stellt es auch den ersten und den letzten Versuch dar, Luther gegen eine englische Regierung zu verwenden.

Bis zur endgültigen Aufrichtung der anglikanischen Kirche im Jahre 1559 wurde Luther also selten vor das englische Publikum gebracht, und zwar eher als ein erfreulich schöner Prediger, nicht dagegen als der revolutionäre Gründer einer reformierten Kirche. Verglichen mit Bucer, Zwingli und besonders Melanchthon war wenig von ihm bekannt; man wußte zwar von ihm, hatte eine gewisse Hochachtung, konnte ihn aber meist nur indirekt kennenlernen und betrachtete ihn keineswegs als den Mittelpunkt der Reformation. An dieser Sachlage änderte sich auch später wenig, obwohl mit der Zeit noch weitere seiner Schriften ins Englische übersetzt worden sind.

Wie wenig die englische Staatskirche mit ihm verknüpft war, tritt gerade bei den beiden Versuchen hervor, ihn populär zu machen, die in den 1570er Jahren und zur Zeit des Bürgerkriegs im 17. Jahrhundert unternommen wurden. Daß es überhaupt nötig war, das nun entschlossen protestantische England an Luthers Existenz zu erinnern, gibt von seiner Stellung einen deutlichen Eindruck. Zu beiden Fällen war der

[18] *A faithful admonition of a certain true pastor* (*STC* 16980).
[19] E. Gordon Duff, *A Century of the English Book Trade* (London, 1948), 48.

Anlaß, daß ein paar sehr ernsthafte Protestanten – um die arme Seele Englands bekümmert und offensichtlich gegenüber dem überwältigenden Einfluß Calvins recht zurückhaltend eingestellte – in Luther einen sympathischeren Geist entdeckt hatten und diese Entdeckung ihren Mitmenschen mitteilen wollten.

Die Lutherwelle der 1570er Jahre wurde wohl durch die Schwierigkeiten veranlaßt, die gegen Ende der sechziger Jahre die Einheit der englischen Kirche von beiden Seiten her bedrohten, als sowohl die Katholiken neuen Mut faßten als auch die unbefriedigten Protestanten (bald Puritaner genannt) eine weiterschreitende Reformation verlangten. Es mag erstaunen, daß Luther, der bekannte Kampfhahn, plötzlich als Friedensstifter auftrat. Zunächst erschienen Übersetzungen, die den schon vergessenen Namen nicht erwähnten, Luthers Buch über den Prediger Salomonis (1573) und seine eigene Predigt über die Wiederkunft Christi (1570).[20] Dann aber nahm John Foxe, der Martyrologe, sich der Sache an. In seinem großen Werk 'Die Taten und Denkmäler' (allgemein als 'Buch der Märtyrer' bekannt) lieferte Foxe den eingehenden Beweis, wie gründlich er mit Luthers Tätigkeit zumal in den Jahren vor 1524 vertraut war und wie überaus hoch er ihn einschätzte.[21] Ganz offensichtlich hielt er es für sehr wichtig, daß das englische Volk diesen bei ihm schon fast vergessenen Helden der Reformation kennenlernen sollte, und unternahm für ihn, was man nur eine Propagandakampagne nennen kann. Die in diesem Zusammenhang bedeutendste Veröffentlichung der Zeit, die englische Übersetzung von Luthers schönem Kommentar zum Galaterbrief, erwähnt allerdings den Name Foxe nicht; doch besteht kein Zweifel, daß er für das Unternehman verantwortlich war.[22] Foxe war der Verfasser der anonymen Vorrede, die Argumente verwendet, die später in von ihm gezeichneten Vorreden wiederholt wurden, und die auch in einer Randbemerkung auf die Lutherbiographie in seinem eigenen Buche hinweist. Zudem beweist der Verleger den Zusammenhang – Thomas Vautroullier, Sohn eines in England angesiedelten Hugenotten, der nachher weitere, von Foxe bestellte Lutherbücher herausbrachte. Die beiden arbeiteten zusammen im Dienste Luthers.

Da Foxe mit Recht annehmen konnte, man wisse nichts von Luther, benutzte er seine Einleitung zu einer kurzen, aber durchaus gründlichen

---

[20] *An Exposition of Solomon's Book Called Ecclesiastes* (1573: STC 16979); *A Very Comfortable and Necessary Sermon Concerning the Coming of Christ* (1570: STC 16997.5).
[21] Besonders, *AM*, IV, 260–325. Auch andere Stellen bezeugen Foxes Ehrfurcht.
[22] *A Commentary upon the Epistle to the Galatians* (1575: STC 16965).

Biographie, in der er besonders Luthers Originalität und Tapferkeit hervorhob. Einen Stein des Anstoßes bildete im calvinistischen England natürlich Luthers Abendmahlslehre, doch räumte Foxe ihn auf die sanfteste Weise aus dem Wege. Gewiß sei Luthers Meinung, die doch nicht mit der Zwinglis übereinstimme, nicht ganz zutreffend, doch sei sie noch viel weiter von der römischen entfernt; also brauche man sich um solche Kleinigkeiten keine Sorgen zu machen. Das Buch beeindruckte den Bischof von London, Edwin Sandys, der die Lizenz zu gewähren hatte, so sehr, daß er darauf bestand, ein Vorwort hinzuzufügen; pompös wie immer, empfahl er das Werk als erbaulich, da 'der Autor gefühlt hat, was er sagt, und von dem, wovon er schreibt, eigene Erfahrung hatte'. Man kann sich denken, wie Luther auf ein solches Lob reagiert hätte. Das Unternehmen war auch geschäftlich höchst erfolgreich; sieben Neudrucke erschienen in den Jahren bis 1635.

Somit war Luthers neue englische Karriere nunmehr im Schuß. 1577 brachten Foxe und Vautroullier den Kommentar über die fünfzehn sogenannten Stufenpsalmen heraus, für den sie einen anderen Übersetzer fanden.[23] Anscheinend machte zu der Zeit die Übersetzerkunst in England Fortschritte. In der Vorrede verfolgte Fox die selbstgewählte Aufgabe weiter, Luthers Größe vor der Welt zu proklamieren. Luther, so schrieb er, sei zwar 'von manchen noch nicht gelesen, von vielen verhaßt und verpönt und von verschiedenen verachtet und falsch beurteilt worden'. Doch 'wenn man ihn sorgfältig liest oder sich entschließt, einmal von ihm zu kosten, und wenn man durch eigene Erfahrung von Schwächen und Leiden das Recht erworben hat, wahre Frömmigkeit zu schätzen, dann wird man einen Mann finden, der unter den Predigern und Lehrern unserer Zeit den größten gleichzustellen ist'. Unsere Zeit, sagt Foxe, benötigt Luther – 'die armen traurigen Seelen der Leidenden können nicht leicht ohne ihn fertigwerden'. Auf zwei Punkte macht er besonders aufmerksam – auf die Hilfe, die Luther denen bietet, die unter der Furcht vor Teufel, Tod und Verdammnis leiden, und auf die Art und Weise, mit der Luther das Verhältnis zwischen Gesetz und Evangelium behandelt. Hieraus erkennt man bereits deutlich, worauf es Foxe ankam. In Luther hat er die Erlösung von den unerfüllbaren Ansprüchen des Alten Testaments gefunden, eine Erlösung, die Calvin, für den das Gesetz auch nach der Inkarnation in Geltung blieb, zurückgewiesen hatte. (Der Unterschied zwischen den beiden Theologen kommt übrigens auch in ihrer jeweiligen Behandlung des Galater-

---

[23] *A Commentary upon the Fifteenth Psalms Called Psalmi Graduum* (*STC* 16975).

briefes zum Ausdruck). Luther war für Foxe also der große Seelsorger, nach dem die verstörten Geister, denen andere nur Zwist und Streitigkeit anzubieten vermögen, sich sehnen. Derselbe Zweck führte im folgenden Jahr zur Veröffentlichung des Büchleins über die vierzehn Trostgründe (*Tessaradecas Consolatoria*), das auch sofort und mehrmals nachgedruckt worden ist.[24] Als dann Foxe ebenfalls im Jahre 1578 eine Vorrede zu einer Auswahlsammlung von 43 Lutherpredigten anfertigte, konnte er nicht ohne Recht behaupten, über Luther müsse man nicht mehr viel sagen, da 'so viele seiner guten Bücher' jetzt veröffentlicht seien.[25] In seiner Widmung an Sir Thomas Heneage, einen einflußreichen Hofmann der Königin Elisabeth, bestätigte der Übersetzer, daß Foxe ihn zu der Arbeit angeregt habe. Wie Foxe selbst betont, hatte er dies getan, weil er 'in diesen heutigen Tagen' fast niemanden kenne, 'der uns besser tröstet als dieser Doktor, der Autor dieser Predigten'.

All diese Bemühungen machten Doktor Martin nicht nur bekannt, sondern führten sogar zu einer kleinen Lutherkonjunktur, da auch andere Verleger die Profitmöglichkeiten wahrnahmen. 1579 erschien endlich eine der großen Reformschriften – die über die Freiheit eines Christenmenschen; es folgten verschiedene Kommentare, besonders die Vorrede zum Römerbrief.[26] Der Übersetzer des Freiheitstraktats widmete das Buch der Gräfin Warwick, einer bekannten Puritanerin von hohem Stande, die offenbar des Geld für das Unternehmen vorgeschossen hatte. Er nannte Luther 'einen Fremdling' und sprach von 'Hochachtung für den Herrn, der dies in Gang gebracht hat' – also wieder einmal Foxe, der ja Luthers Presseagent gewesen war. Über Luther sprach der Übersetzer ebenfalls mit der größten Hochachtung; 'nie hat jemand seinem Herrn treuer gedient; in seines Herrn Anliegen hat kein Mensch jemals größeren Mut gehabt ... Standhaftigkeit, Großmut und Kraft – damit hat er die Feste des Feindes niedergerissen. Niemand ist tiefer in das Wesen der Dinge eingedrungen, hat größere Siege errungen und Besseres erreicht' – und zwar nur, um die armen Christen zu retten, die schon seit Jahrhunderten das Joch 'des abscheulichen Nimrods von Rom' hatten leiden müssen. Vielleicht sollte man den mehrmals wiederholten Ausdruck 'stranger' als 'Ausländer' und nicht als 'Fremdling' übersetzen, denn man muß sagen, daß Luther,

---

[24] *A Right Comfortable Treatise Containing Fourteen Points of Consolation for them that Labour* (1578: STC 16989).
[25] *Special and Chosen Sermons of Martin Luther* (1579: STC 16993).
[26] *A Treatise Touching the Liberty of a Christian* (1579: STC 16995); *A Methodical Preface Prefixed before the Epistle to the Romans* (ca. 1590: STC 16985).

wenn seine Werke so großen Herrschaften wie Heneage und der Gräfin Anna gewidmet werden konnten, dreißig Jahre nach seinem Tod endlich in England angelangt war. Freilich war der Luther, den man in England zur Schau stellte, etwas einseitig, ja man kann sogar sagen sonderlich. Er war rein und nur der Luther, der den Seelen Trost schenkt, indem er ihnen von der Gnade Gottes und der Fürsprache Christi berichtet. Als dogmatischer Theologe blieb Luther weiterhin ohne Einfluß (von dem Streit zwischen den lutherischen Parteien hörte man in England offenbar nichts), und im anglikanischen Christentum lassen sich Lutherspuren nicht finden. Man kann allerdings behaupten, daß John Foxe in seiner Rolle als treuer Seelenhirt den schönsten Luther ausgewählt hat.

Einmal eingeführt blieb Luther auch weiter auf der Bühne, selbst wenn er niemals mit Calvin, Beza oder auch Zwingli als Maßstab christlicher Frömmigkeit konkurrieren konnte. Die führenden Denker der anglikanischen Kirche, ob sie nun Puritaner oder Arminianer oder einfach (wie die meisten) gute, helvetisch beeinflußte Protestanten waren, haben wohl Luther gelesen, wie sich annehmen läßt. Doch ein besonderes Interesse trifft man nicht, und die weiteren Übersetzungen entstammen einem anderen Milieu, dem des frommen Privatmenschen, für dessen Bedürfnisse ja auch Foxe Luther der Vergessenheit entrissen hatte. Recht typisch ist ein Buch, das 1624 erschien und vom Übersetzer 'Das Alltagsopfer' genannt wurde – eine Ausgabe der kurz vor Luthers Tod erschienenen Trostgebete und Meditationen für Kranke und Sterbende.[27] Wie der Übersetzer erklärte, war ihm das Buch zufällig Jahre vorher, 1603, vor die Augen gekommen, gerade als die Beulenpest alle seine Kinder hinweggerafft hatte. Wieder einmal trat Luther also als der höchst eindrucksvolle Seelsorger auf. Doch lernte man allmählich auch andere Seiten von ihm kennen. 1641 brachte Thomas Hayne eine sogenannte Biographie heraus, die hauptsächlich aus dem Buch von Melchior Adamus stammte;[28] und Hayne war bekannt, daß Luther sich nicht immer als ein friedlicher und freundlichter Trostspender benommen hatte. Immerhin dankte Hayne Gott dafür, daß er 'die Vehemenz Luthers durch Melanchthons friedliebendes Temperament so süß gemildert hat' – ein Urteil, das man seither mehr oder weniger in jedem englischen Buch über Luther wiederholt findet. Die Biographie war Sir

---

[27] *Every-Dayes Sacrifice*, translated by W. R. S. (London by Humphrey Lownes for John Parker). Ich kann es im *STC* nicht finden.
[28] *The Life and Death of Martin Luther, the Passages Whereof Have Been Taken Out of his Own and Other Godly and Most Learned Men's Writings Who Lived in his Time*. Translated by T. Hayne (London by I. L. for John Stafford).

Thomas Roe gewidmet, kurz vorher englischer Gesandter im Deutschland des Dreißigjährigen Krieges, und sollte diesen über die Verwüstung, die ihn entsetzt hatte, trösten; allerdings ist mir nicht klar, wie sie das zustandebringen sollte.

Nach dem ersten Bürgerkrieg (1646) interessierten sich die Geistlichen, die beim Westminster Assembly die Religion Englands erneuern wollten, auch für Luther und bestellten eine Übersetzung seiner späten Reflexionen, ehe sie mit Entsetzen entdeckten, wie wenig er zu ihrem Presbyterianismus paßte.[29] Doch auch ohne diese Gönnerschaft erschien die Übersetzung ein paar Jahre später als weiterer Beitrag zu dem englischen Lutherbild (Seelsorger, nicht Reformator). Der Übersetzer war ein gewisser Henry Bell, der sich selber immer als Hauptmann bezeichnete, der aber von anderen einfach esquire genannt wird, also wohl eine Art Kentucky-Colonel, der den im Bürgerkrieg erworbenen Titel nicht aufgeben wollte.[30] Bell hat Luther auch damit einen wirklich großen Dienst geleistet, daß er 1652 eine ausgezeichnete Übersetzung der Tischreden veröffentlichte.[31] Das Buch hatte er in Deutschland kennengelernt, und er ruhte nicht, bis er es seinen Landsleuten zugänglich gemacht hatte. Damit hatte er recht: Mehr noch als die zusammengestoppelte Biographie brachten die Tischreden Luther zum Leben und machten für eine neue Zuhörerschaft in England aus dem erbaulichen Prediger von John Foxe einen abgerundeten, ja sogar vierschrötigen Menschen. Ich füge hinzu, daß der Verleger dieser letzten Lutherwerke, William Dugard, auch ein Sonderling war: ein Pädagoge, der als Vorstand der Merchant-Taylors-Schule in London in dem Schulgebäude eine Presse hinstellte, auf der er die Schulbücher druckte, die seine Schüler dann kaufen mußten. Das machte ihm soviel Vergnügen, daß er neben dem Unterricht berufsmäßig zur Buchdruckerei überging; trotz mancher Schwierigkeiten stand er gut mit der revolutionären Republik und brachte eine Reihe offiziell genehmigter Bücher heraus sowie auch eine wöchentliche Zeitung.[32]

Somit war Luther also mehr oder weniger in England eingebürgert, so daß nach der Restauration von 1660 sogar eine Reihe fragwürdiger Prophezeiungen erscheinen konnten, die sich grundlos seines Namens

[29] Ich bin Herrn Prof. E. G. Rupp für diese Mitteilung dankbar.
[30] *Luther's Posthuma*, translated by Henry Bell (London: William Dugard, 1650).
[31] *Doctoris Martini Lutheri Colloquia Mensalia . . . translated out of the High German into the English tongue by Captain Henrie Bell* (London: William Dugard, 1652).
[32] *DNB*; Lorna Rostenberg, 'William Dugard, pedagogue and printer to the Commonwealth', *Proceedings of the Bibliographical Society of America*, 52 (1958), 179–204.

bedienten. Allerdings kann man nicht behaupten, daß vor dem 19. Jahrhundert oft über ihn diskutiert worden sei. 1687 kam es zu einer interessanten Auseinandersetzung, als ein katholischer Polemiker names Abraham Woodward es etwas verspätet unternahm, Luther der Ketzerei zu überführen.[33] Dies war zwar nur eine akademische Arbeit, überaus langweilig abgefaßt, die gut dem Klima jenes Jahres, in dem Jakob II. Rom wieder nach England bringen wollte, entsprach. Woodwards Bemerkung, daß 'die reformierte Religion hauptsächlich aus mißverstandenen und falsch ausgelegten katholischen Lehren besteht' hätte die königliche Gunst anziehen sollen. Interessant ist die Angelegenheit aber hauptsächlich, weil Woodward sofort von Francis Atterbury eine Antwort erhielt.[34] Atterbury, später der Bischof von Rochester, dem 1720 ein sensationeller Hochverratsprozeß wegen einer angeblichen Verschwörung gegen Georg I. gemacht wurde, war damals erst 25 Jahre alt und noch ein schlichter, treuer Anglikaner. Abgesehen davon hatte er Stil und Schwung; seine Antwort läßt sich mit einem Vergnügen lesen, das man bei allem bisher Zitierten kaum empfindet. Er fand es besonders töricht, daß Woodward Luthers angebliche Irrtümer der englischen Kirche aufs Konto setzte. Wie solle es möglich sein, erklärte der junge Oxforder Gelehrte recht scharf, daß, 'was Luther gesagt oder getan hat, eine Kirche betreffen könnte, die auf eigenem Fuße steht und von allen fremden Autoritäten ebenso unabhängig ist wie die Krone, die ihr Beschützer trägt'. Ein geschickter Appell an den König, auf dessen Gunst der Gegner spekuliert hatte! 'Luthers Stimme', fuhr er fort, 'ist für uns wahrhaftig . . . die Stimme eines Fremdlings': Als hätten John Foxe und Henry Bell sich umsonst die Mühe gemacht. Tatsächlich wollte Atterbury diesen Ausländer aber verteidigen – jedoch (wie er sagt) nur wie man einem Freund zu Hilfe kommt, nicht als wäre man der Sohn dieses Vaters. So wendet er sich heftig gegen die gängigsten Verleumdungen: 'Luther lebte treu dem, was er gelehrt hat, und er ist den Tod des Gerechten gestorben'.

Damit kommen wir zu einer sozusagen hundertjährigen Lücke in dem Verhältnis zwischen Martin Luther und England. Ich muß jedoch betonen, daß ich mich von hier ab auf unvertrautem Gelände befinde und vielleicht manches übersehen habe. Doch scheint mir, als sei im 18. Jahrhundert jedes Interesse an Luther verblaßt. Man war damals weitgehend bemüht, das Zeitalter der Reformation und der großen Streitigkei-

---

[33] *Concerning the Spirit of Martin Luther and the Original of the Reformation* (Oxford, 1687).
[34] *An Answer . . .* (Oxford, 1687).

ten stillzuschweigen; das war eine Vergangenheit, von der man sich loslösen wollte. Zu diesem Urteil besteht allerdings eine Ausnahme. Der dumpfe Religionsfriede des Jahrhunderts wurde bekanntlich durch die Revolution der Methodisten gestört, und da muß man daran denken, daß der Gründer Johann Welsey seine ursprüngliche Bekehrung Luther zu verdanken hatte. Als er im Mai 1738 bei einer Vorlesung von Luthers Einleitung zum Römerbrief zuhörte, machte die Erfahrung ihn zu einem wiedererneuerten Menschen. Das, was mehr als zweihundert Jahre früher zu Luhters Erwachen geführt hatte, spielte also bei diesem neuen Reformator dieselbe Rolle. Jedoch verschwand der Einfluß sehr schnell. Drei Jahre später drückte sich Wesley, dessen Theologie sich immer mehr zur Betonung des freien Menschenwillens neigte, ganz entrüstet über diesen Menschen aus, weil er die Hilflosigkeit der Kreatur gegenüber der Gnade des Schöpfers zum Mittelpunkt der Religion gemacht habe.[35] In das Zeitalter der Aufklärung paßte Luther schlecht hinein, und das traf auch für diejenigen zu, die die deistischen und agnostischen Folgen der Aufklärung bekämpften.

Als nachher Luther wieder auftrat, hatte sich manches geändert. Gegen Ende des Jahrhunderts nahm ja bekanntlich mit dem sogenannten Evangelical Movement der Einfluß der Religion sogar in der Staatskirche wieder zu, auch als Reaktion gegen die fast pelagianische Einstellung des neuen Methodismus. Wieder wendete man sich den Reformatoren zu, was Luther hätte zunutze kommen sollen. Auch stieg gerade um die Jahrhundertwende das Interesse an dem, was in Deutschland vorging, an. Die durch die Revolutions- und Napoleonischen Kriege bedingte Abwendung von allem Französischen verband sich mit der neuen Romantik, so daß immer mehr Engländer intellektuell durch Deutschland angezogen wurden. Wie Goethe Lord Byron entdeckte, so entdeckte man in England Goethe und Schiller, und nebenbei auch Niebuhr und die neue Geschichtsschreibung. Trotz alledem gewann jedoch Luther wenig durch diese Umstände. Die Hauptvertreter des deutschen Einflusses – Samuel Taylor Coleridge und Thomas Carlyle – zeigten kein Interesse an ihm, der erste wohl nicht, weil er nach einer mystischen Religion strebte, die er eher im fernen Osten (und im Opium) fand, der andere, weil er doch im Wesentlichen immer der Calvinist blieb, als der er aufgewachsen war. Es ist schade, daß Carlyle neben sein Werk über

---

[35] Martin Schmidt, 'Die Bedeutung Luthers für John Wesleys Bekehrung', *Luther-Jahrbuch* (1938), 125–59. Vgl. auch Schmidt, *John Wesley* (englische Übersetzung: London, 1962), I, 263.

den alten Fritz neimals ein Buch über Luther gestellt hat: Da hätte man doch einiges erfahren können![36]

Auch die Entwicklung der rein religiösen Auseinandersetzungen wirkte gegen die Wiederbelebung Luthers. Als das Oxford Movement die Reformation angriff, um sie ganz aus der Geschichte der englischen Kirche auszuscheiden, wendete es sich verständlicherweise gegen Calvin, der ja noch immer die Grundlage der anglikanischen Theologie darstellte; und ebenso berief sich auch der Widerstand der Reformationstreuen natürlich mehr auf die calvinistische Tradition, die im eigenen Lande ausgearbeitet worden war. Soweit ich feststellen kann, hat noch niemand in dem religiösen Wiederaufleben des 19. Jahrhunderts ein etwaiges Lutherthema behandelt, und wenn man die Bücherkataloge berücksichtigt, die erkennen lassen, wie wenig damals über Luther gearbeitet und geschrieben wurde, sieht es schon so aus, als ob ein solches Thema nicht existiert. Ein angelsächsisches Interesse an Luther findet man viel eher in Amerika vor, seitdem sich dort deutsche und skandinavische Lutheraner anzusiedeln begannen. Selbst die neue Geschichtsschreibung trug fast nichts bei. Die meisten der neueren Historiker stürzten sich auf das Mittelalter (auch da hat das Oxford Movement eine Rolle gespielt) oder auf die jüngste Zeit; für die wenigen, die sich auf das Zeitalter der Reformation spezialisierten, war Luther von geringer Bedeutung, weil (wie wir ja gesehen haben) sein Einfluß auf die englische Reformation so gering war.

Und dann kam das Zeitalter der Weltkriege. Obwohl es angenehm wäre, darüber schweigend hinwegzugehen, muß der ehrliche Chronist doch etwas sagen. Nach 1914 reihte man Luther in die Schar derer ein, die angeblich das deutsche Volk aus dem rechten Geleise gebracht hatten. Während das 19. Jahrhundert die romantischen Züge des teutonischen Luther noch bewundern konnte, erkannte das 20. in solchen Eigenschaften nur die Vorbedingungen, die, wie man jetzt dachte, zu Welteroberungsplänen und in den Schützengraben geführt hatten. Zwischen den zwei Weltkriegen wurde aus der Geschichte der Reformation besonders auf den Schulen, aber auch auf den Universitäten, immer mehr die reine Geschichte des Calvinismus, soweit man sich überhaupt für die ausländische Geschichte des 16. Jahrhunderts interessierte – und gerade die

---

[36] Man sollte so scharfe Urteile nicht fällen, wenn man außerhalb seines Fachbezirkes nicht genug gelesen hat. Obwohl Wolfgang Franke ('Englische Lutherdeutung von 1787 bis 1984: Reformation, Revolution und Reform', *Luther-Jahrbuch* (1976), 36–91) viel mehr Interesse an der Reformation als an Luther vorführen kann, trifft es doch zu, daß Coleridge sich zeitweilig mit Luther beschäftigte.

führenden Tudorhistoriker hatten damals wenig derartiges Interesse. Luther galt als verwirrt und 'unsystematisch' – und auch als etwas gefährlich. Wie viel besser konnte man doch mit Calvin und seinem 'französisch-logischen' Denken umgehen. Auch zog man Calvin vor, weil man immer auf der Seite der angeblich demokratischen Puritaner gegen den angeblichen königlichen Absolutismus des 17. Jahrhunderts stand. Ich darf auf diese Dinge nicht weiter eingehen, möchte aber nur bemerken, daß politische und soziale Vorurteile zu einer sehr einseitigen und oft einfach ganz verkehrten Geschichtsschreibung geführt haben, die uns heute noch Schwierigkeiten macht. Was Luther angeht, so besiegelte der Zweite Weltkrieg diese verfahrenen und bigotten Einstellungen. Ich brauche nur auf A. J. P. Taylor hinzuweisen, der in Luther einen deutlichen Vorgänger, ja sogar Urvater, des Nazismus entdeckte. John Foxe hatte man vollkommen vergessen, und an die Stelle seines tröstenden Seelsorgers trat nun eine reine Karikatur. Der einzige Luther, den man kannte, war der Verfasser der Streitschriften gegen die brandschatzenden Bauern und der antisemitischen Hetzschriften. Für Doktor Martin waren dies dunkle Jahre, obwohl ich bezweifle, daß er sich darüber, wo er auch sein mag, viel Sorge gemacht hat.

Die Gegenwart hat das Gleichgewicht hergestellt. In England hat man jetzt endlich nicht nur den alten Konfessionsstreit, sondern auch den verallgemeinernden Haß der jüngsten Kriegszeit völlig überwunden. In die Kirchengeschichte – in die Geschichte der Menschheit – hat man Luther wieder eingereiht und ihm seine berechtigte Stellung zugestanden. Selbst wenn der größere Teil der Arbeit in Amerika geleistet worden ist, hat doch auch England einen nicht unwichtigen Anteil an dieser sehr notwendigen Revision. Am meisten verdanken wir Gordon Rupp, dem ersten Historiker der Neuzeit, der den Engländern beigebracht hat, daß die Reformation auch etwas mit Martin Luther zu tun gehabt hat.[37] Gegen alle Erwartung ist jetzt plötzlich Calvin in den Hintergrund getreten! Der leider viel zu früh verstorbene James Cargill-Thompson bürgerte bei uns auch die Erkenntnisse der neueren Lutherforschung aus Skandinavien ein,[38] so daß in England das Lutherbild tiefgründiger und auch reichhaltiger geworden ist. Heinrich Boehmers Biographie hat man 1957 übersetzt, und schließlich konnte man 1963 sogar Gerhard Ritters recht teutschen Luther verdauen. Ich behaupte nicht, daß man Luther heute in England viel liest oder eifrig studiert,

---

[37] E. G. Rupp, *Luther's Progress to the Diet of Worms* (London, 1951) und *The Righteousness of God* (London, 1953).

[38] W. D. J. Cargill-Thompson, *Studies in the Reformation: Luther to Hooker* (London, 1980).

obwohl zu erwarten ist, daß er 1983 plötzlich überall auftauchen wird. Immerhin hat man ihn aber endlich so angenommen, wie er war. Vor fünfzig Jahren wäre eine englische Teilnahme an einer Lutherfeier ungewöhnlich, vielleicht sogar unberechtigt, gewesen. Glücklicherweise hat sich diese Lage noch vor dem 500. Geburstag erfreulich verändert.

62

DIE EUROPÄISCHE REFORMATION: MIT ODER OHNE LUTHER?*

In diesem Jubiläumsjahre bestgeht die Versuchung, die Reformation mit Luther gleichzustellen, in besonderem Maße – oder jedenfalls die Annahme, daß es ohne ihn nie zur Reformation gekommen wäre. Manche Historiker gerade in Deutschland haben dieser Versuchung nachgegeben, was sich leicht entschuldigen läßt, wenn man die Größe des Mannes betrachtet. Aber bedeutet Reformation eben einfach Luther? Auf einem vor etwa 12 Monaten abgehaltenen Kolloquium über Luther in der Neuzeit nahm man sich vor, ihn als eine allgemein europäische Figur zu behandeln, blieb aber immer wieder im deutschen Umkreis stecken. Bei mir erweckte dies den Gedanken, daß Luther vielleicht wirklich nur eine Bedeutung für Deutschland besaß. Anderswo ist er wohl bekannt und vielfach auch verehrt worden, hat aber nur selten Spuren hinterlassen, selbst in Gegenden, die die Reformation mit offenen Armen empfingen. War er wirklich für ganz Europa der Ursprung der Reformation? Diesem Gedanken, der vielleicht in diesem Jahr etwas ikonoklastisch erscheinen mag, möchte ich heute Abend ein wenig nachgehen.

Selbst in Deutschland war ja Luthers Renommée bis zum Ausbruch dieses Jahres etwas im Niedergang. Gewiß, bei den beruflichen Kirchen-historikern und den Beiträgern zum Luther-Jahrbuch blieb er weiterhin im Mittelpunkt, aber in den Gebirgen und Meeren, die diese ein wenig selbstgefällige Insel der Forschung umgeben, donnerte und blitzte es gefährlich. Vom Osten her drohte ein doppeltes Gewitter. Einerseits war man sich dort doktrinär sicher, daß die Unruhen des 16. Jahrhunderts weniger mit der Religion als mit den sogenannten sozialen Verhältnissen zu tun hatten: Religion ist ja marxistisch gesprochen nur ein Paraphäno-menon. Andererseits, falls nun wirklich etws Religiöses bei der Sache mitgespielt haben sollte, fand man dort den Volksreformator Thomas Müntzer anziehender als den Fürstenknecht Luther. (Es erscheint daher etwas erstaunlich, aber auch angenehm, daß man 1983 dort drüben ganz energisch gefeiert hat: Luther hatte ja das Pech, außer ein paar Abste-

* [*Martin Luther: Probleme seiner Zeit*, hrsg.v. V. Press und D. Stievermann (Stuttgart, 1986), 43–57.]

chern, sein ganzes Leben in der Deutschen Demokratischen Republik verbracht zu haben). Wichtiger und überraschender ist die Entwicklung der Reformationsgeschichte im Westen gewesen. Seit Anfang der 60er Jahre hat man sich hier auch auf die wirtschaftlichen und gesellschaftlichen Verhältnisse gestürzt und hat besonders entdeckt, daß die Reformation ihren frühen Erfolg eher den Städten als den Territorialstaaten verdankte. Die Profanhistoriker standen verlegen da, als ein so bekannter Kirchenhistoriker wie Bernd Moeller ihnen dies klarmachte, aber sie erholten sich schnell und folgten den angedeuteten Spuren so energisch nach, daß die bisher oft betonte Anziehungskraft einer religiösen Erneuerung bald vor den Ambitionen unterdrückter oder aufsteigender Schichten zurücktrat. Die Reformationsgeschichte als Sozialgeschichte ließ für Luther wenig Platz übrig, zumal der Vorrang der Städte den unabhängigen Einfluß anderer Reformatoren – Zwingli, Bucer, Oekolampadius – schwergewichtiger erscheinen ließ als den der Wittenberger Nachtigall. Diese Neudeutungen zogen auch Mitarbeiter in England und Amerika an, sodaß die, wenn ich das so sagen darf, altmodische Art der Lutherforschung hauptsächlich in Skandinavien Zuflucht fand. Eine Sondererscheinung bildet jedoch Heiko Oberman, dessen Arbeiten über die Vor- und Frühreformation uns so viel Neues über Luthers eigene Gedankenwelt beigebracht haben.[1] Übrigens hat man auch im Westen Thomas Müntzer, die Bauern und die Täufer nicht vergessen; manche deutsche, englische und amerikanische Forscher haben sogar angedeutet, daß die wahre Reformation in diesen Geländen zu suchen sei.[2]

Natürlich hat das Lutherjubiläum dem Doktor Martinus die Gelegenheit geboten, die Rolle der berühmten sozialen Kräfte wieder ein wenig in den Hintergrund zu rücken. Heute hört man seine Stimme wieder durch den Trubel hindurchklingen, den schwäbische Bauern, mährische Hutteriten, Augsburger Patrizier, Straßburger Constofler, Kolmarer Zünfte angestiftet hatten. Hie und da sehe ich sogar Anzeichen, daß selbst Fürsten und Adel wieder aus den Kulissen hervortreten wollen: Selbst im demokratischen, elitenfeindlichen 20. Jahrhundert gibt es noch Historiker, die verstehen, daß in der Geschichte das gemeine Volk meist Niederlagen erlitten hat und die Reformation sich nur dort festsetzen

---

[1] Namentlich Heiko A. Oberman, *Werden und Wertung der Reformation* (Tübingen, 1977; englische Übersetzung unter dem Titel, *Makers of the Reformation*, Cambridge, 1981).

[2] Vgl. zwei allgemeine Überblicke über die neuere Literatur: Rainer Wohlfeil, *Einführung in die Geschichte der deutschen Reformation* (München, 1982), und *Reformation Europe: A Guide to Research*, hrsg.v. S. Ozment (St Louis, 1982). Einen nützlichen Bericht über die sozialgeschichtliche Auslegung liefert Robert Scribner, 'Religion, society and culture,' in *History Workshop*, 14 (1982), 2–22.

konnte, wo die großen Herren ihre schützenden Hände ausstreckten. So
unterbrach z.B. Volker Press bei einer Zusammenkunft in London, wo
die Städtehistoriker hintereinander das Podium bestiegen, diesen gemüt-
lichen Konsens mit fünfzig überzeuged gefaßten Seiten über 'Adel,
Reich und Reformation'.[3] Doch denken Sie bitte nicht, diese vielsei-
tige Tätigkeit beweise die Streitsüchtigkeit eines furor historicus: es geht
vielmehr um freundschaftliche und gegenseitige Unterstützung. Mir
kommt es vor, als ob der Marktplatz, den wir die deutsche Reformationsgeschichte nennen, heute recht friedlich aussieht. Alle Buden und
Läden untersucht man fleißig, und die Versuchung, die eine oder andere
Entdeckung mit übertriebenem Stolze anzumelden, ist wohl vorbei. Wir
stehen in einer Nachrevolutionszeit, in der sowohl die unverbesserlichen
Konservativen (für die Luther allein die Reformation verköpert) wie
auch krakelende Revolutionäre (für die Luther nur als zufälliger Vertreter der Volksmasse Bedeutung hat) etwas fossil aussehen. Nur ein
Historiker tut mir leid, nämlich derjenige (falls es ihn gibt), der eine
neue, große zusammenfassende Geschichte der deutschen Reformation
zu unternehmen bereit ist. Die neuen und alten Bausteine lassen sich
schon zusammenmauern, aber das Gebäude wird in die Wolken ragen
und wahrscheinlich unter dem Gewicht so vieler Tatsachen und so
raffinierter Theorien letzten Endes zusammenbrechen.

So jedenfalls sieht die Angelegenheit von außen gesehen aus, und von
außen her erkennt man auch das ungelöste Problem, von dem ich am
Anfang sprach. Der Mensch Luther – der Reformator, der der mittelalterlichen Kirche ein plötzliches Ende bereitete – hat sowohl die Enthül-
lung seiner eigenen, recht mittelalterlichen Natur als auch den sozialpoli-
tisch wie auch sozialgeschichtlich begründeten Widerstand gegen die
Rolle des 'großen Mannes' überleben können. Zum Verständnis der
deutschen Reformation bleibt sein Beitrag hervorragend. Jedoch war die
Reformation so rein deutsch? Ist selbst ihr Beginn in Deutschland
unanfechtbar? Und was bedeutet es für unsere Meinung von Luther,
wenn sie sich vielleicht als weder rein noch ursprünglich deutsch
herausstellen sollte? Das sind weitläufige Fragen, die nicht in einem
Vortrag beantwortet werden können. Dennoch möchte ich vorschlagen,
sie sollten einmal gestellt werden: Vielleicht hat es einen Nutzen, an
Hand einer außerdeutschen Erfahrung auf sie einzugehen.

Ich formuliere die Frage genauer und weniger provozierend. Man
spricht gewöhnlich von einer Reformation, die in Deutschland anfing

---

[3] Vgl. *Stadtbürgertum und Adel in der Reformation*, hrsg. v. Wolfgang J. Mommsen (Stuttgart,
1979), 330–83.

und dann in anderen Ländern empfangen oder angenommen wurde. Unter dieser Reformation versteht man den Aufbau von protestantischen Kirchen, die sich schismatisch von der römischen Kirche lostrennten, ihre eigene Theologie entwickelten und die Einheit der vom Papste regierten Kirche auf die Dauer beendeten. Diese Reformation habe mit Luthers Protest begonnen und ihre Vorgeschichte und Vorbedingungen seien in Deutschland zu studieren. Die weiteren Reformatoren erscheinen dann als Mitarbeiter oder Nachfolger Luthers, obwohl ihre persönlichen Beiträge zu der Reformation natürlich stets hervorgehoben werden. Wenn man die Vorgeschichte und Vorbedingungen in den anderen europäischen Gebieten untersucht, in denen sich die Reformation entweder zeitweise oder dauerhaft durchsetzte, nimmt man stillschweigend an, daß der vorbereitete Boden (so nennt man ihn) zum Empfang der aus Deutschland importierten Reformation bestimmt war. Wie mag es aber mit dieser Auslegung stehen, wenn es sich herausstellen sollte, daß diese Vorbereitung nicht der Aufnahme einer vom Ausland eingeführten, kirchlichen Revolution diente, sondern autochthone und einheimische Veränderungen hervorbrachte, die vielleicht mit den deutschen Ereignissen in Verbindung standen, ihnen aber nicht entsprungen waren? Die gewöhnliche Interpretation bietet uns sozusagen einen Familienvater namens Martin Luther an, dessen Abkömmlinge sich in verschiedenen Ländern niederließen. Doch wie wäre es, wenn es sich eher um eine Schar locker verwandter Vettern handelte? Machen wir vielleicht einen Fehler, wenn wir von einer zentralen Reformation reden, inmitten derer sich mit der Zeit örtlich verschiedene Manifestationen entwickelten? Kämen wir der Wahrheit nicht näher, wenn wir örtlich verschiedene, aber prinzipiell einander ähnliche Anläufe voraussetzten, die im Laufe der Zeit in eine Reformation verschmolzen?

Das Beispiel Böhmen liegt sofort auf der Hand. Die Hussitenbewegung war deutlichst eine vorreformatorische Reformation und wird auch als solche gewöhnlich anerkannt. Doch aus drei Gründen hat sie den Begriff einer sich von Deutschland ausbreitenden, echten Reformation nicht untergraben. Erstens hatten die Utraquisten schon lange vor Luthers Auftreten ihr Abkommen mit dem Papst getroffen und brauchten daher die lutherische Reform nicht, die auch zunächst in Böhmen wenig Einfluß erlangte. Zweitens blieb die hussitische Reform auf ein kleines Gebiet beschränkt, in dem sie im 17. Jahrhundert von der Gegenreformation rechtzeitig unterdrückt werden konnte: Außerhalb der Tschechoslowakei stellt man die ganze Episode als ein wenig bedeutendes Zwischenspiel zur Seite. Und drittens, als die deutsche

Reformation doch nach Böhmen kam, übernahm sie die einheimische, tschechische Bewegung so vollkommen, daß in der Krise von 1618 der protestantische Adel sich eher lutherisch als utraquistisch fühlte und die Böhmischen Brüder (den hussitischen Restbestand) im Hintergrund verschwinden ließ. So konnte man also auch die vorlutherischen Hussiten in einer Geschichte der Reformation untergehen lassen, die mit Luther anfängt.

Böhmen war klein und nach der Wahl eines Habsburger Königs im Niedergang. Bekanntlich aber entsprang die Stellungnahme des Jan Hus einer von Böhmen weit entfernten Quelle – sie kam aus England, einem Lande, das im 16. Jahrhundert im Aufstieg begriffen war und trotz verschiedener ehelicher Verbindungen zwischen seinem Königshause und den Habsburgern seine Unabhängigkeit zu bewahren wußte. Und hier machte sich ja auch eine spätmittelalterliche, papstfeindliche Bewegung spürbar, die auf John Wycliffe zurückging – die Bewegung der Lollarden. Dies geschah in einem Lande, das später die sogenannte wahre, von Luther herstammende Reformation empfing und dann zu einem der führenden protestantischen Königreiche wurde. Tatsächlich fängt in der vorherrschenden englischen Geschichtsschreibung die Reformation in den 1520er Jahren an, also mit Luther. Kann das richtig sein? Es mag sich lohnen, das Beispiel Englands etwas genauer zu untersuchen. Ganz ohne Zweifel übte die kontinentale Reformation einen gewichtigen Einfluß auf die Geschichte Englands aus; ebenso zweifellos ist aber auch die vorherige Existenz einheimischer Ideen und Persönlichkeiten, die vor der Reformation eine der lutherischen ähnliche Erneuerung des Glaubens durchzuführen bestrebt waren. Bereiteten, wie man das meist angenommen hat, die Lollarden den Boden für den Empfang der deutschen Bewegung? Oder verhüllt diese Art Formulierung eine komplizierte Wahrheit, nach der die Lollarden und die heimische Tradition ihre eigene Existenz beibehielten und separat zur Geschichte des englischen Protestantismus beitrugen? In der jüngsten Zeit neigt die Forschung eher der letzteren Ausdeutung zu, obwohl das noch nicht weithin bekannt geworden ist – und obwohl das Geschehen mir als noch verwickelter vorkommmt, als es selbst diese Theorie darstellt.

Erlauben Sie mir also bitte eine kurze Übersicht über ein bekannt merkwürdiges Phänomen – die Kirchengeschichte von England im Zeitalter der Reformation. Eine Reformation von eigenartiger Weise, die sich auch eines eigenartigen Ursprungs erfreute. Obwohl sich hierzulande während der 20er Jahre des Jahrhunderts sowohl humanistische als auch frühprotestantische Einflüsse reformierender Art bemerkbar machten, blieben Regierung und Volk im Glauben traditionstreu, bis dann Heinrichs VIII. Streit mit dem Papst der religiösen Erneuerung den Weg öffnete. Also entstand in England (so heißt es) die Reformation aus vorwiegend politischen Gründen: Sie war, wie ein einflußreicher Historiker das einmal formulierte, das Werke des Staates.[4] Infoldgedessen veränderte sich auch wenig an der Organisation der Kirche und an dem offiziell approbierten Glauben, solange dieser König am Leben war. Gewiß gab es schon manche einflußreiche Politiker und Geistliche, die im Kielwasser einer Loslössung von Rom auch gleich den Protestantismus einzuführen versuchten. Die Wortführer dieser zaghaften Bewegung waren der königliche Minister Thomas Cromwell und der Erzbischof von Canterbury Thomas Cranmer; während der 30er Jahre wurden dann auch ein paar lutherische Reformen durchgesetzt, reformierende Prediger erhielten offizielle Unterstützung, und man war bestrebt, mit den Schmalkaldenern in Verbindung zu treten. Doch reichte ein vom König geförderter Umsturz am Hofe aus, diesen Anfängen der echten Reformation ein Ende zu bereiten: Im Juli 1540 machte die Hinrichtung Cromwells öffentlich bekannt, daß die unabhängige, englische Kirche 'altkatholisch' bleiben sollte. Erst während der Regierungszeit Eduards VI. traf also die Reformation in England ein und wurde dann mit Hilfe einiger führender, kontinentaler Theologen durchgesetzt. Nach dem Versuch der Königin Maria, das Rad zurückzudrehen und den päpstlichen Supremat wieder herzustellen, mußte die Regierung der Königin Elisabeth von neuem anfangen. Ab 1558 begann man ernsthaft zu reformieren, unter der Leitung der aus protestantischen Gebieten zurückkehrenden emigrierten Pastoren und mit Hilfe der Ratschläge verehrter Führer in Zürich und Genf. Langsam und mit der Zeit verbreiteten diese Pastoren und ihre Nachfolger den neuen Glauben im Lande, sodaß em Ende des Jahrhunderts England wahrhaftig und nicht nur auf dem Papier ein protestantisches – wenn auch eigentümlich protestantisches – Land geworden war.

Diese Darstellung, hier zu knapp zusammengefaßt, beherrscht die Geschichtsschreibung, oder sie tat es jedenfalls bis zum gestrigen Tag. Nach ihr blieb die Initiative bei den Behörden und mußte der Protestantismus einem recht widerwilligen Volk aufgezwungen werden. Zum Bruch mit dem Papst kam es überhaupt nur, weil Rom Heinrich VIII. seine Ehescheidung verweigerte. Sowohl die erfolglosen als auch die

---

[4] F. M. Powicke, *The Reformation in England* (Oxford, 1941), 1: 'The one definite thing which can be said about the Reformation in England is that it was an act of State.'

siegreichen Bewegungen in Richtung Reformation fingen bei den Monarchen, Ministern und Erzbischöfen an: Religiöses Streben von unten gab es fast überhaupt nicht, abgesehen von ein paar von Luther beeinflußten Universitätsleuten – wenn man das von unten nennen kann. Bei ihrer Politik fand die Regierung Unterstützung durch zwei kirchenfeindliche, aber religiös neutrale Einstellungen – durch den weit verbreiteten Antiklerikalismus in der Laienschaft, der aber meist die Verbesserung und nicht die Abschaffung des Priesterstandes anstrebte, und die noch weiter verbreitete Begierde nach dem kirchlichen Landbesitz. Beide Strömungen halfen angeblich den wenig zahlreichen Vertretern einer protestantischen Reformation, ohne an sich protestantisch reformieren zu wollen.

Trotzdem wird aber auch weitgehend anerkannt, daß selbst im traditionstreuen England gewisse geistige Einflüsse die Orthodoxie zu schwächen begonnen hatten: Ganz ideenlos waren diese recht politischen Machthaber auch nicht. Einerseits hatte die Oberschicht von Laien und Geistlichen den Humanismus des Erasmus und seiner Genossen eifrig umarmt; und obwohl dessen führende englischen Vertreter (der Bischof John Fisher und der Lordkanzler Thomas Morus) papsttreu blieben und daher auf dem Schafott umkamen, wandte sich die nächste Generation der Humanisten auf den Universitäten, am Hofe und in der Kirche dem Programm reformierender Veränderungen zu, das Thomas Cromwell aufstellte. Anderseits schöpfte die offizielle englische Reformation ihren Ideenschatz an Glauben und Theologie meistens aus dem deutschen und helvetischen Protestantismus. Das heißt, man neigt im allgemeinen dazu, die Reformation in England in her Haupstache als eine Weiterentwicklung der von Erasmus vorbereiteten und von Luther ausgelösten Umwälzung anzusehen. Selbst wenn das reine Luthertum in England, wo der Einfluß von Zürich, Straßburg und schließlich auch Genf viel spürbarer war als der von Wittenberg, wenig beitrug, sieht es doch so aus, als wäre es ohne Luther unmöglich und unvoraussehbar gewesen, daß sich ein Land, dessen ungewöhnlich traditionelle Frömmigkeit vor 1529 die Historiker immer wieder betonen, im Zeitalter der Gegenreformation zum Mittelpunkt protestantischer Hoffnungen hätte entwickeln können. Wie sehr man auch die politischen, sozialen und rein zufälligen Faktoren, die zu diesem Endprodukt beitrugen, anerkannte, war man doch überzeugt, daß in Hinsicht auf den Kern der Reformation – d.h. auf die religiöse Revolution – keine namhaften einheimischen Ursprünge festzustellen seien.

So hat die englische Reformation bis vor kurzem als ein Bestandteil, ein etwas verspäteter Bestandteil, der allgemeinen, europäischen Reformation, die von Luther ausging, gegolten. Wenn dies richtig wäre, dann könnte man gewiß auch weiterhin die Reformation mit Luther gleichstellen; dann hätte die deutsche Vorliebe, die Reformation als eine deutsche Angelegenheit zu beurteilen, die später in verschiedenen Richtungen in andere Länder Europas ausstrahlte, das Problem von der richtigen Seite angepackt. Die neuere deutsche Forschung, die das Verlangen von unten, wie man sagt – also die aus sowohl geistlichen als auch sozialen Gründen aufwallende Sehnsucht nach religiöser Erneuerung – stark betont, unterstützt ebenfalls diesen Begriff vor der einheitlichen, in Deutschland fabrizierten Reformation. Ob Luther den Fürsten oder dem Volke eine Stimme verlieh, macht da keinen Unterschied: Die Hauptsache ist die Annahme, die spontanen Ursachen der Reformation seinen nur in Deutschland vorhanden gewesen, während andere Länder auf Einfluß aus Deutschland warten mußten, ehe sie ihre politisch bedingten Probleme mittels einer religiösen und kirchlichen Umwälzung zu lösen im Stande waren.

Wie wahrheitsgetreu ist jedoch der Umriß der englischen Erfahrung, den ich Ihnen vor ein paar Minuten vorlegte? Wie ich schon mehrmals angedeutet habe, wird heute manches an ihm bezweifelt. Ein nicht unwichtiges Ereignis in der Geschichte Englands ist nämlich übergangen worden. Dieses 'traditionell fromme' Land brachte eine der wenigen spätmittelalterlichen Häresien hervor, die bei der Bevölkerung genügend Zulauf gefunden hatten, um dem herrschenden System große Sorgen zu bereiten. 1414 bedrohte der Aufstand des Lollardenführers Sir John Oldcastle die Regierung Heinrichs V. so gefährlich, daß der König es vorzog, nach der nur halbwegs erfolgreichen Unterdrückung dieser Unruhen die Energien seiner Untertanen auf einen Feldzug in Frankreich abzulenken. Als John Foxe, der bekannte Martyrologe des 16. Jahrhunderts, die Geschichte der englischen Reformation schrieb, übersah er die Lollarden nicht: Er ernannte John Wycliffe zum 'Morgenstern', der den Tag Martin Luthers ankündigte. Anderseits aber verehrte er Luther in einer für englische Umstände ganz ungewöhnlichen Weise und ließ daher die vorlutherischen Ketzer nur als Vorläufer auftreten, die dann, sobald es möglich war, zu Lutheranern wurden.

Im Prinzip blieb somit die Geschichtsschreibung bis vor kurzem bei Foxe. Den Lollarden gehörte nur die kleine Rolle der Vorbereiter, deren kaum spürbare, weitere Existenz hie und da den neuen, aus Deutschland hereinkommenden Ideen die Plattform verschaffte. Es galt als bewiesen, daß nur noch kleine Gruppen aus der Unterschicht – Kleinbauern,

Handwerker und Landstreicher – an der alten Häresie festhielten. Solche
Leute konnten natürlich auf die Machthaber – König, hohe Aristokratie,
Landadel, schließlich die in England recht kleine Schicht wohlhabender
Bürger – keinen Eindruck machen. Daher stand fest, daß der ketzerische
Glauben der Lollarden mit dem auf den Universitäten auftretenden
Streben nach dem neuen Glauben nichts zu tun hatte. Ich bin ursprüng-
lich auch dieser Meinung gewesen. Wir waren uns einig darüber, daß der
Angriff auf die Orthodoxie mit Erasmus und den von ihm beinflußten
Humanisten einerseits, andererseits mit den sogenannten englischen
Frühprotestanten wie William Tyndale, Robert Barnes und John Frith
anfing – mit gelehrten Theologen, deren Zweifel am katholischen Glauben von der Wittenberger Reformation, also von Luther, genährt
wurden. Daß die alten, einheimischen Ideen etwas beigetragen hatten,
galt als unwahrscheinlich, eine Ansicht, die man umso leichter annahm,
da die Lollarden und Lutheraner in vieler Beziehung einander ähnlich
waren. Am einfachsten war es daher, jedes Auftreten reformierter Ideen
als lutherisch zu bezeichnen, wie es ja auch die Bischöfe der damaligen
Zeit taten. Bei ihrem Kampf um die Orthodoxie belegten sie gewöhnlich eindeutiges Lollardentum mit dem Schimpfwort der neuen Häresie,
besonders nachdem der Papst über Luther den Kirchenbann verhängt
hatte. In dieser Weise stellte man sich in die Reihen der allgemeinen
Kirche – und übrigens geschah dasselbe auch in anderen Ländern, z.B. in
Spanien und Italien. Wie gesagt, hegten wir Historiker bis vor kurzem
die Überzeugung, daß in dem Amalgam alter und neuer Heterodoxien
das lutherische Element weitgehend das wichtigere gewesen sei.

In den letzten zwanzig Jahren hat sich die Lage verändert, als die
Forschung die Lollarden genauer studierte.[5] Wir wissen jetzt, daß viel
mehr Lollarden die Verfolgungen des frühen 15. Jahrhunderts überleb-
ten, als einst angenommen wurde. Ihre Glaubensthesen waren sowohl
vernünftiger als auch einheitlicher, als das von kleinen, zerstreuten
Gruppen anzunehmen wäre; und obwohl die Häresie meist Menschen
der Unterschicht anzog (Frauen sowohl als Männer), fanden sich
Anhänger auch bei den höheren Schichten und auf den Universitäten.
Lollarden gab es nicht nur im sogenannten fortschrittlichen Süden,
sondern auch im angeblich rückständigen Yorkshire. Die an sich gehei-

[5] Vgl. besonders die folgenden Werke: J. A. F. Thomson, *The Later Lollards 1414–1520*
(Oxford, 1965); Margaret Aston, 'Lollardy and sedition 1381–1431', *Past and Present*, 17
(1960), 1–44, und 'Lollardy and the reformation', *History*, 49 (1964), 149–170, A. G.
Dickens, *Lollards and Protestants in the Diocese of York, 1509–1558* (Oxford, 1959). J. F.
Davis, *Heresy and the Reformation in the South-East of England 1520–1559* (London, 1983).

men Gemeinden in London, Essex, East Anglia, Kent und im oberen Themsetal besaßen ein gemeinsames schriftliches Erbe, hatten regelrechte Vorstände und standen durch fahrende Prediger miteinander in Verbindung: Man darf von einem Netz einer Untergrundreligion sprechen. Natürlich soll man die Ausdehnung und den Einfluß dieses Netzes nicht übertreiben, aber es ist klar, daß die 'traditionelle Frömmigkeit' keineswegs allgemein verbreitet war. Die Dogmen dieser einheimischen Ketzer nahmen den lutherischen Protestantismus in manchen Einzelheiten vorweg: Man versteht schon, warum die Verteidiger der Orthodoxie in den 1520er Jahren solche Schwierigkeiten hatten, zwischen den zwei Phänomenen zu unterscheiden. Für unsere Zwecke reicht aber der bequeme Sammelname 'Lutheraner' nicht aus. Wir wollen doch feststellen, ob die Frühreformation in England wirklich die deutschen Initiativen im Lande akklimatisierte oder einer wiederbelebten alten Lollardei entsprang. Die damaligen Bischöfe konnten es sich leisten, die Unterschiede zu übersehen; uns hingegen kommt es darauf an, die theologischen Begriffe der zwei Bewegungen voneinander abzuheben. Unsere Informationen kommen aus den Ketzerprozessen vor den Bischofsgerichten, bestehen also hauptsächlich aus den den Angeklagten vorgeworfenen häretischen Aussagen. Es wird dabei klar, daß die meisten dieser verfolgten Ketzer einheimisch lollardisch redeten, und nicht fremd lutherisch.

Die Theologie der Lollarden war im Grunde viel weniger raffiniert als die Luthers: Es geht um den Unterschied zwischen einfachen, bibellesenden Laien und scholastisch gebildeten Wissenschaftlern, wie man ihn ja auch anderswo im vorreformatorischen Europa vorfindet. Daß beide Strömungen dem Volke die Schrift zugänglich machen wollten und die Rolle des Priesteramtes abwerteten, bedeutet weniger als die Tatsache, daß die Lollarden nichts vom Solafideismus wußten, nicht an die allgemeine (sichtbare) Kirche glaubten und jede Art von Klerus ablehnten. Mit diesen Vorstellungen waren sie typische Sektierer und standen den späteren Täufern näher – und wir wissen ja, was Luther von den Täufern hielt. Den Lollarden waren aber zwei Grundprinzipien der Täufer fremd: Sie waren zufrieden mit der Kindertaufe und sie schwärmten nicht. Im Gegenteil: Ihr deutlichstes Charakteristikum war eine reelle und sehr nüchterne Einstellung zu den Mysterien des Glaubens. Ein echter Lollarde verpönte alle Heiligenbilder und Statuen als 'nur Stein und Holz', aus denen kein Heil zu saugen sei; er erklärte regelmäßig, die Hostie sei einfach Brot und bleibe es auch immer, was auch der Priester anfangen möge. Recht oft liest man eine Aussage über das Abendmahl, die ein treuer Lutheraner für Gotteslästerung hätte halten müssen: Wenn es wahr wäre mit dem Meßopfer und der Wandlung in den Leib Christi, 'dann würde ich doch beim Abendmahl die Knochen in meinem Munde knirschen hören'. Der echte Lollarde verachtete ganz bersonders jede Art von Heiligenkultus und die Anbetung der Mutter Gottes. Die für mich anziehendste überlieferte Aussage kam von einem derben Londoner Frauenzimmer: 'Warum denn all der Trubel über die Jungfrau Maria? Die hat doch nur das eine Kind gehabt. Ich hatt' sechs davon – und ich weiß wenigstens, wer der Vater war.'

Bei Luther spielte das Problem des Heiligenkultes keine besondere Rolle und die offizielle Reformation widersetzte sich den Bilderstürmen, die die Lollarden unternehmen wollten (und die auch am Anfang der Reformation unter Eduard VI. stattfanden). Daher dienen Äußerungen solcher Art als ein nützlicher Prüfstein.

Bei der Untersuchung der Geständnisse, die die vor den Bischofsgerichten Angeklagten machten, stellte es sich nun heraus, daß sie meist bis zur Mitte des Jahrhunderts deutlich lollardisch gefärbt blieben. Von den typischen Ideen des Luthertums hört man fast garnichts – nichts über die Erlösung allein durch den Glauben, nichts von der Freiheit des Christenmenschen, nichts von der Kirche auf Erden oder der Rolle der Priesterweihe. Hingegen trifft man immer wieder auf den Protest gegen die Heiligenverehrung und den Angriff auf alle Pfaffen, ob sie traditionell oder reformiert waren. In der englischen Frühreformation spielte das Fegefeuer eine etwas überraschende Rolle. Kein Thema kommt häufiger in der theologischen Debatte und in Predigten vor; die Orthodoxen und die Heterodoxen unterschieden sich hauptsächlich dadurch, ob sie dieses Dogma annahmen oder ablehnten. Ob Luther an ein Zwischenstadium zwischen Heil und Verdammnis glaubte, scheint deshalb schon nicht recht sicher zu sein, weil bei ihm das Fegefeuer keine bemerkenswerte Rolle gespielt hat. Hingegen war es schon immer ein Hauptpunkt lollardischer Kertzerideen gewesen, die in der Bibel nicht belegte Lehre vom Fegefeuer zu verneinen.

Also lassen Lollarden und Lutheraner sich schon voneinander unterscheiden, selbst wenn man anerkennt, daß sie sich in manchen Glaubensthesen die Hände reichen. Und wenn man diese Probemittel anwendet, findet man sehr überraschend Lollarden am Anfang der englischen Reformation. Die meisten der damals entdeckten Ketzer waren gewiß kleine Leute aus den traditionell als lollardisch definierten Gruppen, auf dem Land und in den Städten, aber sie standen nicht alleine da. Hinzuzuziehen sind auch bekannte Opfer der Verfolgung, die bei Foxe als echte Protestanten auftreten – solche Leute wie James Bainham, ein Londoner Rechtsanwalt, oder Richard Bayfield, ein ehemaliger Mönch und bekannter Kolporteur ketzerischer Schriften. Besonders wichtig ist die Entdeckung, daß Thomas Bilney auch kein Lutheraner, sondern ein evangelischer Lollarde war, denn Bilney war ein Universitätsmann, ein Theologe aus Cambridge, der 1531 als ein rückfälliger Ketzer verbrannt wurde. Foxe ernannte ihn zu einem der Gründer des englischen Protestantismus. Er nahm das Meßopfer und die meisten orthodoxen Lehren an, was ihn zu einem beunruhigenden Problem für die Historiker gemacht hat: Warum wurde er eigentlich umgebracht? Wie es sich nun herausgestellt hat, erlitt er den Tod, weil er gegen die Anbetung der Heiligen predigte – also aus deutlich lollardischen Gründen. Bilney, zweifelsohne ein besonders einfacher und reiner Geist, hatte auf alle seine Bekannten ungewöhnlich großen Einfluß. Besonders war er für die Bekehrung von Hugh Latimer verantwortlich, und in den dreißiger Jahren vor seiner eigenen Hinrichtung unter der Königin Maria tat Latimer mehr als jeder andere Einzelne, um die Reformation in England zu verbreiten. Latimer, kein sehr gelehrter Mann, aber ein aufreizender Prediger, wurde sogar noch Bischof von Worcester und sammelte eine Schar eifriger Propagandisten um sich, die auch unter anderem traditionelle Lollardenideen proklamierten. Also drang die lollardische Tradition durch Bilney, Latimer und dessen Schüler in den königlichen Hof und in das Episkopat ein. Solchen Erfolg hatten die wahren Lutheraner wie Tyndale und Frith nicht. So gewichtig erwiesen sich die von Deutschland kaum berührten (oder doch erst nachher berührten) Strömungen, daß man die englische Frühreformation fast schon als einen Lollardensprößling bezeichnen könnte.

Natürlich darf man nicht vergessen, daß die verschiedenen Zuflüsse zu dem Hochwasser, das am Ende die alte Orthodoxie hinwegschwemmte, dauernd durcheinander strömten, sich gegenseitig unterstützten und oft in ihren fruchtbaren Mischehen eigenartige Nachkömmlinge hervorbrachten. Die Situation war verwirrend, und die Verwirrung fing sofort an, nämlich bei Thomas Morus, der sich 1528 als Erzfeind der Ketzer und Staatsanwalt für die katholische Orthodoxie meldete. In seiner ersten Streitschrift (Dialog über Ketzereien, 1528) verteidigte er die Kirche eigentlich nur gegen Glaubenszweifel alter Art – Zweifel an dem Heiligenkultus, an den Pilgerfahrten und allen Gebräuchen magischer Art –, die die sogenannten 'Brüder' (die geheimen Lollarden) schon seit hundert Jahren gehegt hatten. Doch hatte Morus schon 1521, als er Heinrich VIII. in seiner Auseinandersetzung mit Luther Hilfe leistete, die neue, kontinentale Häresie kennengelernt und daher knüpfte er an seine Hetzschrift gegen die 'Brüder' eine kurze aber heftige Verdammung der Wittenberger Reformation an. Er machte sich auch nie die Mühe, Luther und dessen Anhänger richtig zu verstehen: Für ihn blieben sie nur eine Abart der ihm zu Hause besser bekannten Brüderchen. Was ihn besonders erregte war, daß geweihte Priester solche antiklerikalen Ideen aufgenommen hatten, und seine genaueste Beschwerde gegen die Protestanten galt der Priesterehe, ein abscheulicher Bruch des Keuschheitsgelübdes, das ihm niemals aus dem Kopfe ging. Doch da er infolgedessen Luther persönlich angriff, erhielt er eine Antwort von Tyndale, und der weitere Flugschriftenstreit wandte sich etwas verwirrend von der Lollardentradtion ab und dem neuen Protestantismus zu. Nachdem Foxe dann alle vorreformatorischen heterodoxen Erscheinungen in die offizielle Aufstiegsgeschichte des elisabethanischen Protestantismus einbaute, vergaß man selbst in England die einheimischen und vorlutherischen Grundlagen.

Dieses Vergessen wurde umso peinlicher, weil der einheimische Ursprung im Untergrund weiterhin einflußreich blieb und manches Eigenartige am Anglikanismus erklären kann. Bekanntlich konnte ja die englische Reformation Luther nicht recht verdauen und fand das helvetische Vorbild überzeugender. Dahinter stecken verschiedene Ursachen, z.B. die humanistische Tradition in England, die sich mit Zwingli, Bucer und Bullinger viel leichter verständigen konnte als mit Luther (aber auch Melanchthon respektierte), sowie auch des Königs besonderer Haß gegen Luther wegen all der Schimpfworte, die der Doktor Martinus seinerzeit über das Haupt des Junkers Heinz ausgeschüttet hatte. Doch bestanden auch rein theologische Gründe für die Hinwendung nach Oberdeutschland und der Schweiz. Wie überall bei der Frühreformation stand das Problem der Abendmahlslehre vor Augen. In dem Streit zwischen Luther und den Schweizern vertraten die letzteren eine Auslegung, deren Verneinung der körperlichen Präsenz den Ideen der Lollarden sehr nahe stand. Die englische Ketzertradition betrachtete die Eucharistie nur als eine Gedenkfeier, nicht als ein die Gnade vermittelndes Sakrament. Ich brauche wohl nicht zu betonen, wie schwer sich diese These mit Luthers Lehre in Einklang bringen ließ und wie vertraut andererseits Zwinglis Lehre erscheinen mußte. Tatsächlich behielten all die verschiedenen Versionen des englischen Protestantismus Brocken aus der lollardischen Tradition bei. Erinnerungen dieser Art stecken noch in der Sakramentslehre der Neununddreißig Artikel von 1563; sie klingen wieder in dem ethischen Imperativ der meisten Puritaner; sie machen sich bemerkbar in der zuerst auf der Universität Cambridge auftretenden Abkehrung von der calvinistischen Prädestinationlehre, die von den 1580er Jahren ab in England der arminianischen Reaktion den Boden Bereitete.

Es wird also deutlich, daß die englische Reformation vieles aus der einheimischen Tradition schöpfte und daher einen eigentümlichen Protestantismus hervorbrachte. Diese Eigenständigkeit schuldete manches auch anderen nichtdeutschen Einflüssen, etwa den Humanisten mit ihrer Konzentration auf die Ethik, auf die Sozialprobleme und das Erziehungswesen, oder erastianischen (d.h. obrigkeitsteuen) Grundprizipien, denen sich eine von einer königlichen Regierung angestiftete Reformation notwendigerweise nicht entziehen konnte. Die Lollardentradition beeinflußte weniger die gesellschaftlichen Ideen und überhaupt nicht die Organisation der anglikanischen Kirche, hatte aber Bedeutung für die Theologie. Sobald man die Möglichkeit ernstlich ins Auge faßt, kommt einem das Fortdauern solcher im Volke verbreiteten Lehren nicht überraschend vor. Selbst die normale, Luthers Rolle betonende Auslegung nimmt ja an, daß die von Deutschland ausstrahlende Reformation überall unter dem Einfluß lokaler Bedingungen unterschiedliche Formen erhielt.

Doch die Frage, von der wir ausgingen, lautete etwas anders. Ich schlug vor zu untersuchen, ob die Reformation in England wirklich genötigt war, auf die deutschen Anstöße zu warten. In diesem Zusammenhang kommt es darauf an festzustellen, was den Lollarden vor dem Auftreten Luthers geschah. Wie ich schon sagte, fing eine energische Verfolgungspolitik mit dem Aufstand von Oldcastle 1414 an und hörte dann eigentlich nie wieder auf.[6] Alle paar Jahre unternahm einer der englischen Bischöfe einen kleinen Feldzug gegen die Häresie, indem er einer Gruppe Lollarden den Prozeß machte und eine Anzahl von ihnen dazu zwang, ihren Ketzereien abzuschwören. Trotz der drakonischen Gesetze von 1401 und 1414, die die weltlichen Behörden zu automatischen Vollstreckern der von der Kirche erlassenen Todesurteile machten, starben jedoch nur wenige Opfer auf dem Scheiterhaufen. Dann aber kam es plötzlich in den Jahren 1511 und 1512 zu einem konzentrierten Angriff in vier Diözesen (London, Canterbury, Coventry und im Süden des riesigen Bistums Lincoln), bei dem zehn Menschen verbrannt wurden und über 150 weitere als erstmalig entlarvte Kertzer schwere Bußen tun mußten. Dann gingen die Zahlen wieder auf die vorher

[6] Vgl. die Liste in Thomson (Anm. 5), 237 f.

gewohnte, niedere Stufe hinunter, bis 1521 der Bischof von Lincoln erneut versuchte, die in seiner Diözese besonders zahlreichen Seuchenherde auszurotten. Der Lordkanzler, der Kardinal Wolsey, der kurz vorher auch eine Bücherverbrennung angeordnet hatte,[7] veröffentlichte ein königliches Rundschreiben, das die Beamten in allen Städten und Dörfern der betroffenen Gegenden zur Unterstützung aufforderte.[8] Die verbrannten Bücher waren die Schriften Luthers, aber die verfolgten Ketzer – von den 54 Verurteilten wurden vier verbrannt – waren Lollarden. Von Anfang an also überschnitten sich die an sich verschiedenen Häresien und zugleich die Probleme, die sie den kirchlichen und königlichen Richtern stellten.

Leider steht mir nicht die Zeit zu, diese neugefaßte Darstellung ausführlicher zu belegen. Immerhin sollte klargeworden sein, daß das Lollardentum anfangs des 16. Jahrhunderts wieder an Gewicht und Selbstbewußtsein zunahm. Die Kirche erkannte die Gefahr sofort und leitete die aus der Erfahrung vertrauten Gegenmaßnahmen ein. All dies geschah mehrere Jahre vor dem Anschlag der 95 Thesen und noch länger vor dem ersten englischen Echo auf Luthers Botschaft. Dieses Echo war eigentlich Heinrichs VIII. Verteidigungsschrift für die sieben Sakramente (1521): Möglicherweise hat nur der königliche Eifer für die orthodoxe Theologie verhältnismäßig früh ein Fenster nach England geöffnet. Jedenfalls, so weit wir das wissen, war der König der erste Mann in seinem Lande, der so schnell die Gefahr erkannte, die durch Luther der einheitlichen, päpstlichen Kirche und dem katholischen Glauben drohte. Hat doch selbst Thomas Morus, der spätere Vorkämpfer für Katholizismus und vielleicht für das Papsttum, uns die ineressante Nachricht hinterlassen, er, der am Anfang der 20er Jahre über den päpstlichen Primat recht unsicher war, sei erst von Heinrich davon überzeugt worden. Aber während der König dem deutschen Ketzer den Kampf ansagte, und sein Kardinal die Bücher des Wittenberger Häresiarchen verbrennen ließ, beschäftigte sich der Bischof Longland von Lincoln mit der Unterdrückung altmodischer, lollardischer Ketzer, die plötzlich wieder hervorgetreten waren.

Also: Das Lollardentum, das später so deutlich zur Entwicklung der englischen Reformation beitrug, gewann zu Anfang dieses Jahrhunderts ganz unabhängig von dem, was in Deutschland vorging, neue Kraft und wurde von der Kirche als wiederauflebende Gefahr behandelt. Die

---

[7] C. S. Meyer, 'Henry VIII burns Luther's books, 12 May 1521', *Journal of Ecclesiastical History*, 9 (1958), 181–3.   [8] *TRP*, I, 133 f.

Sozialhistoriker werden gewiß weise das Haupt wiegen: Nehmen sie doch jeden Fall eines volkstümlichen Widerstands gegen die Obrigkeit als Beweis des bei ihnen axiomatisch gegenwärtigen Klassenkampfes oder wenigstens einer wirtschaftlich bedingten Unruhe. Daher sei betont, daß die damals erkannte Gefahr rein kirchlich und religiös war, und keineswegs politisch oder sozial. Obwohl Anhänger von Oldcastle noch vierzig Jahre lang nach dessen Tod als Anstifter von Aufruhr tätig gewesen waren, verlor die Bewegung nach 1450 jede Färbung politischer Ambitionen oder sozialer Unzufriedenheit. In dem großen, von Jack Cade geführten Aufstand von 1450 spielten die Lollarden und ihre Schismatik nicht die geringste Rolle; und die Ketzerverfolgungen von 1511 bis 1522 entdeckten keine revolutionären Bedrohungen. Auch waren die Lollarden der frühen Tudorzeit nicht die bei sozialistischen Historikern beliebten Opfer der feudalen Herren oder der neuen Kapitalisten. Gewiß bestanden die geheimen Gemeinden der Brüder zum größeren Teil aus Wollenwebern, Handwerkern und Kleinbauern – und aus deren Frauen und Töchtern. Doch sprachen sie nicht vom Unglück des gemeinen Mannes, strebten nach keinem Umsturz und nahmen Herren aus dem höheren Stande (wie z.B. den wohlhabenden Londoner Kaufmann Richard Hunne) willig in ihre Reihen auf. Ein Vergleich mit dem Bundschuh oder dem Armen Konrad wäre völlig unzutreffend. Als es Morus später darauf ankam, die Ketzer als Anstifter sozialer Unruhen und mörderischen Aufruhrs anzuprangern, vermochte er nach Oldcastles Aufstand nichts vor dem deutschen Bauernkrieg anzuführen.

Den Lollarden ging es um die Wahrheit der Lehre und das Heil der Seele. Ich nehme schon an, daß sie mit ihrem irdischen Schicksal nicht besonders zufrieden waren: Sie waren ja Menschen. Aber gegen die Herren wandten sie sich nicht und ihre Teilnahme an der englischen Reformation trug nichts bei zu einem etwaigen sozialen Protest, der ohnehin bei diesem Ereignis in England nicht vorkam. Ihre Abscheu reservierten sie für die öffentliche Macht der Kirche, für den Prunk der Bischöfe und für die Unzulänglichkeit der Pfarrherren – also für die Tatsache, daß eine korrumpierte Kirche (angeblich) von Gottes Lehre und Christi Beispiel abgewichen sei. Sie wollten die Bibel auf englisch lesen dürfen und nach dem Heil ohne die fragwürdige Hilfe der Pfaffen suchen. Wie unbequem auch immer die Armut sein mochte, verlangten sie keine Neuverteilung allen Reichtums, sondern nur die Konfiskation des als überflüssig geltenden Kirchengutes, damit der Klerus seine Weltlichkeit verlöre. Daher konnten sie mit der offiziellen Reformation in den 30er Jahren, als die ein Jahrhundert lang erstrebte Säkularisierung plötzlich einsetzte, auch zufrieden sein, abgesehen davon, daß ihre theologischen Standpunkte dem neuen Oberhaupt weiterhin die Haare zu Berge stehen ließen. Als dann aber nach Heinrichs Tod eine religiöse Reformation anfing, die manche Ideen von Zwingli, Bucer und Melanchthon übernahm, näherten sich altes Kertzertum und neue Orthodoxie einander so weit, daß die Lollarden ohne Schwierigkeiten in der protestantischen Kirche unterkommen konnten. Ganz integriert in die reformatorsche Kirche wurden sie freilich auch nicht: Das Überleben lollardischer Begriffe läßt sich noch in der allmählichen Entwicklung separatistischer Sekten von den 60er Jahren ab erkennen.

Ein altes und sich im Niedergang befindendes Ketzertum wurde also gerade vor dem Anfang der deutschen Reformation wieder stärker. Etwas muß man da auf die Erfindung des Buckdruckes schieben, der die Vervielfältigung der geheimen und verbotenen Lollardenschriften ermöglichte und damit ihren Propheten eine neue Waffe verlieh. Dies erklärt aber nicht, warum gerade damals solche Propheten wieder auftraten und beim Volke Anklang fanden. Wohl blieben sie zahlenmäßig in der Bevölkerung eine kleine Minderheit, aber um 1500 hatten sie mehr Anhänger als um 1480. Um das zu verstehen, muß man an ein Phänomen denken, das fast europäisch genannt werden darf und jedenfalls auch aus anderen Ländern – einschließlich Deutschland – bekannt ist. Ehe noch Luther auf die Bühne trat, findet man verschiedentlich Bewegungen zur Erneuerung der Kirche und des Glaubens vor, die manchmal den Namen Evangelismus erhalten haben. Diese Bewegungen mögen ihre wirtschaftlichen und sozialen Seiten haben, aber im Prinzip spiegeln sie eine religiöse Sehnsucht wieder. Es handelt sich um einen Protest gegen eine verweltlichte Kirche, eine verfahrene scholastische Theologie, eine verwirrte und verwirrende Lehre über die Heilsmittel. In Deutschland erkennt man all dieses Streben als Vorbereitung zur Reformation Luthers an. Wie ich hier nur zeigen wollte, kamen solche Vorbereitungen ganz unabhängig voneinander auch anderswo vor – in Gebieten, in denen dann eine von Luther höchstens teilweise berührte Reformation stattfand.

Wenn wir von Luther reden, sprechen wir vom Reformator der deutschen Lande. Das ist wohl Ehre genug; und es ist eine Ehre, die auch andere Völker anerkannt haben, inem sie ihm bei ihren eigenen Reformationen mehr Platz einräumten, als ihm eigentlich zusteht. In England, wo eine Art von Reform kommen mußte, sobald sich der König in einen unlösbaren Streit mit dem Papste verstrickt hatte, war Luthers

Einfluß besonders gering, obwohl dank John Foxe der Versuch gemacht wurde, ihm auch hier eine führende Stellung zuzuschreiben. Darf man hoffen, daß gerade im Lutherjahr die Sachkenner auch anderer Länder die Frage genauer untersuchen, wie weit ihr Protestantismus dem deutschen entstammte.[9] Niemand bezweifelt Luthers Größe: Wie Thomas Carlyle sage, er war eine Heldenfigur. Doch der Mann, der sein Leben lang die Wahrheit des Wortes predigte, würde doch hoffentlich die Wahrheit der Geschichte einer gedankenlosen Ehrfurcht vorziehen. Und diese Wahrheit heißt: Wenn wir von der Reformation reden, sprechen wir von viel mehr als von Martin Luther.

[9] Für Frankreich ist dies gerade getan worden: D. J. Nicholls, 'The nature of popular heresy in France', *HJ*, 26 (1983), 261–75.

II

ON HISTORIANS

63

HERBERT BUTTERFIELD AND THE STUDY OF HISTORY*

In 1931 Herbert Butterfield, precisely as old as the century, published a short book entitled *The Whig Interpretation of History*. It made him famous, and for the next forty years or so he stood forth as one of the leading voices in the profession. His voluminous writings in books and essays were read avidly by schoolmasters and their pupils, by students and – less regularly – by dons; to a wide range of educated and reflective people not themselves historians he represented the voice of history in England. He added a further dimension to his image when single-handedly and with considerable courage he engaged the then dominant Namierite school of eighteenth-century studies; though he cannot be said to have triumphed in that battle, he emerged from it with honour and with the satisfaction of having been able to crack the crystalline self-regard of the opposing party in several places. Those who knew only the voice, on paper at that, were liable to be profoundly disconcerted when they encountered him: no whitebearded old testament prophet after all, preaching stern simplicities, but a clean-shaven (often somewhat razored) man permanently about thirty-five years old, brisk, cheerful, responsive, entertaining, variously chain-smoking or sworn off cigarettes altogether, always courteous, never pompous. It might be thought that today, less than four years after his death, it is yet too early to venture upon an assessment of his achievement, but it seems to be desirable that the task should be attempted by one who still remembers the famous Butterfield giggle while reading the Butterfield writings. My own special qualification, I would claim, lies in the fact that I knew him but not all that closely and did not belong to his circle (which tended to be based on Peterhouse); in thirty years of sharing the same history faculty with him I do not remember ever once seriously talking history with him. And since I come most definitely not to bury him but not altogether to praise him either, this mixture of acquaintance and detachment may serve better than closer ties would have done. Let me say therefore at once that, though I cannot judge his labours to have always been well directed

---

* The first Sir Herbert Butterfield lecture, delivered at Queen's University, Belfast, on 29 April 1983 [reprinted from *HJ*, 27 (1984), 729–43].

or successful, I regard him not only as a man of goodness and charm but also as a fascinating thinker about the labours in which both he and I have spent our lives.

There can be no doubt of Butterfield's influence on the study of history in this country. By his own choice and by that of his readers, he delivered for decades a stream of analysis, instruction, suggestion, judgement and warning. He discharged this life's work in three different ways. He wrote history himself, not indeed a great mass of it (he rarely troubled the editors of learned journals) but quite enough to show his principles at work in practice. Secondly, he produced a plethora of writings on history – on the method and the past growth of the historian's enterprise, on the relationship between history and religion, and on new themes to be opened for historical study. Lastly, he devoted such free time as he had to promoting the study of history in others. I propose to look at these activities in the reverse order.

First, then, Butterfield the cherisher of other people's historical labours and interests. He taught research students across a notable range of subjects, though his dread of becoming the master of a school and his honourable refusal to impose himself even on students who needed firmer direction probably reduced his influence where it might have done most good. He knew what he was doing: 'some of the worst examples of teaching tyranny I have known', he once wrote, 'have occurred . . . at the stage of actual research, where serious situations have occurred because a pupil refused to be enslaved to a teacher'.[1] A very true and suitably ominous remark, but there are stages between slavery and anarchy, and Butterfield seems to me to have let the reins hang a bit too loosely. However, in his teaching and guidance of students at all stages of development he did much for history, especially at Cambridge and more particularly at Peterhouse (he was always a dedicated college man); his aura endures sufficiently for that college still to be generally regarded as an historians' preserve long after it has ceased to be one. He was an indefatigable servant of the Historical Association, especially but by no means only during his three years as its president; few if any men of his eminence, with such endless calls upon their time, could be relied on more regularly to accept invitations to address branch meetings. In calling him a man of eminence I offend against his memory: he would have hotly repudiated any such description, and it was above all his simplicity, his total lack of affection, that made him so impressive and

---

[1] *George III and the Historians* (London, 1957), 15.

influential in all this activity. More specifically, we must on this occasion remember his lion's share in the founding of the Wiles Lectures. It was his voice that captivated Mrs Boyd; it was his proposals for a series of historical lectures that she accepted and turned into the annual reality which has so enriched both the profession and Queen's University. In all these doings this unassertive Methodist lay-preacher (though by 1950 he had ceased to preach) displayed surprising powers of political craft and administrative skill: after all, the author of *Christianity and History* also wrote one of the most perceptive books on Machiavelli. Butterfield in fact enjoyed a refreshing realism about people – the sort of thing that narrower minds called cynicism. Peterhouse flourished during his mastership; I recall him as one of the most efficient chairmen of the history faculty board I have known – the only one who would abruptly terminate the customary and irrelevant ramblings of one of my (on this occasion nameless) colleagues; some officers of my university still remember their astonishment when this supposedly unworldly scholar turned out to be the most businesslike vice-chancellor in memory. And it was Butterfield who contributed one of the main props of the Wiles Lectures, the one provision without which even good discourses might have wafted away on the wind: the provision which withholds the lecturer's fee till the manuscript is delivered to the press. Butterfield, as a good historian should, understood people, and as the best historians do he treated their less attractive foibles with firm but not unkindly remedial measures.

These time-absorbing activities should never be forgotten when we try to assess Butterfield's contribution to the study of history, but of their nature they do not extend beyond the generation of Butterfield's contemporaries, listeners and pupils, and thus leave few manifest reminders behind. What he wrote obviously had the power to extend that influence over times thereafter. And most of what he wrote belongs to what I shall call his prophetic role rather than his work as a practitioner. As his bibliography shows, however hard and frequently he tried to get back to simply writing history he could not escape the demand that he should instruct by reflecting rather than by demonstrating: in particular, when he was invited to lecture he was expected at least to skirt topics of a philosophic or pedagogic import.[2] Not surprisingly, he came rather to repeat himself, though his message – in essence plain

---

[2] See the list in the Festschrift presented to him: *The Diversity of History*, ed. J. H. Elliott and H. G. Koenigsberger (London, 1970), 315–25.

enough – deserved and probably required hammering home. From first to last he wished to establish the right function and the necessary limits of historical study. In particular he fought against two errors: the writing of history in the service of a present-day cause, and the conversion of historical assessments into superior moral judgements. The past asked to be studied for its own sake, and the historian had neither right nor duty to punish past misdeeds by present censure. These convictions formed the content of his first exercise in the genre, *The Whig Interpretation*, and they recur thereafter in variations whenever he thought about the nature of history – though in due course he was to recognise that the possession of a Christian faith rendered adherence to them problematic and to try to come to terms with an internal tension. However, all his remarks on historical method aimed to establish those early tenets. Time and again he pointed to the need to look at the past in its own terms and to grasp the meaning of words and ideas in the context of their own time, to the essentially relativist character of historical interpretation, to the absence of foreknowledge in the historical agent, and to the weight of the unpredictable and contingent.

These wise prescriptions cannot be repeated too often, in Butterfield's time or our own, though in his case their force was somewhat abated by his concentration on a particular area of malfeasance. The false history which he was attacking – Protestant whiggery in the history of politics and religion – belonged, as it happened, to an age already passing away when he started to uncover it. Even by 1930, the presence of what I may call socialist history – Tawney and the Hammonds (to link the admirable and the deplorable) – with its desire to influence the present and to do so by means of history written out of carefully selected materials (J. H. Hexter's 'source-mining') should have caused him more concern than the ghost of Lord Acton or the presence of George Macaulay Trevelyan. The newer siren voices were no less vulnerable to his critical weapon, which yet he seems never to have turned upon them. He may have been subconsciously influenced by his sympathy with the working classes and his notion that whiggery equalled not only biased history but the bias of the country house, but I think there was an additional reason which shows up something about his limitations. Despite his promotion of what he called total history (knitting together all the strands which the specialists develop) Butterfield never really showed much informed interest in economic or social history and, if his published writings are anything to go by, does not seem to have understood them all that well. His one attempt to come to grips with Marxist history, for instance, strikes me as confused and rather superficial: devoid of specific analysis or even citation, it welcomes Marxism for allegedly demolishing a linear progress–oriented history well dead even when the essay was written and in fact seriously maintained only, in altered form, in Marxism itself. Recognising that all was not well with the history written by Marxists, Butterfield preferred to think that the manifest failings of the school reflect individual inadequacy rather than a geological fault in the system itself.

No doubt, as Maurice Cowling says,[3] Butterfield at that time was trying to cope with the crude Marxism boiling up among his students: he was perhaps falling over backwards, never a position which makes for clear or cogent thinking. Still, to quote Cowling again, he could regard Marxist history 'as a valuable ally in the fight against Whiggery and Liberalism', which shows that he mistook what he had before him. The essay does indeed breathe the spirit of the 1930s, when English historians for the first time, belatedly and bemusedly, began to take Marx's followers seriously and found in them the depth of analysis and realistic force which Butterfield accused the conventional historians of his day of lacking. Later, I must point out, after the war, Butterfield grew more apprehensive of Marxism as a threat to free thought and historical truth. Nevertheless, it is surprising that the hammer of the whigs did not more immediately and more successfully diagnose the teleological and deterministic error in Marxism – whiggery's spiritual descendant.[4]

Butterfield's relationship with Acton – alternatively repelled and attracted as he was by him – deserves a brief word. In 1931 there was still some point in attacking Acton's demand for moral judgements in history, though even then Butterfield was giving the *coup de grâce* to an enfeebled and elderly doctrine. Having once looked at Acton, he could not, however, thereafter bestow on him that honourable oblivion which that unproductive monument really deserves, though his one direct engagement – the pamphlet he wrote for the Historical Association's series in 1948 – hints that he had an inkling of the unwisdom of the obsession: it reads like the half-finished torso of a draft for a sizeable book. I incline to think that Butterfield felt unwilling totally to write off the time and labour he had invested in actually working on the mass of often highly enigmatic notes which Acton's failure to write his own great book on liberty had left behind as the chief record of his ideas.

[3] In his obituary notice of Butterfield: *Proceedings of the British Academy*, 65 (1979), 598.
[4] 'Marxist history', in *History and Human Relations* (London, 1951), 66–100 (reprint of an essay first published in 1933).

Butterfield encouraged young students to look at Acton too, and I remember once really shocking the research-studies committee of the Cambridge history faculty by proposing a firm resolution to permit in future no more than three students at any one time to work on his lordship. Butterfield, I suspect, really thought this a deplorable attempt to limit academic freedom. None of those dissertations, I may say, ever came to anything, and neither did Butterfield's endeavour to turn Acton into an important source of inspiration or, alternatively, a terrible warning to historians. All this was Acton's fault, in a way, but I could wish that Butterfield had forgotten about him after 1931: he wasted much time, effort and subtlety in that doomed enterprise to make something of a bogus enigma.

However, apart from his needless involvement with Acton and his insufficient confrontation with the chief challenge in his day to the open and empirical historiography in which he himself believed, Butterfield's advice and guidance were sound and needed. The fact that he repeated himself so regularly over the issues he had raised matters the less because the battle did in fact need to be fought over and over again – nor is it yet won. He was absolutely right in his insistence that historians must recognise and respect the limitations which the nature of history and the characteristics of historical evidence impose on their endeavours. He was right in drawing attention to the importance of the unforeseen and unforeseeable in history, to the right of every age to be studied for its own sake, to the duty not to confuse a right to arrive at conclusions about people and events with a right to deliver judgements based on some universal principle. Though he had indeed arrived at the essence of his professional beliefs by the time he was thirty-one, he did develop and deepen them for a time, and there is benefit to be gained from comparing *The Whig Interpretation* of 1931 with *The Englishman and his History* of 1944.

A common opinion seems to hold that the first was a brilliant and incisive essay, while the second, a piece of wartime spirits-raising, embodied a surrender to the kind of purposes the first had attacked. Butterfield, we are told, in 1944 adopted precisely those whiggish attitudes which in 1931 he had condemned, and he did so because he felt urged to preach a patriotic sermon.[5] It is true that in the second book he pointed to the gain in self-confidence and contented assurance that a whiggish conviction about the growth of liberty in one country had

[5] Maurice Cowling, *Religion and Public Debate in Modern England* (Cambridge, 1980), 227.

offered to Englishmen, and it is true that facing Hitler he found the effect propitious. But it is not true that he had come to approve whiggery as a right way to read history. In analysing the (historically true) advantages gained from those enduring attitudes he did, I think, a proper historian's job on them without turning whig himself. Maurice Cowling points to the little book of 1944 as the first sign of a transformation in Butterfield. Until then, he maintains, Butterfield had been purely the professional historian, conscious of the limitations of his craft; henceforth he was to become more and more the prophet who wished both to find in history an aid to present action (especially in the field of international relations) and to achieve the amalgamation of, as the title of the later book says, *Christianity and History* (1949). I agree that from the 1950s onwards Butterfield increasingly wrestled with the problems of a beleaguered Christianity in an historically adverse world, but I cannot agree that he ever departed from his honest conviction that history does not prove the truth of universals or support the cause of any ideology or even religion. I do not propose to say much about Butterfield the Christian – though I shall have to come back to him – because, so far as I can see, Butterfield always, even when he came to look at forms of history arising from the sort of religious beliefs that he himself shared, remembered the difference between historical study and the demands of the faith. I should not be surprised to hear that sometimes he wished he could more completely assist his faith with his history, but in the book he devoted to the effort he showed himself effectively unable to do so because he refused to deny the truths about history that he knew so well.

What impresses me about *The Englishman and his History* is the gain in solidity. *The Whig Interpretation* proves on rereading to be really perilously thin – truly an essay, lacking in substance, and in particular lacking in history. The range of examples used is surprisingly narrow, even for a man of thirty-one; one gets very tired of Martin Luther popping up on page after page, with nothing said about him that indicates serious study. In 1944, instead, there is evidence of research, patchy no doubt and full of starting points rather than achievement, but by comparison a demonstration of genuine labours on the materials of history. I would particularly draw attention to one new insight which seems to me to show up the chief weakness in *The Whig Interpretation*. A good many critics had already pointed out that there was little cause for saddling one historical party with the false view of history attacked in the essay. As Bernard Manning remarked at the time, whigs and Protestants (both of which he proudly claimed to be) were not the only purveyors of history twisted to their own purpose.[6] In fact, though we still use the language that Butterfield taught us, we have long since divorced the term 'whig' from its party-political associations. By a neat trick of fate, the malfeasance which Butterfield identified too narrowly with one ideology has been widened until the soubriquet attached to that ideology has turned into a term descriptive of the historical malpractice in general. As a matter of fact, Butterfield was mistaken in 1931 when he picked on the whigs, and by 1944 he seems to have known better. Typically enough, like most of us at some time or other, he had profitably gone to school with F. W. Maitland.[7] There he had learned that what he had called whig history was really lawyers' history, justifiably practised by them when thinking about the law in which the latest meaning of an event is the only meaning to matter, and in which new opinion abolishes its predecessor – neither of which is true in historians' history. To a lawyer the doings of the past signify only inasmuch as they persist into and have life in the present. All very fine for them, but this teleological preoccupation, which ruins genuine history, they had imposed on the historians. What Butterfield had been attacking, though it took him some time to find it out, was the readiness with which from the seventeenth century onward historians had accepted the lawyers' interpretation of the history of law, government and constitution. The battle to break those shackles (assuredly reinforced by the satisfaction which the notion of successful progress brings) has been long, and the current disputes over the history of the civil war and its antecedents still represent a terribly belated effort to free that bit of history from the same old thraldom. But at least Butterfield nearly forty years ago put his finger on the cause of it all.

There are some serious doubts that I shall later have to express about the range and depth of Butterfield's advice to historians and their readers, but for the moment let us be clear that, often in the face of well-entrenched perversions and thesis-ridden convictions, he rightly, firmly and consistently asserted the way in which the historian distinguishes himself from the propagandist. It is therefore a trifle ironic – though it is really only an effect of first sight – that in the second of his prophetic activities he turned propagandist himself. He did so in two sets of lectures, turned into books, which may well now be his best-known writings – *The Origins of Modern Science* (1949), and *Man on his Past* (1955: his Wiles Lectures). Here Butterfield endeavoured, with consider-

---

[6] Cited by John Derry in *The Historian at Work*, ed. J. Cannon (London, 1980), 176–7.
[7] *The Englishman and his History*, 35.

able success, to guide the study of history into new channels, or perhaps it would be better to say, to open new themes for treatment by the tried and true methods of historical scholarship. I speak of considerable success in one particular sense: he succeeded in stimulating others to follow the signposts he had set up. The history of science has become an active and respected enterprise especially in England and America, even though it has developed in what seems to me an unnatural and unfruitful marriage with the philosophy of science. There is no sign that Butterfield would have thought the connection desirable, a connection which may yet threaten the future of the history of science as the philosophers affect its preoccupations and, worse, its vocabulary. (The reason for this mis-alliance is not clear, but I think the muddle arose – whatever may afterwards have been invented to justify it – from grounds common-place in academic politics. Departments of history proving insufficiently welcoming to what is in fact only a branch of the history of ideas and sometimes of economic history, and practitioners of the specialty being too few to stand by themselves, they joined up with similar outcasts who had found philosophers and scientists equally uninterested in them. A case of little acorns and so forth, but the offspring is no solid oak. I am glad to hear that both partners increasingly apply for *divortium a mensa et toro*.) The history of history, another branch of the history of ideas, has at least remained with the historians, many of whom have joyously opened their arms to it – admittedly too often only because it can serve as a substitute for teaching an understanding of history to undergraduates anxious to get away from the dates of the Seven Years War and the details of Lloyd George's people's budget. Butterfield, who with reason regarded the subject as unsuitable for the beginning researcher, rather welcomed its intrusion into the undergraduate syllabus,[8] though whether he would still do so some twenty years later if he were to encounter the not uncommon students to whom historical problems resolve themselves exclusively into debates between historians I do not know.

In any case, abuses of things good in themselves are inevitable and should not be blamed on the promoters of what is good in them; and the history of science and historiography is essentially a very good thing. However one defines either complex of ideas, they both quite clearly underlie the modern view of the world, a view conditioned by science and history far more than by philosophy or theology. Since natural

[8] *The Present State of Historical Scholarship* (inaugural lecture, Cambridge, 1965), 6–7.

science and historical relativism are the two pillars of twentieth-century thinking, we might as well inform ourselves properly about the history of science and the science of history in order to understand what part they may have played in past views of the world. However, in this very fact lurks a manifest danger – the danger that past science and past historical thinking will be studied with an eye to what has since become of them both. That is to say, they are in danger of falling victim to the whig interpretation of history. And it has to be said that the man who identified that danger in the history of politics promptly succumbed to it when he entered these new paths. The consequences were more manifest in the history of science, where even the title of the book betrays the baffling truth. Like a good lawyer-historian, like a faithful disciple of Sir Edward Coke, Butterfield devoted himself to discovering the *origins* of modern science instead of seeking to understand the place of an age's science in that age's totality – in its social, intellectual and even political make-up. Perhaps it is even more surprising that he knew beforehand where those origins lay – in the so-called scientific revolution of the seventeenth century – and thus came to describe essentially only those elements in seventeenth-century science that could be defined as leading to modern views of the physical world. In his three references to Giordano Bruno he turns him into some sort of moderniser, and Paracelsus does not appear at all; hermeticism and Newton's alchemy remain equally unmentioned. The fact that Butterfield wrote before the comet-rise of Frances Yates to some extent explains these shortcomings, but it does not excuse his failure to realise that he was writing beautifully clear whig history.

The case is unquestionably less serious in *Man on his Past*, though even here past labours on history are too manifestly measured against the yard-stick provided by what is seen as the great age of true historiography, the nineteenth century. (Butterfield rightly admired Ranke, and it is sad to see him censured for this by some who would perhaps prefer him to have worshipped dubious gods at the shrine of the *Annales*.) On the other hand, whereas after one effort he left the history of science to others, his excursions into historiography occurred frequently through-out his life, and it would be wrong to confine an assessment of his understanding of the theme to the one book. A concerned interest in the historiographical aspect of historical problems is perhaps the most obvious hallmark of all his writing – the footprint from which you can always infer the lion's presence. Indeed, at the end of his life he was once more engaged on a book dealing with the history of history, and while once more its title (which, I understand, is the editor's and not the author's) speaks of origins, the term here does not carry the whiggish meaning that it had in the lectures on science. In this posthumously published work Butterfield was looking into origins in their own right – into the first efforts to write history that we can find – and not into the prehistory of later achievements measured by anachronistic standards.[9] He was there not writing about the origins of *modern* history, whereas he had expressly been writing about the origins of *modern* science.

In any case, whatever may be alleged against the achievements of the pioneer, what matters is his pioneering: he did put on his boots and venture into those barely trodden regions. By stirring up a professional interest in the history of two of man's most fascinating intellectual occupations Butterfield did great service to the study of history and became the progenitor of very important developments. Even those more recent practitioners who have done much to render especially the science book rapidly obsolete have commonly acknowledged his courage and enterprise in showing the way. They have rightly joined the ranks of those who have seen Butterfield possessed of something he would have been horrified to think vested in himself – the charisma of leadership.

Butterfield led by exhortation and by opening new doors: did he also lead by example? His output of what may be called straightforward history was not, in fact, very large: two early and slender books on the peace tactics of Napoleon (1929) and on Machiavelli (1940) – both interesting and impressive but in sum too brief to form the foundation of a major reputation; and two substantial books dealing with the reign of George III. Of these last, one – *George III and the Historians* (1957) – put his preoccupation with historiography to good use; the other – *George III, Lord North and the People 1779–80* (1949) – constituted the one truly sizeable work in which he displayed in practice the prescriptions touching research which he had pronounced several times. A few notes and articles discussing particular problems of diplomatic history (especially his Creighton lecture of 1962 on *Charles James Fox and Napoleon: The Peace Negotiations of 1806*) complete the tally. It has to be admitted that for a man of his standing the yield was not large, though all the writings in question achieve high standards of technical competence, learned precision and sensible analysis. They are good history, but not outstandingly good. The book on a two-year crisis in the reign of George

---

[9] *The Origins of History*, ed. Adam Watson (London, 1981).

III showed that Butterfield knew a range of sources very well and possessed the far from common skill to marshal a mass of detail in an interesting fashion; it showed that he could indeed write the sort of technical history which he advocated in his prophetic guise, and it broke through current conventions by restoring to the politics of that age those elements of political motivation which Namier's attack on the old whig legends had removed twenty years before. More particularly, Butterfield once again pioneered by drawing attention to the growth of radical politics outside Westminster, a growth which at the time he wrote had in effect been forgotten; that concern with those nationwide manifestations is now commonplace only underscores his insight.

The effect and effectiveness of Butterfield's direct clash with the school of Namier, in the book on the historians who had previously written about George III's reign, is harder to assess, the more so because his opponents reacted with pointless obloquy rather than argument, and because other scholars familiar with the period preferred not to get involved. However, there is no question that Butterfield successfully demonstrated how variously the reign had been interpreted long before Namier and his followers swept aside most earlier writers in order to assail a particular line; they should have accepted the fact that much of what in their own interpretation was made to appear novel and revolutionary followed guidelines plainly laid down earlier. Here Butterfield's ability to render the history of history fruitful showed to the best advantage, and the first part of the book sweeps the reader along on a brilliantly executed rehearsal of pointed analysis. However, the second part, in which Butterfield directly confronted Namier, was less successful even as plain controversy because he did not succeed in clarifying and resolving any of the substantive issues touching the nature of politics in the eighteenth century that lay between him and Namier. *George III and the Historians* thus highlights both the potential and the limitations of the historiographical approach. The method illumines current debate by placing it in an evolving context, but it does little for the actual study of history, which must be tackled from the problems and the sources, not through the writings of predecessors.

For most historians of the last two generations one would regard this record of production and achievement as entirely respectable, but it has to be admitted that in the case of Butterfield, a man possessed of so much imaginative power and concern for the recreation of the past, even the friendly critic feels a certain sense of disappointment. Something, it seems, stood in the way of his very genuine intention to depart from prophecy and turn his mind to events, facts, people – to the study of the past for its own sake. No doubt some of the obstacles were not of his own making. Having almost inadvertently acquired the prophetic mantle he was for ever in demand as a prophet; and his deep concern for the troubles of his own day drove him increasingly into a distracting search for the use of history and the historian's mind in the solution of current problems. But even when age and retirement produced a slackening of such pressures, the barriers remained. As is well known, he had been thinking for a long time about writing a book on Charles James Fox – an excellent theme and a much needed book. Yet when he died he left behind him nothing on Fox of any substance; instead there was an uncompleted but publishable book once more on the history of history which revealed that in his last years his interests concentrated on the manner in which men first came to write history at all. And while his passionate discussion of 'The originality of the Hebrew Scriptures' and 'The establishment of a Christian historiography' demonstrated how powerful and stimulating his prophetic insight remained to the end, this posthumous book also confirmed that Butterfield still could not see his way to producing substantial work on the past as it was, rather than as it was thought about and manipulated by others. Creative critic that he was on the outer limits of history, he lacked the power to create at the heart of the story.

Why? Why did he not complete his study of Fox? The reason most certainly did not lie in declining powers, as any regular visitor to the University Library, easily outmatched by Butterfield in regularity, will testify. Nor can I accept the quirky answer offered by Denis Brogan who professed to think that so upright a man could not bring himself to grapple with rakes and rascals.[10] Butterfield in fact rather liked to make an historian's acquaintance with less than worthy persons: his sense of fun and of the cosmic irony responded well to people who showed up stuffy narrow-mindedness. He did not shy away from John Wilkes, his Napoleon is no moral hero, and Charles James Fox was really rather made for him. Nor did he find it at all impossible, as some do, to cut the string when the time comes – to call an end to research (which, we know, is never really complete) and let the result take its chance in print. The question, as I have raised it, may not be answerable, especially by someone who did not possess any access to Butterfield's inmost being, but I should like to put before you two reasons which seem to lie at the

---

[10] See *The Diversity of History*, 13.

heart of his failure to become the major historian – as distinct from Clio's prophet – which repute and expectation should have made him. One of these is highly technical: deficiencies in Butterfield's understanding of historical evidence and its treatment, just the area in which he is reckoned to have been learned and illuminating. The other is the conflict within him between the historian and the Christian.

I have already said several times that Butterfield's advice to students is sound at heart: he correctly grasped the problems of authenticating historical facts, the need to eliminate the effect of the historian's inescapable personal intervention, and the demands of each part of the past to be studied on its own terms and for its own sake. That a sound recognition of basic principles is not, however, quite enough is well demonstrated in his most explicit engagement with these questions – in the opening chapter of *George III and the Historians* entitled 'The historian and his evidence'. Rereading it now I am struck by what I am forced to call its insufficiency. The long discourse on the shortcomings of memoirs and autobiographies could have been compressed into half a page: by the 1950s no half-trained scholar needed reminding that people do not tell the simple truth in their apologias, and no one, surely, any longer wrote the sort of history that treated memoirs as works of impartiality. (It may not, however, be irrelevant that when Butterfield worked on Napoleon in the 1920s such fundamental errors had still been current.) Butterfield devoted two pages to demonstrating, by means of Magna Carta, that words change their meaning and documents must be interpreted within the age that produced them: very true, but the discussion itself carries an air of remoteness from the very document employed to make the point. Did Butterfield ever really study Magna Carta? The question matters because the Charter runs like a thinnish thread through much of his writing, turning up again and again as some sort of exemplar; its historiographical fate (once again!) forms the theme of his not very satisfactory Stenton Lecture at Reading.[11] Altogether, reading Butterfield's work in bulk brings home the disconcerting fact that his range of historical examples, used to point the moral of his teaching, was really quite narrow: the same bits of history do duty over and over again. In a man whose actual range of interests and knowledge was so wide this is surprising: but it points to a fundamental gap in this historian's equipment. Despite his wide reading and his roaming over the centuries, despite his high respect for what he himself called technical

[11] *Magna Carta in the Historiography of the Sixteenth and Seventeenth Centuries* (Reading, 1969).

history, he had a limited acquaintance with the diversity of historical materials.

Of course, Butterfield pursued research in archives and read his sources, in manuscript and in print. But as his discussion of the historian and his evidence shows, and as the footnotes of the book on 1779–80 amply confirm, his sources (apart from commentaries upon the event in memoirs, pamphlets and occasionally newspapers) were all of one kind. They were letters. It is about letters that he tells the young student, distinguishing between official and what he calls policy-making documents (those not intended for public consumption). That distinction has little weight: all the material that he analyses is of one kind: writings intended, either directly or indirectly, to create information for and influence action by recipients. Of course, such materials constitute an important sector of the historical evidence, but they are very far from exhausting it; and about all the rest Butterfield is silent. He began life as a diplomatic historian in the school of Temperley, a powerful and sometimes overbearing teacher, and an influential though, as we now know, often very unreliable historian. Butterfield rightly fought for his freedom from Temperley's dictatorship, but he remained a diplomatic historian. He continued to believe that diplomatic history offered the best training ground available to the research student in modern history;[12] and since diplomatic history provides precise and manageable topics, readily separated from the confusing complexity of the day's events as a whole, he was entirely right about this. But that is for the beginner. Butterfield, with his call for total history, knew the dangers of unreality that hang about that kind of history; he endeavoured to free himself from them by extending the range of his interests, which grew very wide without becoming total and especially increasingly embraced intellectual history. However, it would appear that his understanding of sources did not keep pace with his interest in problems; he apparently did not realise that the second would not be successful unless he could also enlarge his acquaintance with historical evidence beyond what diplomatic history had told him were the characteristic sources. Even when he noted the important point that some evidence has been produced with no thought that it might become useful to an historian – the fundamental distinction between his evidential range (letters and memoirs) and the rest – he still has confidential letters and private memorials in mind for which this characteristic is in fact doubtful. He

[12] See Derry in *The Historian at Work*, 180.

never considers the enormous range of historical materials produced by the daily processes involved in managing men's earthly existence. So far as his own discussions show, he never looked at financial records, whether of states or individuals, at the records of counting house or estate management, at the massive records of litigation of all sorts: what people told one another in correspondence formed for him (and he was certainly not alone in this) the true foundation of historical reconstruction. Like Namier – in whose case the omission was markedly less excusable – he did not even use the Journal of the House of Commons, where much of the history he found himself writing actually happened.

This failure to recognise the true variety of historical source materials was his chief weakness as an historian. No one can read everything, but everyone should be consciously aware of all that exists waiting to be read. Whenever Butterfield turned to the technical tasks of the professional historian, a theme on which he spoke with firmness and sense, he talked only about letters and dispatches and gave no indication that he knew anything else to exist. History written on that basis cannot help but remain restricted and limited, and no major work of reconsideration, innovation or wider-ranging authority can be thus written except perhaps within the realm of that diplomatic history which Butterfield so rightly regarded as insufficient for a life's work. I do not think he ever realised how firmly his early training had put its stamp on him: the influence of Temperley, the memory of Ranke (seen only as the man who read ambassadors' dispatches), and the encounter with Acton (affected by the same limitations).

The problem posed for Butterfield the historian by his profound and unchanging commitment to the Christian religion are more delicate, and I do not know that one who did not know Butterfield at that level ought to discuss them. On the other hand, they are central to an understanding of this historian, and he in effect permitted their discussion when he wrote at length about them. Is it not strange that a man who throughout his life adhered to his faith, a faith which (as he very well understood) had always been involved in the earthly existence of mankind, should never have devoted his historian's labours to the history of church and religion? There are indications in *The Whig Interpretation* that in his younger days he felt the need to come to terms with the historical facts of the Christian experience. As I have already noted, he had Luther very much on his mind at that time, and he spoke of him in terms which suggest that he might have been attracted to the history of the Reformation. And in his honesty he at once tried to face the fundamental problem: he tried to identify the manner in which an historian committed to a faith might be able to write proper history about such an event. 'His role', he said, 'is to describe; he stands impartial between Christian and Mohammedan; he is interested in neither one religion nor the other except as they are entangled in human lives'.[13] Well said and true – but is it possible for a believer?

The difficulties do not lie in the danger of partisanship; that can quite readily be dealt with by a genuine historian and especially by so unsentimental a Christian as Butterfield was. Rather they lie in the much more fundamental problem of reconciling history as the human experience which to Butterfield it was – unplanned, unforeseeable and contingent, with no outcome capable of being foretold from the record of the past – with faith in an omnipotent and omniscient creator. In that very influential book (influential especially in Christian circles), *Christianity and History*, Butterfield made a determined effort to resolve the dilemma and indeed thought he had done so, though to my mind he gives along the way rather too many hostages to the notion that the Christian historian discerns and witnesses the hand of God in history. The last sentence of that book is quite often quoted, apparently to indicate that he had indeed arrived at a solution: 'Hold to Christ, and for the rest be totally uncommitted'.

'Hold to Christ, and for the rest be totally uncommitted': nobly said and a ponderable maxim to live by. But to live by as an historian, especially as the kind of historian Butterfield so rightly believed to be the only true historian? If as an historian you hold to Christ, what lack of commitment remains for you? If you hold to Christ, the son of God sent to earth to save mankind, are you not totally committed to a history which presupposes that God is at work in all human experience? And how can that commitment leave you uncommitted as an historian? Can you then really avoid that interpretation of history, however disguised, that sees it as the working out of the creator's plan, foreordained perhaps or at least foreknown, and certainly directed to an ultimate purpose: the form of historical interpretation which Butterfield's definition of history so firmly declares to be wrong and unacceptable? It was the kind of history which, as Butterfield himself shows in *The Origins of History*, included the future within the province of the historian whose task it is to illumine the will of God. That Christian history, whose high point may be found in the schematising of Joachim da Fiore or in the confident

Puritan belief that the Old Testament offered a blueprint for all past and future happenings, dominated Western historiography for a millennium, but it was not, of course, Herbert Butterfield's history. What was he to do? At the very least, if he was to stay uncommitted in his historian's labours while holding to Christ, he could not, it seems to me, engage himself in those phases and issues in history which unavoidably raise the dilemma, as the Reformation certainly does. He would of necessity find himself driven back to those tighter, lesser, more restricted topics towards which his early experience as a research scholar was also driving him. I must confess that even for the history of George III, Lord North and the people I find Butterfield's maxim very difficult, perhaps even strictly impossible. Why did those events not also form part of the divine plan? And if they were that, can they be historically evaluated – that is, treated in their own right, without teleological considerations? However, I readily admit that good historians, devout in their faith but less given to honest self-examination than Butterfield, have managed in their time to cope with the dilemma; and I can see that by concentrating on a very specific topic, preferably one in which questions of the Christian religion are not directly raised, one may be able to subdue the dilemma even though it is not really exorcised.

Butterfield was a great enough man, and a good enough historian, to deserve an appraisal that is weighed seriously and not coloured by adulation. And to me the verdict must be that as a practising professional historian, of the kind that he himself valued above the other roles he found himself playing, he failed to produce absolutely great work because professionally he never progressed to a full understanding of the nature, range and problems of historical evidence, and because his faith remained at war with his deeply held convictions concerning the practice of history. Such a verdict, however, must raise to an even greater height his real contributions to the study of history. These consisted, on the one hand, in his fight against cant, his proclamation of honest labour, and his repeated opening up of new territories and themes to be explored. On the other hand – and here lay his outstanding service – they consisted in his daily labour to bring the reality of history and the historical understanding to others. In the last analysis, Butterfield's monument will not be found in his books either of history or of prophecy, striking and valuable though the latter in particular are in so many respects, but in the memory of men and women who came under that demanding but cheerful and benign influence. Men and women pass away. It is therefore both pleasing and reassuring that the memory of

Herbert Butterfield and of his service to the study of history will remain alive in the more permanent form that at one point he was enabled to give to his personal influence. The memory will remain alive in the Wiles Lectures of the Queen's University of Belfast.

64

HISTORIANS AGAINST HISTORY*

Not to beat about the bush: I am talking about the current influence of that dominant group of French historians called the *Annales* school and especially about its Latter Day Saint, Emanuel Le Roy Ladurie. However, this is not another tedious attack on the use of the social sciences by historians. Quite enough evidence and arguments have by now accumulated around the virtues and limitations of quantification, model-building, anthropological analogies and all the rest: *Requiescant, sed non in pace.* I willingly add my mite to the lip service paid to those early *Annalistes* who persuaded so many scholars to forsake their storytelling and dive into the analysis of tax registers, shipping registers, parish registers and so forth. It would seem to be true that by the 1920s French historical writing had got stuck in a stultifying preoccupation with political, military and diplomatic history, all of it treated with relentless rigour and impressive absence of imagination; and though a historiographical tradition which from William Camden to William Hoskins had shown much concern with questions of economic and social import did not really need to cross the Channel for inspiration, English historians have unquestionably drawn some benefit from their love for all things French. Nor has that recourse stopped. At present a good many are showing a disquieting inclination to throw themselves into the deep morass of the *Annalistes'* latest fashion, the history of *mentalité*, and no more than the French do they look likely to escape the death by a thousand words of meaningless verbiage which that morass promises. Still, we should all of us like to know about 'climates of opinion' and such-like things, and perhaps our people can yet show their mentors how a humble scepticism and a reluctance to use grandiose flourishes in place of reason may succeed in finding the way from tussock to tussock.[1]

---

* [The *Cambridge Review*, 18 Nov. 1983.]

[1] For an excellently balanced evaluation of the *Annales* school – its past victories and present defects – see an essay by one who had his training there: René Pillorget, 'From a classical to a quantiative study of history: some new directions in French historical research', *Durham University Journal*, new series 38 (1976–7), 207–16.

Have we, however, really ceased to be threatened by the dangers which lurk within the *Annales* school's attitudes and methods? They did far more than simply draw attention to new questions or suggest new methods of research; at the heart of their thought lies an influential scheme of historical phenomena which is disquietingly rigid and hierarchical. They despise *événements*, love *structures*, and exalt *conjonctures*. The terms are flexible, to varying degrees. Events do occur, even in *annaliste* history where they are liable to be honoured by selectivity; the original objection lay against the kind of narrowly empiricist history which parades happenings and occurrences in isolation, content to record the event without trying to understand it in context or relate it to background, implication or wider significance. So far, most historians would agree: no halfway respectable practitioner will give the prize to the purely anecdotal or antiquarian treatment of the past. A lot, however, depends on where the line is drawn. Those whose shrine lies within the Seizième Section would now seem to frown upon any telling of the story and to accept only the most static of analyses as worthy of the true scholar. Taken to its logical conclusion, their attitude produces what Ladurie has called 'history that stands still', the title of the inaugural lecture he delivered at the Collège de France in 1973.[2] History that stands still? History that ceases to move ceases to be history.

The occasion for this peculiar notion lies in the devotion to structure. Now it must be said that studying structures – systems, organisations, settings, the shape of both events and thoughts – is no *annaliste* preserve: we all do it. The historian even of war and diplomacy cannot explain battles and negotiations without a (preferably instructed) understanding of the scheme of things within which these events take place. He wants to know about the 'structure' which produced those armies and their meeting, those ambassadors and their manner of proceeding; he wants, for instance, to know about the economic realities which determined a choice between waging war and treating for peace. There is nothing mysterious about structure which seems simply to signify understanding the context so as to explain the particular. Or rather, there was nothing mysterious about it until it was made the end rather than the means of historical understanding. Again, Ladurie provides an excellent example of this aberration. In an essay on the court factions of Louis XIV, he offers an intricate picture of interrelationships between individuals and groupings in one given year – actually a year very near to the end of the

---

[2] E. Le Roy Ladurie, *The Mind and Method of the Historian* (London, 1981), 1 ff.

'structure' analysed.[3] The essay teems with the hallmarks of the refined *annaliste* method: much pointillist detail (static, not moving), simple as well as exceedingly complex graphical representations of the links between the entities studied, and that predilection for metaphorical forms of description (in this case clockworks and the game of billiards are brought in) which constitutes Ladurie's playful but habitual evasion of the duty to explain. A structure is assuredly laid before us, whether or not one finds those explanatory techniques convincing. However, nothing happens. The structure stands there, full of detail frozen at one point in time. There is no movement: the clock has stopped, the billiard-ball rests in the pocket. So what is the point of it all? We are told that it would be interesting to discover how the constituent parts of the structure had come into existence, and so it would because it would set the particles in motion: but the interest is not pursued. The question of why the structure should be studied at all – a question which can be answered only by introducing motion – is not even asked. Structure, itself a concept which the mind has imposed upon reality, turns out to be a dead or at best a sleeping thing: and so is history that stands still.

Worst of all, there is *conjoncture*, a term, we are often told, that defies translation. Actually, so far as I can judge, its basic meaning in French is the same as in English – the concurrence of various events, developments, circumstances, even people, that produces a particular situation of high promise or dire danger: the point (to adopt the metaphorical methods of the adversary) where streams meet to produce either a great and useful river or a vast and destructive flood. The only difficulty in translating *conjoncture* arises from the fact that the word is so rarely used in English while it can be given a special and idiosyncratic meaning in French. (As it can in German. *Konjunktur*, meaning a pregnant moment, acquired this meaning by way of the stock exchange where it signified a point of upswing.) And the meaning which the *Annales* school has assigned to it is mystical: it would seem to signify the global theme, the structure of structures. It is the ordered, predictable and predicting dance of those elephantine entities into which the past has been resolved; or, since structures stand still, it might be better to speak of the great jigsaw puzzle into which they have been fitted until a picture – a sacred picture viewed with rapture – emerges. If I find it difficult to be more precise, this is because I cannot discover any very precise meaning for the thing. *Conjoncture* is the myth of the historian, the dream (or nightmare) which

---

[3] 'Versailles observed: the court of Louis XIV in 1709', ibid., 149 ff.

opens to his vision as he contemplates the past and moves from lesser abstractions to the ultimate. As the mystic seeks oneness with God, so the *annaliste* historian seeks *conjoncture* with Clio.

I suppose Arnold Toynbee's gyrating civilisations belong to this category of description, as the Marxist class struggle certainly seems to do; and so does Braudel's subordination of two centuries of history to a clash of empires which resembles nothing so much as the famous battle of the monsters in Conan Doyle's *Lost Continent*. It all, I make no doubt, sounds better in French; but there is no room here also to consider the rhetoric with which the school has imposed the rule of its empty concepts upon so many historians.

The ultimate outcome of these classifications and hierarchies has been the opposite to what its propagandists have claimed for the school and its methods. They started by denouncing the superficiality and thinness of the history they inherited, deficiencies they wished to remedy by studying the underlying movements and structures on the top of which the conventional themes of history played their allegedly meaningless games. They called for the analysis of economic facts and behaviour, of social structure and its influence upon action, ultimately also for the investigation of that common world of ideas and often unconscious convictions within which the historical processes moved and from which they draw their characteristics. Tools were legitimately borrowed from students concerned with matters economic, social or anthropological, though it should be said that the tribal god of the 1980s, quantification, reached France and the *Annales* only after preoccupations had solidified. From these ambitions and their apparent fulfilment descended most of the currently popular endeavours: demographic history, history from below, history of minorities, history of women. All share the *annaliste* reaction against a history predominantly centred upon males, and European males at that, and males, moreover, belonging to a thin top layer of society; and sharing the reaction, they have all gladly partaken from the store of grace laid up by the saints and distributed by *annaliste* indulgences. The reaction, let it be said, in its day was healthy and desirable. Certainly the founders of the school demonstrated possibilities of historical enquiry and understanding that had been thought unattainable. Having one's doubts about the long-term effects of this school does not exemplify a desire to return to Ranke; nor will even a marriage of Ranke and Burckhardt (or Buckle?) satisfy our needs any more.

Then, however, things began to go wrong. Worshipped as gods, the

Annalistes succumbed to the sins of covetousness and pride to which gods are prone. The worshippers copied their idols' less pleasing characteristics of arrogance and exclusiveness. It is sad to see cliometricians who will not allow any other kind of historian to put up his shingle; to see historians of women who are only concerned to do down men; to see 'ethnic' historians who seek to redress past neglect by current wild invention: and all such things are justified by the claim that a greater cause entitles the historian to do as he pleases so long as he avoids events and plumps for structures. The *Annalistes* taught this lesson when they first elevated one form of history to absolute power and exiled all other forms, first in their writings and ultimately in their academic politics. They set themselves to capture the citadels – professorial chairs – and to execute non-believers, and other historians so encouraged have been trying to do the same. (The hierarchical structures – how useful the analytical tool can be! – of the French and American universities helped to produce this disaster.) And in those poisoned centres of historical research, evidence retreats before theory: theory rules, for theory, however unlikely or unilluminating, is *conjoncture*. Instead of widening and deepening the study of history, the school came needlessly to delimit it with bigoted narrowmindedness, when they damned the event, kissed the feet of structure, and crowned with laurel the cloudy brow of *conjoncture*.

We are approaching a point when only historians of peasants and criminals will be accorded respectability – a true triumph for *annaliste* principles because while peasants and criminals have lives they have almost no history that moves. I think myself that this decay of the good *Annales* work can already be discerned in Fernand Braudel's study of the Mediterranean world, especially in the rather pompous elaboration of the obvious in geography, in the notable selectivity applied to the available facts of the past, and in the artificial building up of a universal concept into which all things are forced. However, Braudel also can still prove his descent from Marc Bloch and perhaps Lucien Febvre. The effects of a self-satisfied vision crossed with power and uncontrolled by scepticism or resistance are now beginning to show in that charming, witty and to all appearance lighthearted scholar, Le Roy Ladurie. Leaving aside *Montaillou* (no one should be judged on a book that brings in money, even when it ignores the first principles concerning the criticism of sources), the signs of the disease keep breaking out all over his short essays. That metaphor has a special aptness because Ladurie seems to have persuaded himself that global history is the history of epidemics.

It would be painful to analyse the absurdity of his breezy treatment of that theme; let it suffice to note that where once fear of cholera and plague allegedly created one world the same end is now achieved by worry about carbon monoxide, lead in exhaust fumes, and pesticides.[4] Of course, Ladurie can still produce good and stimulating remarks, flashes of insight. But predominance has undermined the determination to understand as well as the humility which seeks a way by means of the evidence. Where others try for argument, simile and metaphor are allowed to take over. Western expansion 'had come to seem like an exploding galaxy':[5] really? to whom had this vision come? An historical crisis is best understood by being compared to the San Francisco earthquake of 1906.[6] Indeed, in this kind of history crises crop up all the time (sometimes lasting quite comfortably for a couple of centuries) and are then explained by a metaphor involving the 'critical mass' of the nuclear physicist. Perhaps it should be noted that all those great big *conjonctures* attract a treatment that it would be generous to call superficial.

In 1972, Ladurie expressed regret that the triumph of a historiography devoted to 'the quantifiable, the statistical and the structural' had virtually 'condemned to death the narrative history of events and the individual biography'.[7] Outside France, at least, his obituary was premature, but on the other hand those regrets do not sound terribly sincere. A few pages further on we find him hoping for a history from which all events and chance happenings have been exorcised (as he puts it); indeed, we find him claiming that the apparently unpredictable would always, once it had become visible, fit entirely and predictably into the pattern previously, and predictingly, discerned.[8] This is to give the game away. The devotee of *structure* and *conjoncture* must not only despise the event but is at need entitled to adjust its particularity. The exorcism will produce a history that is 'entirely logical, intelligible and predictable', an end to be fought for by no more than hard work. What an ambition! The event to be exorcised is humanity.

The structural historians – and that includes the historian of mentality – must come to understand their true function. No one wishes to kill them off or would dream of denying their impressive achievements.

4 Ibid., 28.   5 Ibid., 273.   6 Ibid., 288.
7 E. Le Roy Ladurie, *The Territory of the Historian* (London, 1979), 111.
8 Ibid., 113–14. I hope I have got this right: the passage rather bewilderingly plays around with biological metaphors.

Their place is secure, so long as they know their place. Those achievements do not equal the writing of all history, and in a way they do not equal the writing of history at all. Historians of structures act as clearers of the ground, illuminators of the scene, indicators of the conditions within which the historical past operates, delimitators of the possible and sometimes of the probable. They do not in that role tell us what happened and why: they cannot tell us history, though they may create much better pointers to where the what and the why may be found. The event without structure may well be no more than thin and dull history, but it is history of a sort; structure without the event is not history at all. As for *conjoncture*, let us amend it to conjecture and leave it to the prophets.

65

WOMEN'S HISTORY*

The turmoil in the universities in the later 1960s produced, among other things, an addiction to so-called minority history – history seen through the eyes of minority groups and rewritten to suit their supposed needs and interests. Of the specialities then introduced only women's history has survived as a serious academic preoccupation. Neither gays' nor blacks' history, for instance, ever settled into a regular part of the curriculum, whereas women's history has become an accepted feature in many American institutions and in publishers' lists. Nor is this surprising. Women, after all, are the only human minority that forms a majority of the population, and – however fiercely feminists may deny this – they started from a position of power not available to other groups. The men whose supposed distortion of history they attacked could hardly avoid frequent contact with them. Moreover, men (especially American men) had for long regarded women as a sex with a mixture of respect and apprehension which reflected their understanding of female power and induced them to accept the often unrestrained criticism hurled at them. The common reaction of the liberal mind is to feel guilty when accused, and most historians, especially in the United States, are of a liberal mind. Women's history also benefited from the contemporaneous and powerful swing towards social history, as it is called – the somewhat static study of social groupings in the past and their relationships to one another. Thus women's history had little difficulty in achieving academic recognition.

The combination of passionate assault and conscience-stricken response produced, predictably, a state of affairs in which women's history has received little serious criticism. No one will doubt that the history of women merits as much attention as the history of any collection of human beings, but it has to be said that its claims to scholarly validity have in the main been taken for granted too readily. The issue is not whether women's history should be written, but whether what is being written is good. The publication of Joan Kelly's essays offers an

* [Review of *Women, History and Theory: the Essays of Joan Kelly* (Chicago, 1984), in *The American Scholar*, Autumn 1985.]

opportunity to review the quality and accuracy of the history purveyed, that is to say of the history as it is being shaped not by women, or indeed men, but by feminists. I well know the risks one runs in applying the normal critical standards to people who write with passion and for a cause. Such people cling together, praising the members of the group and deeply resenting anyone who looks at their premises and performances from outside the charmed circle. It will be interesting to see whether women's history has grown up sufficiently to permit a voice to one who approves its aims but is not committed to its current results.

On the face of it, the test case of Joan Kelly looks a little feeble. The book consists of a mere five essays of which only two discuss plain historical problems; the remaining three attempt to set up a general theory of feminist history. Kelly, who died in 1982 at the age of fifty-four, never produced a vast quantity of historical research. Before she turned to women's history – and it should be noted that the title of this book disguises the fact that several earlier essays are excluded – she wrote a book on Leon Battista Alberti, a relatively minor figure in the Italian Renaissance, as well as a few pieces on topics in Renaissance humanism, all of which showed her to be a reasonably competent product of Garrett Mattingly's teaching at Columbia University. She had a well-developed social conscience and actively hated the war in Vietnam, so that the years 1968–9 naturally enough found her joining the students' rebellion from the professorial camp. Round about 1970 she turned to feminism and was received there as a valuable recruit and potential leader. Her chief contribution, we are told in the lengthy prefatory matter in this volume, consisted of the discovery that women's history could provide a 'vantage point' (the term seized upon by her followers) from which to inspect the whole of history. What, therefore, makes this small collection of five articles worth serious consideration is the opinion, expressed in the prefaces, that after her conversion and owing to her proclamation of a 'theory' she acquired the status of a true prophetess in the movement. Insiders regard her work as exceptionally important in the advance of women's history.

The term 'prophetess' is strictly applicable. In her own introduction – a third piece added to the preliminary matter – Kelly tells us how she came to turn to feminist history. Here (pp. xii–xiii) she makes it plain that what happened resembled a religious experience much more than the working out of a rational train of thought. She did not surrender easily. Saul had his revelation in a flash on the road to Damascus; Kelly, more resistant, underwent a four-hour harangue from a dedicated missionary (Gerda Lerner) whose preaching prepared her for 'the most exciting intellectual adventure' she had ever had. But by her own account that adventure was not exactly intellectual; she describes it as resembling the experience of adolescence when despairing confusion retreats before a 'restoration', an instinctive trust in a new dogma revealed to the recipient. No new reading, she says, no archival find, no additional knowledge contributed to the process. In fact, what by her own description had happened to her was a form of what since has come to be known as being born again. Perhaps she was readier than some to undergo this rebirth, having acquired all the conventional liberal reactions to the events of the day and, as a species of Marxist, already being accustomed to following a faith.

Feminism of this kind is thus manifestly a form of religion, not a rational tool of historical analysis, even though a critique of the history written under its banner must apply rational standards. Adherence to it involves conversion, the comfort of the sect, and proselytising; the end sought its salvation. Once received into the faith Kelly became a typical convert – more zealous even than existing followers of the spiritual teaching offered. Her sadly early death (a victim of cancer, a charismatic disease in such circles) made it likely that from prophetess she would be promoted to sainthood, and the manner in which the two prefaces speak of her indicates that she has at any rate already been beatified. She is presented to us in the language which forms the dogmatic framework of feminism – male oppression, female virtue, free sexuality, heightened consciousness, and so forth. Her special role is defined: it was she who transformed articles of belief into positive action. 'For Kelly', we are told (p. xvi), 'politics was everywhere: it involved more than active opposition to economic injustice, sexism, racism, and the hierarchical relationships in the larger society and in the university; it involved both writing and teaching'. (It is not clear whether the disconcertingly anticlimactical structure of this sentence was intentional.) She receives adulatory praise for organising seminars and conferences, and for adding an awareness of class relations to the understanding of the gender-based oppression suffered by women. In short, she is seen as the active, even activist, prophetess the movement needed; to the outsider she therefore represents a good guide to the sort of intellectual standards in the production of women's history that the movement approves of. It should be added that her own writing remained free of that stridency born of hatred which one otherwise encounters so frequently; if it were not for one citation from her private diary, in which she 'passionately' prayed for 'an end to patriarchy' (p. xv), one would not understand the charisma attaching to her. But it was clearly circumambient.

Naturally this suffices for the believer. The non-believer, willing to be persuaded, must ask whether the substance of thought and learning behind the charisma makes Kelly's kind of feminism a sound foundation for women's history. She herself defines that compound as possessing 'a dual role: to restore women to history and to restore our history to women'. There is a characteristic woolliness about that phrase. Women have never been omitted from history; what Kelly meant (as the rest of the essays shows) is to write history not only exclusively from a women's standpoint but also as though only women had mattered in the history of human experience. It is this desire that fuelled her claim to attention – her discovery of a 'theory' which allegedly opens one's eyes to an entirely new, and entirely true, way of interpreting the past. The search for a 'theory' constitutes one of the more aberrant preoccupations of American historians, anxious not to be laughed at by the more obtuse practitioners of the social sciences, and Kelly's 'theory' possesses the qualities generally demanded by women and men alike who have surrendered to this quest: it is very simple, it is very absolute, and it precedes the actual work of historical research. What this 'theory' proposes is that a supposedly general and conventional view of the past turns out to be unusable when the fortunes of women, as a human group, are given proper attention: the world turns upside down. At first sight one cannot quite believe that Kelly is serious about the supposed conventional interpretation which she attacks; she seems to suppose that male historians all underwrite the most simplistic of progress doctrines according to which humanity has steadily and by stages moved from barbarism to a condition of freedom and self-fulfilment. This, Kelly maintains, holds good if you confine history to men, but in her view men achieved their progress by oppressing and exploiting women, so that every stage of their advancement equalled a stage in the downgrading of women. The first part of the world which is turned upside-down is paradise in which Eve was perfectly happy before Adam provoked the fall; and while he has been struggling upwards ever since he has done so only by treading on Eve's head.

Kelly works out her theory of step-by-step decline in essays on 'The social realities of the sexes: methodological implications of women's history', 'The doubled vision of feminist theory', and 'Family and society'; substance is adduced in two historical essays on 'Did women have a renaissance?' and 'Early feminist theory and the *Querelles des femmes'*. Unhappily, in this limited corpus of work, the theoretical discussions, apart from being tendentious, can only be called jejune, while the historical investigations are flawed in just about every particular.

It is really quite astonishing to find an historian in the later twentieth century who can suppose that prevalent teaching concentrates on simple notions of progress and identifies (so Kelly says) three nodal points in this march through time: Periclean Athens, the Italian Renaissance, and the French Revolution. Who on earth thinks thus? The answer is that Marx did and that Kelly, enemy to patriarchy, unhappily chose to exempt that quintessential patriarch and oppressor of women from the curse of Adam. Conceptually, she stopped somewhere in the middle of the nineteenth century, and it cannot encourage belief in the new theory to find that the enemy that has been overthrown has been dead and mouldering for decades. The point comes out most starkly in the essay on 'Family and society', an attempt to link the history of the family (as women's history) to the consequences of class war. Admittedly addressed to students, it employs a breathtaking oversimplification at every point touched, using a totally unsophisticated version of the Marxist sequence of dominant classes to move from 'feudalism' to 'capitalism', from 'preindustrial' to 'industrial' and so to the bright hopes of the present, with a proletariat of women about to save the world. Along the way we learn such new marvels as that private property, as a concept and a fact, emerged in the fifteenth and sixteenth centuries during an alleged transition to what are called 'state-organised' societies, and we get a sadly outdated child's guide to the industrial revolution. Occasional good insights come as a welcome relief but tend to vanish in the general morass of textbook history at the 'world civ.' level or below it. In all that range of history which she here tries to make her province, Kelly's knowledge and reading were strictly minimal. For example, she offers an array of confident assertions – some highly doubtful, more still certainly wrong – about medieval society (a thousand years of experiences varying enormously in time and place); for all this the reader is calmly referred to one of G. C. Coulton's compilations and to Henri Pierenne's general history. Coulton's work appeared in 1928; Pirenne's, first published in 1936, was written in an internment camp in the last year of the First World War; here they are cited, misleadingly, from reprints dated 1960 and 1958, so as to pretend much more recent composition. Altogether, the historical information offered in this essay varies from the bad to the inadequate; it is used to support a scheme devised a century and a half ago; out of this we are to gather a revolutionary modern 'theory'.

Doubts are unfortunately only reinforced by what would seem to be the most important essay in the book, that on women and the Renaissance. This apparently incorporates the moment of revelation which first provided Kelly with her new 'vantage point'. The Renaissance, she says, is generally regarded as a great age of liberation – socially, politically, in matters of art, learning and literature. No doubt, she agrees, it was all that for men, but for women it marked a moment of repression which reduced their powers of action and self-expression well below the level attained earlier. It did so mainly by introducing a 'bourgeois morality' of chastity and seclusion, and by inventing the notorious 'double standard'. Here again Kelly's starting point is wildly out of date: to her the male interpretation of the Renaissance stands now where Jakob Burckhardt supposedly fixed it in 1860. Whole libraries of learning, much of which has cast comprehensive doubt upon the whole concept of the Renaissance as a unique and liberating movement even in matters of the mind, have passed her by, as has a general movement away from 'the Middle Ages' as an identifiable stage in human development. She maintains her argument by paying attention to very minor manifestations of the sixteenth and twelfth centuries respectively which are given the status of universally held views of the role of women. On the one hand, there is Baldassare Castiglione's *Courtier* (1513–18); on the other side stands the idea of 'courtly love' celebrated by the troubadours and the writers of *chansons*. Here allegedly we find a contrast between the condemnation and the worship of adulterous (extra-marital) sex, and with it the growing incarceration of women, who in the days of the *Minnesänger* could strike up sexual relationships where they pleased, in a freedom which reflected their independence in general. The extraction of massive conclusions touching all social, economic and political life from a few writers of books is unfortunately typical of Kelly's method, and it will not do, as every beginning graduate student is surely made to learn. Working with so little material, she easily manipulates the evidence to suit her purpose. Though she mentions the problem whether 'courtly love' represents real experiences or a literary convention of pretended adoration, she thinks the question of no importance: what matters is that there was a society which promoted an ideology of free and extra-marital love. A society? She admits that the supposed experience seems to have been confined to women of the aristocracy, but then calmly applies her vision of free women to centuries of time and millions of people. The multiplicity of those societies comes to be assessed from a few poems and romances, from the light literature which some people in the south of France liked to read. (Lancelot's involvement with Guinevere was treated much less tolerantly in the northern tradition!) Even if one were to give to courtly love a place of modest importance in judging social attitudes, a very different interpretation offers itself which is no less convincing and no less romantically insecure. Freud has failed to impress Kelly, whose psychology of people is distressingly simple. But looking at all that submission to noble ladies, all that kissing of feet, all that adoration of *belles dames sans merci*, one must be struck by the powerful strain of masochism, of a desire to be dominated by women. A theory of history resting on such foundations is, even by the standards of what passes for theory in history, exceptionally ill-grounded and, frankly, rather silly.

Too much, far too much, gets ignored in these essays. How can Kelly damn Castiglione for preaching chastity to women and never once mention the medieval nunnery from whose constraints (others have argued) the Reformation freed women? How can she reduce the practice of a humanist education, experience of which in fact gave intellectual liberty to many women, to the imposition on helpless girls of a classical culture 'with its patriarchal and misogynous bias'? Does she really suppose that only the Renaissance made women suffer from what she regards as the patriarchal and misogynous bias of Christianity? We hear something of the chance given to the medieval noblewoman to participate in business, estate management, and politics; nothing is said of the much greater share that women of all classes demonstrably took in such labours in the three centuries after 1500. The essay on the *Querelles des femmes* (the growth of literary feminism from Christine de Pisan to Mary Wollstonecraft), relying on better guides, offers sounder history, but major claims are again made on very modest evidence elicited by a single-track enquiry.

The trouble with Kelly's history is, at heart, threefold: it is far too limited, too poorly informed, and too American.

Limited: her concerns practically never extend beyond traditions of literature and art. She gives no sign of knowing any economic history, or anything specific about government and politics. Her socialism is the socialism of a pathetic illusion. Marx, though mentioned, is never cited: for all the evidence of these essays, she did not read him, which is perhaps just as well since Marx's attitudes do not suit well with feminist predilections. Like many present-day socialist theoreticians, she takes refuge with Engels, a much nicer man. I see no sign that she has thought seriously about the meaning or reality of the concept of class, her chief analytical tool; she uses the term as a conventional prop for her gender-based schema; she never analyses it or comes to grips with the proliferation of debate which Marxian simplicities have called forth. She does not seem to have noticed that the lot of women, public or private, is markedly less fortunate in socialist countries than in the strongholds of capitalism; indeed, at least the upper-class women of Tsarist Russia, where European *mores* had penetrated, were 'freer' in the feminist sense than are the women of the USSR. Kelly operates by means of a tunnel vision created out of illusions.

Poorly informed: by the ordinary standards of historical research and method, the work presented in these essays is thin and poor. Kelly uses a tiny sample of primary sources, all of them in print, to rest enormous interpretative theories upon them; she employs a very selective range of secondary writings in which books by men nearly always feature only if they were written long ago. After her conversion in about 1970 she seems to have read only the writings of fellow feminists. Yet on this utterly inadequate basis of learning she confidently reorganises half the world's history. It would be unkind to analyse her notions concerning fifth-century Athens, of which, it seems, only the fact that respectable women supposedly remained out of the public eye has struck her. Occasional references to anthropological enquiries are applied without any of that sense of relative values depending on historical circumstances which the study of history is supposed to create. Plain howlers abound. On three successive pages she equips manorial courts with the power to inflict the death penalty, assigns such 'children of serfs' as entered the priesthood to invariably inferior positions in the church, ascribes the use of the term 'middle class' to the Middle Ages, and supposes that farmers' wives called their husbands 'masters', a term reserved for the gentry (pp. 118–20). Some of her errors derive from the tendentious mistakes of the social historians she relies on: even the feminist historian can be the victim of her male contemporaries.

American: this may well be the touchiest aspect of this critique. Kelly's point of view, the position where she drops anchor, remains throughout very specifically governed by notions and convictions developed within the United States and drawn from the experiences and attitudes of American women. These ideas have certainly been making inroads elsewhere, but their American aspect always stands out to the observer from outside the United States. The interpretation here offered of women's needs and desires is American, or perhaps Anglo-American at most, in terms of the contemporary scene, and it makes no attempt at all to understand the great majority of women of the past in their own right. Feminist historiography, like all the history written by fanatics, knows best what women of the past should have wanted and indeed would have wanted if they had not been 'socially conditioned' into submissive attitudes. This splendidly universal escape-hole denies the right and the power to think to myriads of women who understood the problems of existence in the miserable life to which God had, by creating them, condemned all mankind better than the privileged women of the North American continent can grasp. But it is the duty of historians to understand the people of the past, not to invent an alternative existence for them.

In such work as Kelly's, the standards and experiences of present-day America are universalised in a totally unhistorical fashion and without much display of historical understanding or empathy. This accounts for the recital of forerunners like Christine de Pisan and the ignoring of the many educated and effective women who were not feminists. It looks very much as though feminist historians do not wish to write history as history, but to seek sisters in the past and posthumously to liberate the unenlightened. In the process they regularly impute their own characteristic discontents to people who frequently lived happy lives in ways which the doctrine asserts cannot lead to anything but misery. There is nothing whatsoever wrong with the history of women, provided it is not written by feminists but by female or male historians. Real history results when the past is studied without rigorous preconceptions, studied in all the available sources, studied in full consciousness of variety and change, and studied for the sake of understanding the past, not for the purpose of today substituting female dominance for male. Joan Kelly wished her history to assist in freeing humanity from suffering, from indignity, from 'the cruel and stupid political world'. We can all share her idealism and her hopes, but we cannot but wonder why she should ever have learned from history that only men corrupt, or why she should have thought that the unsound methods she pursued in the writing of history would help to save mankind.

By the evidence of this collection of essays, women's history needs to take a long look at itself. But then feminism is a religion, and feminist history constitutes an attempt to underpin a dogmatic for that religion. Like all dogmatics it now and again hits on true points and valuable insights, but like all dogmatics it is miles away from real history. This is not in the least to say that men are right and women wrong, as no doubt I shall be accused of holding. All it means is that religious faiths are poor guides for historians.

66

THE NEW HISTORY*

Both these books consist of collections of essays and reviews that have
previously appeared in print – ten of them in Professor Himmerlfarb's
volume and twenty-one in Professor Stone's. However, anyone thinking of spending his money on the latter should note that of those twenty-
one fifteen appeared in an earlier collection a few years ago.[1] Though
we are assured that on this second appearance those fifteen have been
rewritten 'to focus attention upon broad historical problems and issues
and away from the merits and defects of the particular book under
review', the changes are minor. While it is good to have Stone's second
or third thoughts on some themes, the fact that the bulk of the book
originated in book reviews remains obvious. Stone has for some time
enjoyed the lavish patronage of the *New York Review of Books*, which
allows him enough space for the display of much learned detail,
sometimes enlightening and sometimes confusing. In this era of historical
revision even he can fall behind the times: chapter 12, on 'the new
eighteenth century', is in fact about the old eighteenth century, before
the Jonathan Clark revolution. If there is a general theme holding these
pieces together it is Stone's conviction that a recent great age of historical
studies, one of whose ornaments he was, has passed away, to be
succeeded by an age of pettifoggers who now subject the buildings
erected by the heroes to quibbling questions about the soundness of the
foundations and the quality of the brickwork. Though the range of his
reviewing is as awesome as his verdicts are positive, let us humbly hope
that Stone will not revisit the past and the present a third time.

By contrast, Himmelfarb has collected pieces, written between 1975
and 1986, that have not before appeared in book form. They also possess
more of a thematic unity. Coming at it from various directions, they all
consider the growing tendency among historians in the United States and

---

* [Review of Lawrence Stone, *The Past and the Present Revisited* (London, 1987), and
  Gertrude Himmelfarb, *The New History and the Old* (Cambridge, Mass., 1987), in *HJ*, 31
  (1988), 761–4.]
[1] *The Past and the Present (1981)*. My review of this in *The Times Educational Supplement* in
  July 1981 will, I hope, excuse me from going over all the ground again.

On Historians

Britain to follow the lead of the *Annales* school by embracing the siren of social history and relegating to an old people's home the sombre muse of political, constitutional and intellectual history. Himmelfarb confronts 'anti-elitist' history from below, the curiosities of psychohistory, the triumph of an analysis innocent of chronology, and the importation of 'scientific' techniques into the study of the past: and she finds that she cannot much like these manifestations of the 'new' history. Specifically she dislikes the claims made by the new history to be the only admissable and permissible history. Such claims are noisy in the States, where professorial ascendancy in the departmental structure can offer too many opportunities to the monopolist; fortunately, they have not yet made very serious inroads in England, now a beleaguered bastion of empiricist and non-ideological history. A disconcertingly large number of American historians tend to be in thrall to some universal theory, often Marxist or crypto-Marxist, sometimes Freudian, sometimes Geertzian, sometimes feminist and so forth, and always predictive. In this country genuinely Marxist historians remain few, but they form the subject of an interesting essay (chapter 4) on their self-proclaimed 'Group'. Himmelfarb's cool, elegant, restrained but probing analysis here brings out the risks which political commitment poses to the freedom of the historian's mind.

Both Stone and Himmelfarb write well – lucidly and compellingly. There is, however, a difference of tone. Stone tends to patronise the scholars he discusses, while Himmelfarb, her measured phrases notwithstanding, is right in there, battling against demons with fists and feet. Stone welcomes the novelties presented by the social historian of, say, death or madness, though he does not swallow everything by any means; there is a good deal of criticism, often shrewd and accurate. But in principle he adheres to that camp. Himmelfarb, while lambasting the absence of sound research and the arrogant exclusiveness of that sort of history, by no means wants to return to the alleged earlier exclusiveness of the old political history. Thus both allow for the possibility of a rapprochement, though it will be a long time before they really come to terms. What neither of them seems to realise is that the new history is really as old as Herodotus and was, for instance, expressly embraced by quite a few historians in the seventeenth century. They too had grown tired of bishops, kings, wars and diplomacy; they too wished to study social structures, social habits and beliefs, maypoles and ale houses, the law and its practices. For their pains they have usually been dubbed antiquaries.

By a happy coincidence we now possess each of these authors' view of the other. When Himmelfarb reviewed the earlier collection of Stone's essays she headed her piece 'Reflections of a chastened father' (chapter 5). She had in mind his conviction that things had been best in social history when he was young, and his decision that his heirs and successors needed disciplining – a discipline which he then applied with some energy. She noted that he had not reprinted some of his more vitriolic reviews (a fact which accidentally left this reviewer as the sole target of Stone's well-known power to savage), and she praised him for his willingness to recognise deterioration in areas that he himself had been instrumental in opening up for historians. But she also noted that he did not call for a return to the old history but for a transfer to 'the newest ship in the armada of the new history, the flagship sailing under the banner of *mentalité collective*'. She was being kind. Stone's career is signposted by a series of very large books using successive social-science techniques. A devotion, in turn, to economics, sociology and anthropology erected great structures that tended to collapse as soon as they were closely examined, leaving behind a mass of often very impressive building materials. Stone's 'crisis of the aristocracy' in the earlier seventeenth century (which enabled lesser landowners to get at a king no longer protected by his great vassals) has vanished from the scene: we are learning that a powerful and increasingly discontented aristocracy led the attack on Charles I. Relationships between husbands and wives, and between parents and children, have refused to observe the time-table constructed for them by Stone out of his (borrowed) thesis that the Reformation produced the oppression of women and sin-suppressing punishment for offspring: the thesis incorporated fundamental errors, though Stone still (in one of the additions to his collection) sticks to his scheme and will not cite the works that have shown up the faults in quite a few of his basic assumptions.[2] The 'open elite' which he closed down in his last book is in process of being opened up again.[3] He tells us that his conversion to the study of *mentalité* will now take him to the history of sexuality, perhaps the most overworked and least engaging of all the ways of humanity to be trampled by the social historian. Shall we see another great structure put together out of hard work on detail and the

[2] E.g. Steven Ozment, *When Fathers Ruled: Family Life in Reformation Europe* (Cambridge, Mass., 1983); Linda A. Pollock, *Forgotten Children: Parent–Child Relations from 1500 to 1900* (Cambridge, 1983).

[3] See reviews by Harold Perkin (*Journal of British Studies*, 24 (1985), 496–501) and Eileen and David Spring (*Albion*, 17 (1985), 149–66): one friendly, the other not. Both agree in their doubts about the arguments and conclusions of the book.

use of highly dubious categories? The essay on sexuality in the present volume certainly points that way.

The interesting thing about Stone's relationship with social history is his nose for the imminent collapse. Time and again, he has made his major contribution to some aspect of it, only to follow up with an attack on the underlying principles that he himself had made attractive to others (though he has never recanted on his earlier conclusions). He has denounced the sociological model used for *The Crisis of the Aristocracy* and the anthropological model followed in *The Family, Sex and Marriage*. He has called for narrative in place of analysis, though (as Himmelfarb points out) the meaning he gives to narrative still does not involve the telling of a tale. His readiness (in his own words) to call 'for the historical rats to leave . . . the social scientific ship' into which he had originally enticed them is not, however, a sign of true repentance because he now offers a leakier vessel still for his organised cruise in pursuit of the truth: it is a manœuvre designed to extricate himself from past error without having to admit to it. If precedent is anything to go by, his next excursion will in due course be followed by a disavowal of his present passion for the champions of *mentalité*, who have dumped on the historians' desks a remarkable pile of dubious constructs. Stone's future conversion cannot come too soon. Himmelfarb, who shares these doubts, expresses them without the severity she uses against psychohistorians or against a more surprising target for her arrows – Theodore Zeldin and his pointillist history of France, denounced rather convincingly for discarding the notion of nationality.

In *The New York Review of Books* for 17 December 1987, Stone in his turn reviewed Himmelfarb's collection of essays, by and large in a spirit of kindly reproof towards an erring colleague; only occasionally did he unsheathe his claws. He set her down to begin with by stating that the purpose of her book had to be extracted with some difficulty because it consists of collected reviews and is not a single volume constructed around an argument. I find this an odd remark for an author who also uses reviews to lay out his historian's faith. However, he managed to identify her purpose quite correctly – it is in fact crystal-clear – as an attack on the predominant styles of social history. Much of this he accepted, though he repeated at some length his own credo that 'the last forty years have seen an astonishing explosion of the so-called "new history" ', and he provided a very mixed bibliography of those seminal and liberating writings. He agreed with some of Himmelfarb's critique but blamed her for concentrating 'exclusively upon the defects of this outburst of energy', accused her of bitterness and passion, and in the end, returning to his patronising pose, thought her insufficiently familiar with what she was attacking. In this crossfire between two determined fighters, Himmelfarb shows the greater courtesy as well as a greater willingness to admit some virtue on the other side, while Stone displays his superior skill in the slitting of jugulars.

I shall be reckoned no impartial umpire in these disputes: I am known to incline towards Himmelfarb's position and against the new history, and she correctly cites me to that effect. But I hope that this does not disqualify me from drawing attention to what she is actually saying. Perhaps she overstates her case; perhaps there is more than a touch of passion in her assault on a treatment of the past which, in its preoccupation with structures and conditions, tends to eliminate humanity. But what she denounces deserves to be assailed passionately. She specifically homes in on two features of this kind of history: on the downgrading of reason and the elevation of one kind or another of predestination. In both respects, she seems to me to have right absolutely on her side. The new social history, whether it is quantitative, psychological, class-dominated, or interested solely in the fortunes of previously neglected groups, tends to eliminate the operation of the human mind and to construct schemes which determine the course of events independently from human action. In itself, this is not necessarily all wrong; it becomes all wrong when it is proclaimed to be the only good history. Theory-based history can be enlightening, but it works by inverting the true process of enquiry: it knows beforehand what the outcome will be and selects from the historical record such detail as will validate the prophecy. It is for this reason that its products are so vulnerable to a proper enquiry (despised as empiricist or historicist). The recognition that at every moment in the past the future was essentially unpredictable and subject to human choices lies at the heart of a study which respects the past and allows it a life of its own. If men (and women) are treated as devoid of choice, their reason is demolished; the product is a history which dehumanises mankind and gives dictatorial powers solely to the mind of the historian wielding his theory.

There is another problem about this new (and not so new) history which arises from Himmelfarb's analysis but is not expressly discussed by her. It depends on a very inadequate, because uncritical, treatment of the evidence. The case of Le Roy Ladurie's famous *Montaillou* is instructive. The materials he used were produced by the technical processes of a court of law: they are the results of visitations and constitute a body of allegations which it was then the task of the court to sift and assess. The historian took them at face value: accusations were treated as though they equalled convictions. Yet even when a historian's uncritical or incompetent handling of his sources has been established, the dedicated disciples will not give up conclusions based on such shaky ground. Stone, in his essay on sexuality, fully accepts that both Ariès and Foucault treated historical evidence in a thoroughly unsatisfactory manner so as to support their large schemata, but he nevertheless discusses the subject as though the theories so created deserved credence and could be used. The myths are allowed to survive even after their mythical foundations have been exposed. An interesting variant of this methodological error is gaining ground in the historiography of seventeenth-century England in the wake of the increasing respect shown to literary critics venturing into problems outside their normal territory. Of necessity they borrow some interpretations constructed by some tendentious historians who then cite those derivative conclusions as though they constituted independent confirmations. The questions which the new history asks are, of course, often important enough, but their very importance calls for the use of exceptionally tricky materials which have not before this been subjected to the normal tests of historical science and should not be used until they have been so tested. The old historian marvels at the insouciance with which the new historian flings his finds about, until he realises that too many more or less old historians have also shown much loose recklessness in their treatment of the sources. There is an awful lot of clearing up to be done, but knowing beforehand what the outcome must be will prove the most serious hindrance of all. In such circumstances, we can do without the belief that man is a creature without powers of reason and thought.

67

OBJECTIVITY*

Nowhere do historians go in for so much self-examination as they do in America: it is a part of American culture to examine the self. The same conglomeration of habits also accounts for American historians' exceptional willingness to listen to self-appointed guides, some of them sane but more of them not evidently so. The profession therefore lends itself well to the sort of analysis that Peter Novick has undertaken in this fascinating, if rather over-long, book. (Excessive length in books is another American habit.)

However, this passion for commitment, this accumulation of fretful worries and serious night thoughts, has made a splendid story. Novick has chosen the recurrent desire of American historians to provide an objective account of the past, in the face of contemptuous complaints that such a thing is impossible, to structure his description of a century of learned endeavours. That is the noble dream of his title, a dream which again and again, just when it looked likely to turn into a waking experience of reality, turned into a nightmare. He opens the story in the late nineteenth century when a first generation of American historians aspiring to professional status learned their trade in Germany, returning full of Ranke and the cult of the objective study of the past. Their preoccupation with the search for a pure truth then suffered two set-backs. The 'progressive' historians (Robinson & Co.) demanded that the historian subordinate everything to providing a social service to his time, and the Great War demonstrated that even the much admired champions of the unprejudiced study of the past, on both sides of the divide, were only too willing to discard their principles in the service of nationalist propaganda. The noble dream was gone for a time, to be replaced by the long ascendancy of relativist views, propagated elegantly by Carl Becker and thumpingly by Charles Beard: it became axiomatic that the historian always writes under the direction of his own day and his own personality. The moral certainties of the Second World War enabled scholars to return to a more positivist stance, and the 1950s

* [Review of Peter Novick, *That Noble Dream: The 'Objectivity Question' and the American Historical Profession* (Cambridge, 1988), *Journal of Economic History*, September 1989.]

laboured under the sign of a somewhat anodyne 'consensus'. This collapsed crashingly in the upheavals of the sixties. Between them, rebellion against authority and the passionate search for new prophets among the practitioners of various social sciences produced the present state of rudderless confusion, or at least multiplicity of tactics. Novick, wisely refraining from turning prophet in his turn, leaves things there, though he seems to regret a state of affairs which strikes me as healthily devoid of assertive authority.

Along the way we meet many seductive byways as well as moments of high comedy. Novick has found some fairly amazing cases of brutal antisemitism, usually among eminent scholars willing to adopt Karl Lueger's principle of claiming the right to decide who is a Jew. The fortunes of black Americans have meandered around since the days of Social Darwinism, with its certainty that there are inferior races, through the separatist days of Black Studies, to the peace created by the present conviction that skin colour has nothing to do with intellectual equipment and that history equally attends to the fortunes and labours of everybody. (John Hope Franklin emerges as the one man who throughout adhered to the only right principles.) And then there came feminist history, about which it may be best for a mere male to say nothing. We get a very frank account of David Abraham's battle with Henry Turner and Gerald Feldman, a battle from which none of the combatants emerges with his honour untarnished. Novick has searched both public prints and private archives, unearthing many remarkable statements of bigotry as well as long-suffering, and much of the book is strikingly funny. If the noble dream of objectivity at times disappears behind the billowing smoke of the battlefields, it always returns in time to give the story continuity and coherence. At the end, it does so by evidently having ceased to be the central aspiration: if Novick is right, American historians have now given up even the ambition to tell it *wie es eigentlich gewesen*.

But is this so? Of necessity, only a minority of the thousands of scholars who have studied history in the United States make their appearance here, and the sample is biased by two inbuilt conditions: it consists of people who have involved themselves publicly in these debates about methods and ends, and it is virtually confined to historians of the USA, that is to say, scholars who have never concerned themselves with any aspect of the past more than 200 years distant from their own day. Indeed, in the main debates – about, for instance, Reconstruction, the causes of the First World War, or the nature of the

New Deal – they dealt with matters which impinged directly on their own times. Novick himself is a student of fairly recent French history, a fact which assists the predominance in these pages of modernists thinking about issues close to their own lives. Among the many non-historians parading as influential thinkers, Americans again predominate, with Frenchmen looming across the Atlantic; English historians who have tried to think about the nature of history escape unmentioned. (Novick does cite a curious trio of writers from England – Imre Lakatos, a conservative social thinker, Terry Eagleton, a Marxist literary critic, and Mary Hesse, a philosopher of science – none of them at all influential among English historians.) Moreover, economic history proper, not to mention cliometrics, puts in hardly any appearance. The whole analysis applies much more to modernists and to social historians than to Americans involved in medieval or early-modern history, or engaged in the less fashionable aspects of the game.

Yet the much despised demand that the past be studied for its own sake makes much better sense for people who need to consider times more distant from their own experience – who *have* to think more historically. In any case, American historians seem regularly to misunderstand that demand. They have from the first to the present been subjected to pressure to do service to their own society, a pressure made only more severe by the absurd passion for supposed relevance thrown up by the 1960s. Studying the past for its own sake does not mean forgetting the present or overlooking the fact that historians are human beings equipped with personal experiences and preferences which render the noble dream of total objectivity an unattainable ideal. It does mean trying to understand the past from within itself and not by the standards and fashions of one's own day; it does mean respecting the past and its people ahead of oneself and one's own concerns. Both Hayden White, for instance, and too many feminist historians have never grasped this last point. It is in these duties that so many present-day historians, not only in the United States but more regularly there, have gone astray, under the influence of two somewhat pernicious misunderstandings.

The first of these imposes a moralising duty on the historian: he is instructed to assist in one way or another his contemporaries' desire to be thought just, socially involved, morally improving. Unless, it is held, he gives a leg-up to the conventional virtues of his day he is not doing his social duty. But his real duty is to the past: he must make that past and its inhabitants comprehensible to the present rather than use that past and those people in order to offer to the present day consolation or exhortation. The other error, again very flourishing among Americans, arises from the conviction that other people's generalising theories should guide the historian's posing of questions and offering of answers. This review cannot fully explore the consequences of these two aberrations. But is it not remarkable that the claims of so many dubious prophets obtain deference from historians needlessly troubled by the well-established fact that their own proper concerns do not yield great general schemes to interpret, and perhaps to forecast, the human experience? Thus, to take two wildly different examples, Marx and Foucault continue to command adherence in a great many quarters when yet they, like many such, have time and again been convicted of merely abusing historical evidence by employing it selectively and inaccurately to underpin what can only be called lies. History should be sceptical of theorisers and should not submit to mere human dictate: it is here that its proper 'service to society' lies.

The first professionals of the nineteenth century very often, for understandable reasons, gave an impression of childlike simplicity. The idea of total objectivity was a product of immaturity and inexperience, though it did provide a measure of self-confidence and a suitable start to the enterprise. The harmless impossibility of knowing all the truth emerged quite naturally from the conflicts of understanding which are an essential concomitant of advancing historical comprehension. Unfortunately, too many of the scholars discussed in this excellent book seem to have advanced from childhood only into adolescence – into that condition which thirsts for universal theories and will fit the past into them. Procrustes marks no improvement on Herodotus. Has not the time come to grow up? The claims of the people of the past to be understood in their own right must come before the claims of the operator to promote his own self. And the proliferating gurus of the day call for critics, not for disciples.

INDEX OF AUTHORS CITED

GENERAL INDEX

General Index

Cade, Jack, 261
Caernarvon, 93
Calais, 25, 94, 237, 239
Calthorpe, Charles, 114
Calvin, John, 134, 169, 175, 206, 229,
  236–8, 243–4
Calvinism, 204–5, 228–9
Cambridge, 45, 54n., 161, 206, 211, 221,
  231–2, 272; Pembroke College, 161–2,
  167, 174; Peterhouse, 167, 267–9
CAMPION, EDMUND, 185, 189, 191, 195,
  204
Carafa, Gian Petro (cardinal), 175
Cardiff, 97–9
Cardigan, 99
Carey, Henry, lord Hunsdon, 102
Carlyle, Thomas, 242–3, 263
Carmarthen, 103–4
Carr, Robert, earl of Somerset, 30
Cartwright, John, 184
Castigilione, Baldassare, 298–9
Catherine of Aragon, 38–9
Cawood, John, 106
Cecil, Robert, earl of Salisbury, 6, 8, 17,
  29–30, 32
Cecil, William, lord Burghley: control of
  government, 6–7, 28–33; 'his fast', 112;
  and Parliament, 102, 106, 126; and
  propaganda, 191–3; also 17, 148, 221,
  229
Chamberlain, John, 165
Chancery, court of, 10–11, 27, 55, 73,
  155, 220
Charles I, 26, 81, 157, 171, 305
Charles V (emperor), 38, 149, 159
Chatham (Kent), 115
Chaucer, Geoffrey, 133, 173
Cheke, Sir John, 204, 220
Chepstow, (Mon.), 97, 99
Chester, 25, 100, 137
Church of England, 5, 7–8, 33, 52, 71,
  199–208; Convocations of, 18, 43, 49;
  courts of, 18–20, 51; organisation of,
  18; principles of, 170–2 vicegerency in,
  19; and see Supremacy
Civil war, 139
Clement VII (pope), 38–40
Clitheroe (Lancs)., 114
Cloth manufacture, 95–6
Coke, Sir Edward, 11–12, 173, 276
Coleridge, Samuel Taylor, 242
Colet, John, 210, 219, 222–3
Colonialism, 65

Common Prayer, book of, 52–3, 105–7
Cornwall, 135
Corruption, 17, 28
Cosin, John (bp of Durham), 165
Coverdale, Miles, 232–3
Cranmer, Thomas (abp of Canterbury),
  51, 171, 192, 202–3, 230, 251
Cromwell, Thomas (diarist), 125
Cromwell, Thomas, earl of Essex: career
  and character of, 144–60; and the law,
  42–3, 56; and Parliament, 52, 54, 91,
  137; and propaganda, 89, 233; and the
  Reformation, 41, 46–50, 171–2, 202–3,
  232; reforms of, 5, 9, 97, 133, 220–1,
  228, 252; also 19, 46, 55, 71, 90, 106n.,
  192, 230, 252
Crown, see Monarchy

Danes 132
Daniel, Samuel, 158
Davies, Richard (bp of St Asaph), 104–7
Dee, John, 115–16
Denham, Henry, 107
Derby, earl of, see Stanley
Devereux, Robert, earl of Essex, 32
Devon, 135, 138
Digges, Leonard, 116
Digges, Thomas, 116–17, 119
Dispensations, act of (1534), 47–8
Dispensing power, 68–9
Donne, John, 163
Dort, synod of, 169
Dudley, Edmund, 216
Dudley, Robert, earl of Leicester, 28, 30,
  32–3, 102, 116, 119
Dugard, William, 240
Durham, 25, 100–1, 137
Dutch, see Netherlands

Education, 60, 64, 66, 73, 103, 202, 211,
  219–23, 228–9, 240, 268, 299
Edward I, 25, 88–9, 132
Edward III, 80, 137
Edward IV, 77–9, 85, 136
Edward VI, 52, 92, 94, 99, 101, 108, 154,
  199, 204, 234–5, 256
Egerton, Thomas, lord Ellesmere, 12
Elizabeth I: and the church, 19–21, 53,
  185–6, 199, 251; long life of, 85; and
  Parliament, 24–5, 56–7, 92, 95, 117,
  141; as ruler, 5, 8, 29–35, 84, 192,
  196–7; also 7, 51, 88, 136, 157
Elizabeth Stuart, 34

316

83; *Utopia*, 177–80, 183, 189, 212–17, 227; *also*, 192, 194, 220
Morgan, Francis, 101
Morison, Richard, 134, 151, 204, 220
Morton, John (abp of Canterbury), 87–8
Morton, Thomas, 194
Mulcaster, Richard, 162
Müntzer, Thomas, 246–7
Murray, William earl of Mansfield, 73

Napoleon I, 277, 279–80
Navigation act (1563), 112
Navy, 12, 115–16, 118
Netherlands, 13, 34, 110, 115, 122, 130
New Zealand, 58, 226
Newborough (Anglesey), 99
Newcastle, 115
Newfoundland, 115, 117, 122
Newton, Sir Issac, 276
Nietzsche, Friedrich, 60
Norfolk, 135; duke of, *see* Howard
Norman Conquest, 132
Normandy, 13
Northampton, 101
Norton, Thomas, 114, 119, 124–5, 127, 140

Oecolampadius, John, 247
Oldcastle, Sir John, 180, 253, 259–61
Ordnance Office, 12
Outlawry, 100–1
Owen, George, 133
Owen Tudor, 86
Oxford, 213, 232

Pace, Richard, 222
Padua, 210, 218
Paine, Thomas, 65
Painting, 200–1
Paracelsus, 276
Parker, Matthew (abp of Canterbury), 204
Parliament, 5, 7, 21–6, 37–57, 68–9, 71, 91–108, 111–15, 117–26, 137–43, 152, 156, 187–8; and the church, 18; elections to, 14; management of, 23; and politics, 25–6; *and see* Legislation, Taxation
Parsons, Robert, 171, 192, 194
Patronage system, 27–8
Paul, St, 60, 203
Paynell, Thomas, 232
Peace, justice of the, 14

Pembroke, Jasper Tudor, earl of, 86–8; *and see* Herbert
Perkins, William, 171, 197
Persecution, character of, 175–96; victims of, 66, 190–1
Peterborough, 114
Petition of right, 4, 72–3
Petrarch, Francesco, 201
Petyt, John, 190
Philip II (king of Spain), 134, 234
Pisan, Christine de, 299, 301
Plato, 215, 217
Pole, Reginald (cardinal), 93, 146, 153, 173, 204, 210, 218
Praemunire, 47
Presteigne (Rad.), 96n.
Price, Richard, 102–3
Printing, 106–7
Privy Council, 5–7, 12, 15, 33, 53, 111–12, 119, 140–1, 165, 173, 186–7; factions in, 31; in Parliament, 23, 26, 102
Probate, 10, 51, 55
Proclamations, 21, 106, 117
Purgatory, 256
Puritanism, 20–1, 166–7, 175, 206–7, 239–40, 284

Radnor, 96n.
Rastell, John, 153
Ratcliffe, Sir Henry, 125
Religion: diversities in, 20–1, 29; and history, 282–4; *and see* Calvinism, Church of England, Luther, Puritanism, Rome, Supremacy
Renaissance, 297–9; in England, 200–8
Requests, court of, 10–11
Revolution: American, 61, 63–4; English, 64, 67–9, 80; French, 61–3, 297
Rhys ap Gruffydd, 94
Rhys ap Thomas, 89
Richard II, 80
Richard III, 77–9, 83, 85, 136, 212–13, 215
Richmond, Edmund earl of, 77, 86
Rights, human, 58–67, 75–6; in law, 67–75
Robinson, Ralph, 216
Rochester (Kent), 99, 114
Roe, Sir Thomas, 240
Rome, 148; Church of, 38–42, 85, 185, 191–8; sack of, 40, 180
Roper, Margaret, 146